Money Can't Buy Us Love

Everton in the 1960s

Money Can't Buy Us Love

Everton in the 1960s

Gavin Buckland

deCoubertin
BOOKS

First published as a hardback by deCoubertin Books Ltd in 2019.

First Edition

deCoubertin Books, 46B Jamaica Street, Baltic Triangle, Liverpool, L1 0AF.

www.decoubertin.co.uk

ISBN: 978-1-909245-59-4

A CIP catalogue record for this book is available from the British Library.

Cover design by Thomas Regan/MilkyOne. Typeset by Leslie Priestley.

Printed and bound by Replika Press Pvt. Ltd.

For my wife, Joan,

and children Faye and Andrew

Contents

Introduction

THE PARABLE OF THE MERSEY MILLIONAIRES IS REALLY A TWENTY first century football story that took place more than fifty years ago. The arrival of a rich and powerful benefactor from the business world, who uses their wealth to reinvigorate the fortunes of a club, is a scenario that has been played out regularly over the past decade or more. In contrast, the arrival of John Moores at Everton in 1960 was taking English football into unchartered territory at the time.

Oligarchs and sheiks may now be the benefactors of choice in a globalised game, but in the early 1960s it was the local businessman made good. But Moores, as head of the powerful Littlewoods organisation, had far greater means than the local butcher or car dealer, and in many ways he – and his story at Everton – is the first link in a chain that runs from the insular world of English football of the 1950s to the multi-billion pound global money-making machine it has become today.

There was literally a price to pay though. A ruthless and ambitious chairman with designs on buying and being the best may have delighted Evertonians, but it instilled a degree of mistrust and animosity within the footballing community and elements of the press. Not only that, but the story begins at a time when the country was on the cusp of enormous cultural and economic change. Civil unrest and youthful rebellion bred football hooliganism, whilst the growth in tabloid journalism led to newspaper revelations about the rich and powerful. Everton, with big support and even bigger ambitions, were to become the victims of both. To add another dimension, the media saw the rise of Bill Shankly's Liverpool – with their loveable and witty Kop and charismatic manager, plus a close association to the feel-good factor in the city at the time – as a welcome antidote to Big Brother at Goodison Park. If Liverpool were the clean-cut Beatles, then Everton played the part of the early Rolling Stones to perfection, although the truth as ever lies somewhere in-between, as the book shows.

But every ruthless leader needs a hatchet man, and in Harry Catterick, Moores recruited for many the perfect A-lister for the role. In his review of Rob Sawyer's autobiography of the Everton manager in 2014, the *Guardian's* Daniel Taylor wrote that 'Catterick was difficult, impenetrable, deceitful, frequently unpleasant and pulled some fairly despicable stunts. He was also brilliant, a football visionary,' which is a fair summation. Catterick's mistrust of virtually everybody did not exactly help the club's popularity, but that should not disguise his wide range of talents as a football manager – he could win ugly or with beauty, was a strategist with an attention to detail and could handle both big stars and turn promising youngsters into international players. Most importantly of all, in his two decades and more as a manager, Catterick showed the ability to operate successfully with either a shoestring budget or blank chequebook, whilst under extreme pressure to succeed. At the time, that was pretty unique.

Money Can't Buy Us Love therefore attempts to make sense of all of this, telling the story of the Mersey Millionaires from Moores' arrival to Catterick's departure 13 years later. Amongst the main cast are Johnny Carey, Alex Young, Roy Vernon, Gordon West, Derek Temple, Colin Harvey, Howard Kendall, Joe Royle and Alan Ball. There are walk on parts for Shankly, Matt Busby, Don Revie, Bill Nicholson and Brian Clough – plus Dennis Skinner, the legendary MP. Alex Ferguson's first public 'hairdryer' – with Catterick only feet away – gets an unexpected outing. The script takes the story from London's Café Royal to Goodison via Anfield, Wembley, Blackpool's Bloomfield Road and Athens. The main part of the plot both starts and ends in farce, beginning with a famous sacking in a taxi and finishing with a horse biting a spectator outside the Baseball Ground, Derby. Thankfully, the tales that filled the interim depict one of the most fascinating and revolutionary passages of English football history.

1.
In the Beginning

THE HOTEL CAFÉ ROYAL IN LONDON HOLDS A UNIQUE PLACE IN THE history of Everton Football Club. When the Everton chairman John Moores and his manager Johnny Carey left the Grade II listed building just after 4 p.m. on 14 April 1961, it set off a chain of events that set the agenda for domestic football in the rest of the decade and beyond.

At that point in their history Everton had not won a trophy for 22 years, after their League Championship triumph in 1938/39 – the club's third title in twelve seasons. When organised league football returned in 1946, Everton failed to recreate the momentum of the pre-war years. Losing players like Tommy Lawton and Joe Mercer was never going to be easy and with the club unable to sign top quality replacements then decline was inevitable, especially as several of the ageing 1930s team remained.

If 1945-1950 was the Age of Austerity, as the country struggled to rebuild after the end of World War Two, then the same description could easily have applied to events at Goodison Park. After a reasonably solid tenth place finish in 1946/47, there was a decline in the next two seasons and in 1948/49 the club finished just three places above the relegation places. The introduction of former player Cliff Britton as manager during that campaign failed to halt the slide and despite a losing FA Cup semi-final appearance to Liverpool in 1950, by the end of that year relegation was a distinct possibility, Everton taking just nine points from their opening eighteen games. A renaissance at the year-end took Britton's side clear so that by early April they were six points above the drop zone, albeit having played more games than the two teams below them – Sheffield Wednesday and Chelsea.

Two defeats meant they travelled to Hillsborough on the final day needing a point to survive. The result was a humiliating 6-0 defeat and, for only the second time, Everton slipped into the abyss. 'Let us not shirk from the stern fact that unless there is a drastic overhaul of Goodison affairs it is going to be a long time before we see Everton back in their rightful sphere,' were the words of Ranger in the *Liverpool Echo*. 'It has taken them five years of consistent decline to get into the Second Division. In the absence of an all-out effort at rehabilitation it may take them as long to work their passage back.'

In the event it took them three years to claw their way back into the top flight, following statistically the worst season in the club's history in 1952/53 when Britton's side finished a lowly sixteenth. Promotion as runners-up in 1953/54 was primarily down to the forward partnership of Dave Hickson and John Willie Parker, who struck 55 goals. With the board showing no signs of investing in the squad, elevation to the first division failed to light the fires of success at Goodison, and manager Britton left in 1956 after two disappointing finishes outside the top ten. His successor Ian Buchan – infamously regarded as a 'chief coach' rather than manager – fared no better and when the Scot was sacked after a poor start to the 1958/59 campaign, the board turned to Carey. The only consolation during this period was future stalwarts like Brian Harris, Derek Temple and Brian Labone all made their debuts. Meanwhile one of the most important men in Everton's long history began to make his presence felt.

2.
'The King is Dead, Long Live the King'

John Moores – the Manchester Messenger

Born in Eccles, Greater Manchester, in January 1896, John Moores was one of a family of eight children. Even from an early age the future Everton chairman showed the entrepreneurial skills that would make him one of the richest people in Britain. Encouraged by his mother, Moores moved quickly after his first job as a six-shilling a week messenger boy for the Post Office, where the self-confidence and single-mindedness that characterised his rise to the top ultimately lead to his departure. After Moores objected to instructions to work during his break, the head messenger warned him that 'In future you'll do as you're told.' Moores replied 'I won't,' and left by the end of the week.

Moores' next job was as a trainee telegraphist with the Commercial Cable Company, which in many ways shaped everything that came afterwards. Shortly after World War One ended, the role took Moores to Liverpool for the first time, for training in Bixteth Street. The visit began a love affair with the city and its people that was to last more than seventy years, but typically one that worked both ways; asked once why he had never moved south, Moores replied: 'I have made money out of this area and I like the people here.'

With training complete Moores was then stationed to Waterville Cable Station in County Kerry, Ireland. Following complaints over food, Moores was elected Mess President – effectively granting him overall management responsibility for catering – where for the first time he displayed the leadership skills and business acumen that would define him. Moores picked the committee members himself and after discovering that suppliers were overcharging, formed the Waterville Supply Company to source their own food, reducing costs and improving the standard of cuisine. Other Moores-led initiatives included the purchasing of books for the station's library and, with the local golf course having no club shop, agreeing a deal with Dunlop to become their agent for 'the supply of golf requisites' in the area. With these lucrative sidelines, at a time when the average wage was £3 per week, Moores was earning nearly ten times as much, thanks to his hard work and gift for identifying gaps in the market.

With his appetite for success and wealth whetted, Moores was continually looking for additional ways of generating money. One of his companions in Ireland was Colin Askham, a friend from his days as a messenger boy in Manchester. After 18 months in Ireland,[1] both men returned to Liverpool and teamed up with another former messenger boy, Bill Hughes. Taking their lead from a football pool run in Birmingham, they devised their own venture, putting up £50 each as start-up costs. The company's name of Littlewood originated from the adopted Askham's actual surname at birth, his business partner having been orphaned at a young age.

The first 4,000 coupons were distributed before a Manchester United game at Old Trafford in February 1924. Famously only 35 coupons were returned, the three founders' income after the dividend not even covering their costs. Midway through the 1924/25 season, after contributing £200 each with little return, the trio convened a crisis meeting. After his two partners suggested they cut their losses and close the business down, Moores surprisingly disagreed, and offered to pay back both their original investment in return for all their shares. 'I still believe in the idea,' he informed them.

The Mersey Millionaire

Moores' hunch proved correct: within three years the company was turning over more than £200,000 annually and by 1932 he was a millionaire. By then Moores was expanding into mail order catalogues and chain stores on the way to creating the largest private company in Europe.

---

1 There was one curious tale about Moores' time across the Irish Sea. According to his biographer Barbara Clegg, in her book *The Man Who Made Littlewoods*, there was a possible attempt made on his life. Returning to his camp after a night out Moores discovered bullets that had been fired through a window at his bed. The reasons were unknown, although they could have also been a warning over his business activities.

As well as running the business, Moores had always been a man with a wide number of outside interests, including golf and painting. Moores had also watched Everton from his early days in the city and was a spectator when Dixie Dean scored his record-breaking sixtieth league goal in 1928. After acquiring shares in both Everton and Liverpool, he began a family association with football in the city that still exists today. The Littlewoods chief later explained why it was Everton, and not their rivals, who put the connection on a more official footing. 'I was asked to put money into Everton, which they were to repay,' Moores said in 1964. 'At first it was £36,000 for floodlights then came more money for players. They also began to ask my advice on business matters. Soon it was suggested that I join the board to see my money spent. That's how I came to join the one club rather than the other.'

Two years earlier Moores had told Bob Ferrier of the *Observer* that there was another motive for getting involved. 'I've always been an Everton man[2] – can't tell you why. For ten years I watched the club flounder in management. It got so bad I took to going to St Helens to watch Rugby League.' Moores later told Ian Hargraves of the *Liverpool Echo* of an unexpected shock when he joined the board in March 1960, 'I was surprised to find the club was actually in the red, and I was struck by the amount of waste and the money that was being lost by inefficient use of resources.' For a man used to being in charge, being a board member was always going to be a temporary appointment.

The chairman, June 1960

Unsurprisingly, within three months Moores was appointed chairman, at the annual shareholders' meeting in June 1960. The people who ran football clubs, before Moores arrived, had traditionally been the local businessman made good. That was about to change when the multi-millionaire joined the Everton board. Whether it was intentional or not, Moores gave the impression of wishing to run the club on the lines of the continental giants – Littlewoods underwriting expenditure in the same way that, say, the Agnelli family had used their Fiat fortune to support Juventus. This was taking English football into new territory, and it was a vision that Moores reiterated when he entered the boardroom.

[2] Two years later though Moores told Brian James in the *Daily Mail* that, before joining Everton, the Liverpool chairman T.V. Williams 'would have liked me to join the Liverpool board. I had a leaning towards Liverpool.'

'We want the best players, the best coaches, the best trainers and the best directors,' he proclaimed, 'Whether I shall prove to be one of the best directors will be answered in time.' Moores immediately brought his business expertise to bear, making the financial changes required to bring some stability – a loss of £49,504 in 1959/60 becoming a profit of £25,504 in 1960/61.[3]

With his corporate business background, Moores was very much a modernist who also remained frustrated at the archaic structures at the top of the English game, which hindered the progress of the big clubs, especially when compared to those overseas. The biggest source of his frustration was the 'three-quarters' majority rule in the Football League, derived from each club in the top two divisions having a single vote each, with the bottom two tiers having four votes collectively. Of the 48 votes available, 36 was the amount needed to instigate change, but this rarely happened as the smaller clubs grouped to scupper the plans of the elite.

'If we want really big professional football as a spectacle, that is one thing,' he told Bob Ferrier, 'but it is very different from what we have at the moment.' Moores also believed that the big teams should have the best players appearing in modern stadia. 'As it is now, we are at the mercy of clubs who cannot compete with us, but can veto our progress,' he said. 'The three-quarters majority rule is crippling the future of the game, we cannot tolerate amateur minds sitting in judgement on us.' Moores tried to bend his counterparts' views to match his own by widely circulating his correspondence with the Football League to fellow chairmen – and usually succeeded.

In August 1960, Moores led the protests over the £150,000 ITV television deal with the Football League to show matches live on a Saturday evening, as their management committee did not consult with the clubs. The Everton chairman voiced his fears in writing to all those in the top two divisions, and the agreement was effectively scrapped in the opening months of the season. Six months later, when the proposed 'new deal' with players may have allowed them to walk out at the end of their contracts, Moores – fearing the loss of his expensively assembled assets – wrote to the Football League for an assurance that there was no right to a

3 Although a reduction in transfer expenditure contributed to this change, Moores' business acumen was behind an increase of £28,000 in ticket receipts from home league games, following price rises, and savings of £10,000 in miscellaneous outgoings like travelling, training and matchday expenses. Pitifully small amounts in the modern era, but almost sixty years ago Everton's annual income was around £200,000. In comparison Littlewoods' revenue was more than £90m in 1960, having doubled in five years.

transfer when contracts ended, circulating the letter to all 92 league clubs. The move proved highly influential and at their extraordinary meeting in April 1961[4] the clubs voted to resist the change.

Moores reserved his biggest gripe for the insular view of the game in England. In business Moores had been a regular traveller to the United States, visiting their equivalent companies to Littlewoods, returning to England with new plans to drive the firm forward. On cruises Moores would sound out fellow businessmen from across the Atlantic in an exchange of ideas and opinions. Moores was keen to apply the same principles to running Everton, but the ruling bodies and clubs in this country were averse to allowing overseas influences, protected by the restrictive employment practices operating at the time – there had been a longstanding Ministry of Labour and FA rule that overseas players had to serve a two-year residency period in this country before becoming eligible to play in the Football League. Such blinkered thinking annoyed the visionary Moores, as the sight of Real Madrid winning five European Cups with a cosmopolitan outfit had clearly fired his imagination, as did the Inter Milan side that faced Everton later in the decade.

The Everton chairman bitterly fired off his frustrations to Mike Langley of the *Daily Express* in August 1962, 'Real Madrid, with naturalised Hungarians and Argentinians, are almost helped by the Spanish government to build the world's best team. Our government has no interest in football apart from taking millions in pools money out of the game and putting none of it back.' That had not stopped Moores trying to match the continental giants, even prior to joining the board. In December 1960 he spoke about trying to sign the great Ferenc Puskás, having six months earlier told shareholders about the barriers he faced:

It is no use people telling us to go out and buy world-class players like Real Madrid can do. The League rules will not allow it. If I had offered Puskas a £15,000 signing-on fee when he left Hungary, and made him a director of Littlewoods at £10,000 a year, I still could not have signed him for Everton because the Home Office would not have admitted him into the country as an alien, the Players' Union would have objected and the League would have vetoed it too.

---

4 The meeting took place on an infamous day, of course, in Everton history.

That did not deter Moores from trying to put together a deal to sign the great Hungarian again later in the decade, as he admitted in 1972. 'I tried all I knew to get Ferenc Puskás when there was still a lot of football in him. He would have been given a top job as well as football. We could have satisfied him, but we just could not get permission,' he claimed.

Shares across the Park

One of the more unusual aspects of Moores' time at Goodison was his close links with their rivals across Stanley Park. Littlewoods' involvement with the Anfield club began when their managing director Eric Sawyer joined the board as finance director after Bill Shankly arrived in 1959. 'Liverpool wanted to revitalise their club so I suggested Mr Sawyer should join them as financial expert,' Moores disclosed. Sawyer was to prove a hugely influential figure, prompting Bill Shankly to claim he was 'the man who revolutionised Liverpool'. Previous business experience almost certainly influenced Moores' thinking. After their initial success, the Littlewoods' chairman fully understood that the competition provided by those rivals who copied their lead – such as the other major pools companies of the time, Vernons and Zetters – was not only good for the industry but it drove his company to work in more efficient and imaginative ways. Moores therefore always believed that a healthy rivalry between the two clubs was mutually beneficial. 'I would like to see both Merseyside clubs as good as Spain's Real Madrid and Barcelona,' he admitted after becoming chairman.

However, as an Anfield shareholder Moores was always keen to ensure there was no conflict of interest, so after joining the Goodison board he ceased attending the Liverpool shareholders' meeting. 'I know I must never interfere,' he said in 1964, 'I have not given Liverpool money nor would I help them buy players to beat Everton.' That said, the influence of Everton shareholders across both clubs was remarkable. By November 1966 individual shareholders in Everton also possessed 40 percent of Liverpool's share capital, which was considerably more than the Anfield club's directors. Furthermore, shareholders across the Park also owned 25 percent of the Goodison club. A total of 29 members of the Moores family and their Littlewoods associates collectively owned more than a third of the two clubs – if it happened today there would be examination of the rulebooks to ensure there was no conflict of interest. Moores' benevolence to Everton's closest rivals extended to indirect financial and other assistance – his architects designed the

Anfield Road and Kemlyn Road stands for no charge, while Littlewoods found jobs for several amateurs on Liverpool's books and freely gave time off for training.

Although there were a number of ambiguities with Moores' association across both clubs, there was no question that Everton were his only love. 'Split loyalties?' he said early in the decade, 'I don't think so.' To that end Moores wanted Everton to be the most successful club in the land, and on becoming chairman he repeated a previous statement about only employing the elite, this time with a twist. 'Everton must have the best players, the best coaches, the best manager and the best directors,' he informed the shareholders, before warning, 'if any of them fail, they must go.'

Johnny Carey – the genial Irishman

Johnny Carey was an amiable and easy-going Irishman who during a brilliant playing career had captained Manchester United to the FA Cup in 1948 and was a member of their championship-winning side four years later. Carey was really a footballer by default, having youthful designs on being a tennis player – he was on speaking terms with the pre-war greats like Fred Perry. On retirement, the man who in the words of one journalist 'smoked a pipe through each and every crisis, major or minor,' made the successful and seamless transition into management, taking Blackburn out of the second division in 1958. The Everton directors noted Carey's progress at Ewood Park and later that year gave him the opportunity to re-awaken a sleeping giant after the ill-fated reign of Ian Buchan. Improvement was slow, with the 1959/60 campaign particularly a struggle as the Toffees failed to accrue a single away win in eventually finishing fifteenth, just three points above the relegation zone.

Carey was fortunate that Moores wasted no time in giving Everton access to his fortune, albeit via an interest-free loan of £56,000. The Irishman had already signed Roy Vernon from previous club Blackburn and when Jimmy Gabriel and Alex Young were recruited from north of the border the Toffees were finally in a position to challenge for honours. A 3-1 victory at champions Burnley on Boxing Day 1960 left Carey's men occupying third place in the table, but within 24 hours the Lancashire side had strolled to a 3-0 win in the return. The defeat triggered a depressing sequence of seven successive defeats, including removal from both cup competitions to lower division opponents.

Before Christmas 1960 Moores had been supportive of the manager. 'John is very good. He knows how to deal with the players. I leave that side to him,' he admitted publicly. The reality was that the chairman quietly disapproved of the Irishman's 'arm across the shoulder' style. 'Carey had many outstanding qualifications,' Moores later said, 'but let me say that we thought he lacked in one or two areas we considered essential in our plans for rebuilding Everton. One was that we thought him not to be tough enough.' The chairman had originally decided to terminate the Irishman's contract during the depressing run in the early months of 1961, but Everton flowered in the spring and a sparkling 4-0 win at Newcastle in early April was part of an impressive sequence which saw them pick up nine points from five league games. The former Manchester United stalwart was seen to be popular and regarded as more than capable within the game, but Moores had other ideas.

14 April, 1961

In her biography of the Littlewoods boss, author Barbara Clegg quotes Moores on the secret of his company's success: 'The facility for the quick training of employees, coupled with the organising ability of the directors and executive staff.' Moores wanted strong leaders who were accountable for their actions. 'If you live on high hills, you must expect high winds,' was a favourite quote. In Moores' world, if an employee was not doing their job properly then it was important to find out the reasons why, but ultimately their manager was accountable if they had done nothing to address the issue.

To ensure full oversight at Littlewoods, Moores took the extraordinary step of interviewing all their buyers from their mail order division personally, over the course of a week. These were strictly planned at 20 minutes in length, as Moores had an obsession over not wasting time and prompt timekeeping.[5] The interviews were probing and managers were told in no uncertain terms if they were underperforming. One employee who was given a hard time later saw a Rolls Royce following him on the motorway, and was wrongly convinced Moores was chasing him. The keen football fan therefore established a reputation as being 'ruthless with his executives. He didn't slate the poor fellow down there, it was the management,' according to one of his staff. Elsewhere, although there was a

5 After retiring, Bill Shankly had an appointment to interview Moores for radio, but found it cancelled after turning up late. 'I'm sorry you are behind schedule,' Moores explained, 'and I have a schedule to live to.'

general warmth for Moores, some employees of Littlewoods consequently spoke of a climate of fear in the company, of staff going into hiding when supervisor checks were performed, for fear of being accused of some misdemeanour.

Nevertheless, Moores was cognisant that managing a football club was a different affair to Littlewoods, with players collectively given greater freedom to control their destiny than workers on a shop-floor. 'I know, of course, that running a team of footballers is different from running a business,' he told the *Liverpool Echo* in December 1960, 'If you give players too explicit an order it spoils them, puts them in a sort of straitjacket. We try to get them to talk matches and tactics among themselves and act on the advice of teammates.' Yet for all that talk, Moores struggled with that comparative lack of control during the early years, with the chairman being a regular visitor to the training ground, where he was not shy in passing on his limited knowledge to professional footballers. 'They don't head the ball these days as they used to,' he told the *Daily Mail's* Jack Wood shortly after becoming chairman, 'There are no Lawtons or Deans around. But the right neck exercises and constant heading practice will make them all better in the air.' Carey also resented the chairman's regular presence in the dressing room before and after games, especially on one occasion in early 1961 when Moores clearly undermined his manager with a public rollicking of the players.

Although there were big differences in running Littlewoods and Everton, it was still inevitable that once Moores arrived at Goodison that some of his management principles would follow him and have a similar impact, particularly around job security. Having a significant amount of money to spend and with a ruthless chairman, players and staff were understandably wary of their immediate futures, as the press quickly realised. Speaking of the 'club's apparent policy to be one of unconcern for the individual,' a *Sunday Telegraph* editorial warned that 'Mr. Moores has more than once submitted that his aims are short-term, so perhaps the club's tradition in personal relations is not paramount among his objectives. One can only say that Everton will find it hard to live at the top without internal harmony.' In many ways that proved to be the case in the years that followed. However, in the short-term it was not the players who were vulnerable – in typical Moores' style it was their manager.

His biographer, Barbara Clegg, said that during the 1960s Moores 'seemed to have a speed demon behind him … he was always hustling, always pushing. And the first thing he did was to give the push to John Carey.' When they travelled to London together for the Football League's extraordinary meeting on Friday, 14 April 1961, Carey was probably conscious of the chairman's cold-blooded treatment of his senior managers in business but unaware that for more than thirty years the last day of the working week was known as 'sacking time' in Littlewoods. On one Friday, Moores culled the firm's buyers from thirteen to four in an almost Stalinist purge. Whilst in the capital, Moores therefore applied one of his standard business practices to the running of Everton Football Club. After leaving the meeting, the two men headed towards the Grosvenor House Hotel by taxi, at Moores' behest. By the time they had finished talking ninety minutes later, Carey had been sacked.

The Everton directors was unprepared for such a development. Although they had voted unanimously for Carey's dismissal from his £3,000 a year post, there was an agreement that they should offer the manager the chance to resign with some dignity. After the news broke, there was still confusion on the circumstances of Carey's dismissal. Moores later claimed that the board had agreed to give Carey the chance to resign but 'the opportunity was turned down and the action of last Friday was taken'. If that was the case then the sacking should not have come as a surprise, but Carey was in the dark. 'The first I knew of the decision to finish as manager of Everton was after the meeting in London on Friday, when Mr Moores told me in a taxi,' Carey claimed. Given the circumstances, unsurprisingly the legal ramifications associated with Carey's dismissal lasted a long time, as Moores later admitted: 'I was very naïve when I sacked Johnny Carey. The newspapers asked me to give my side of the story, but I refused because I did not want to hurt Johnny any more than was absolutely necessary. My lawyers said it would be a seven-day wonder. They were wrong.'

There was six years of legal wrangling to reach an agreement over compensation – the parties settling out of court just before a hearing at Liverpool Assizes in March 1967. At the time of his sacking, the general feeling was that Carey had been unlucky. Injuries to key players had blighted the second half of the campaign and his development of young talent – which was highly prized at Blackburn – again showed signs of promise, with Everton in the semi-finals of the FA Youth Cup. However, behind the scenes there were rumours of unrest and of a clash of personalities and methods. Although Alex Young said, 'He [Carey] was very knowledgeable and a very nice, gentle man. If he had a sergeant-major type on his right-hand side he might have been more successful,' that view was not necessarily shared by his teammates. Moores consequently felt that discipline was not as strict as it should have been. 'I'd be a bit tougher than John Carey on training and things like that,' his chairman confessed to the *Liverpool Echo* in December 1960.

Widely booed by the Goodison crowd before the Cardiff City game, 24 hours after the dismissal, in an attempt to curry favour with supporters Moores later denied that he was the driving force behind the sacking of the manager. 'People have the idea that it was me who was determined to get him sacked from the time I took over,' he claimed, 'but on the contrary I was very much for him and defended him at first against the directors.' Carey for his part largely kept his own counsel, save for an interview with the *Daily Mail* ten months later. Asked if there were any disagreements between the two, Carey replied:

You don't have rows with him. There was talk about a Moores-Carey partnership at Everton. This seemed to upset him as there was no question of a partnership. He was not a partnership man. I think two things lead to my sacking. Mr Moores wanted a man who he had appointed as manager – I was there before him. And he wanted a tough man, someone to crack the whip. Whip cracking is not for me.

Intriguingly, four weeks after Carey's departure, Wolves manager Stan Cullis revealed that Moores had approached him earlier in the year with a view to taking over at Goodison, on a huge annual salary of £5,000. 'I told my chairman of the offer as soon as it was made,' Cullis revealed, 'but turned it down on principle.' The Wolves boss did not elaborate on the principle in question, although it may have been that Moores made the offer when Carey was still in the post. Given Cullis' career declined swiftly in the first half of the 1960s, it could have been a blessing in disguise for the Everton chairman.

By the time he sacked Carey, Moores had a new managerial target. Like Carey said, it was somebody in his own ruthless, disciplined and hardworking image. 'I knew who was our man,' he said, 'we had taken the trouble to make a detailed check on him and his methods. I would say there are only about a dozen good managers in the league and he is one of them.'

Harry Catterick – the chosen one

Born in Darlington in 1919, Harry Catterick joined Everton as a player in 1937, but due to World War Two had to wait nine years to make his debut. After scoring 24 goals in 71 games as an effective, if not top-class, centre-forward, Catterick joined Crewe Alexandra as player-manager in 1951. At Gresty Road the novice manager took the Cheshire side to tenth place in the old Third Division (North) in 1952/53.

The achievement was enough to bring Catterick to the attention of other clubs and that summer, having now hung up his boots, the 33-year-old took on the job at Rochdale. The financial struggles at Spotland were symptomatic of the time in the lower divisions – a tale of a shortage of players and unpaid bills. The journalist Eric Todd later recounted interviewing Catterick at the Lancashire club. Writing in the *Guardian*, Todd remembered a card on his desk that said 'take care of the pennies and the pounds will take care of themselves'. Bringing it to the new manager's attention, Todd provoked a curt response from the Rochdale boss. 'What,' Catterick asked, 'is a pound.'

After five years of steady progress at Spotland, Catterick moved to Sheffield Wednesday in September 1958. The Hillsborough outfit were universally regarded as a 'yo-yo' club in the immediate post-war years as they oscillated between the top two divisions, and had just been relegated from the top flight for the third time in seven years. Wednesday romped to the second division title in Catterick's first campaign with 62 points. In 1959/60 the Owls reached the FA Cup semi-final while finishing fifth in the league – which could have been better. Two points off the top with five matches remaining, they won just one more game.

It was during the 1960/61 campaign that Catterick really made his mark. At the beginning of April, Wednesday were in second place, albeit with no chance of catching runaway leaders Spurs. However, it was an open secret that all was not well behind the scenes, and the expectation was Catterick would leave at the end of his contract in August. Therefore, it was no shock that on 10 April 1961, Catterick announced his resignation. 'Mr Catterick's decision did not come as a surprise,' wrote the *Yorkshire Post*, 'although he later said that he had not got any other work.' Inevitably, talk turned to a return to Goodison although there appeared to be little chance. With Carey still in the manager's hot seat, the *Liverpool Daily Post* headlined, 'Forget Catterick For Everton Rumours,' two days after his resignation from the Sheffield club.

When asked about the stories linking him with the role, Catterick's line was that 'I have had no official approach.' Nevertheless, Everton officially offered their former player the job he coveted within 48 hours of Carey's sacking. Tackled by the press outside his parents' house in Stockport on that Sunday, Catterick confirmed his interest. Later that day club secretary Bill Dickinson issued a statement that the appointment of Catterick was expected on the Monday. The former Sheffield Wednesday manager made his position clear that evening. 'Everton's offer looks very attractive,' he said, 'and subject to certain details I am prepared to accept. There's no doubt about it. I should get a tremendous kick out of managing a club I used to play for.' The board ultimately considered the merits of four managers – Catterick, Cullis and Everton legend Joe Mercer, then at Aston Villa, with the other candidate unknown – but the club's former centre-forward was the unanimous final choice from a shortlist of two, with interest in Cullis understandably cooling.

Catterick's demands were mainly around total control over team matters and when they were satisfactorily resolved, he was presented to the press at 5 p.m. on Monday, 17 April. Returning to Goodison brought out the warm side of the manager. 'I am terribly proud to have had this job offered to me. I think you could say it has been one of my ambitions to return to my old club,' he told journalists. Asked about his level of authority, Catterick replied, 'I have as much control as any manager should need. I am very happy about that side of the job. There is no point being called a manager if you are not one.' His arrival certainly pleased the chairman. 'The king is dead,' Moores told the press, 'long live the king.'

The challenge

During his welcoming press conference, Catterick alluded to the belief that 'Everton is now being referred to in some quarters as the new hot seat of management in the football world.' That was certainly correct. In the eighteen months prior to his appointment Everton had undertaken one of the biggest spending sprees in English club history. During that time, the Toffees had paid more than £200,000 for Tommy Ring, Roy Vernon, Mickey Lill, Jimmy Gabriel, Billy Bingham, Alex Young and George Thomson. The massive shopping expedition certainly raised the stakes, with now only Tottenham having the financial means to compete with the Moores-backed Merseyside club. The wider challenge though was to break the monopoly of the 'big five' clubs who had largely dominated post-war domestic football. At the end of the 1960/61 campaign Arsenal, Burnley, Manchester United, Spurs and Wolves had claimed eleven of the previous fourteen league titles, with nine runners-up places. Those clubs had also collectively won the FA Cup five times in that time with three other final appearances.

A super-rich, powerful and publicly ambitious backer with substantial funds available may be commonplace in the upper echelons of the modern game but in the early 1960s it was unknown in England. Moores' money presented an opportunity, but it also brought overwhelming pressure on the manager that, by extension, spread to the players. Jack Wood in the *Daily Mail* once described John Moores with the words 'his ambition is limitless, and uncompromising'. At his new manager's unveiling, one scribe asked Moores, with some hesitancy, why the sacked Carey was classed as a failure, given the club was in fifth position. Moores replied coldly: 'Fifth place is no good to us.' Asked what would happen if Everton remained in no better than fifth under Catterick, Moores was even more blunt. 'Then Harry will go,' the chairman said.

The subsequent internal weight of expectation on Catterick as the first managerial alchemist, the boss capable of turning invested cash into trophies, was therefore immense and for many an alien concept. With Everton at the vanguard, critics claimed greed and financial muscle were creating an unhealthy environment for the domestic game. More than a half a century later and they are still saying the same things, albeit in a financial setting light years away. The modern equivalent of Everton in 1961 is probably the scenario played out at Stamford Bridge in 2003–04. For Moores read Roman Abramovich, while Claudio Ranieri mirrored Carey's role as a gentleman considered, at the time, good but not good enough. Their new employer, who evidently required someone with more steel, sacked both managers after a single season. Catterick and Jose Mourinho were poles apart in many ways, but they possessed the single-mindedness and confidence of natural managerial winners. As the Football League secretary Alan Hardaker[6] once said, an ideal manager must be 'devious and ruthless and selfish', and those characteristics sit easily with both. The man from Portugal was also, like Catterick, able to call on a gifted roll call of players bequeathed by his predecessor. Nevertheless, Catterick still felt the pressure placed on his shoulders, as he later outlined in a self-penned article in the *Liverpool Daily Post* in 1971:

Success. That was my brief when I came to Goodison. To earn it quickly without sacrificing Everton's high standards of football. Mr John Moores made no secret of

6 Asked in 1969 on the integrity of the game, the man dubbed 'the Great Dictator' famously said, 'I wouldn't hang a dog on the word of a professional footballer.' A statement to remember when considering some of the claims made later in the decade about Everton.

the fact he expected results. It was a tall order. I needed no reminding of Everton's history for I grew up with it as a player. They had been starved of success. It was something like twenty-five years since they had seen a trophy. The club were becoming a bit like Villa, trophies were antique. This is wrong. You want modern trophies and this club simply has not had them.

The moniker of 'Mersey Millionaires' did Everton no favours. Like Chelsea in the twenty first century, their unabashed spending attracted wide criticism and accusations of trying to buy success.[7] Although Everton were not the first to do this – Sunderland were once known as the 'Bank of England' club – they were certainly the first to do so with a hugely wealthy and ambitious benefactor from the world of big business. Not lost on opposition fans was the fact that Littlewoods' wealth was founded upon their pools' activities, effectively meaning that Everton bought players using money that indirectly came from supporters of other clubs. This brought a certain amount of negative attention, not least from the southern press, who saw them as a threat, especially to their beloved Tottenham Hotspur – conveniently ignoring the fact that the White Hart Lane outfit had been no strangers to the chequebook themselves before Moores' arrival.

A 2-1 defeat at Fulham early in Catterick's first season gave an indication of the negativity of the press. The post-match coverage featured a withering attack on the club and its ambitions by Desmond Hackett of the *Daily Express*. 'If Mr Moores is not trying to by success, I am slightly puzzled at the way they are lashing their money around as though they were the lira lunatics of Italy,' the flamboyant pressman wrote, 'even millionaires do not beam upon the expenditure of £218,000 just to keep the natives friendly. As I was saying, Mr Moores, you cannot buy soccer success. There can be no price tag for the loyalty and ability of players like Johnny Haynes.'

Hackett's simplistic view that Everton were attempting to buy titles misread Moores' understanding of the game. The chairman knew that success on the pitch, first and foremost, required the right footballing infrastructure off it. 'If the administrative, management and coaching sectors of Everton are on the right lines, then buying the best players can guarantee success,' Moores told Bob Ferrier

7 In the first two years after Moores joined the board to the end of the 1961/62 season, Everton spent in excess of £250,000 on 13 players. In the same period Spurs bought one player (Jimmy Greaves) for £99,999 and Manchester United three for £70,000 in total.

in the *Observer* later that season. Getting the club on a sound financial footing and appointing the best available manager (Catterick) was one half of the equation – the future development of Bellefield as a training centre of excellence was also part of this – but it did not necessarily follow that buying the best players guaranteed success, as the subsequent history of other clubs showed. Nevertheless, the cynicism of the press gathered speed as Everton threatened to lift the title in 1962/63. Following a vital 2-1 win late in the season at Upton Park, Mike Langley stated in the *Daily Express*, 'Everton, at £300,000 soccer's most expensive cast, openly declared at Upton Park that they are in the business of winning matches and not necessarily of entertaining anyone.' Not only was the statement factually incorrect (Spurs' team at the time cost £350,000), it unwittingly explained why victory was everything – the money coming into the game made success the sole priority.

3.
Catterick: His Managerial 'Philosophy'

Balancing the scales

WHEN CATTERICK BECAME MANAGER, THE GENERAL BELIEF WAS that he was inheriting a squad of talented but temperamental players. There was a feeling that Carey had failed to make the team add up to the sum of its parts. However, Catterick felt the overall strength of the squad was lacking. 'I had a number of good players – vintage material – players who had been around several clubs,' he later said, 'but they didn't blend together. But perhaps I had better explain that I am probably the most difficult man in the business to satisfy.' The squad inherited from Carey was also unbalanced: between right and left, and in the mix of artists and artisans. Counting the stricken Tommy Ring, who had broken his leg at Chelsea in October 1960, four players had appeared on the right wing (Ring, Mick Lill, Derek Temple and Billy Bingham). Only the recently signed Jimmy Fell provided a natural a left-sided option.

Aside from the unbalanced squad, Catterick quickly detected the other roots of the club's underachievement. 'There was an air of complacency about the place, everyone seemed too easy going,' he later recalled, 'some of the staff seemed afraid to make even minor decisions affecting training and coaching. I had to make changes and I didn't like what I had to do because I had known some of them as players.' Bingham in particular picked up the immediate change in atmosphere, 'I had gelled well with Johnny. He was a tracksuit manager who could play with us. Harry was a much harder man and more ruthless. Maybe that's where his success came from. In army terms, Harry was a sergeant-major and Johnny an officer.' One of the early casualties was long-serving trainer Harry Cooke. 'He was nearly seventy years-old and I had been a boy under him,' the 41-year-old Catterick said of the man who served Everton loyally over a period of almost six decades. That said, for Catterick the transition was initially not as problematic as it may have been. The manager later pointed to the 1961 summer tour of the United States as vital in terms of building a rapport with the squad, telling the *Liverpool Echo* on his return:

I have got to know them pretty well. Contrary to some stories that I had heard that I would find a lot of 'temperament' at Goodison Park, I found nothing of the sort. I find them a sound bunch of fellows all trying to do their best for the club. That's what I aim to get from all my staff… if we strike a happy blend of team spirit and method we are liable to topple any club in Britain. That Everton can play brilliantly I know from what I saw at the back end of last season. I aim to get them playing well consistently.

Catterick liked a first-team squad, or 'pool' in his words, of about eighteen players of which at any time he was looking to replace two. The squad also required a steady influx of youth, but this initially proved difficult. 'We have a number of good young players,' he told the *Liverpool Echo's* Leslie Edwards in August 1961, 'but some of them are not quite ready yet, in my opinion, for slipping into the first-team. This is a matter that causes me a little concern. We are not as well off numerically for players in certain positions as I would like.' Unlike later in the decade, Catterick was reluctant to use any homegrown youngsters in his early days, even though the side had played in the final of the FA Youth Cup just after his arrival. Only half of the line-up in that final went on to make a first-team appearance, and none became a regular. One of the reasons for this, he later explained, was that the reserve and youth teams played and trained in a vastly different manner to the senior side. Introducing younger players he felt would damage the 'blend'.

The case for the defence

In the early 1960s, virtually all English club sides played the classic WM (3-2-2-3) formation: a centre-half flanked by two full-backs, two wing-halves (approximating to today's defensive midfielders), two inside-forwards and a centre-forward between two wingers. Nevertheless, the game was changing. With increased exposure to European and international football came fresh ideas on tactics and formations. The effect was to make teams more defensive and, as the decade progressed, most deployed an extra centre-half within a 4-2-4 formation, one first pioneered by Brazil in the late 1950s, although Catterick resisted the change longer than most.

For all his proclamations on the need to play attractively, Catterick was in the early 1960s, like most managers, primarily a pragmatist. 'My basic aim is to ally attractive football to complete defensive efficiency,' he admitted, 'I would be happiest winning a game 1-0 rather than 6-5 for it means greater efficiency in getting a result.' This was shorthand for saying that effectively his primary aim in any match was not to concede – a surprise given the general feeling since is that Everton had a reputation for playing progressive football throughout the decade. This was not necessarily the case, especially in the years before the FA Cup win in 1966, when the manager had a reputation for negative, robust play. 'Harry Catterick, a brilliant defensive manager, has not found it easy to give Everton a really consistent look in attack,' said James Wilson in the *Sunday Times* after a 1-0 victory over Spurs in October 1963.

Catterick inherited a reasonably stable back-line, with Albert Dunlop as the resident goalkeeper, Brian Labone as the single centre-half flanked by two Scots, Alex Parker and George Thomson. The signing of inside-forward Dennis Stevens in March 1962 was an important aspect of Catterick's desire to instil increased defensive stability. Bringing in the disciplined and mobile Bolton man was a key part in steadying the right-hand side of the pitch and improving the defensive set-up, one founded on zonal marking. Catterick told the *News of the World's* Bob Pennington of his required defensive shape in the summer of 1963: 'Each player is schooled to take position at once in strict relation to the ball and his immediate opponent, irrespective of that player's number. It means judging distance and angles, defending an area rather than marking an individual.'

Catterick could also be flexible in his approach. The tactics deployed in the crucial league game at Spurs in December 1962 was certainly a pointer to the way Everton – and the game in general – was going in the rest of the decade. Against a team that had scored in every home game in the previous two-and-a-half years, Catterick was taking no chances. In the hotel before the game, he dug into his pocket and pulled out two pennies and two half-crowns. Placing them on the table, he used all four of them to demonstrate to the two full-backs that they needed to play deeper than usual and that, at all times, Brian Harris and Jimmy Gabriel (the wing-halves) were to take a position where the ball was always in front of them. The result was a goalless draw between the two most expensively assembled teams in English football history. 'Everton became even more concerned with strategic defence,' wrote Albert Barham in the *Guardian*, 'such tactics, though admirably executed, leave little for chilled supporters to cheer.'

Like other managers, Catterick also had a short memory. Seven days after the dour draw at White Hart Lane, Ron Greenwood's West Ham side employed a similar defensive shield and their reward was a 1-1 draw at Goodison on an afternoon when the teams were slow-handclapped off the pitch at the end of the game. Conveniently forgetting he had used the same tactics a week earlier, Catterick cut an unhappy figure afterwards. With no hint of irony, he told the press, 'Surely we ask ourselves how long the public will tolerate this defensive approach to the game?'

The increased emphasis on defence away from home bore fruit. After conceding 46 league goals on the road when finishing fifth in Carey's final season, Everton's back-line let in just 25 in the title-winning campaign two years later. However, John Moores was not always in favour of Catterick's tactics. 'We have disagreed on playing style – I'm the old school, a purist,' he said at the end of the championship season, 'He is in charge completely of the playing side and I learn by listening to him after every match. His forte of course is defence as our record shows.'

'You must have control of the midfield'

After signing Alan Ball and Howard Kendall, Catterick told author Peter Morris for his book *The Team Makers*: 'You must have control of midfield. That's where it all starts. For me, that is largely what the game is about and that is why I have concentrated on good midfield footballers. A brilliant attack is useless without them.' In that context it is not surprising that Catterick focused on improving the quality in that area. When the Everton boss spent big, it was for players in the middle of the park. But the process was more evolution rather than revolution. 'He was an assembler of teams rather than a manipulator of the moving parts,' wrote David Lacey in the *Guardian* after Catterick's death in March 1985.

Although the WM formation in theory allowed for mirrored positions on the left- and right-hand sides of the pitch, that was not the case in practice. Of the two inside-forwards, the inside-left (number 10) played a more advanced, creative role – hence the number ten shirt has historically been allocated to the playmaker – while the equivalent on the right flank (number 8) was known as a 'fetcher and carrier', the workhorse link-man between defence and attack. When Catterick arrived Bobby Collins still posed an attacking threat at inside-right, but the advancing years seriously threatened his capacity to track back and defend. Catterick quickly identified that the Scot was now too old to perform that role, leaving the team badly exposed, particularly away from home.

After replacing Collins with Dennis Stevens in March 1962, Catterick created the pivotal title-winning partnership between the former Bolton man at outside-right and Jimmy Gabriel, playing directly behind him at wing-half. The combative and versatile Gabriel brought a powerful presence to the right-flank – when the Toffees were on the defensive, the Scot would retreat into a deeper, central position, with Stevens moving to right-half. With the ageing Collins, the reinforcement of the back-line would not have been possible. Displacing a fans' favourite is not always the easiest job and Stevens was a regular target for abuse from the terraces – the home crowd barracked him unmercifully in the April 1963 encounter against his former club – but he played his role as midfield toiler to perfection.

Jimmy Gabriel was equally influential. The Scot took time to settle after moving from Dundee in 1960 but was grateful to Roy Vernon for the transformation into a battle-hardened midfield enforcer, as he later admitted, 'In England you had to give everything. Roy Vernon taught me that ... he got the anger in me and got me stirred up. Roy got up your nose and that got you going. But he meant to do that and it was for my benefit in the end.' Like Stevens, Everton's future coach and caretaker manager stuck diligently to his designated role, that of vigorously breaking up play and using the ball simply.

On the opposite flank, Brian Harris filled the left-half role up until the Christmas of the championship-winning season. Naturally right-footed, the hugely versatile player shifted to the left to accommodate Jimmy Gabriel. Like his wing-half partner, Harris provided defensive steel but Catterick felt he was unable to dominate and impose his personality on games. That led the manager back across the Pennines in December 1962 to acquire Tony Kay, the Sheffield Wednesday wing-half who was a significantly more vigorous presence. Like the sale of Collins, the acquisition of Kay raised a few eyebrows, as Harris had enjoyed an excellent first half of the campaign. Catterick showed a sense of his own history when asked how about Harris' place being under threat. 'Similar to the way I felt when Dixie Dean was about to retire and the club went out and bought Tommy Lawton. That is the way it is at Everton,' he told the press. Catterick later explained further the rationale behind his thinking to Charlie Lambert in the *Liverpool Echo* before his testimonial game in May 1978:

The game at the time was changing from 'wing-halves' to 'midfield players'. We had in midfield Gabriel, Dennis Stevens and Tony Kay. Getting past that was like getting past a brick wall. All could play, all were hard, all would work. Stevens, whom I signed from Bolton, was not a popular signing. He didn't have the frills of the others, but his work-rate, determination and sheer guts away from home added to the artistry of Alex Young and Roy Vernon.

Kay's initial absence and then ultimate departure, following the betting scandal, plus the acquisition of Fred Pickering, disrupted the balance of the team. With Pickering operating as a central striker, the only way Catterick could accommodate both the former Blackburn player and Alex Young was to move the Scot into a deeper role, whilst trying to replace Kay. The strength and resilience of the right-hand axis of Stevens and Gabriel had been the foundation of the championship side, but Catterick had little choice but to break up the partnership if Young and Pickering were to stay in the team. Consequently, during the 1964/65 campaign Catterick constantly chopped and changed his midfield with Harris, Stevens and youngster Colin Harvey all tried in Kay's role, with Young taking Stevens' place at inside-right, a role for which he was palpably unsuited. As expected it was an unpopular move with supporters. A letter to the *Liverpool Echo* summed up the prevailing mood, 'Why should an unorthodox ball player like Young play like a workhorse Stevens?' It was unfair to impose a style of play that was alien to the Scot and to stifle his natural flair. The statistics told their own tale that the experiment was a failure. In the first four months of the season, Young started fourteen league games in the inside-right role without the side recording a single victory. Despite the FA Cup win in 1966, it was only when Alan Ball and Howard Kendall arrived after the Wembley triumph that Catterick possessed a settled midfield.

From the front

Ironically, given that he was a former striker, Catterick had continual problems in selecting a suitable front-line in his twelve years at Goodison. Only for two periods – after Fred Pickering joined in 1964 and when Joe Royle's talent bloomed at the end of the decade – did he appear satisfied with his options in attack. Indeed, one of the features of his Goodison career was the fruitless hours on either scouting missions or speaking to other managers seeking a solution to his forward problems, with an endless list of strikers linked with a move to Goodison.

Yet, the team Catterick inherited had one of Goodison's greatest partnerships in any part of the pitch: Alex Young and Roy Vernon. In the championship-winning campaign of 1962/63 the two netted 46 league goals, rising to the challenge at the business end of the season – at least one of the pair scored in each of the last nine matches, sharing thirteen of Everton's eighteen goals in that time. The Scot's partnership with the Welsh international fired the imagination of all Evertonians, as the former Hearts player later recalled:

Vernon was one of the greatest Everton players, and certainly one of the best I have ever played with. He was an exceptional player who had brilliant acceleration over ten yards. He was a natural athlete who could run for long periods. We would play the wall pass together. He would play the ball to me and I would flick it past the defender backing onto me for him to run on to and exploit his explosive pace.

It was no secret that Catterick wanted a big target man leading the attack, but to Young's credit his form for large parts of the title-winning season largely made that wish academic. Nevertheless, time would show that Catterick rarely viewed the Scot as a long-term fixture as the attacking spearhead. The push for a big striker quickened after the ineffectiveness of the forward line against Inter Milan in the European Cup and their failure to come anywhere near breaching one of the continent's best defences. The encounter against the Italian side had shown Catterick that the team was too reliant on the intuition and individual skill of Vernon and Young. Against better and smarter opposition, something more potent was required.

The aftermath of the loss to the Italian giants provided Catterick with an opportunity to review his striking options. Despite being linked with several forwards, including Joe Baker, Sheffield Wednesday's David 'Bronco' Layne and Ray Crawford of Ipswich, the Everton manager felt there was little value or quality in the home market for strikers, including his own, until purchasing Fred Pickering for £85,000 in March 1964. With Vernon slipping out of the first-team picture, the challenge for Catterick was linking Young and the newcomer. The two players provided contrasting styles. The deep-lying Scot drifted in and out of games, was delicate and acted as both a goal-maker and goal-taker, while Pickering had legs like tree trunks, possessed a powerful physique and was interested only in scoring. Catterick found it difficult to generate a partnership between the two – basing tactics around a big striker resulted in players like Young naturally appearing in a deeper, more defensive role.

Pickering finished the 1964/65 campaign with 37 goals from 51 appearances, but the reason for the team's failure to mount a championship challenge was due to a lack of goals elsewhere. After Temple's fourteen goals, the next highest was the seven scored by Alex Scott. This polarisation of goalscoring supported claims that Catterick was interested in solely serving Pickering's strengths. Consequently, the variety in attack that was a feature of his title side had disappeared and the suspicion remains that the purchase disrupted the balance and playing style of the team, in the same way that Gary Lineker's did two decades later.

But the move to 4-2-4 in 1965/66 allowed Catterick to integrate Pickering and Young into the same side as twin strikers. With the Scot fully fit for the first time in twelve months and having blended well in pre-season trial games at Bellefield, initially the change worked perfectly, Everton scoring five goals in each of their first two home games. In the second of those matches, a superb display of attacking football demolished Sheffield Wednesday 5-1. Young was the star man, a hat-trick confirming his rehabilitation as a centre-forward after the dark days as a midfield fetcher-and-carrier twelve months before. The Scot's first took the breath away, a pacey run almost half the length of the pitch, a body swerve past his namesake Gerry Young and a crashing finish. 'Young is no grafter. He is an artist,' proclaimed Leslie Edwards in the *Liverpool Echo*. But as the early season optimism faded, Young's form faltered and the former Hearts player scored just three league goals in the rest of the campaign, while Pickering's season ended in injury to finish his cup final chances.

Lessons from the master

Helenio Herrera is one of the most contentious club managers of all time. Although the man brought up in the slums of Casablanca is associated mostly with the dreaded *Catenaccio* tactical system of playing – usually involving the removal of a midfielder to play as a spare man behind the defence – he was in fact an advocate of attacking play. Before joining Inter Milan in 1960, Herrera had been the boss of a sparkling Barcelona side that destroyed English champions Wolves 9-2 on aggregate in the European Cup. After winning 5-2 at Molineux, Herrera told an English journalist at Birmingham airport: 'You in England are playing in the style we continentals used so many years ago, with much physical strength, but no method, no technique. When it came to modern football, the Britons missed the evolution.'

During their victory over Wolves, the Spanish side had revealed the inadequacy of the tactical thinking of the English game, locked to the WM set-up, with the inherent weakness of playing three at the back against four or more forwards. Teams across the continent were now moving to flexible formations and ways of playing that were literally foreign to domestic sides, including Everton, who Herrera faced with Inter in the 1963/64 European Cup. Catterick later said that the biggest lesson he had taken from the defeat was the way their opponents deployed players to undertake specific roles 'without the slightest deviation'. It took Catterick three days after the defeat in the San Siro to put into practice what he learned. In the Anfield derby Stevens played as an extra man in defence with Harris utilised as a 'sweeper' behind Brian Labone, who was earmarked to man-mark Ian St John. These unfamiliar negative tactics did not bear fruit, the visitors enjoying only a consolation goal from Vernon in response to two earlier strikes from Ian Callaghan.

The Inter defeat still sowed the seeds of the tactical blueprint that ultimately lead to the 1970 title triumph, which originated on the pre-season trip to Norway in August 1965. With players far fitter than their predecessors and a greater emphasis on defence, the modern 4-2-4 formation was gradually replacing the outmoded WM set-up, and Catterick used the visit to Scandinavia to develop the system in readiness for the start of the new campaign. The new tactical shape featured Brian Harris as an extra man at the centre of the defence but after unveiling the formation in the 5-2 home win over Northampton, the back-line struggled to adapt. The watching Hugh McIlvanney highlighted the issue in the *Observer*. 'They remain vulnerable through the middle,' the esteemed Scot commented, 'especially when the ball is aimed diagonally into the heart of their defence.' It was to remain a long-term weakness.

Surprisingly Harris settled far more comfortably into the central defensive partnership than Brian Labone. One of the pair was expected to move out to stifle any attacking threat; Harris was more comfortable in that role having played in front of the defence as a wing-half. For Labone, having spent his entire career up until that point as a lone centre-half marking a centre-forward, it was not a natural way of playing, and when the defender moved out opponents exposed his weakness on the turn. Labone later explained the difficulty of the transition. 'When it changed there was a problem of understanding and at first a lot of messages went astray between partners,' he said. 'However, when it settled down and we got used to the new system I found it easier for there was always cover.' By new year the previous uncertainty arising from which of the pair should move out to attack the ball was now resolved, the more mobile and industrious Harris allowing Labone to be more static in his positional play, using natural instincts to snuff out threats.

Although the move to 4-2-4 provided defensive stability and allowed forward roles for both Pickering and Young, there were too many square pegs in round holes, especially in the middle of the park, where the two players acted as both defenders and when in possession had to move the ball quickly and intelligently up to the forwards. Catterick's problem was there was nobody on the playing staff capable of performing that role, especially since Kay's demise. Colin Harvey could certainly do it in time, but the youngster was still learning his trade. For Catterick the midfield was always the most important part of the pitch, so any system that reduced numbers there was always going to have a limited shelf life. The Everton boss addressed the issue by moving to a formation that would produce his best footballing side.

The move to 4-3-3

With several players injured for a meaningless league game at Newcastle in April 1966, Catterick experimented with the new-fangled 4-3-3 formation, one that brought back an extra midfielder at the expense of a central forward, a tactical set-up more accustomed to his thinking. In the Good Friday encounter, the midfield trio of John Hurst, Harvey and Gabriel lined up behind an attacking trident of Jimmy Husband on the right with Derek Temple playing on the opposite flank. Mike Trebilcock filled in as centre-forward in the absence of record signing Fred Pickering.

The three men in attack did not necessarily have to incorporate two wide men – hence the 'Wingless Wonders' description of England after Alf Ramsey used the system in his ground-breaking 2-0 win in Spain four months before – and the selection of Jimmy Husband on the right-hand side was therefore an interesting move. The Geordie had first come to the attention of the senior players when scoring five goals as a guest in a first-team six-a-side match in late 1963. The forward was then one of the star turns in the FA Youth Cup victory eighteen months later, making his first-team debut near the end of the same campaign. Although placed on the right flank, the 20-year-old was not a natural wide man – his style was to move inside and make diagonal runs from the wing towards the penalty area in a style so common today. In doing so, the youngster was crucially also able to provide vital support to the central striker.

As it happened the experiment was a qualified success, the game ending 0-0. Significantly it took Everton's unbeaten run to fourteen games, though that ended less than 24 hours later with a 3-1 home defeat by Sheffield United. The afternoon in the north-east pointed the way to the future – although it would take the arrival of Alan Ball and Howard Kendall to bring glory with the system.

4.
Vindication

Prelude

EVERTON FINISHED FOURTH IN CATTERICK'S FIRST SEASON IN charge, a place higher than what had effectively been Carey's last campaign in 1960/61. Formidable at home, the team struggled on their travels, summed up in March 1962 when Everton overran Chelsea 4-0 at Goodison only to play poorly in a 3-1 defeat at Spurs seven days later. After the loss at White Hart Lane, Michael Charters wrote in the *Liverpool Echo* that 'the difference in them home and away has to be seen to be believed'.

Nevertheless, the key game in the campaign was at Burnley in the FA Cup fifth round. Ahead through a Bobby Collins goal, Catterick's side disintegrated completely in a 3-1 defeat. Some away fans left the ground in the second half, believing the players had effectively given up. One supporter pulled no punches in a letter to the *Liverpool Echo*. 'I was disgusted,' the angry fan complained, 'this was one of the most gutless Everton performances it has been my misfortune to attend. The towel was thrown in as soon as [Brian] Miller scored and the next two goals were almost formalities.' Catterick obviously learned enough that afternoon to realise that the core of the team needed toughening up – starting with the recruitment of Dennis Stevens three weeks later. With the pressure off Catterick's side improved dramatically in the final weeks of the campaign, finishing with a nine-game unbeaten run, which included an 8-3 thrashing of Cardiff City in the final home match and only a third away victory at Arsenal on the last day.

With the Burnley experience still fresh in his mind, the issue for Catterick in the summer of 1962 was adding to his squad. The manager complained clubs were holding onto their players 'like leeches' and provided his usual refrain regarding upsetting the squad equilibrium. 'It is no use signing great players merely because they are great. There is a question of whether they would blend with other famous footballers on the books,' the manager said. His caution frustrated supporters, especially when Denis Law returned from Italy to sign for Manchester United in a record £115,000 move. One fan saw fit to write to the *Liverpool Echo*, 'Yet again we are fed with the annual promise of jam tomorrow, but of course tomorrow never comes.' Catterick responded to the lack of transfer activity by claiming that 'the reason that players like Law, [Ray] Crawford and [Joe] Baker are not considered is that they are in positions were Everton are not weakest.'

Attempts to prise Chelsea's Peter Brabrook came to nothing when, after meeting Catterick at Edge Hill station, the winger initially accepted the terms offered, only to backtrack after being worried about leaving London. (One cynical observer noted that if the Everton manager wished to give a better impression of the area, he should have met his transfer target at Allerton station instead.) The manager was frustrated because not only had the 24-year-old turned down a basic salary of £75 a week, plus a house in Southport, but had clearly used the offer to force the hand of a club in London, which proved successful – Ron Greenwood taking him to Upton Park in a £30,000 deal.

Brabrook's about-turn left Catterick little time to strengthen before the season started. A move to bring in the Southampton winger Terry Paine floundered when the two clubs could not agree a fee and a trip to Glasgow to enquire about the Rangers wingers Davie Wilson and Willie Henderson brought no joy. Asked by the Scottish press if there were alternatives, Catterick required rhetorically, 'You tell me where there is another we could go for?' However, with the previous campaign's strong finish still fresh in the memory, the Toffees were 13-2 second favourites to win the title behind Spurs, priced at 2-1.

Early days – 'It's getting together and is ready to click'

With promises of new forwards unfulfilled and Derek Temple sidelined through injury, the Toffees had a tough opener, away to a Burnley side whose late season collapse had allowed Ipswich to clinch the 1962 League Championship. In beautiful sunshine, for probably the first time under Catterick the side reproduced their incisive Goodison form on their travels. Everton had folded in their cup encounter six months before, but this time it was the home side's turn to surrender in the second period, after leading through a Ray Pointer goal on ten minutes. In the previous campaign, this may have resulted in a collapse, but showing the fight that would be a trademark of the season ahead, the visitors replied with a Vernon penalty nine minutes later. Just after the hour, the Welshman's devastating acceleration allowed him to take a return pass to the bye-line, where he squared for an easy Bingham tap-in from six yards. Vernon helped seal the game near the end, the forward seizing an uncharacteristic loose pass from Jimmy McIlroy to put Young clean through and the Scot finished perfectly with a chip into the corner.

Four days later, Everton treated a 69,500 crowd at Goodison to a superb opening home game of the season, against a Manchester United side close to completing the rebuilding process after the Munich air disaster.[8] Catterick withdrew Gabriel to the back-line to man-mark new signing Law, effectively meaning something close to a 4-3-3 formation, the Scot playing the role to perfection in an opening half dominated by the Toffees who strolled into a 3-0 lead. After twelve minutes, two goals by Young had put the home side 2-0 up and when Alex Parker struck with a rare effort just before the break, it seemed the match was over. United threw caution to the wind in the second period and with Law freed from Gabriel's vice-like grip, Matt Busby's side dominated but only had the new striker's effort to show for a stirring fight-back.

After signing Johnny Morrissey from Liverpool, the winger made a quiet debut in a 4-1 home victory over Sheffield Wednesday, and three days later the Toffees established their title credentials in the return at Old Trafford. In a searing, blistering encounter that occasionally bordered on the edge of lawlessness, the visitors displayed their newly found resilience first apparent at Turf Moor. With Labone outstanding in the centre of defence, Catterick's side kept the home team at bay and twelve minutes from time got their reward, as Shay Brennan felled Morrissey in the area and Vernon coolly converted the spot-kick. Top of the league with maximum points from four games constituted the club's best start to a season in 24 years. Alex Young was now convinced that the glory days beckoned, as he later admitted. 'In 1962 we regarded Spurs and Manchester United as our main challengers for the title and having done the double over United we were certain we could lift the championship. We had some great players in that side.' But the

[8] There was not just football supporters travelling from Manchester that night to the city. A Granada television crew also paid a visit, filming the increasingly popular Beatles at the Cavern for their *Know the North* programme.

100 percent record ended in the capital on the first weekend in September. On his arrival the London based daily newspapers ambushed Catterick at Euston station before their game against Fulham. The Everton manager was in bullish mood when asked about the team's prospects. 'Top of the league means nothing,' he admitted, 'until you have played twenty matches, but this team has great potential ... this side has been reformed. It's getting together and is ready to click.' Asked what would happen if that did not occur, he replied, 'We're prepared to buy any great player who comes on the market – in any position. Provided, of course, he entertains the crowd and strengthens the side.'

Such hubris proved misplaced on this occasion, as the home team – without England internationals Johnny Haynes and Bobby Robson – won 1-0 against an Everton side unrecognisable from the team that had already triumphed twice on their travels. The visitors were the prime contributors to a particularly bad-tempered game; Gabriel was spoken to four times by the referee before half-time alone. It was also a nightmare afternoon for Gordon West. Kicked in the face and the body, the keeper was at fault for the only goal, failing to collect a long throw and watching helplessly as Stan Brown crashed the ball home. After the game, Catterick wore a mask of frustration, especially as television had filmed the match. To many, the defeat simply reinforced the southern press view that Everton's success was largely down to a large and vocal following at home. Taking his anger out on the players on the following Monday, Catterick carpeted those he claimed were responsible for an 'ill-tempered' performance in the capital. 'Their lack of control was not in their own interests or in the interests of the club,' he said. The manager pointed out to one player – Jimmy Gabriel, who had been lucky to stay on the pitch – that their international future was in jeopardy if there was a repeat performance.

There was some redemption as the next two games saw Goodison victories over Johnny Carey's newly promoted Leyton Orient (3-0) and an excellent Leicester City outfit (3-2). The latter victory was particularly noteworthy for the burgeoning understanding on the left between Morrissey and Brian Harris, who played behind the new signing in the wing-half position. Harris had an interesting, if fitful, Everton career. Born in Bebington, on the Wirral, Harris moved to Goodison from Port Sunlight in 1954 having previously turned down Liverpool in strange circumstances. Having been told to turn up at Melwood for a trial game at 2.45 p.m., he assumed it was for the second half only, so rejected the invitation, only to be told later it was a misprint and it should have said 12.45 p.m. and he was due to be playing the full ninety minutes. The error benefited Everton, Harris making his debut in 1955 as an inside-forward – ironically in the same game as his namesake Jimmy – and only moved to his favoured left-half role after the arrival of Gabriel. His strong tackling, clever ball control, and effective distribution, combined with Morrissey's penetration, added an extra dimension to the Everton attack. Another aspect of the game, apparent after the Leicester City encounter, was the challenge of hooliganism, with fighting in the Gwladys Street end after the match.

The golden autumn – 'I have always known they had the talent'

With six wins from seven matches, confidence was high for the return to London and an away game at Leyton Orient. After a goalless first half in front of 21,847 spectators, a misunderstanding between Harris and Labone led to the home side taking the lead through Norman Deeley and the visitors were eventually humbled 3-0, after heroics by the 34-year-old home goalkeeper Bill Robertson. The watching Mike Langley of the *Daily Express* said with some glee, 'For Orient chief Carey, the manager Everton sacked in a taxi last year, it was a night of public revenge. His unrated team matched expensively assembled Everton for pace, fight, football and were explosively ahead in shooting power.' Everton's defeat certainly delighted the southern press and the result meant that the Toffees had won just one of their last thirteen trips to the capital – the meaningless victory at Arsenal five months before.

Three days later it was normal service resumed, with a fine run and finish by Bingham plus a Gabriel header enough for a 2-0 victory at Bolton. The triumph left the Toffees second in the table, but revealingly it was the side's third win on their travels, matching the whole of the previous campaign. A frustrating 2-2 derby draw at Goodison left the Toffees two points off the summit, behind Wolves. Stan Cullis' side had made a brilliant unbeaten start to the season, with eight wins and three draws, and were formidable opponents. Yet, when the teams locked horns at Molineux in front of the watching BBC cameras, for the first time Catterick's men looked like genuine title contenders. In the autumn sunshine, the visitors produced a display that mixed sophistication with powerful commitment. After Brian Harris and Jimmy Gabriel had annexed the midfield, Young displayed the full range of his art, dictating the pace and the shape of the game quite beautifully.

Dominant for an hour, Everton went ahead when Bingham headed home Morrissey's cross from the bye-line and fifteen minutes later the visitors wrapped the game up in classical fashion as Mick Meagan fed Vernon, whose delightful through ball from the centre-circle fell perfectly for Young and the Scot finished easily. In a brilliant team performance, Vernon particularly impressed the watching Eric Todd of the *Guardian*. 'He arranged the variations of pace at which the game was contested, under this astute and experienced general, Everton scarcely could help but thrive, and their teamwork never will be forgotten by the 44,506 people who saw it.' Catterick was overjoyed after the game. 'I have always known they had the talent,' he proclaimed, 'now I know they have the heart.' In modern parlance, it was a real statement of intent.

Catterick then watched on when a poor Blackpool team were beaten 5-0 at home, but Vernon's removal from first-team action for the preceding Manchester City game had heightened speculation that the manager was preparing another sortie into the transfer market. The press mooted several names to Catterick's frustration. 'I deplore these rumours, which cause as much trouble to us as they do to the other clubs they concern,' he said. Yet, two weeks later he told the *Liverpool Echo's* Leslie Edwards that the club had made enquiries about a dozen players. One approach to Sheffield Wednesday to sign star forward Johnny Fantham ended in failure. This was a huge disappointment, for the gifted player (who scored 166 goals in 434 games for the Yorkshire side) would have brought an extra dimension to Everton during the decade, being able to switch play quickly with accurate cross-field passes as well as possessing one of the hardest shots in the game.

On the pitch, three days after the thrashing of Blackpool, the side showed the powers of recovery required by all champions during a 4-3 victory at Nottingham Forest in a chaotic encounter at the City Ground. Two-nil down after fifteen minutes, the visitors were 3-2 ahead by the break and then conceded an equaliser before Gabriel headed the winner. On the last Saturday of November, a 3-0 win over Sheffield United made it eighteen points out of a possible twenty at Goodison in an unbeaten home start to the campaign. The victory also took Catterick's side back to the top of the table and set them up for possibly the highest-profile league game in the club's history at that juncture.

In completing the first league and cup double of the twentieth century during 1960/61, Tottenham Hotspur had established themselves as one of the greatest of all English club sides. Now including Jimmy Greaves in their star-studded line-up,

Bill Nicholson's men added to their legend by defending the FA Cup twelve months later. Although some of their star names were now ageing, they were still formidable in every sense of the word. Allied to a strong defence were Danny Blanchflower and Dave Mackay, two of the finest midfield players in the post-war game. As an attacking threat, they had the tenacious and graceful inside-forward John White and the wonderful Welsh winger Cliff Jones, a player with infinite powers of acceleration and superb crossing ability – as well as Greaves, who scored more career top-flight goals than even Dixie Dean.[9] The White Hart Lane outfit were a real balance of silk and steel, so when the Toffees took a two-point lead over Spurs to north London in early December, the eagerly awaited encounter took place before a sell-out crowd of 60,626 – the gates locked a quarter-of-an-hour before kick-off – as well as the BBC cameras.

In the week that the British and French governments agreed to develop the Concorde supersonic airliner, the two most expensively assembled teams in English history were also pointing towards a glamorous future. Spurs and Everton were taking part, it could be argued, in the first modern league game – a forerunner of the regular 'Super Sunday' clashes of today. John White was missing for the home side, while Catterick was still without the services of the injured Morrissey. Backed by a huge and vocal travelling army of 8,000 supporters, the visitors' stifling tactics – understandable as they had conceded 27 goals on their six previous visits to White Hart Lane – worked to perfection as Spurs struggled to break down the resolute five-man back-line, with Labone in outstanding form. Only once did they allow Nicholson's men a sight of goal, when Greaves took a pass from Blanchflower and thundered a shot against the underside of West's crossbar. For the home team, Bill Brown made three point-blank saves in rapid succession from Bingham, Vernon and Young. With the end result of a goalless draw justifying the means, Catterick beamed with delight as he left for the journey home after the game. The scoreline was satisfying, but not for the first time a big game disappointed. 'Expectations mocked by cold reality,' proclaimed *The Times* headline, 'Spurs and Everton reduced to defensive stalemate.'

After a dour 1-1 draw with West Ham on the following Saturday, seven days later those frustrations were forgotten as Everton produced an excellent

9 Curiously Dean and Greaves share the record for the youngest player to reach 200 league goals, remarkably both achieving the feat at the age of 23 years 290 days.

performance to defeat third-place Burnley at Goodison Park. Three goals up after less than half-an-hour, the match was a personal triumph for Alex Young. After missing two chances against West Ham, the home support had roundly booed the striker at the end of the game, but the visit of the Lancashire side saw the Scot at his artistic best. While others struggled in the biting wind and slanting rain, Young's spectral presence in a roving forward role was the contrast between the two teams. After Stevens and Vernon had put the home team 2-0 ahead, the Scot scored a delightful third with a header that looped over a crowd of players after the goalkeeper's punch had found him in the penalty area. 'Everton now have that repetitive machinelike method which is the blueprint of success,' wrote David Miller in the *Sunday Telegraph*, adding that Young 'in every game I see him he has at least two or three moments which are indelibly memorable'.

The Big Freeze

The 3-1 victory over the Lancashire side took the Toffees three points clear at the top. It was to be their last home game for ten weeks, as one of the coldest winter spells in history started just before Christmas. January 1963 was the coldest month of the twentieth century and the big freeze continued until the end of February when the temperature in the city of Liverpool reached forty degrees Fahrenheit for the first time in nine weeks. Between 23 December and 2 February, there were postponements in 369 of 477 games in England. With sheets of ice covering pitches, clubs used novel methods to make ground conditions playable. Everton officials travelled to Widnes and returned with a five-gallon drum of chemical solution to apply to the frozen Goodison pitch, with pneumatic drills also used in a fruitless attempt to crack the ice.[10] Training sessions took place on Formby and Leasowe beaches.

After a 2-2 draw against Sheffield Wednesday on 22 December, Everton did not play a league game until the middle of February. By then Catterick had added a further two players to his line-up in Tony Kay and Alex Scott. Catterick's signing of the Scottish wide-man was another example of incrementally improving the side in an area of strength, as Billy Bingham was having an excellent season on the right wing. Nevertheless, at 31 years of age, the Ulsterman was also nearing the

[10] Other unusual approaches to beat the deep freeze included Norwich City using military flamethrowers, which only succeeded in flooding Carrow Road.

end of his career and Catterick was a big fan of the greater penetration and speed of Scott's direct approach.

The latest additions to the squad made their league debuts at Leicester in the middle of February. Strengthened by the signing of Frank McLintock during the previous summer, the Midlands side were proving to be a real threat. With the canny Scot Matt Gillies in charge, Leicester employed a system of playing perfected by Austria thirty years before. Called the 'Whirl', it was a style reliant on the constant switching of positions. Away from the game they were equally inventive. Whereas others were taking up to ten weeks to get their pitch in good condition, imaginative work by their groundsman Bill Taylor had produced a playable surface at Filbert Street in five. There was no surprise when before the fixture Catterick described the playing conditions as 'remarkably good'. Whether he had the same view at the end of the ninety minutes was doubtful as Leicester dominated after comfortably adapting to the bone-hard playing surface, the home side victorious 3-1 on an evening when Kay put in a reasonable display but Scott hardly got a kick. The victory took the capable Midlands outfit third, just a point behind Everton, who trailed Spurs by the same gap. There was more frustration in a goalless draw against Wolves and, with a thaw ending the big freeze, Nottingham Forest treated a 45,000 crowd at Goodison to a desperately defensive display in early March. Remarkably deploying their centre-forward Peter Hindley as a man-to-man marker on Alex Young of all people, the unusual 3-4-3 formation made no difference as the visitors lost 2-0.

In the FA Cup, having disposed of Barnsley and Swindon Town[11] in the frozen wasteland of the opening weeks of the year, the Toffees travelled to West Ham United for a fractious fifth-round encounter, but returned empty-handed following a 2-1 defeat. Three days later the vanquished side were impressive in a 3-0 win at struggling Ipswich, when goalkeeper Gordon West did not have a save to make, before the home supporters witnessed a familiar tale against Manchester City four days later. Whilst the country's youth were enjoying the first Beatles album, released the previous day, the visitors withdrew their two wingers and, with their full-backs, they double-marked Morrissey and Scott in a strange 2-5-3 formation. City went ahead through Dave Wagstaffe and, with keeper Harry Dowd in

[11] Where Tony Kay had an embarrassing start to his Everton career, slipping as he entered the pitch and falling full length onto the turf.

magnificent form, it eventually took goals from Young and Morrissey to thwart the visitors. The victory left Everton third on 41 points from 28 games, a point behind Leicester and three behind Spurs, who had both played two games more. However, the fixture backlog effectively forced the playing of two league games every week for the rest of the campaign, placing extra pressure on their two rivals – Leicester were still in the FA Cup and Spurs had European commitments. Despite that advantage, the following week saw Catterick team's title chances melting away like the winter's ice.

With Spurs leading the table, it was ironic that their north London adversaries Arsenal would do them a big favour by defeating one of their rivals, with Everton going down 4-3 on a night of real drama at Highbury. After Tony Kay had scored his side's first goal of the season in the capital, the Toffees went 3-2 down but looked like taking something when Young equalised with a delicate lob twenty minutes from time. To the visitors' horror, straight from the kick-off the home side went up the other end and Alan Skirton forced the ball home from a corner for a winner. It was a nightmare game for West, who was at fault for two of the goals. The result was a massive boost too for Spurs, whose victory over Leyton Orient 24 hours later took their run to eight wins and two draws from ten league matches.

Although it was too soon to panic, Catterick's teams liked to play to a decent tempo and the manager voiced concerns that the downtime over the winter had damaged the rhythm of his side. For the first time critics were voicing concerns over the signing of Tony Kay – a less disciplined player than Harris and at Highbury guilty of playing too wide and deep and ceding midfield control to George Eastham and Geoff Strong. That was part of a perceived wider malaise within the team, as the accusations returned of a lack of leadership, discipline under pressure and a cutting edge up front. Those concerns were not allayed on the following Saturday, the Toffees going down 2-1 at Sheffield United in a disappointing display. The defeat left them six points behind Spurs, with two games in hand. For the first time the title was out of Everton's hands.

Two days later the forward line recaptured their early season magic with a fine display at Villa Park when the star of the show was undoubtedly Alex Young, who scored one goal in a 2-0 victory and created countless opportunities for others. 'Young's artistry is the delight of the Goodison crowd. He does not often show it away from home. Last night, however, he gave a display of genius,' wrote Michael

Charters in the *Liverpool Echo*. Catterick went a step further. 'One of the finest centre-forward exhibitions I have ever seen,' the Everton manager proclaimed. At this stage of the campaign it was a case of two steps forward and one back, as Blackburn's defensive shield was enough to secure a point at Goodison, followed by a derby stalemate at Anfield, the goalless draw not doing justice to an outstanding game in which the respective centre-halves, Labone and Ron Yeats, were impeccable. Catterick's previous club did their former manager a favour though on the same night, inflicting a 3-1 defeat on Spurs at Hillsborough, leaving Leicester City now top. At that stage the midwinter hiatus had masked the distinctly less than championship form of Catterick's side, with just six victories in sixteen league games.

The run-in

Like many a campaign the Easter period proved crucial. Teams played up to three games over four days, with the usual practice of facing one side twice. In 1963 Everton were due to play relegation-threatened Birmingham City on two occasions, Spurs were away and at home to Liverpool while leaders Leicester City faced Manchester United twice. The tide started to turn in Everton's favour on Easter Saturday – the Toffees' trip to Blackpool resulted in a 2-1 victory, thanks to goals from Young and a free-kick from Scott, who had his best game for the club since moving south. Elsewhere Leicester lost 2-0 at West Ham United while Spurs could only manage a 1-1 draw at home to Fulham. The London club had lost heavily 5-2 at Liverpool on Good Friday when the others did not play – a defeat avenged with a 7-2 thrashing of Shankly's men three days later.

Labone was missing for the home game against Birmingham City on Easter Monday, replaced by Gabriel at centre-half, and the Scot was clearly at fault for both the visitors' goals, an equaliser from Scott thirteen minutes from time salvaging a draw. Within 24 hours Catterick wisely selected understudy George Heslop in Labone's absence, the side returning from St Andrews with two precious points, thanks to a late goal from the edge of the box by Vernon following a clever pull-back from Kay. That took the Toffees tally to five points from the three games, against three each for Spurs and Leicester.

At this stage there was an intriguing three-way fight at the top: Leicester 51 points from 37 games with Spurs and Everton locked together on fifty having played a game less, the two teams facing off on the following weekend in arguably the biggest league game in Goodison history. Nicholson's side were taking a run of poor form into the historic encounter, having garnered just four points from five games. At the same time, Everton had remained in contention through a series of resilient away performances; at home, they had won just two of their five league games since the big thaw. On an intriguing afternoon that would be a gift from the gods for broadcasters in the modern era – although there was no regular televised coverage at the time – Leicester were also playing fourth-placed Wolves.

Catterick set his team a target before the big match. 'I reckon we are ten points away from winning the championship,' he reckoned, 'there are six games to play – four at home – and if we get ten points from those games then nobody will catch us.' Realistically that would have to include a victory over Spurs, who were without Blanchflower and had their eye on the first leg of the European Cup Winners' Cup semi-final four days later. As it happened, on a bleak, windy day on a hard pitch without grass, the match was a no contest. A ruthlessly determined Everton dominated the London side from the moment Greaves squandered an easy opportunity inside the first fifteen minutes. The only goal of the game came within sixty seconds of the miss. Vernon's cross from the left hung in the wind and as the Spurs keeper Bill Brown came out Young rose imperiously above Tony Marchi to head home. The hugely significant goal brought celebrations, rarely seen on the ground, from a passionate 70,000 crowd. Thereafter Catterick's side maintained an iron grip in the middle of the park, with the inspirational Kay, Gabriel and Stevens all outstanding and full-back Mick Meagan having one of the games of his life against Cliff Jones. Up front, they were equally effective. 'Everton's attack, indeed, bestrode the whole match,' wrote Brian Glanville in the *Sunday Times*, 'It's mastery symbolised by the greyhound elegance of Vernon.'

With the Spurs goal leading a charmed life – Young, Morrissey, Stevens and Vernon all striking the woodwork – the final half-hour was agonising for the huge crowd, who had created a wonderful atmosphere. Pandemonium ensued when the referee Mr Crawford blew for full time to end a gripping game that justified all the hype. With Leicester held to a 1-1 draw on the same afternoon, Everton were now top on goal average, having played a game less than their rivals. The encounter also marked the end of an era for Nicholson's great Tottenham team. Never again would his side contest the title, and Spurs would have to wait until 1985 to seriously challenge for the crown again – when Everton again ended their dreams.

The spare game came four days later, but a far tougher Arsenal side made

Everton fight all the way for a point at Goodison, with an injury to West effectively ending the season for the big keeper. It was then a case of returning to the scene of the crime on the following Saturday: a trip to Upton Park, venue of the chaotic FA Cup tie six weeks earlier. With Leicester beating Liverpool in the semi-final on the same day, it was a chance for Catterick's side to put some distance between themselves and their rivals. Albert Dunlop replaced the injured West and Derek Temple (who had hardly played due to a cartilage problem) came in for the dropped Morrissey. The visitors played and, just as importantly, acted like champions. Eschewing the belligerence that had characterised the cup game, the Toffees won far easier than the 2-1 scoreline suggests. It was also a personal triumph for Tony Kay. With memories of the FA Cup game still fresh in the memory, the home crowd booed the midfielder throughout, but the new addition to the team was the dominant figure in a game where Everton were a goal down after twenty minutes. 'The credit goes entirely to the indestructible Kay, who on this evidence, put his £55,000 transfer fee into the bargain basement variety,' said the *Sunday Times*, 'He wasted not a single ball, his tackling was breathtakingly effective and fair, and he gave tremendous inspiration to his colleagues.'

On the first Saturday in May, 52,047 spectators witnessed another rugged home fixture, as visiting Bolton put up a fiercely defensive shield on a day when the result was more important than the performance. 'Everton were positively tame,' wrote Arthur Hopcraft in the *Observer*. The home side had to wait until deep into the second half for their winner, when Young flicked on Gabriel's long ball for Vernon to finish sweetly past Eddie Hopkinson. With Leicester out of the running after losing at West Brom and Spurs three points behind with a game in hand, the result left Everton effectively needing four points from their last two games to become champions for a sixth time.

Champions – 'An explosive mixture of fire and pace'

Before Spurs had played again, Catterick's side gathered two of those points at West Brom three days later, when they were recipients of the good fortune that occasionally favours champions. With their opponents down to ten men after just six minutes when full-back Ron Bradley fractured an elbow, the visitors scored first on 39 minutes in bizarre fashion. Whilst goalkeeper Ray Potter was busy protesting to the referee that Young was not ten yards from a free-kick in his own penalty area, he failed to notice that full-back Graham Williams had flicked the ball to him, the Everton forward did however and nipped in to score. After the Scot added a fine second in the second period, Vernon converted a penalty and the 4-0 rout was concluded by a Williams own-goal. The manner of the win may have been fortuitous – 'a hollow victory,' according to *The Times* – but that did not matter to the gleeful Evertonians who flooded the Hawthorns at the end of the game. Catterick virtually admitted they were now champions and gave a clue why. 'This was our eleventh away victory, which is far as I know equals the club record,' he told the waiting journalists, 'when you consider Everton used to be known as the team that could not win away from home, surely this represents striking progress.' Although the signings of Stevens and then Kay had added greater steel to the side, the previously misfiring forward line had come good at exactly the right time.

With a chance to win the title, the game against Fulham on the second Saturday in May 1963 remains one of the Goodison's greatest days, as the home side duly delivered the victory that ended almost a quarter-of-a-century without a major honour. Clearly influenced by the fact their opponents had nothing to play for, it was also a rare example of the manager allowing his head to rule his heart, in permitting full-back Alex Parker to start and be part of the occasion. 'I remember Harry Catterick asking me if I was fit,' the Scot later said, 'and though I said "yes" I couldn't understand why he allowed me to play. He must have known I wasn't a hundred percent.' Parker later provided a picture of the scene in the dressing room beforehand:

Most of the lads suffered from nerves before a game but this day the tension in the dressing room was unbelievable. Harry Catterick and Tommy Eggleston were having a quiet word with each of the players. Tony Kay was bawling and shouting about the place, trying to make people think he was not nervous. Roy Vernon was trying to crack jokes, Alex Young just sat there, and I remember Jimmy Gabriel was particularly nervous.

Any apprehension had surely disappeared after the first ten minutes, by that time Vernon had scored twice and although the visitors pulled a goal back, a further strike by Scott restored the two-goal margin before the break in front of a wildly partisan crowd. Although the home team lost their way in the second period, Vernon produced a suitable climax to the campaign by completing his hat-trick before the end – the third successive season that the Welsh maestro had achieved the feat in the final home game. The carnival spirit took over when the referee blew the final whistle, the 4-1 victory meaning Everton had finished the season in a manner befitting champions – twenty points out of 24 producing a club record 61 points.

The performance characterised the season as a whole. 'Everton crowned their season with an explosive mixture of fire and pace, which has been their trademark,' said the *Daily Telegraph*. With Spurs failing to win any of their last three matches, the gap between the sides of six points did not reflect the small margins at the top for most of the campaign. That mattered little as the spectators greeted their heroes as they walked round the ground after the game, with Vernon's speech from the Main Stand to the crowd a particularly nice touch. Uniquely, Everton remained unbeaten at home as more than one million spectators passed through the Goodison turnstiles in league matches for the first time.

Even John Moores was duty bound to acknowledge the crowd as they chanted his name, but afterwards the chairman was quick to place on record who was to receive the full credit. 'Harry has done the work,' he said, 'he has chosen the players he wanted for the club, and we have merely helped him to get them. His judgement has been vindicated over and over again … I don't see where we could have found a better man for the task we had in mind for him.' Catterick himself used the championship celebrations to reaffirm his connections to the club. 'I like to think I am just as much an Evertonian as any of our crowd,' he said after the game. 'Remember I was just a kid when I came to Goodison Park as a player and even when I left them, the only result I wanted to know after my own games were over was that concerning Everton.' He also paid tribute to trainer Tommy Eggleston, brought over from Sheffield Wednesday. 'He has done a first class job, and I know of no better man for it.'

The champions

So how had Catterick taken the team that had under-performed under Carey to league champions within two years? Geoffrey Green in *The Times* described the side thus:

As it is this team of royal blue functional efficiency, supported by a host of fanatical clans – was there ever such a ceaseless roar battering the eardrums as at Goodison? – possess in Parker a chivalrous, canny right back of Scottish vintage; a powerful half back line in Kay, Labone and Gabriel; and a pair of talented forwards in Vernon and Young, who have claimed 46 of their 84 league goals this season. Vernon, an advanced inside left, is a central dagger of attack; Young is the roaming, creative centre forward, a player of poise, polish and sensitivity, a footballer of pure quality.

The goals from Young and Vernon certainly contributed to the title triumph, while Morrissey and Scott provided greater steel and penetration on the flanks, but the answer was really in the middle of the park. Critics scoffed when Catterick sold Bobby Collins to Leeds United, but replacement Dennis Stevens was an integral part of the team's success. Everton had a more resilient edge reflected in the vast improvement in their away record.

Full-backs Alex Parker and Mick Meagan (who had replaced George Thomson), were marshalled superbly by the polished and composed Brian Labone. The future club skipper enjoyed an excellent campaign and was named by Matt Busby as one of his five footballers of the year. 'He is very good in the air. His positional sense is good. He never seems flurried and it is rare to find such assurance in so young a player,' the Manchester United manager said in the *Daily Express*. Labone's protection of goalkeeper Gordon West resulted in a formidable defensive barrier. The 42 goals conceded were a new club record low for a single campaign, counterbalanced by 84 scored – 27 fewer than Spurs but reflecting Catterick's desire to win efficiently.

Away from the pitch, however, the biggest difference was Catterick himself. The title-triumph was the high point of his golden period as a manager, one that started when he took over the reins as Sheffield Wednesday and lasted probably until the middle of the decade. At Hillsborough, he had been very much a tracksuit manager. In February 1961, the *Daily Mail's* Jack Wood asked Catterick whether he deserved his reputation as 'too much of a players' man'. Catterick's response was surprising given his later reputation at Goodison. 'I am proud of the label. Success on the field depends largely on the close bond between manager and players.' After leaving south Yorkshire, Catterick astutely made the smooth transition to becoming a directors' manager – someone who was just as comfortable in the boardroom as on the training pitch. With a powerful, ruthless chairman, it was a wise move.

Moving seamlessly into the hierarchy, Catterick thus became more of a general manager, the arch strategist with a clear sense of purpose, his plans including the youth programme at Everton that would bear fruit later in the decade with the development of Bellefield. There was no waste. His dedication was absolute, as Moores later admitted. 'Catterick puts in more hours and miles with his scouting than anyone I know, wearing out a car a year,' the Everton chairman said. 'I'm sorry for his family, but he is a professional, a complete professional, and would have it no other way.' Catterick, for his part, appreciated the role of his chairman, as he admitted to the *Liverpool Echo* more than a decade later:

He [Moores] had a Godfather-like image, but I always found him approachable and prepared to discuss matters concerned with the club, be they to do with players or the financial side. He always gave logical reasoning to all our discussions...he was quite knowledgeable on the game, and was always prepared to discuss the technical side of it.

The alliance of Catterick and Moores was thus a key element of the title triumph, as Donald Saunders of the *Daily Telegraph* noted. 'Everton, a business-like, methodical and progressive club, thoroughly deserve their prize. Their consistency on the pitch has been matched by the singleness of purpose shown by their board and manager.' Not lost on Saunders was the biggest challenge of integrating an expensively assembled group of players into a single formidable unit. In the modern era such a talent is taken for granted amongst elite managers, but then it was very much a unique achievement. Saunders succinctly described the key skills Catterick required:

Handling a collection of temperamental stars and working under a powerful chairman would obviously require tact as well as strength of character. I was not alone in wondering whether the forceful Mr Catterick would master the art of diplomacy. He evidently has done so.

5.
Trouble in the Ranks

Pricing the pay

LONG CONSIDERED BY PLAYERS AS A RELIC OF THE VICTORIAN AGE, the maximum weekly wage for footballers was £20 when Catterick joined Everton in April 1961. The FA had initially set the ceiling at £4 a week in 1900, with the intention of curbing the powers of the big clubs. The wage then was approximately double that of skilled tradesmen, which was still the case when organised football returned after the end of World War Two. By the end of the 1950s the gap had narrowed, and a maximum weekly wage for footballers of £20 was now only £5 more than those supporters with a trade who watched them. Frustrations increased amongst players as the vastly increased income, generated by clubs due to the post-war growth in attendances, was not passed on. Players consequently looked elsewhere for employment. Neil Franklin (Colombia) and John Charles (Italy) moved abroad with varying degrees of success, Charles earning upwards of £25,000 a year at Juventus. At home, under-the-counter payments to circumvent the rules proliferated, with Sunderland later discovered to having disguised their illegal spending as expenses on straw to protect the pitch during winter.

Mobilised by Jimmy Hill, in 1960 the PFA invited players to strike on the issue, and the 'yes' vote proved a pivotal moment in the domestic game's history. Following a very real threat of industrial action, in April 1961 – at the very meeting Carey was attending in London with Moores on the day he was sacked – club chairmen ratified the earlier Football League decision to remove the maximum wage from the start of the 1961/62 campaign. There was a further concession of allowing the extension of contracts to a maximum of two years. Strangely, considering they would undoubtedly benefit from the change, Everton actually voted against it – for reasons that were not made public. However it is easy to speculate that, as a businessman with patrician values, Moores would reject a move that effectively increased costs and granted players more power at the expense of the manager and chairman, something which ultimately happened of course.

The new rules allowed players greater freedom to negotiate their own deals, but it also raised suspicions that the best attracting the highest wages would naturally gravitate to the wealthiest and biggest clubs. Those fears were realised in time, although not immediately as clubs still endeavoured to set their own ceiling, resulting in several localised disputes. The PFA were called in to arbitrate at Anfield, while Manchester United's policy was not to pay more than £50 per week, against the £100 a week provided by Fulham chairman Tommy Trinder to England international Johnny Haynes.

The greater rewards also came at a cost to the game as a whole. With pay incentives increasingly linked to success on the pitch there is no denying that raising the stakes created a more pressurised and competitive environment, indirectly causing more on- and off-the-field violence, with Goodison Park a focal point on more than one occasion. As the *Guardian's* Eric Todd said at the time, 'The footballing public will look forward to an increase in the standard of play commensurate with the increase in wages. Spectators now have a right to expect that there is no repetition of some of the shoddy stuff produced last season [1960/61] under the guise of first-class football.' The Everton manager was also wary of the freedom to pay the market rate for footballers. 'It will make big clubs bigger and smaller clubs will become nurseries for their bigger counterparts, ultimately leading to a super league,' he said at the time, 'but you must give the public what it wants, not what it thinks it wants. It wants good football, played in a sporting manner, with better amenities.'

Setting aside these negative aspects, ironically the abolition of the maximum wage opened the door for the club and Catterick to build a team capable of winning major honours, by allowing an even greater use of Moores' financial backing. In the summer of 1961, Catterick was also encouraged by the squad's willingness to agree their new deals when they returned to training – the club setting a maximum of £35 per week with a further £1 extra for every 1,000 spectators more than 40,000 for home games. The uplift meant that annual salaries for the top players at the club in a successful season would double at least.

The lifting of the maximum wage benefited players, but there is no doubt that that it brought about a divisive and destabilising effect on clubs. Even for wealthy ones such as Everton there was a need to balance the books, whilst paying the market rate and without letting the growing disparity in wages affect dressing room morale. During the 1961/62 season only Tottenham had paid more than Everton and armed with the knowledge that Danny Blanchflower was now earning around £6-7,000 per year, a number of senior players entered in negotiations at the end of that campaign aiming for a significant increase compared to twelve months before. The impact rippled through the entire staff, as those less experienced players delayed signing new deals until they saw what the club offered their star performers.

Alex Young was the first to break ranks in May 1962. The Scot announced that he had rejected a new contract and wanted to move to Italy, where there was more money and therefore greater security. Like a domino effect, other established players followed suit. By the end of June, Roy Vernon and Alex Parker had joined Young in rejecting the terms offered (which were the best in the club's history) and expressed a wish to depart. Jimmy Gabriel and Billy Bingham also refused the proposed deals. Vernon's case summed up the situation perfectly. After expressing a personal hearing with Catterick, the Welshman's suggestion for an increase in wages was turned down by the manager. When told his request was unacceptable, the forward produced a letter from his trouser pocket asking the club to transfer him.

The perceived greed of his star men dumbfounded Catterick as, like his managerial peers, he had grown up in the poverty of the 1920s and 1930s and the bleak years of the post-war era. The Everton manager made clear where he thought their priorities should lie. 'These players should be thinking more of giving value for money than of asking for more money,' he said. 'We have the best supporters in the land at Goodison Park, fans who are behind the team all the time, home or away. Players should be seeking to win for them the honours their support deserves.' Most fans, conscious of a number of away games in 1961/62 where the forwards appeared to show no heart, shared his view.

Leslie Edwards summed it up well in the *Liverpool Echo*. 'Players who were on twenty pounds per week as recently as two seasons ago should think again before they turn down terms which will give them more than twice as much. By withholding their signatures they are not only losing money, but, much more important, the goodwill of the public.' Fans were also cognisant that, in addition to their salaries, players received other benefits such as free housing. The impasse lasted until the end of July 1962, when the club announced improved terms. In addition to the basic salary of £35 per week, players would also receive £2 for every 1,000 spectators over 35,000 at Goodison if in the top two places in the league, down to a sliding scale of £1 per week. Although these numbers appear trivial in the modern era, it meant that a successful season near the top of the table could drive annual salaries to £3,000 and above.

The enhanced terms proved attractive enough for all players to re-sign, with Young and Vernon doing so on two-year terms. From that point players' financial rewards increased dramatically, and by 1971 Alan Ball was receiving a weekly wage ten times greater than his predecessors a decade before. The impact of this spending, by Everton in particular, drew criticism of clubs buying success and that money was distorting the game's priorities. At the time, Spurs' Danny Blanchflower was the highest paid player in the game, and there was a degree of irony in his regular criticism of Everton's spending power, one that hinted at an underlying agenda. However, his comments (in 1964) about Everton are still relevant today. 'I feel the talk about what players earn has confused everyone's sense of values,' he said in the *Sunday Express*, 'it gives the impression that the rewards at Everton were somehow more important than the achievements.'

Ice Cold with Alex

There is a paradox underpinning Alex Young's time at Everton. How can someone whose career on Merseyside was blighted by inconsistency and injury arguably be the most worshipped and beloved player in the club's history?

The Scot's career at Goodison contained two distinct halves. From 1960-64, he was a focal point of the revival under Carey and then Catterick. At home, the man dubbed 'the Golden Vision' was a match-winner capable of producing performances of sublime beauty, yet on away grounds the forward was a source of frustration to both manager and supporters, being accused, sometimes unfairly, of 'hiding' in matches. This aspect of his game continually frustrated Catterick, who wanted a steelier approach, but always puzzled the Scot. 'For five years with Hearts, nobody said I couldn't play well away from Tynecastle. Why should they say these things now?' Young pondered to James Mossop of the *Daily Express* in 1965.

Young had moved to Everton in November 1960, but niggling injuries had interrupted the rest of the campaign, before the Scot eventually reached top form in the early months of the 1961/62 season. Following a 4-1 win over Arsenal in September 1961, Leslie Edwards wrote in the *Liverpool Echo*, 'He may not be endowed with great stamina but his occasional touches of genius mark him as a player-and-a-half able to infiltrate, almost magically, into a defence with a deceptively quick dart.' Seven days later the fragile Scot earned even more praise from the same journalist. Following one of the best performances of the Catterick era, a 6-0 home humiliation of a capable Nottingham Forest side, Edwards wrote: 'The finest exhibition of centre-forward play since the days of Dixie Dean and Tom Lawton ... like [Stanley] Matthews and other men of football genius he always seems to have time to think and space in which to move.'

Young continued his fine form into the title-winning campaign twelve months later, netting 22 goals in a league season where he was ever-present. Ironically, given his reputation for not giving his best on opposing grounds, the forward saved some of his most valuable performances for the crucial away games at the end of the season. After starting the 1963/64 campaign reasonably well, by the beginning of January both Young and strike-partner Vernon had lost form and were both suffering a relative goal-drought. Nevertheless, Everton supporters were unprepared for the bombshell news before the visit to Burnley on the second Saturday in January – in what was an astonishing move at the time, Catterick dropped both forwards. Regardless of the motives, it was a brave decision leaving out his two biggest stars. But one of the features of Catterick's first four years as Everton boss was to publicly lay the blame for the team's failings on his most famous players – if things were not going according to plan then Young and/or Vernon were sidelined.

Young's complaint that Catterick favoured players he bought, at the expense of those inherited, was understandable. Dennis Stevens and especially Alex Scott were struggling and were not providing either the goals or the ammunition for their forward colleagues, yet Catterick dropped the Scot and Vernon. Having said that, there was not much opposition from supporters, although a fair few were present at Goodison to see both perform for the reserves in a 5-3 home defeat by Burnley – Vernon missing a rare penalty – while the first-team vindicated Catterick's educated gamble by winning 3-2 in the encounter at Turf Moor, when Jimmy Gabriel captained the side. Tellingly, despite the financial implications of Catterick's decision, neither Young nor Vernon asked for a transfer, although the manager did not show any sympathy to Michael Charters in the *Liverpool Echo* when told they were unhappy. 'That is the way it should be,' he said, 'I like discontented players in the second-team. That gives them the incentive to produce the dynamic performances which could help them back into the first-team.'

Young returned to the starting line-up at the end of February with Everton's charge to retain their title gathering momentum. Having bought Fred Pickering, the next sign that all was not well between Catterick and the Scot was in the Good Friday fixture against West Brom at Goodison. With Vernon suspended and Kay ill, Catterick kept Young out the squad in another decision that pointed to a hidden agenda – on this occasion the forward was entitled to ask why yet again he was the victim, especially having scored in the crucial wins over Aston Villa and Spurs on his return to the starting line-up. The result was no service to Pickering, whose finishing prowess relied exclusively on the work of others. A goal up, the home team were frustrated when the Midlands side equalised from a corner with nine minutes left, Everton dropping a vital point and passing the initiative to Liverpool in the title-race.

A significant number of the 61,187 crowd showed what they thought at the end of the game, standing in front of the directors' box chanting 'We want Young, we want Young.' Their anxiety was understandable. Those who criticised Catterick for having a vendetta against the striker, one that had the potential to derail the Toffees' title challenge, had a point. One supporter wrote in the *Liverpool Echo*, 'I may have quite the wrong impression but I can't help feel that someone is trying to prove something and the ultimate result could make Everton a two-time loser.' The injured Young did not help his case with a club fine for failing to show up at a treatment session a week later, attending the Aintree race meeting instead.

Recalled to the side, Catterick then played Young as a right-winger in the return fixture at the Hawthorns and, after a poor performance in this unfamiliar role, unfairly dropped him again for the 3-2 defeat at Stoke. The loss in the Potteries effectively handed the title to their bitter rivals. Everton fans showed their loyalty in the final game of the season against West Ham, when one entered the playing area with the now famous banner 'Keep Young, Sack Cattrick (sic)'. Ironically, the manager was not at Goodison that day – he was at Huddersfield watching Ray Wilson.

Unsurprisingly Young requested a transfer by the end of the season. 'I have felt for a while though that the doors have been closing against me,' the Scot said.

Everton circulated Young's details, but other clubs made no firm offers, or indeed made a serious enquiry for the Scottish striker. Ironically, by that stage the Scot may have already crossed Stanley Park. In the days following the signing of Fred Pickering, well-informed sources claimed that Liverpool had made a move for the striker but Everton had rejected the bid as too low. Indeed the Anfield club subsequently sent two directors to the match against West Brom on a scouting mission. There may have been some substance to the story. Speaking on BBC Radio Merseyside in 2008, Young made it clear who was his favourite manager in the city: 'I got on better with Shankly, when I was going training he was coming out of his house going to Liverpool's training ground. He always used to stop his car and speak to me, he called me Sandy so it would be "How's it going, Sandy?"'

With little interest from other clubs, at the end of May the Scot asked Everton to take him off the transfer list. Displaying typical bloody-mindedness when it came to Young, Catterick sat on the request for two months before removal. 'His initial request was made in haste. We have given him plenty of time to consider the withdrawal of it,' the manager pointedly said afterwards. This stubbornness with Young was a long-standing issue and continued throughout the Scot's career at Goodison. 'He preferred a big, bustling centre-forward-type,' Young later said, 'the guy who signed me, John Carey, liked the way I played, which was by using skill to play the ball around. Harry and me just did not get on well. I was in the team, but if he could have got away with it he would have left me out.'[12] That said, Catterick was still a fan, as he told Colin Wood of the *Daily Mail* in 1966. 'I am a great admirer of him [Young] for his skill. He is unfortunate in having to play against the packed defences. He is the target of the tough boy in any opposing defence because he is so skilled.' The further point Catterick made about the Scot in the same interview gave an insight into why he was becoming dispensable. 'I feel that Alex Young is unlucky in many ways because the modern game, which builds up these packed defences, is demanding more and more contact and leaving less space for the accomplished ball player. A fellow of Young's physique and style doesn't have the same sort of opportunity as he would in an open game.'

In the 1964/65 campaign Catterick had tried to keep Young in the side by

[12] There is actually no evidence to support this argument, the Scot made 262 appearances under Catterick and only Brian Labone (331) had played more games by the time of Young's departure in 1968. The fact that Catterick also changed the shape of the team on at least one occasion to accommodate the forward also points to the manager wishing to retain Young's services.

deploying him in the inside-right position as the 'link man' between defence and attack, the role requiring both durability and selflessness, through sacrificing personal ambitions for the wider needs of the team. Young, whose strength was primarily acting as a hugely gifted solo performer, capable of individual moments of brilliance, was clearly not a suitable candidate for the job. In the crowded midfield area, bigger players found it too easy to block the worshipped but fragile Scot out of the game and those graceful runs that left opposing players trailing in his wake were now infrequent. Brian Clough used to say that the biggest crime in football was giving jobs to players who did not have the tools to do them, and this was a classic case, with Catterick clearly at fault.

Although the move to 4-2-4 midway through the decade allowed Young an opportunity to once again play in a central striker role, Catterick's negative stance in public continued. After the dreadful 5-0 mauling at Anfield in September 1965, Catterick responded to the challenge of picking a team against FC Nürnberg in typical fashion. Alex Young was out. 'I was so disappointed with Young's display on Saturday that he would have been dropped whatever the game was,' the Everton manager told the *Liverpool Echo's* Michael Charters on the plane journey to the continent, the defeat reopening the debate about the Scot's role in the club. 'Young is certainly a Goodison problem boy,' wrote James Mossop in the *Daily Express*, 'he is such a gifted player that it hurts to see him drift into the shadows of a game when things go wrong – as in last Saturday's derby game. Is there any real future for him with Everton?' Although the Scot could feel yet again that he was the scapegoat, club officials supported Catterick's view that Young's performance was unacceptable and that he should be dropped. The forward returned for the second leg, with some supporters claiming that the 28-year-old had only been included in the game to boost the attendance. When the Scot was an unused substitute for the 2-1 home defeat to Leicester in early November, there was ironic cheering when a genuine loudspeaker announcement for a man wanted urgently at home seemed strangely apt. 'Here is an SOS for a Mr Young ...' Supporters then showed their displeasure by engaging in a mass exodus before the end.

Following the departure of Pickering, Young enjoyed a new lease of life, the arrival of Alan Ball enabling a 4-3-3 formation with the Scot as the attacking spearhead. Even so, there were still issues. After a 3-2 defeat in the classic FA Cup quarter-final at Nottingham Forest in March 1967, the performance of one Everton player drew familiar criticism. 'The great disappointment was Young. He was so aloof from the fray that I cannot recall him making one important contribution in such an important tension-packed game,' wrote Michael Charters in *Liverpool Echo*. Catterick concurred, 'I thought the team played really well, but I was disappointed in Young.' Unsurprisingly the forward was dropped and did not re-appear until the final game of the season. Not only was Catterick, in Young's eyes, making life difficult at club level, but the manager had also harmed his chances of international recognition. Young won only two caps at Goodison, although that was also due to the acknowledged bias in Scotland selecting players from north of the border. 'How Scotland continue to overlook his talents is past understanding,' Geoffrey Green once wrote in *The Times*. Young felt the attitude of his manager was largely to blame, as he told Aiden Smith of the *Scotsman* in 2012:

He [Catterick] and I didn't get on. There were quite a few Scots in the team, the likes of Jimmy Gabriel, Alex Parker, Sandy Brown and George Thomson who'd come down with me from Hearts, and he hated that ... if a [Scotland] selector ever did show up at Goodison, the manager would tell him: 'Don't bother looking at Young.' I just wasn't Catterick's kind of centre-forward – he liked them all rumbustious – and he was always right on top of me about something.

For all these public displays of dissatisfaction, Catterick still valued Young enormously, moving him to a wider position following the introduction of Joe Royle as a central striker. Young played brilliantly on the opening day of the 1967/68 campaign, scoring a wonderful goal against champions Manchester United at Goodison. The watching Arthur Hopcraft in the *Observer* succinctly outlined why he was such a magnetic presence for Everton fans:

Young ... produced most of the tricks – pulled with that effortlessness of touch which brings out the delight in the Goodison Park roars. But he added a little iron to his play as well, no doubt necessary if he is to hold his place. Winning the ball in tackles, and then using it with such delicacy, made him as much an asset to his side as he was a joy to watch. The trouble with Young in the past has been that he was not always both at the same time.

Catterick was now selective in picking Young, leaving the gifted Scotsman out of the more challenging away matches – depending on the opposition or state of the pitch – as a defensive move and keeping the forward fresh for games suited to his mercurial talents. A good example was the fourth-round FA Cup tie against Burnley in January 1967. The fans' idol did not play at Turf Moor but returned for the Goodison game with devastating effect, scoring two brilliantly taken goals in a hard-fought victory. This policy meant that in his final five months at Everton, in the 1967/68 season, Young played seven matches, but four were in the FA Cup. For all their differences, Catterick still thought Young could offer something.

However, this was not enough for Scot. Feeling he was still in the shadows, Young left the club in the late summer of 1968. The forward turned down a move to the New York Generals for family reasons, after the two clubs had agreed a financial package,[13] and then refused a transfer to second-tier Huddersfield Town for financial reasons. After another move to Wrexham failed to materialise, the mercurial striker moved to Glentoran for a fee of £12,000.[14] It was a low-key end to the career of a player who arguably, in the eyes of supporters, embodied the traditions of the School of Science more than anybody else did. The move was not a surprise, for after 1964, Young's career went into steady decline, on his own admission. 'Everton saw me at my best for about three years because of injuries … I never played those last five years as well as I would have liked, although I had lots of good games and good spells,' the Scot later admitted. 'I never really played consistently well. Many players played well into their thirties, but they didn't have knee or ankle injuries.' As one of the players who was placed under public scrutiny, Young later confessed that the worries from the *People* newspaper's allegations about Everton, that made headlines in 1964, effectively took a year out of his career.

Much has been made of the fact that Catterick was not the biggest fan of

13 Young later claimed that Catterick scuppered the move but that was certainly not the case, based on reports at the time. The two clubs had agreed a fee equivalent to £12,500 and the Generals manager Bill Bergesch said, 'Everything had been agreed upon between Generals and Everton for Young's transfer in an exchange of cables. Young was financially well satisfied and was to receive part of the transfer fee as a bonus.' But the Scot told the manager that he could not cross the Atlantic. 'I was stunned,' said Bergesch at the time, 'We are deeply disappointed, but Young could not bring himself to leave England.' Given the forward would also not move to Sheffield for family reasons, this would appear to be the correct version of events.

14 Young's move to Glentoran was a source of friction between the player and Everton. Sheffield United had previously offered £22,000 for the Scot, which Everton accepted, but Young did not wish to relocate his family. As a gesture of goodwill, a reduced £12,000 transfer was then agreed with the Irish club as Young was going as a player-manager, on the proviso that if sold back to a league club a further balance of £10,000 was due to Everton, to match the amount lost when Young turned down the move to Yorkshire. After two months in Ireland, Stockport made a move for Young but were unable to pay the £22,000 fee Glentoran required to break even. After much negotiation, Everton kindly waived all but £2,000 of the amount due to expedite the deal and Young went for £14,000.

Young and this contributed to their difficult relationship. There were times when the Scot wanted to leave Goodison but Catterick had no wish to sell and vice versa. When Young and Catterick agreed that the gifted forward could depart, there were no suitable bids. For a long time it was an unsolvable puzzle. The manager gave the Scot more than enough opportunities to prove himself, albeit in a variety of positions. The fact that Young – by his own admission – went missing in far too many games for a player of his ability undermines any pretensions to true greatness,[15] as does the perceived inability to attune to the changing demands of football. As the Scot admitted, 'There were other times when I exasperated myself and must have stretched the patience of manager Harry Catterick.' Although supporters criticised the Everton manager for his treatment of Young, Catterick could point to the number of games he did play, and the fact that when placed on the transfer list other big clubs did not show an interest, apart from Manchester City in 1967. 'We would use him, he has terrific skill. I think he would be a very good player for us,' said coach Malcolm Allison. City promptly bought Francis Lee instead.

Although the press voiced their bewilderment at this lack of activity, in retrospect this was no surprise. Supporters have since portrayed the Scot as a victim of Catterick's managerial whims but in reality, the absence of interest was a consequence of him being a casualty of the shifting mood of the game, where the opportunities for flair players were becoming scarce. His manager made this point in a column for the *People* in 1966. 'This is the era of team play, of players who sacrifice their own individuality for the sake of the other ten,' he told the paper. The former Hearts player's problem was that as a naturally deep-lying operator his skills were more suited to the inside-forward's role, but that required a more physical presence that simply did not suit his build. What you cannot deny was that, on the right day, his beautiful balance and touch made him one of Everton's greatest and most beloved players.

Welsh wizard, wayward Welshman – Catterick and Vernon

In his masterful 1966 portrayal of post-war football, The *Soccer Syndrome*, the journalist John Moynihan perfectly described the inherent contradictions within

15 Young however was included in the list of '100 league legends' unveiled by the Football League as part of their '100 seasons' celebrations in 1998.

Roy Vernon. 'A man with fine control of the ball, and sometimes a temper which flooded in bursts of hot saliva round his lips,' the author wrote. Moynihan was not alone in that view – Arthur Hopcraft in the *Observer* once described him as the 'dark and sinister darling of the fans'. Whether Vernon was indeed the Prince of Darkness is open to debate, but to Everton supporters he was their Prince of Wales, a potent mix of the instinctive creator with razor-sharp finishing powers. The forward was perhaps the key player for Everton in the first half of the decade. Intelligent and cultured – later becoming an antiques dealer – Vernon also possessed a notorious rebellious streak that, combined with self-confidence bordering on arrogance, was always going to mean he was poles apart from the strict disciplinarian Catterick. Like most of his ilk, taking away that edge also reduced his impact on the pitch.

Vernon's journey to Goodison was in many ways a series of false starts. Invited for a trial in 1952, manager Cliff Britton thought he was too small to make the grade. Vernon signed for Blackburn after his father, who was a scout with links to the Ewood Park club, recommended him to Johnny Carey, who was then in charge. His progress was rapid, scoring 49 league goals in 131 games before Carey – having now moved to Goodison and seen bids for Denis Law and Joe Baker rejected – agreed terms with Rovers to bring him to Goodison in January 1960. Although Vernon inspected club houses, he turned down Carey's overtures before changing his mind four weeks later, moving to Goodison in a £35,000 deal that saw Eddie Thomas travel the other way. Although Vernon settled quickly and dovetailed beautifully with Bobby Collins in his early days at the club, the striker's partnership with Alex Young has passed into Goodison legend.

Off the pitch Vernon could be trouble. Catterick first clashed with the Welshman on the trip to the North America in 1961, to appear in the grandly titled 'International Soccer League'. The brainchild of an American businessman, the tournament was primarily based in New York and involved the importing of European teams in the close-season to join selected local outfits in two leagues of seven, with the group winners facing each other in the final. The Everton board, attracted by a guarantee of $2,500 per game, had accepted an offer to play in the 1961 tournament scheduled over three weeks in May and June. After an arduous domestic campaign and alarmed by stories from previous visitors of ill-disciplined players, inadequate refereeing and poor training facilities, Catterick's suggestion to withdraw was rejected by the directors due to the possible legal consequences – although he later welcomed the opportunity to see the players' mettle tested in unusual circumstances.

Vernon played in the first game against Canadian side Concordia in their home town of Montreal, where Billy Bingham was sent-off after just 22 minutes of a 1-0 victory for the visitors, in a bitterly contested encounter featuring no less than thirteen minutes of injury time. 'Fists flew faster than at Liverpool Stadium,' Catterick told puzzled local journalists afterwards. The game was Vernon's only appearance due to fitness problems, and two weeks later Catterick, infamously, ordered the striker home for reputedly breaking a curfew. 'I felt it would be in the boy's best interest and the interests of the team,' the Everton manager said, although the other suggestion was that the punishment was related to Vernon's refusal to sign a new contract. The Welsh international was uncharacteristically diplomatic after returning home. 'Mr Catterick is the boss,' he announced, 'he has given his verdict and I accept it without the slightest bit of acrimony.' [16]

There had previously been rumours that the players were not happy about the sacking of popular Carey, and the demotion of coach Gordon Watson following the appointment of Tommy Eggleston.[17] In that context, the decision to send Vernon home was Catterick clearly imposing his will (and expected standards of discipline) on the playing staff – whether the punishment matched the crime is a moot point, and it is doubtful he would have taken the same course of action if Vernon had been fit to play. Nevertheless, the dismissal of the forward from the tour was a pointer to how Catterick handled relationships in the years that followed. Like his chairman, Catterick was a man who was more comfortable in giving messages via actions, not words, and it is not coincidental that those players who were on the receiving end – Vernon, Alex Young and later Alan Ball – were his biggest stars, as a way of a warning to others. Vernon's behaviour irked Catterick to the extent that the new manager privately made clubs aware he was available for transfer, and a planned move to Arsenal three months later only fell through when Everton were hit by a sudden injury crisis. Strange,

16 A paradox that characterised Vernon's Everton career was his measured comments to public humiliation. Those expecting a combustible response to his dropping – a big thing at the time – by Catterick for the trip to Manchester City in October 1962 were disappointed. 'I admit this dropping is a blow to my pride,' he admitted, 'but it will only increase my determination to recover my form and my place.'

17 One of the accusations Albert Dunlop made in the *People* in 1964 was that the players had to be talked out of boycotting the American tour, such was their anger at Carey's sacking.

therefore, that the career of one of the most important post-war Everton players was very nearly strangled at infancy.

Nevertheless, Vernon was superb in Catterick's first two seasons in charge. In 1961/62 the Welshman netted 26 goals in 37 league games, drawing this tribute from the *Liverpool Echo's* Leslie Edwards after a marvellous display against Burnley in February 1962: 'Having seen most of the great inside-forwards over the past forty years ... I have come to the conclusion that we have, at Everton, one to beat the lot. He's only starting his career, weighs little more than ten stone, has rather a knock-kneed stance which makes him look anything but a player and has a characteristically Celtic temper and temperament. Name? Roy Vernon. Position? Anywhere and everywhere.'

Vernon was just as potent in the 1962/63 championship-winning season, scoring 24 goals, after Catterick had made him club captain in an attempt to instil a sense of discipline. That was a temporary fix and Catterick never really forgave Vernon for missing three crucial games at the end of the ill-fated 1963/64 campaign through suspension. Booked against Birmingham in the February, the Welshman received a 'blue notice' – warning that a further caution would produce a ban – only to pick up another for retaliation against Nottingham Forest. One of the games Vernon missed was the costly 1-1 home draw against West Brom. That said, Vernon on his day could still be immensely valuable, earning public praise from Catterick after switching to right-back – having previously played for only half-an-hour in that position as a professional – in the 1-0 win over Spurs in October 1963. The striker's admirable discipline and application on the day was proof that the Welshman's naturally rebellious and individualist streak could be harnessed without damaging his contribution to the team.

But by the end of 1964 Vernon continued to try the patience of the Everton manager. Having scored just one goal in eleven games, Catterick fined the Welshman for arriving late for training and then there was a further breach of club discipline for giving an interview, without permission, to the press. The last straw was oversleeping the day before an away match at Spurs – Catterick dropped him, in his words, as 'a disciplinary measure for a breach of the club and training regulations'. Asked if he had taken full responsibility for the action, Catterick sneeringly responded, 'I am the manager, not the tea boy.' Vernon struggled in the reserves, threatening to play with an umbrella in one windswept game. 'We'll all get pneumonia in that,' said the Welshman in the tunnel beforehand, 'I'm taking my brolly with me.' Asked by the trainer if he was serious, he replied, 'Dead right I am. If I can't take this I'm not playing.' Fortunately, Vernon threw the umbrella into the dugout just before stepping onto the pitch.

The disciplinary measure accelerated his release from the club and the Welshman requested a transfer shortly afterwards. A move to Blackpool floundered when the two teams could not agree terms but Vernon eventually got his desired move from Goodison, to Stoke City fifteen minutes before the March transfer deadline, fittingly reaching a century of league goals (in 176 games) during his final match against Aston Villa. After leaving Stoke five years later the Everton hero ended his career in non-league football, where his sharp mind remained undimmed. Once told by a non-league boss that his midfield could not find him because he was standing still, Vernon responded, 'If they can't find me when I'm standing still, how the hell do you expect them to find me if I'm running around?'

Truculent and mercurial in equal measure, the former Blackburn player spearheaded the revival under Carey and was a key component of the 1963 title triumph. Vernon may not have seen eye to eye with his manager but there was no denying his respect for Catterick, as he later admitted, 'Everton came before everything else with him. At times he seemed to do certain things that the players – and sometimes the supporters – didn't like. But in his heart it was always the best for the club.' Brian Labone later paid tribute to the Welshman, 'Roy Vernon made it very easy for us. "Taffy" could do that, which took the pressure off the defence. He had a shot like a cannon with a very short backlift. He was built like a bag of bones and he smoked very heavily – all the things you shouldn't do.' Although his five years witnessed personal success and some unsavoury moments, as one of Everton's finest and most influential post-war players there was no doubting his fondness for the club when departing:

I cannot leave a great club like Everton, and they are a great club, without some pangs. However the time has come to make a break. Don't expect me to say anything critical about Everton, for I am not going to do it. I genuinely appreciate what Everton have done for me and cannot speak too highly of the way the crowd have appreciated my efforts.

6. Flexing the Millionaire Muscles

THE PERFECT COMBINATION IN FOOTBALL IS KNOWLEDGE AND money, something that Everton had in abundance in the first half of the decade. This came from chairman and manager, as Donald Saunders noted in the *Daily Telegraph* after the 1963 title triumph. 'Many an industrialist, flirting with the game, has poured thousands of pounds into a club and achieved nothing but disappointment. Mr Moores has made sure that his money has been spent wisely … Mr Catterick rarely picked wrongly, Mr Moores never failed to produce the cheque when his manager explained what position needed strengthening, what player could do it and what the price would be.'

Gordon West and Dennis Stevens, March 1962

Although Catterick's inherited squad had more than a touch of excellence, it still needed reinforcement and a ratcheting-up of quality in key areas. Yes, in the years that followed there were often expensive purchases, but there was certainly no scattergun approach to buying, indeed the policy was to be careful in transfer dealings, acquiring players only where there was value and with a specific role in mind, so they would not damage the 'blend' of the team.

The Everton manager waited until early March 1962 to make his first major move in the transfer market, and did so with dramatic effect. Catterick had been on the lookout for a new goalkeeper for most of the season, a need that became more pressing when reserve Willie Mailey broke a leg in January and a feeling that

Albert Dunlop, who was thirty-two, was not a long-term option. Knowing that Burnley had three top-class keepers in first-choice Adam Blacklaw, plus Harry Thomson and Jim Furnell, an approach was made to sign the latter for £22,000 only for the Scot to turn down the move at the last minute. This led Catterick back to Blackpool and the 18-year-old Gordon West, having first enquired about the 6 feet 1 inch, 14-stone England under-23 star six months before. This time negotiations moved quickly and West was signed for a record fee for a goalkeeper of £27,500. It was to prove an inspired choice, with the Darfield-born keeper going on to make more than 400 appearances.

Within 72 hours of signing West, Catterick struck again in the transfer market, bringing the Bolton inside-forward Dennis Stevens to Goodison for £25,000. Famously a cousin of Duncan Edwards and one of twelve children, the Dudley-born player's main contribution to Everton history until then had been his feisty contribution to a reserve game at Goodison several seasons before. [18] That was all forgotten as Stevens made his way to Everton. Catterick had been a long-term admirer of the man whose big heart and work ethic sat perfectly in the context of the changing game, especially as Stevens could also play across the middle or in a forward role. Consequently, Catterick singled him out for praise at the end of the 1962/63 championship-winning season: 'Stevens is the hard-working type essential to all sides – unsung yet rating the major recognition.'

Johnny Morrissey, September 1962

Attempting to resolve the long-standing problem on the left-hand side of the pitch, at the start of the 1962/63 campaign Catterick pulled off one of his celebrated transfer coups. Johnny Morrissey's move from Anfield remains one of the Merseyside football's most divisive affairs. Like many outstanding Liverpool schoolboys from the 1950s, Morrissey originated from the Scotland Road area and could number Larry Carberry – who had ironically just won the title with Ipswich – Willie Carlin, Bobby Campbell and Jimmy Melia amongst his contemporaries. A Liverpool fan from birth, he came home from Wembley in

[18] Everton reserves' 2-0 defeat to Bolton in November 1954 witnessed some of the worst scenes ever of supporter unrest on the ground. The referee, later alleged to have been drunk, appeared to dismiss Stevens after a clash with Everton's Harry Potts, only to change his mind. After he sent off Potts and teammate Ken Birch, a crowd of some 200 spectators invaded the pitch to remonstrate with the referee and Bolton players. Impromptu games of football between small boys took place in the penalty boxes and a woman struck a linesman with an umbrella. It took 15 minutes for police and Everton officials to clear the playing area.

tears after Arsenal had beaten them 2-0 in the 1950 FA Cup final. As a youngster Morrissey modelled his style on Billy Liddell, only moving to the wing when a player failed to turn up for his team. Recruited to the Anfield ground staff after leaving school, Morrissey made his debut against Everton, ironically, in a Floodlit Cup match in 1957 but after 37 appearances across four seasons, Shankly froze the wide-man out for the entire 1961/62 campaign. Morrissey spent the season in the reserves on a weekly contract and although Everton's Johnny Carey – hugely impressed by Morrissey's performances in Liverpool Senior Cup matches between the sides – had previously made enquiries, it was still something of a surprise when Catterick struck.

On the Monday after the opening weekend of the 1962/63 season, Everton representatives were at Anfield watching Morrissey terrorise Manchester City for Liverpool reserves, scoring in a 4-2 victory. Subsequent negotiations moved quickly and Morrissey signed three days later for a reported fee of £10,000. When quizzed about the move, the local-born player made his position clear. 'When I played for Liverpool I gave them everything I had,' he said, 'but there is no question of divided loyalties. From yesterday onwards I became an Evertonian.'

Catterick had his man but across the Park, the transfer famously had far-reaching consequences. T.V. Williams, the Liverpool chairman, handled the sale without the prior knowledge of his manager and did not consult Bill Shankly at all about the deal. Incensed, the Scot typed out a letter of resignation and left it on his desk. Walking out of the club, he informed Bob Paisley, amongst others, of his departure but staff persuaded him to stay and burnt the letter. Shankly, unsurprisingly, demanded more of a say in future deals. Given the future rivalry between the two, it is somewhat ironic that Catterick played a key role in Shankly strengthening his powerbase within the Anfield corridors – one of the first acts the Scot did subsequently was to enquire about signing Alex Parker, but Catterick rejected the request.

Although the former Liverpool player won a championship winner's medal in 1963, the winger's Everton career was something of a slow-burner. Indeed in the autumn of 1963 Morrissey was on the transfer list, but remarkably there was no prospective buyers. Three years later, Morrissey – who had played just once in the victorious FA Cup run and was not considered for the final – again asked for a move when his contract finished but with no interest again, the local-born player remained. It was only afterwards, when Catterick moved to a 4-3-3 formation, that he flourished in a blue shirt. Although not necessarily the quickest wide-man, the Liverpool-born player used his excellent touch and strength to bully his way past markers and, unusually for the time, could cross with both feet.

The other attribute Morrissey possessed was a penchant for intimidation that was legendary. In an area known for its militancy, there was some truth to the observation that Morrissey was the most combative left-winger in the city. One of a new generation of wide-men, Morrissey was capable of both taking it and giving it out – although in his case not necessarily in that order. Ironically, it was former teammate Tommy Smith who summed up the sense of dread that Morrissey instilled in opponents. In his *Liverpool Echo* column in October 1976, the Liverpool player was uncharacteristically charitable towards the wide-man:

The Everton player that Liverpool feared the most during my time was Johnny Morrissey. When we went over the Everton team before the game the word was always: 'Don't get involved with Morrissey.' The reason was that Johnny, a good friend of mine, was truly a hard man. On top of that he was a good player. He'd been brought up in a hard environment and that had taught him how to look after himself. You never took liberties with John. He was feared because he had no fear and he was clinical about any revenge that had to be taken.

Feared he may have been, but unsurprisingly it was Leeds United undoubtedly who drew the best (and worst) out of the Everton player. Even for a time when petty feuds were commonplace, his rivalry with Jackie Charlton, in particular, was renowned. Brian Labone once remarked that 'John was a dirty little bugger. He was about half the size of Jack and when he was around, you had to look out.' More than twenty years after their last meeting the World Cup winner detailed the origins of their enmity, following a bad challenge by Morrissey in a game at Goodison:

Picture the scene – my foot is in plaster, and I'm hobbling towards the coach with the aid of a stick. He's stood at the door asking, 'How's the leg then, big fella?' And I look across at him and see this cynical smile on his face – and I nearly flipped. I mean, if I could have done him then, I would have. 'I'll tell you something,' I said, 'if it takes me ten f---ing years, I'll get you back for this.' And I did. But then he got me back, and I got him back, and so it went on till we finished playing.

In the interim, Charlton had recorded his infamous October 1970 television interview, during the course of which he revealed that 'I have a little book with two names in it and if I get the chance to do them I will.' There was no black book, Charlton later admitted, but over the years there has been much speculation on the possible contents, if it had existed. When interviewed by the *Independent* in 1996, Charlton still left no doubt which opponent left the biggest impression. Asked for the names in his fabled book, he refused to oblige, before saying, 'I wouldn't want to embarrass anyone now. Apart from Johnny Morrissey.'

The local-born player therefore retains an almost mythical presence in the memories of those who played and watched football at that time, his name unfairly used as a symbol of the increasingly aggressive nature of the English game.[19] Even the Premier League obsessed Sky Sports News asked Charlton's teammate, John Giles, in 2010 about the winger's reputation. 'Johnny Morrissey first of all was a top class player, he was a terrific player,' the Irishman admitted, before adding that Morrissey's combative style could also survive in the sanitised modern game because of his cunning. 'Why I made him so dangerous was that he was so clever at it,' Giles said, referring to the winger's capacity for the dark arts.

Tony Kay, December 1962

Sheffield Wednesday may have rejected Everton's bid for Johnny Fantham two months earlier, but they found a £55,000 offer for club captain Tony Kay too good to refuse at the end of December 1962. This was in spite of the fact that the initial negotiations between Catterick and his successor as Wednesday boss, Vic Buckingham, broke down and it was ten days before Moores finalised the deal with his opposite number at Hillsborough.

The 25-year-old Kay had original designs on being a goalkeeper and even had a trial at Wednesday in that position. Having made his debut as a 17-year-old in 1955, two years of national service delayed his first-team aspirations and a permanent run in the team coincided with Catterick's arrival in 1958. A year later he appointed Kay as club captain at just 22 years of age and during the next four years the Sheffield-born player established himself as a top-class and supremely

19 By the late 1960s Morrissey was the only regular first-team player on Merseyside without an international cap at any level from youth upwards. The winger was called up by England under-23's whilst at Anfield but in the interim was punched in the jaw by an opponent and cracked a bone, forcing his withdrawal. It is safe to assume that he dealt with the miscreant on a later date.

competitive wing-half with the personality and drive to dominate big games – the sort of player supporters despised but secretly wanted on their team.

Press and spectators raised eyebrows at the move as Jimmy Gabriel and Brian Harris had proved a hugely consistent and solid wing-half partnership, but one of Catterick's great strengths as a manager was making incremental improvements – albeit at some cost – in areas that were already working extremely well. The move for Kay also reflected the wider changes within the game; managers had noted how Bill Nicholson, in particular, had skilfully manipulated his strength within midfield by resting players and deploying reserve Tony Marchi as a replacement. For Catterick it was the most important part of the pitch and, following Nicholson's lead, the chance to bring his former first lieutenant to the club was therefore an opportunity he could not miss. Kay later recalled, 'Harry Catterick, Everton manager at the time, said he wanted me to win the title for him. I turned him down because I was a Sheffield lad and I'd just bought a house there for my wife and kids. Harry came back a bit later and told me Roy Vernon would be captain for the toss-up, but I'd be the real boss of the team.' The fact that the move doubled his salary was also a factor, as the midfielder later admitted.

It was also a transfer endorsed by his chairman at the end of the season. 'It was hard on Brian Harris who Kay replaced, but we knew it might be another ten years before a wing-half like this was available,' Moores admitted. The big cheque also brought with it more disapproval that Everton were effectively trying to buy the title, which left Catterick annoyed. 'I was amazed at the amount of criticism that came the way of myself and the club at his [Kay's] signing,' he argued, 'but I have always believed that if I feel the team can be strengthened then it is my duty to do so.' There was some justification in his complaint. Other teams had also spent big money previously – not just Spurs, but others like Manchester United – without the same attention. It was money well spent too, as the Everton manager later told the *Daily Express*. 'I bought Tony Kay from Sheffield Wednesday when Brian Harris was already playing very well at left half. That signing probably clinched the championship.'

The 27-year-old seemed to have a long and profitable Everton career ahead, but events surrounding a game played at Ipswich on the same day as his new club's hard-fought draw at Spurs on the first day of December 1962 would return to haunt Kay, Everton and football.

Alex Scott, February 1963

Six weeks after signing Kay, Catterick struck again. The Everton manager was one of the many long-time admirers of the Rangers right-winger, Alex Scott, and with the Scottish international sidelined through the rise of the prodigious Willie Henderson, both Everton and Spurs were on alert when the Glasgow club put the 26-year-old on the transfer list in the first week of February. On face value, the transfer saga was classic Catterick as the cloak-and-dagger chase literally spanned the whole of Scotland, but he later admitted that was not the case:

The implication has always been that I pulled a fast one on Bill Nicholson of Spurs, but that isn't so. Bill is one of the straightest men in football and typically when Scott became available he phoned me. 'Are you interested?' he asked. 'Yes' I said … We exchanged prices and they were the same. 'Right' I said. 'It's up to the player.'

Both men travelled north of the border and, with the rail and road network virtually paralysed through bad weather, their trips proved hazardous. Nicholson arrived first while Catterick endured a nightmare journey. 'I drove up and got caught in a snowstorm. I got stuck in a drift, tried to dig my car out and finally abandoned it near the border and took a train from Carlisle.' Although Catterick and Scott spoke briefly first, when the Spurs manager took Scott away to the port of Grangemouth, where they breakfasted together on the morning of Thursday, 7 February, it appeared the deal was made. Meanwhile Catterick was left kicking his heels in room 232 of a Glasgow hotel. 'I'd hardly checked into my hotel when the telephone rang,' he later admitted, 'A reporter was on the line. "You've lost Scott," he said.'[20]

Catterick's fears appeared to be realised when at 12.20 p.m., Scott arrived at Ibrox and told the waiting reporters he was a Spurs player. Twelve minutes later, a beaming Nicholson turned up at the ground to clinch the deal. In the interim Scott had agreed to write an article for a newspaper, 'Why I chose Spurs', while his wife agreed to another, 'Why we chose London.' Evening newspapers in Glasgow, Liverpool and London set their presses for a back-page headline: 'Scott for Spurs.' However, the winger was heading to Everton within two hours. Initially,

20 The journalist in question was Jimmy Rodger, a confidant of Bill Nicholson, who was later involved in one of football's most famous verbal exchanges. Meeting Sir Alf Ramsey at Prestwick Airport, Rodger greeted the World Cup winner with the refrain 'Welcome to Scotland, Sir Alf.' The England manager's caustic reply has gone down in legend. 'Welcome to Scotland. You must be f------ joking.'

Nicholson's decision to let Scott tell Everton that he was moving to London backfired. From his vantage point outside the glass-fronted main entrance at Ibrox, the Spurs manager first realised there was a problem as he watched the Rangers manager, Scott Symon, and the in-demand player deep in conversation. Then at 1.45 p.m. Nicholson left abruptly, muttering 'the deal is off as Spurs are concerned. I'm going home.' Nicholson must have regretted not signing Scott in Grangemouth. Ten minutes later Catterick arrived at the ground and at 2.15 p.m. announced to the press that the Rangers man was Goodison bound. 'I always thought I'd get him. Scott thinks it will be better at Liverpool because he's nearer home. It's all a question of timing your negotiations right.' Asked why the winger had changed his mind – meaning Nicholson had lost a bidding war for the first time – the Everton manager said: 'Scott realises Everton are a good team, and we have fifty thousand supporters who think so too.'

Sandy Brown, September 1963

Sandy Brown's move from Partick Thistle in the early stages of the 1963/64 season is another part of the Catterick legend. Brown was, like Bobby Collins, a former cobbler who had impressed as a defender for the Scottish side, having spent five months at Spurs as a 15-year old before returning home through homesickness. One of Catterick's scouts at the time was the legendary Harry Storer,[21] whose no-nonsense style appealed to the Everton manager. Storer had been tracking utility man Brown for a considerable time and with injuries to both left-backs, Mick Meagan and George Thomson, by early September the time came to strike again in the transfer market. Catterick was attending a banquet to celebrate the championship triumph in the Adelphi hotel in Liverpool city centre and later described what followed:

It was midnight ... the players were celebrating and a cabaret was on stage, but neither I nor the Everton directors were watching it. We were huddled in a corner holding an emergency board meeting. 'We need more cover at full-back,' I said, 'and

[21] Storer's homespun wisdom during his time as a manager had been a significant influence on a young Brian Clough, then a player in the north-east. The man born in the West Derby district of Liverpool also taught the tricks of the scouting trade to one of the greatest judges of footballing flesh: Clough's sidekick Peter Taylor. Doubtless Storer's scouting assessments on Brown were more positive than one for an Everton target he was sent to assess. The report had one word in capitals: 'COWARD'. His statement on the vagaries of football management, 'Nobody Ever Says Thank You', was the title of Jonathan Wilson's 2011 biography of Clough.

I've just heard where I can get someone.' The directors gave me the O.K. and I left the hotel immediately, to drive alone to Scotland. At breakfast time I was changing clothes at a small hotel in the Lowlands. At nine, I was parked outside Partick Thistle's main entrance. At ten, I'd signed Brown and was driving home again.

Fred Pickering, March 1964

With Alex Young and Roy Vernon struggling, in the early months of 1964 Catterick turned to the powerful Jimmy Gabriel to spearhead the forward line. The Scot enjoyed a purple patch, netting in three successive games, including an FA Cup victory over Leeds and a derby win at Goodison. The run reinforced to Catterick the importance of having a strong and powerful target man. Three days after a 4-2 victory at White Hart Lane on the first Saturday of March had left the Toffees with a good chance of retaining their title, Catterick pulled off another transfer coup.

During the season, the Everton manager had run the rule over more than twenty centre-forwards. By the time of the crucial win at Spurs, some had moved on and his shortlist was now down to less than ten strikers who were theoretically available. Of these, Dundee's Alan Gilzean was unlikely to move with his team still in the Scottish Cup, while Burnley's Ray Pointer – who Catterick would have signed – was out injured. Bobby Smith of Spurs was in his thirties and considered only a stop-gap due to his age and Stoke's John Ritchie was considered too inexperienced. The Everton manager also passed over opportunities to sign Sheffield Wednesday's David 'Bronco' Layne and Carlisle's prolific Hugh McIlmoyle. Catterick felt that Ron Davies, then at Norwich City, was not up to the mark. It was a rare error of judgement. With Southampton, the gifted and powerful Welshman would become one of the best and most prolific strikers of the next decade.

That left one man available, Blackburn Rovers' deadly Fred Pickering, a scorer of 26 goals in league and cup thus far in the campaign. Catterick was an acknowledged fan and speculation was rife when the Everton boss was spotted at the local derby between Rovers and Bolton. Approached in the following week about a possible approach for the striker, he was typically evasive. 'We have not been in contact with Blackburn Rovers, nor have we made any approach for their player Fred Pickering,' Catterick told journalists. 'Because I attended the match on Saturday, I'm automatically said to be about to sign Pickering.' Yet when rumours of interest emerged about a possible move to Spurs, he quickly made an initial offer six days before the end of the transfer deadline. The deal moved quickly when the amount involved scared off other clubs. Pickering was actually on international duty at the time and training with England at Sheffield when Rovers recalled him to Ewood Park where the two parties agreed a fee of £85,000 – a record cash deal between two English clubs. 'I had become unsettled at Blackburn and wanted to join a club with big ambitions,' the player said later, 'when I was thinking of leaving Blackburn I remembered the football fever on Merseyside. So when I had the opportunity of joining Everton it didn't take me long to decide – in fact within ten minutes of meeting Mr Catterick I had signed for the club.'

The 23-year-old had joined Rovers from school and although nominally a striker, had actually started as a left-back in the first team, before reverting to a forward role as late as March 1961. From that point Pickering's progress was swift. Although not the complete forward, he was a natural goalscorer. Horace Yates in the *Liverpool Echo* felt the move was a catalyst for regaining the championship crown. 'My rating of Pickering is the best centre-forward in the country today and the man is ideally suited to end the biggest weakness in the Everton side. A big, strong bustling leader, and a deadly finisher must confirm Everton in the role of favourites for the title.' Catterick though took the opposite view. 'This is a signing for six seasons, not six weeks,' the Everton manager told waiting journalists, 'this is not just a move to the clinch the championship this season. Pickering has been brought to fit in with our long-term policy to keep Everton right at the top.' However, the Everton manager had complete confidence in the striker. 'Pickering could be another in the great Everton tradition of centre-forwards like Dixie Dean and Tommy Lawton,' he said at the new signing's unveiling.

One other man impressed by the deal was one of Pickering's predecessors at Blackburn. 'The greatest stroke of business since Manchester United signed Denis Law and Spurs bought Jimmy Greaves,' proclaimed Roy Vernon. 'Great as Pickering was with Blackburn, I feel convinced he will be greater still at Goodison Park.'

Nevertheless, the acquisition raised more questions than answers. Why, having waited so long to bring in the bustling centre-forward he had craved for three years, did Catterick wait to move until near the end of a campaign disrupted through constant selection headaches? Was Pickering able to fit in with the style of the team that had scored eighteen goals in seven games? Most pertinently – what was Alex Young's future? The press, as expected, asked the Everton manager about the Scot's prospects when the new signing was paraded. His response was typically world-weary and philosophical. 'What is anybody's future in this game, player or manager?'

Pickering was an immediate hit, scoring a hat-trick on his debut in a 6-1 thrashing of Nottingham Forest, but with the balance of the team disrupted, form slipped and the championship, which seemed there for the taking, slipped across the Park.

Ray Wilson, July 1964

When second division Huddersfield announced they were happy to release their England international left-back, Ray Wilson, the Everton manager moved quickly. With weaknesses on the left-hand side contributing to defensive frailties in the previous campaign, Catterick was keen to add the world-class full-back to the squad, having previously courted the 29-year-old when he was Sheffield Wednesday manager.[22]

Catterick had competition though from Liverpool. When he was manager at Leeds Road, Bill Shankly had moved Wilson into the left-back role from the wing. Now alerted to his availability, Shankly immediately visited the player, who ironically was living in the Liverpool manager's old house. However, the Huddersfield manager, Eddie Boot, was not keen on selling Wilson to his predecessor and immediately contacted Catterick, the two men sealing the deal within 48 hours. The final fee was £35,000 with Mick Meagan going across the Pennines in exchange. Although a significant amount for somebody close to thirty years of age, Wilson was worth every penny, as a player of undoubted international quality. The player also welcomed the deal, because of the frustrations arising from plying his trade outside the top-flight. 'I would have come to Huddersfield on my hands and knees to sign … I could have kissed my old club for letting me go to Everton, after playing against Brazil at Wembley on a Wednesday it wasn't easy to adapt to turning out at somewhere like Scunthorpe the following Saturday.'

Wilson was the finished article, the author Ivan Ponting summing up the England international perfectly. 'Light, compact and wiry, he was devastatingly quick in short bursts, could either tackle crisply or jockey his winger into blind

[22] At Sheffield Wednesday, Catterick wanted to prise Wilson from Bill Shankly, who was happy to sell in exchange for cash and reserve midfielder Don Megson, who then graduated to the first team causing the deal to collapse.

alleys as the situation demanded, and was blessed with positional flair that hinted strongly at a sixth sense.' Catterick was more than satisfied with the deal. 'We want only the best,' he said, 'and he is the best.' Wilson, having waited so long for his top-flight debut, strained a hip muscle in the opening home game and missed the next three months of the campaign. That was a minor blip as over the next five years the club's greatest ever full-back made more than 150 appearances, never falling below the highest standards. His Everton career effectively ended on the eve of the 1968/69 season as he later recalled, 'I jumped to head the ball in training, I felt my knee go as I landed and at thirty-four I knew my time was up.' On his departure, Catterick paid tribute to the Yorkshireman, 'Wilson is one of the finest professionals I have ever known. His behaviour on and off the field is a model to every player. It has been a great pleasure to me to have him on the playing staff.'

And one that got away ... Joe Baker

Like Mark Hughes more than thirty years later, striker Joe Baker always seemed destined to play for Everton. Born in Liverpool to Scottish parents, Baker's family returned north of the border when he was just six weeks old. After impressing with Hibernian, Johnny Carey tried and failed to bring Baker to Goodison before signing Roy Vernon in 1960. However, during the 1960/61 season both Carey, again, and Catterick, whilst at Sheffield Wednesday, tried to bring him back to England. (Catterick later felt that the failure to push through a £50,000 deal effectively cost the Yorkshire side the title.)

Catterick rekindled his interest within a week of becoming Everton manager, and on the final day of the campaign the new boss missed the easy 4-1 home victory over Arsenal as he was in Scotland trying to negotiate a deal. On this occasion the new manager lost interest when the Scottish club's £75,000 price tag proved prohibitive and the widely coveted Baker eventually went to Torino. That was not the end of the club's quest to sign the forward. When the striker was thought to be keen on coming home in early 1962 after his spell abroad proved troublesome, Everton were rumoured to be making a fourth attempt to sign the former Hibernian man. Catterick naturally denied the claims, 'Baker is a signed player of another club. We are interested in all sorts of players, sometimes as many as the forty our scouts report to us, but whether we sign any of them is a different matter.'

Such indifference was a Catterick trademark of course; the reality was that he had secretly ordered the club to negotiate with the Football League – a requirement of the time, given Baker was abroad – for him to come to Goodison. At 5 foot 7 inches and twelve stone, the pugnacious Baker was not the ideal forward Catterick was looking for, but still was an adept goalscorer who literally packed a powerful punch, once knocking an Italian press photographer clean into a Florence canal. Baker eventually moved to Arsenal, where he later floored the Shankly colossus Ron Yeats following a skirmish at Highbury. The deal eventually hit the buffers when Torino would not budge from their original valuation of £78,000.

There was one final act between Baker and Everton. By the spring of 1967 the striker was plying his trade at Nottingham Forest, then in the running to complete a league and cup double. Their FA Cup quarter-final encounter with the Goodison side at the City Ground was one of the games of the decade, Forest victorious 3-2 in a heart-stopping encounter. To this day Forest fans claim that Brian Labone's uncharacteristically nasty challenge on Baker irreparably damaged their chances of silverware. Within ninety seconds of the start the Everton skipper clobbered the Forest dangerman and his thigh injury not only ended his active involvement in the game and season but some on the Trent say Baker was never the same player again.

Whether that was true is one to debate but perhaps there was no coincidence that Catterick's side targeted their biggest threat early on. 'I have no doubt that foul was pre-meditated,' Forest's former Everton player Frank Wignall told the author Andrew Dolloway for his book *Nottingham Forest in the Sixties: The Forgotten Decade*. Afterwards, Alan Ball then took the unusual step of entering the Forest dressing room to apologise. It was a strange way to end to the game, but Everton and Baker were never meant to be.

And one who went ... Bobby Collins

The Scot was the most influential player of the Carey era, ironically one who had come to Goodison for a second time in the final days of Ian Buchan's reign. Born in Glasgow in 1931 and a cobbler by trade in his early years, Robert Young Collins had first come to the club as a shy teenage amateur but soon returned north of the border when learning of Celtic's interest. After ten years at Parkhead and with the team in transition, Collins made clear his ambition to play in England, and in September 1958 moved to Everton for a fee of £23,500.

For the 5 foot 4 inch Collins, the playing area was a battlefield and despite his lack of height, it was never a case of David against Goliath. The opposition was the enemy who, despite his lack of inches, were to be destroyed with extreme prejudice. During a playing career that lasted close to a quarter of a century, the granite Scot made aggression an art form, clearly ruled by fear while firmly believing it was a case of kill or be killed. Collins once raked his studs down George Best's shins *before the game* and in his later years single-handedly reduced testimonial matches to kicking contests. Teammate Billy Bingham said of him that 'Collins was the most competitive player for his size I have ever come across, he would kick his granny if he had to.' Like his compatriots from a rich seam of Scottish footballing talent that has long since dried up, Collins could also play, and with Alex Parker and Bingham formed a powerful triumvirate on the right-hand side.

By the time Catterick arrived and bought Dennis Stevens in March 1962 there was one unanswered question. The Everton manager was adamant that the former Bolton man would go straight into the team, but as he was a like-for-like replacement for the Scot, what did it mean for the man who had almost single-handedly kept Everton afloat for two seasons? Asked about Collins' future on the day he bought Stevens, Catterick said, 'What is the use of our building up our strength if we are going to let players go wholesale. It would take a very tempting fee indeed for us even to consider letting Bobby go.' The enticing offer came within 48 hours.

Across the Pennines, Don Revie was moulding his second division Leeds team into a side whose ruthless professionalism would become a major feature of the domestic game for the next decade or more. In Collins, the Elland Road boss identified somebody who could propel his young outfit into the top-flight. Catterick turned down an initial bid from Revie but on receipt of a second, he put it before the board. The directors reluctantly agreed and Collins – who had several business interests in the area, one curiously being a pig farm in Aintree – had no hesitation in moving for a club record outgoing fee of £30,000, a considerable amount at the time for a 31-year-old. The deal made sense for both manager and player. Catterick was never going to build a new side around someone who was gradually losing both touch and fitness, whilst it provided the former Celtic player with a new challenge. Collins himself knew the writing was on the wall. 'Harry Catterick didn't think I was as good as I had been and that upset me a bit. I was surprised to go, but he said he wasn't too happy with my form even though I had just scored a couple of goals in a win over Fulham. In that situation I had no choice so off I went.'

In a slightly surreal development, Liverpool tried to hijack the deal at the last moment. Bill Shankly attempted to phone Collins, but his target was out and the Scot's brother-in-law failed to recognise the Liverpool manager. Shankly got in touch again, but by then Collins had left Everton. As the midfielder later recalled, 'The phone went again. I was bowled over when this voice growled: "Son, is it true yev signed fae Leeds?" I could only say: "Yes, Mr Shankly". To his credit, he replied: "Arra best anyway, son". I don't know what would have happened if I'd been in when he first called.' There was another aspect of the move that Catterick revealed in the *Liverpool Echo* in 1978. The Everton manager claimed that Revie had previously been in contact about Collins, and that in return he wanted the young Billy Bremner:

I was interested in Bremner, but Don Revie was very browned off with him. The lad was homesick and he had been going home to Scotland at weekends and not coming back until several days later. Don spoke to me about Collins and we agreed a fee of around £20,000. At the same time I asked about Bremner and it was agreed I could have him for the same amount. But Leeds had a series of matches coming up and they wanted to keep Bremner for a couple of weeks longer. I agreed, the lad played for them, did exceptionally well and the deal was off.

Without doubting Catterick's side of the story – and in many ways he was publicly trying to justify the sale of the Scot – that was not necessarily the case. There was no chance of the ginger-haired youngster leaving, as Revie confirmed himself to the *News of the World* in 1980. The former England manager recalled his response to the Leeds board after they informed him that they were willing to accept Everton's £25,000 offer:

'He's one of the best players we've got,' I pointed out. They remained adamant about letting him go and I told them: 'That's me finished!' And I stormed out of the room. One of the directors, Harry Reynolds, came after me: 'You win,' he said, 'We'll keep him.'

Like the transfer of Alan Ball nearly a decade later, the sale of Collins bemused supporters, although the same fans had just given the Scot 'the bird' (in his manager's words) when he had returned from injury. The club captain also enjoyed a notoriously difficult relationship with John Moores, and two months before

Collins had confronted his chairman after he had slammed his performances. 'As captain I was the first to receive his opinions and I was not happy when Mr Moores inferred that I wasn't giving my all,' Collins later admitted. 'Nobody criticises my work rate, winning was everything to me. I was fuming and I let him know.'

After his departure supporters' fears were realised when Collins, keen no doubt to prove Catterick wrong, more than repaid his new manager's faith. In the words of Rob Bagchi and Paul Rogerson's excellent study of the Revie years, *The Unforgiven*, 'He constructed the DNA pattern that has defined it – the myth of "dirty Leeds."' The Elland Road side were promoted two seasons later and they became a dominant force in the domestic game, while in 1965 Collins was voted Footballer of the Year. Without the same incentive and in completely different circumstances, the Glaswegian would never have flourished to the same degree at Goodison. At Leeds, Collins played higher up the pitch in the inside-left role as playmaker – the number ten jersey – requiring less defensive work than on the opposite side at Everton. The Scot was not going to become the creator at Goodison while Roy Vernon was with the club. Comparisons of Collins at Everton and Leeds are therefore invalid to a degree.

Having said that, Catterick later admitted to a rare error of judgement in letting the Scot depart. 'Of all the decisions I've made the sale of Collins to Leeds was the only one that would have been better delayed,' he admitted. The success that came Everton's way after he left, and his contribution to the dramatic rise of Revie's side, succeeded in airbrushing out the enormous contribution made by Collins as one of Everton's greatest ever players. Brian Labone later acknowledged the influence of the man whose size four boots he would later fill as captain:

Bobby Collins made the biggest impact on me during my career. When I broke into the side on a regular basis in 1959, Bobby was skipper and the key player in the first team … Bobby was the ultimate professional. He taught me a lot during the early stages of my career. I remember challenging him for a ball during a training match. I was over six foot tall, so you'd think it would be a mismatch going in against Bobby, but he went in hard and took me out. I was amazed by his strength, aggression and desire. Next time I went in a lot firmer and he said with a wry smile, 'You're learning, son,' but that was Bobby, no quarter was given on or off the pitch. I learned a lot from him.

7.
Travels and Travails in Europe

ENGLISH TEAMS ENTERED EUROPEAN COMPETITION FOR THE FIRST time in 1955, enjoying mixed fortunes until Spurs became the first to lift one of the three major trophies eight years later, after a 5-1 destruction of Atlético Madrid in the Cup Winners' Cup final (ironically in the Feyenoord stadium where Everton lifted the same trophy 22 years later to the day). Everton's opportunities on the continent were hindered by one of the more ludicrous rules of the time, the 'one city, one club' diktat that applied to the Fairs (later UEFA) Cup, where entry was based on league position. In 1968/69 Everton failed to qualify for the competition having finished third, as Liverpool were runners-up, while seventh-placed Southampton did. Having waited seven years to test themselves against the continent's finest, after qualifying for the first time in 1961/62, the Toffees were ironically only required to make a relatively short trip north of the border.

Dunfermline, Fairs Cup, September 1962

The Greek side, Salonica, were Everton's original opponents but following their withdrawal, Dunfermline stepped in as their replacements. Their manager was Jock Stein, who was taking the early steps in a career that would establish him as the leading contender for the greatest British manager of all time. Critics gave the side from north of the border little chance in the first leg in Liverpool against the team that was now topping the table. 'I have a feeling that they may be somewhat overawed by the Goodison crowd and are likely to go home with a five or six goal deficit,' said a local press columnist.

The optimism proved misplaced. With the Cuban missile crisis escalating the threat of nuclear war, the outcome of an early round European fixture at Goodison seemed insignificant in comparison. On the night, the visitors' strong-arm tactics bridged the gap between the ability of the two teams as Catterick, not for the last time in Europe, failed to make the required tactical adjustments to counter the visiting team's massed defence. (Unlike Stein, who realised that the best way to counter a massed defence was massed attack, tactics he brilliantly deployed later in the decade with his magnificent Celtic side.) In a contest screaming for some width, the manager deployed Young as the attacking spearhead, a ploy easily countered by Stein, who fielded an extra central defender to smother any threat through the middle. The only goal came after 25 minutes when Stevens connected cleanly with Bingham's corner and saw his header go in off the crossbar. Despite almost constant pressure from the home team, there were no more goals in a game marred by cynical play from both teams. Five players were booked in an encounter described by the *Liverpool Echo's* Horace Yates as 'the most nakedly ill-tempered match I have ever seen'.

The return in the Scottish town seven days later was more entertaining than the pitch-battle at Goodison but equally controversial. The home team were more enterprising and took an early lead through a twenty-yard strike from George Miller. With a third game looming, four minutes from time came the defining moment of the tie. The home side's Harry Melrose looked clearly offside when running onto a long pass from the back and to the delight of the 21,000 crowd slipped the ball past West. Despite the protests of the Everton players, the referee allowed the goal to stand and Catterick's men were out. Although Everton could count themselves unfortunate, Stein's side had outplayed the English champions-elect on a night when their attacking vanguard failed to create a single opportunity, with only the magnificent Jimmy Gabriel posing a goal threat. Later in the championship-winning season, Catterick viewed the defeat as what modern managers now call 'a blessing in disguise.' The manager said, 'One can feel relieved that Dunfermline did us a good turn when they defeated us in the Fairs Cup. At least we were relieved of those extra games.' The title victory guaranteed qualification for the European Cup, but the draw produced a tie against the toughest opponents imaginable.

Inter Milan, European Cup, 1963

Unlike the stage-managed Champions League of today, there was a degree of naivety in the approach to the competition fifty or so years ago, primarily borne out of the political divisions on the continent at the time. To restrict travelling and minimise meetings between clubs on either side of the Iron Curtain, the draw split those from west and east Europe into separate pots.

As English champions, Everton were included in the draw in Zurich during the first week of July. Others in the 31-team competition included the holders, AC Milan, and the five times champions, Real Madrid. The team to avoid was Helenio Herrera's Inter Milan, the Serie A champions. Although politically understandable, the division of entrants increased the risk of the big clubs from the traditional powers of the west meeting early on in an otherwise open draw. So it proved. The pairings resulted in Glasgow Rangers matched with Real Madrid and next up came Everton, drawn against Inter. Four of the biggest names in the competition were to meet at the *preliminary* stage.

Although Moores was optimistic – 'I think this is a grand match for our followers' he said in the aftermath – in reality it was a horrible draw. Catterick later said, 'It is going to be an extremely hard test for Everton. In fact, we could not have had a harder tie.' To put the draw into context, twelve months earlier the previous English champions, Ipswich Town, scored fourteen goals over the two legs against Maltese minnows, Floriana. The only consolation was their opponents shared the same sentiments. 'Everton! What a terrible draw for us,' Herrera told Everton coach Ron Lewin during a course at Lilleshall, 'This was the team I feared above all and hoped to keep away from at this early stage.'

Everton encounter the 'great fixer'

The two-legged tie against Inter was due to take place at the end of September. Before the meeting, there had been the usual scouting missions. Herrera attended the Burnley home game – when Everton suffered their first loss in 44 games at Goodison – and identified their biggest threat in the first leg. 'It will be a hell of an ordeal for us at Goodison, for I have just seen what a din the local crowd kicks up. They are tireless and sometimes turbulent – quite an effective twelfth man for a very strong team. Believe me I'll be happy to settle for a draw there.' Meanwhile Catterick, Moores and Eggleston had all travelled to Italy in the first weekend of September and saw their weakened cup opponents beaten by city rivals, AC Milan,

2-0 in a friendly. In truth they learned little. With Serie A starting a month later than the league programme in England, Herrera felt that his side's rusty edge was to Everton's advantage.

While in Italy the managerial trio spent eight hours in teeming rain searching for suitable accommodation for the second leg. Their only companion was one of European football's most infamous figures, Dezso Solti. The Inter president, Angelo Moratti, first worked with the Hungarian during the 1950s but only made him a permanent presence at the club after Solti helped set up the appointment of Herrera. However, managerial positions were not the only thing Solti arranged. According to the testimony of several figures within the shadowy world of 1960s European football, Solti was also proficient in helping to 'fix' games. In their brilliantly researched exposé of alleged match-fixing published in the *Sunday Times* during the mid-1970s, the hugely experienced football journalist Brian Glanville, with his colleague Keith Botsford, placed Solti and Inter firmly within a tangled web of corruption of match officials. Included in their revelations was the bribery of the referee in a European Cup tie against Borussia Dortmund in 1964, and they reported Solti's failed attempt to bribe the Hungarian referee, György Vadas, at the same stage against Real Madrid in 1966. In between those two fixtures had been their notorious semi-final against Liverpool, when referee José María Ortiz de Mendíbil allowed Inter two controversial goals in the San Siro as they successfully retrieved a two-goal deficit from the first leg. Solti later left Inter, but the Portuguese referee, Francisco Lobo, told the journalists of the Hungarian's bribery attempt before the first leg of the 1973 European Cup semi-final between Juventus and Derby County.[23] Although UEFA subsequently suspended Solti, both Italian giants disgracefully escaped sanction.

During their investigations, the two journalists failed to uncover anything untoward about the clash between Everton and Inter. However, they did expose the undue influence that Italian clubs had on the selection of match officials and in that context, it is easy to be cynical about the two referees for the tie (Gyula Gere and Lajos Horvath) being Solti's compatriots. The great 'fixer' did visit Liverpool twice, according to Glanville, to agree a favourable date for Inter for the game at Goodison. On the first occasion he failed – and was sacked by Moratti – but then succeeded and was reinstated. Of their Italian meeting, John Moores later

23 By coincidence during the course of this game, on 11 April 1973, Catterick was sacked as Everton manager.

said that Solti made 'a very good job' of providing facilities in Milan. Catterick held a different view, as he later recalled, 'Perhaps it was just a coincidence, but, when I went to Milan to help in arranging that second leg against Inter, all the hotels we were shown overlooked tram routes, railway lines or scooter-infested streets. "You no like?" sighed the Italian representative [Solti].'

The first leg – stalemate

All these accusations of skullduggery, of course, were yet to happen when the two teams lined up at Goodison Park on 18 September 1963. Inter flew into Manchester and were then whisked away to their luxury hotel in Birkdale, where Herrera again repeated his thoughts on the opposition. 'Sure it's going to be a difficult game. I still think English training methods are out of date – but we fear Everton more than any other team in Europe.'

Whatever his public thoughts, the Inter boss had no reason to feel apprehensive, for his team dazzled with performers of genuine quality. The key figure was the former European Footballer of the Year, Luis Suárez, a hugely gifted Spanish playmaker brought from Barcelona for an eye-watering fee, even for a club of Everton's stature, of £204,000. Elsewhere there was 'the Jaguar', the swift and deadly Brazilian right-winger, Jair, and the deep-lying playmaker Mario Corso on the left. The young and equally gifted Sandro Mazzola completed the flexible attacking spearhead. Inter's twin full-backs, the majestic Giacinto Facchetti and Tarcisio Burgnich, were so accomplished they were still playing for the national side at the World Cup eleven years later. Although *Catenaccio* is regarded as a defensive tactic, Herrera exploited the attacking principles, allowing Facchetti licence to move forwards. If Catterick wanted an insight into the continental way of playing, then he should have been at Anfield two weeks before the Inter encounter, where West Ham United's progressive manager, Ron Greenwood, deployed Bobby Moore as a spare man in defence and swapped systems during the game. The home side, used to a rigid tactical approach, were bewildered and succumbed to a 2-1 defeat.

Herrera reminded the press of his wariness of the home support before the game and on the night a gate of more than 62,000 for the first leg – paying British record receipts of £31,450, far exceeding those of £27,500 for the Spurs and Rangers clash in the same competition twelve months before – would have impressed the Inter boss. Although nominally at full strength, Everton went into the opening leg with some players off form or carrying knocks – Young in particular had lost his turn of speed while Vernon, Gabriel and Kay had all missed games though injury – but the only replacement was Harris for the injured Thomson at left-back. Inter brought in Horst Szymaniak[24] for Corso, to provide extra defensive resilience, although the German had not impressed Catterick when playing for Karlsruhe against Everton in America two years before.

It turned out to be a night of frustration for Everton, in a tense and tight goalless draw that confirmed two things, that the fearsome home crowd were magnificently partisan and Inter were a top quality side, arguably the most accomplished to visit Goodison in its long history. Desmond Hackett, writing in the *Daily Express*, was one impressed by the home support. 'On this night of roaring noise and an undaunted faith in their team, I can salute only the quality of the Everton fans. To the last minute, they were invincible and unquenchable as they filled the black skies with a cannonade of noise.' Nevertheless, winning games occurs on the pitch, not the terraces, and Hackett said that 'Milan played football in a language Everton could not translate.' He was correct, although Inter's game was far more expansive than expected, the precision and control of the play was no different to what Herrera usually set out to produce – keep it tight at the back, make sure Suárez has enough of the ball and exploit the pace of the menacing Jair on the right. What Catterick failed to do was to develop a game plan to counter Inter's fluidity and subtle positional play. The midfield allowed Suárez too much space, and they did not exploit the pace of Scott to get round the back of the defence. With the forwards neutralised by the Italians' defence, Everton's biggest attacking threats came from full-backs Alex Parker and Brian Harris. Although Vernon had a late goal disallowed for what looked like a marginal offside decision, ultimately the home side relied on the classic British tactics in Europe – long, aimless balls into the box that provided no threat to a superbly drilled back-line.

After the game Catterick put down his side's below-par performance to their difficult preparations and inexperience at this level. The manager said, 'We suffered from not being able to train together in recent weeks due to injuries and Vernon might have been a little sharper with more recent match practice … our forwards in particular have a lot to learn from this kind of football.'

[24] To put into context the difference in the wealth of the two clubs, Inter admitted that they had paid £115,000 for Szymaniak – twice the fee for Tony Kay – 'simply to counter Everton's strength'. Herrera himself was paid £25,000 per year, seven times Catterick's salary.

Asked about the home side, Herrera replied, 'They played very hard, but I think they will not reach the next round. The score in Milan? I don't know – perhaps two nil.' The statistics at the end of the game told their own tale. At the end of a home European tie against a team content for a draw, Everton had fewer shots (10 against 11), fewer corners (6 against 8) and conceded more fouls (18 against 12). For the champions of England, it was a salutary experience and such were the unusual demands of continental football that in the next few days players reported aches and pains associated with pre-season.

The second leg – San Siro zero

'No hope,' the *Daily Mail* proclaimed after the first game and Everton's preparations for the second leg in Milan a week later were hampered by further injury problems, Gabriel tearing a hamstring in a 3-2 home victory over Sheffield Wednesday on the Saturday. That left the manager with a conundrum before leaving for Italy, as Gabriel's natural replacement Brian Harris played at left-back in the first leg. The odds against succeeding were high. In the seven previous seasons of the European Cup, English sides had won just three times on the continent and not one had moved into the next round after drawing the first leg at home.

The club's travel preparations for the second leg were not the best, with their original departure from Manchester airport scheduled for as late as Monday evening – less than 48 hours before the kick-off. However, bad weather in France caused the cancellation of their flight and eventually they had to fly to Italy from London, arriving in Milan at 4.30 a.m. on the Tuesday morning. The tired and hungry squad essentially missed a night's sleep before the biggest game of their lives in a piece of poor planning, which typified the approach of some English teams in Europe at the time. Big continental clubs had long since taken steps to getting preparations right – Inter had been given permission to cancel their league game before visiting Goodison. The naivety associated with European football was also apparent on the day of the game. Told by home officials to leave in good time for the journey to the San Siro for traffic reasons, the Everton party watched helplessly as the driver sped through the back streets, arriving at the ground more than two hours before kick-off, which only added to the tension.

With Corso returning to the Inter line-up, the return leg in front of 59,128 spectators, including a party of 130 away fans who had paid the princely sum of

£26 each for the trip, was an altogether feistier affair compared to the Goodison encounter. In spite of their erratic travel arrangements, Everton were far more competitive in the San Siro, in difficult conditions, as Alex Young said at the time. 'It is the most terrifying stadium I have ever played in,' the Scot admitted, 'Even if you have only got possession the crowd will start that hideous whistle or go completely silent until Milan regain the ball.'

Catterick set the team up more defensively, pulling Dennis Stevens back in defence, with Young and both wingers deployed in midfield, leaving Vernon as the lone striker. Famously Colin Harvey made his professional debut for the club, replacing the absent Gabriel. The visitors held firm in the first half with Catterick happy to employ these negative tactics – including double-marking Suárez – with the intention of taking the tie to a third game at a neutral venue, should the scores be level after two legs. With the crowd reacting to the visitors' spoiling methods with a mixture of boos and whistles, Inter still fashioned a number of chances before the crucial moment of the tie in the opening minutes of the second period, Carlo Tagnin freed Jair on the right hand side and the Brazilian shot fiercely into the roof of the net.

The rest of the game developed into an ugly scrap, with four players booked and a number of running feuds. Everton had one excellent opportunity to draw level but Scott, after a 40-yard slalom run through the Inter defence, shot wide from twelve yards out. The last few minutes saw the home side employ time-wasting tactics before the Hungarian referee Lajos Horvath blew the final whistle. After the game, Catterick put on a brave face. 'This was a wonderful show, considering we had a makeshift eleven,' he told the press, 'To hold Inter to one goal in three hours of football is something Merseyside can be proud of. Everything I asked of the lads they did and the tactics we employed almost came off.' Despite the good performance in Italy, Everton were out of the premier European competition at the first hurdle.

The Inter encounter taught Catterick and Moores that, to compete with cosmopolitan foreign clubs in European competition, then limiting their horizons to home talent meant they were fighting with one hand tied behind their back. Football League rules dictated that Everton were simply unable to go abroad and buy a Suárez or a Jair, even though they had the resource. As Catterick said before the tie, 'Apparently they [Inter] cannot find home grown products to satisfy their needs, so, because their regulations are more elastic and co-operative than ours, they are able to tour the world and spend to the limit of their purse.' Catterick and Moores would revisit the theme regularly during the decade.

Manchester United, Fairs Cup, January/February 1965

The early months of 1965 were difficult times at Goodison. Out of the championship running and in the midst of a gruelling fourth-round FA Cup tie against Leeds United, the third-round Fairs Cup match-up against Manchester United was possibly the last opportunity to salvage something from a disappointing campaign. With the Toffees outside of the top six, for the first time there appeared to be widespread negativity around Catterick's management and playing style. The team was gradually losing the gloss of the Carey era, Catterick accused of replacing it by tactics that were becoming slavishly defensive – predictable results at the expense of negative, no risk football.

Europe was providing respite, and having defeated Norwegian side Vålerenga and Kilmarnock in the first two rounds, Everton travelled to Old Trafford at the end of January 1965 with a weakened team, missing Sandy Brown, Brian Harris and Roy Vernon. Supported by a travelling army of 12,000 fans, the visitors snatched the lead when centre-half Bill Foulkes missed a clearance from Tommy Wright and Pickering, ever the opportunist, nipped in to score. The home side replied in similar fashion. This time it was Jimmy Gabriel's turn to commit an error in defence – John Connelly seizing upon the Scot's loose back pass to Gordon West to equalise. With Labone a central defensive rock and Tommy Wright – not for the last time – shackling the menace of George Best, the visitors comfortably held onto their away draw that left them marginal favourites to progress to the next round.

Before the return game on Merseyside, the Toffees went out of the FA Cup after two bitterly fought games against Leeds United and with supporter dissatisfaction growing, matters came to a head in the home encounter against lowly Birmingham City three days before Matt Busby's side arrived at Goodison. 'Catterick must go' proclaimed one banner at the ground but, fortunately, the Everton manager was not there to see it, being on a scouting mission. Even more luckily, he avoided the catcalls at the end of the game when the home side could only draw 1-1. Although there was no danger of Catterick losing his job, there were enough concerns amongst the directors to arrange a meeting with the manager 24 hours before the United game. The Board expressed their concern with poor performances on the pitch and some unwelcome events off it. A break in Blackpool had resulted in complaints from a hotel manager over players' behaviour, which were leaked to the national press, and a number of reserves had requested transfers.

Like the first game, the season-defining encounter at Goodison was fast-paced and entertaining. With Vernon returning to the team for the first time in two months, the difference on the night was his counterpart on the United side, the electrically charged Denis Law. The Scot operated on the periphery of the game for the entire ninety minutes, choosing to involve himself on two occasions. The first came on six minutes when his brilliant pass set up Connelly to open the scoring. After Pickering – who had earlier struck a post – equalised via a deflected free-kick, Law struck again when his sweeping run from the halfway line was followed by another perfect pass to Connelly, whose shot West saved before David Herd followed up the rebound. United held onto their 2-1 lead and the result ended the last chance of silverware for the home team. 'This is not time to harry or harangue Everton officials or players. This is a time when followers of the club must show they appreciate that the ball does not run kindly,' admitted Leslie Edwards in the *Liverpool Echo* afterwards. It was the low-point of the campaign though, the Toffees rallying to finish fourth after a difficult season.

FC Nürnberg, Fairs Cup, September/October 1965

Three days after the debacle of a 5-0 derby defeat at Anfield in September 1965, Catterick took his side to Germany for a rendezvous with FC Nürnberg in the first round of the Fairs Cup. With Brian Labone out injured, the manager responded to the derby defeat in familiar fashion by dropping Alex Young. The Germans were a tough and disciplined outfit, who had beaten Manchester United 2-0 in a pre-season friendly. Matt Busby warned Catterick before the game that 'they are one of the toughest sides we have faced in continental football; Everton will have to work very, very hard to get through'.

With Dennis Stevens replacing Young and Catterick recalling Sandy Brown to reinforce the fragile back-line, the first leg was a brutal battle from start to finish. To most observers the man to blame was the Czech referee Dr Gelba, somebody with a medical background who had no issues with players inflicting physical harm on their opponents. 'We shall be making a report on the referee who was the poorest I have seen,' Catterick said after the game. The Everton manager had a point. The primary instigator of the violence was the German team's striker and captain, Heinz Strehl, who kicked and punched Brown within seconds of the start in full view of the referee, who took no action. The visitors were no angels though, conceding twenty free-kicks to the sixteen of their opponents, but there were countless other fouls that went unpunished.

The two teams of combatants exchanged fouls and a goal apiece – Harris heading an equaliser for the visitors on fifty minutes – before a moment of high comedy. Fifteen minutes from time, two Everton players simultaneously found themselves lying injured, Morrissey twenty yards from the goalmouth and Harris in the centre of the pitch. Trainer Tommy Eggleston ran towards Morrissey, the others in attendance being two men with a stretcher and the Nürnberg goalkeeper, Roland Wabra. Eggleston later recalled what happened next. 'When I reached Morrissey the men with the stretcher were pulling at him to get him off the pitch. I thought they might break his leg so I stopped them. At that moment the German goalkeeper intervened and swung a punch at me which missed, so I pushed him away. Then the referee ordered me out of the ground and the goalkeeper picked up my medical bag and hurled it off the pitch.' The referee allowed Eggleston to stay in the ground only following the intervention of the Nürnberg technical director, Herr Riemke, but farcically reserve goalkeeper Andy Rankin undertook trainer's duties for the rest of the game, which eventually finished 1-1.

At the end of the ferocious encounter, only three Everton players were free from injury, the rest wearing bandages and bruises following the harsh treatment of the home team. 'I am no softie but this is the toughest team I have ever seen, As far as these fellows are concerned the war is still on,' Catterick told the *Daily Mirror's* Frank McGhee after the game. 'The players of both sides were unnecessarily hard and there was too much pushing. In the second half the fouls became too severe all together,' said the referee in his own defence. In total, six players were booked in a game of obstructive tactics, vicious tackling, provocation and retaliation – typical of many English sides' encounters with teams from the continent in the first two decades of European football.

In the *Liverpool Echo*, Michael Charters' view afterwards that 'this game became a disgrace to football and made one wonder if European competition is worthwhile' was part of a wider outlook shared by many journalists at the time. Elsewhere in that round of European games, Chelsea were subject to stormy and savage abuse in Rome while Bobby Collins, of all people, effectively had his top-class career terminated following a horribly fractured leg after a vicious tackle at Torino. 'The game more and more is being brought into disrepute and cynical mockery … the monster looks to be rapidly getting out of control and something needs to be done about it,' said Geoffrey Green in *The Times*. Indeed, the great man advised that the British should threaten to withdraw from all European football. Before the return leg, Everton drew 2-2 at home to Blackburn – Catterick missing the game after an emergency abdominal operation – and enjoyed an encouraging 3-1 victory over Spurs, while Nürnberg's home game against Karlsruhe required police helicopters and water cannon to disperse fans angered by the referee. Before the second leg, the noises coming out from Germany would have encouraged the stricken Catterick. 'As long as we are not beaten by too many goals, we do not mind, we have little hope,' said the Nürnberg coach Jeno Czakandy.

It is probably exaggerating to say the eyes of the football world were on Goodison Park, but given they were the first English team to renew European combat after the anarchy of the first leg matches there was greater interest than usual in a game between two middling Anglo-German sides. There was also the reputation of the Everton crowd – and with Liverpool also playing at home 24 hours later, the city's supporters in general – to consider. As ever, pre-match hype of another Anglo-German bloodbath proved to be without foundation. 'All quiet on the Goodison front,' said the *Guardian* headline, Albert Barham adding 'peace was declared in the second leg of this Inter-Cities' Fairs Cup first round match which had such an ugly baptism in Nürnberg a fortnight ago.' Although the visitors were on their best behaviour, their spoiling tactics of playing both wing halves in a blanket five- or six-man defence contributed to a sterile, passionless encounter. Alex Young returned to the side in the inside-right position for his first appearance since the derby loss, Jimmy Gabriel was now up front with Fred Pickering and the Scot scored the only goal of the game on 63 minutes. Brian Harris headed Tommy Wright's cross against a post and, while the German defence stood motionless, the emergency centre-forward pounced for his fourth goal in three matches. The only black spot in a game expertly controlled by the Frenchman, Marcel Blois, was Gordon West's broken collarbone after the goalkeeper had fallen while clearing the ball in the first half. Fortunately, a recent rule change allowed the provision for a replacement and Andy Rankin, the substitute trainer in the first leg, fulfilled his usual role in slightly less controversial circumstances. Everton's reward for the 2-1 aggregate win was a tie against a very accomplished Hungarian side, Újpest Dozsa.

Újpest Dozsa, Fairs Cup, November 1965

The three weeks following the victory over the German team were symptomatic of a difficult first half of the 1965/66 season. Catterick was still recuperating at home following his operation, missing the Nürnberg encounter at Goodison and getting any scraps of information off the radio and television. His mood did not improve in the next two matches, a 3-2 defeat at Fulham and a goalless draw at home to Blackpool, when the crowd jeered the home side off. Having campaigned all season for Everton players to improve their image on the pitch, the manager was irate when Colin Harvey was sent-off at Craven Cottage after clashing with the home side's John Dempsey. 'I thought I had buttoned them up so far as the question of retaliation was concerned, but apparently not so. As I am not able to see any games, I thought it best that I should leave team matters, including the selection of the side, to Tommy Eggleston. So except for advice on the Fairs Cup fixtures, I am playing no part in the club's affairs.'

Catterick may have been thankful that he did not take the trip beyond the Iron Curtain for the first-leg trip to Budapest, a visit that left the team's European dreams in tatters. Preparations were not ideal, Everton's decision to stay in monastic seclusion in the hills, some five miles of narrow roads away from the city, baffled home officials. 'We do not think it is good for footballers to stay so high up,' one said, 'we cannot understand why Everton didn't stay in the city.' The visitors were without the injured Gabriel for the encounter against the powerful home side, featuring nine players who had played for their country at either full international level or the Olympic Games. Star attraction was the hugely gifted Ferenc Bene, a beautifully balanced and pacey player who, despite a slight build, was deployed as a central striker for his club side. With the game shown live on television, there was a crowd of just 5,000 in the cavernous but impressive Nep Stadium, built for 100,000 spectators. Their absence added a surreal atmosphere to an evening when the visitors were undone by the typical tactics and style of the top continental sides, the Hungarians displaying better ball skills, speedy transition from defence to attack combined with precise, accurate passing.

Having set out with a packed defence in a rigid 4-4-2, with Harris sweeping behind Labone, Everton were a goal down within nine minutes, when Ernő Solymosi's strike from 25 yards flew past a startled Rankin. By the half-hour the gap was two goals when Wright blocked a free-kick from the same player only to see the ball bounce back to Bene, who scored easily. Everton were as good as out of the tie when Béla Kuharszki scored a third in the second half. Like Inter Milan two years before, the visitors did not show enough against players and tactics of a type they rarely faced in domestic football, drawing just one save from the home goalkeeper over the ninety minutes. 'We were found wanting in the forward line,' said Eggleston afterwards, which was a clear understatement. The abject display even shocked the visiting Everton directors.

Catterick returned from his enforced absence after the away leg, initially for a few hours a day, with Eggleston remaining in charge for the trip to Sheffield United on the Saturday before the return. It was a familiar tale. The visitors were poor in a demoralising 2-0 defeat while a few of their followers who invaded the pitch at the end chanted the now familiar refrain of 'We want Young' in front of the directors' box. 'It was dreadful; a disaster of a game,' said Michael Charters in the *Liverpool Echo* afterwards. To be fair Eggleston was finding it difficult in fulfilling the unfamiliar manager's role and after the loss in Yorkshire he cut an exasperated figure. 'I have done my best to choose a successful team from the players available and I am sure they have all tried their best, but unfortunately that has not been good enough. Nobody can complain that they have not been given every chance – now changes are inevitable.'

Eggleston was correct. Catterick wrung six positional changes for the return leg against the Hungarians. Pickering was out and Young in. Ray Wilson was back for Brown, while Catterick dropped Scott and Stevens with Gabriel returning from injury and Jimmy Husband stepping in for only his fourth senior start. For Stevens it was the sign that his Goodison career was over, the utterly dependable midfielder making only two more appearances before leaving for Oldham in a £30,000 deal, in typical low-key style, before the end of the year.

Faced with a seemingly impossible task, for half an hour it appeared that Catterick's bold experiment might pay off. After just four minutes, Harris directed a header from a Wilson free-kick beyond Antal Szentmihályi in the Újpest goal. The keeper then made two outstanding saves before Gabriel headed against an upright. Nevertheless, the classy Hungarians gained control of the match and equalised on 31 minutes. From then on, it was a typical Everton performance at Goodison in Europe during the decade, the home side's hurried approach contrasting with the methodical and tactical style employed by the continentals. The game fell away after the bright opening as the visitors broke dangerously, but surprisingly the home side scored again before the end when Ernő Noskó turned a fast cross from the dangerous Temple into his own net.

Real Zaragoza, European Cup Winners' Cup, November 1966

Before they started the 1966/67 European campaign, Everton had further experience of the diverse nature of football on foreign shores. After winning the FA Cup, the team travelled for an end-of-season visit to the Eastern Mediterranean. After defeating AEK Athens 1-0, they moved to Israel, a journey punctuated by incidents representative of overseas tours. In Haifa, Gordon West spent the best part of one day filming a TV commercial for their hotel, while Brian Harris' version of 'San Francisco' had hotel guests screaming for an encore. On their last night in Tel Aviv a businessman bet Sandy Brown £15 that the Scot could not swim ten lengths of the pool. The Everton player did just that, the man handed over the money in silence and then disappeared into the night. There was a serious side as well. The last game of the tour, against Turkish side Fenerbahçe, degenerated into a kicking match. Hundreds of home fans hurled bottles at Fred Pickering after the striker was sent-off in a game settled by Jimmy Gabriel's penalty. 'The referee was bad, the spectators were even worse,' claimed Catterick after the brutal contest.

After defeating the Danish side, Aalborg, in the opening round of the 1966/67 Cup Winners' Cup – 'the roughest team we have met in five years of European football' said Catterick – Everton's unfortunate habit of attracting good-quality teams early in the draw continued. This time it was a dangerous outfit from Spain, Real Zaragoza. The side from the Iberian Peninsula had won the Fairs Cup in 1964, in a 2-1 victory over Valencia, before losing in the final to Barcelona two years later – after scoring three times in the opening thirteen minutes at Elland Road in their semi-final play-off against Leeds, as they strolled to a 3-1 victory. As well as a strong defence featuring three internationals, their penetrating attack, nicknamed *Los Cinco Magnificos,* featured Carlos Lapetra and Marcelino from Spain's 1966 World Cup side, as well as the rangy and graceful Juan Manuel Villa on the wing.

Everton approached the first leg in northern Spain in good form, on the back of a six-game winning run, their best for three years. The opening half at La Romareda again typified matches in senior European club competitions at the time – a brawl overseen by weak officials, with some football in the interim. After some initial posturing between the two teams, the Spaniards lit the blue touch paper just before the break. The home side had targeted Alex Scott for some heavy treatment and when Lapetra felled the Everton player, the winger threw the ball at his assailant. The referee responded by booking the Scot. As the teams lined up for the free-kick, Jose Violeta – who had been sent off against Leeds United seven months before – went down and was rolling around the pitch, seemingly following an incident involving Johnny Morrissey. When West moved out of his area to speak to his teammate, the goalkeeper was pursued by three Zaragoza players aiming punches. West then retreated towards the bye-line, becoming the centre of an ugly skirmish in which all but two of the players from both teams were involved – Alan Ball and the home goalkeeper watching on from the centre-circle. The referee dismissed Morrissey, with cushion-throwing fans targeting the winger as he walked around the pitch. The *Daily Mirror's* Frank McGhee described the events as 'one of the most incredible scenes I have ever seen on a football field'.

Thankfully the break allowed tempers to cool on both sides, at the end of a half where Zaragoza had scored the only goal on fourteen minutes, when inside-right Eleuterio Santos headed home after West had misjudged the flight of a corner. With order restored, the visitors staged a brave rearguard action with ten men in the second period, only to concede a second on 65 minutes. West was again at fault, the goalkeeper badly out of position as a Marcelino header gently dropped in off the crossbar. To sum up a frustrating night, the man in black turned down what appeared to be two clear penalties for fouls on Temple. Catterick was livid after the game, although he did pay tribute to his players, 'I am proud of them all, the way they played after being one man short. So far as the Morrissey incident was concerned he was kicked twice by Violeta before the Swiss referee saw anything. When the referee did turn round he saw Violeta rolling on the ground in apparent agony and all that Morrissey had done was to push him in retaliation.' Alan Ball said, 'We weren't allowed to play football tonight. When we are we should show them how goals are scored.'

The midfielder had a fortnight wait for the opportunity. The fixture in Spain typified the problems of the time of dirty play and weak refereeing, but these were not just limited to European games. At Manchester City just before the second leg, it was even worse than the Zaragoza match. The newly promoted team – or Dave Connor in particular – targeted Ball for special attention and a running feud followed between the two players, only ending when Catterick moved the England man up the pitch, where Ball continued his dispute with Tony Book. 'Sad to see an instinctively brilliant footballer squandering his talents in the cause of reprisals,' wrote Eric Todd in the *Guardian*, who would not be the last journalist to caution Ball over his fiery temper. *The Liverpool Daily Post* described it as 'football, in between bouts of wrestling and rugby league'.

Nevertheless, matters came to a head when the referee, Mr Bill Handley, disallowed what appeared to be an Everton equaliser from a corner, rightly informing the players that he not blown for the restart, being too busy clearing up debris thrown by supporters. A swarm of jostling players and spectators then submerged the City goalkeeper Harry Dowd. Ironically, the referee's actions resulted in fans throwing even more missiles onto the pitch – in the end officials removed more than 100 coins, a wheelbarrow full of broken glass and several darts from the playing area. Police were required to break up fighting spectators and they escorted several from the ground covered in blood. There were more than fifty arrests. 'This was a disaster for football,' said Horace Yates in the *Liverpool Echo*. One of Manchester's leading surgeons was Sidney Rose, a City director who showed a little black humour amidst the chaos. 'It is a long time since I saw so much blood,' he admitted after the game, 'and I'm used to it.'

The second leg against the Spanish side was four days later. Whether their experiences in Spain influenced the Everton officials' behaviour when Zaragoza arrived in the city is unknown, but they were hardly welcoming. Only the club secretary met the team at the airport and Everton refused permission for the Spanish side to train at Goodison, meaning the visitors were left using the Liverpool Baseball Association playing fields in Aintree as their training base.

The game took place on a brilliantly floodlit and misty Goodison night, and echoed the heartache of the Fiorentina game more than four decades later. With queues forming around the ground from mid-afternoon, a 56,000 crowd spurred the home team on against a side happy to defend after a bright start. With marker Santiago Isasi initially shackling Ball and Scott fading quickly, it left Young – six years to the day after joining Everton – to provide the first-half inspiration. Despite the Scot's promptings, the home team created only limited chances against a defiant Zaragoza rearguard and were left waiting until ten minutes from time to reduce the arrears. Catterick wanted penetration in attack so Sandy Brown played as a centre-forward and when Gabriel flicked on Harvey's long pass, the auxiliary striker reacted first and fired high into the net. The final minutes contained more drama than the rest of the game combined, but following some narrow escapes and outrageous timewasting from the visitors, Everton went out 2-1 on aggregate.

'How Zaragoza survived we shall never know,' wrote Eric Todd in the *Guardian*, 'but survive they did and that was the end of Everton.'

European Inquest

The defeat to the Spanish side meant that Everton had failed to reach the quarter-finals in their first five seasons of European competition. During that time their only victory over any team with a pedigree was the 2-1 aggregate win over FC Nürnberg in the 1965/66 Fairs Cup. Why a club with Everton's financial resources, experienced playing staff and a manager capable of winning the championship had such a disappointing record in Europe is up for debate. Discounting the defeat to Manchester United, as all English ties always have an artificial feel in Europe, Everton were unlucky when drawn with eventual European Cup winners Inter in 1963. Jock Stein and Dunfermline had outwitted Catterick tactically twelve months before, while the aggregate losses to Újpest Dozsa and Zaragoza were directly the result of poor performances in the first leg. Újpest and Zaragoza were both good sides, but not in the top tier of European teams – Leeds beat the Hungarian side convincingly on aggregate after they had knocked out Everton and an ageing Zaragoza went out to Rangers on the toss of the coin.

It is true that the more tactically advanced and better-prepared foreign teams held an advantage over their English counterparts in the early part of the decade, so by 1966 only Spurs and West Ham had lifted European trophies. Liverpool had reached the European Cup semi-final in 1965 and Cup Winners' Cup final twelve months later, but then repeated Everton's poor form in the rest of the decade, when sides like Újpest's Hungarian stable-mates Ferencváros overcame the Anfield side.

Nevertheless, Everton should really have done more. The first problem was scoring goals against the better teams. In the ten matches played in the five ties they lost on aggregate, Everton scored just six times and only one in five games away from Goodison – and that was at Old Trafford. These problems primarily lay in Catterick's reaction to the tie against Inter in 1963. The Italian defensive set-up hugely impressed the manager, in particular the use of a left-winger as an auxiliary defender, and this lay behind his move to a 4-2-4/4-3-3 system from a three-man defensive unit. After the attacking momentum of 1962/63, his teams became increasingly more defensive, sitting back more. The best teams, like Inter, used this to their advantage, by employing pace on the break. Catterick's problem was that his sides lacked that characteristic by the middle of the decade – Morrissey certainly was not the quickest and preferred to receive the ball deep in the opponents' half while Scott's speed dissipated following a series of injuries. When sitting back in away games, creating scoring opportunities became a problem.

At home, Everton struggled against deep-lying defences, a pattern repeated in league games in the years after the first title-winning season. Like many English sides, Catterick's team were unable to vary their way of playing. The lack of pace and penetration on the flanks and through the middle produced largely aimless balls in the direction of a big target man, tactics that were meat and drink to opposition defences, particularly those from abroad, who were expert in shuffling attackers into areas of the pitch where there was no threat. 'The blanket type of defence means a club has elected that the game will be played in one-third of the pitch by two-thirds of the players. This is not easy to master,' Catterick admitted.

The manager himself was probably the other issue. His frustration that Everton were unable to compete with the cosmopolitan giants of Europe, first aired after the defeat to Inter Milan, did not necessarily create a positive attitude. With the associated bureaucracy, Catterick therefore treated continental soccer with a certain amount of disdain. 'European competitions are not competitions at all,' he later confessed, 'playing games over two legs isn't football. It does nothing but create negative play that is something we cannot abide.' The manager also took an arrogant approach to his foreign rivals, 'Some of the supposedly brilliant continental sides would not last five minutes in this [English] league – the pressure would be far too great. There are teams who have won the European Cup who would never win the English League Championship, the toughest competition in the world, with forty-two games to play in every possible conditions.'

To say that the best continental sides of the time, like the two Milan clubs and Benfica, would not flourish in England was a ludicrous statement. Even though the Everton manager was not alone in that opinion, it was still a myopic view. Other more progressive English club managers – Matt Busby, Bill Nicholson, Don Revie and Ron Greenwood – embraced European football and made a success of it. Catterick's failure to do either is one of the factors why commentators regularly omit his name from the list of great managers of the time.

8.
Home is Where the Hatred is

IN *THE SOCCER SYNDROME*, JOHN MOYNIHAN DESCRIBED STROLLING round the touchline at Goodison Park on a perfect summer's day. Even then, Moynihan noted, the ground carried a certain amount of menace. 'Walking behind the infamous goal, where they built a barrier to stop objects crunching into visiting goalkeepers,' he wrote, 'there was a strange feeling of hostility remaining as if the regulars had never left.' Even someone as experienced as World Cup winner Jack Charlton admitted the Everton crowd was 'the worst before which I have ever played ... there always seems to be a threatening attitude, a vicious undertone to their remarks.'

Why, then, did Goodison Park inspire such feelings of fear? The answer is probably a complex one, and is not necessarily all football related. As the level of crime and violence increased after the War – the 1960s was the only decade in the twentieth century where criminal offences doubled – press coverage rose commensurately.[25] There were particular concerns over rising juvenile crime, as 1950s teddy boys morphed into the mods and rockers of the following decade. Inevitably, these anxieties affected the public perception of football, with its inherent youthful fan base. With supporters now organised into larger groups,

[25] The *Liverpool Echo* headline 'Young Hooligans turn Liverpool Streets into Battlefields' is not from the past five years but from March 1963.

followers became increasingly tribalistic, particularly those associated with the big city clubs like Everton. The *News of the World's* Bob Pennington spoke of the 'lunatic fringe of support that fastens onto them [Everton], seeking identification in a multi-national port where roots are hard to establish.' The same newspaper later described Everton supporters as the 'roughest, rowdiest rabble who watches British soccer'.

The working population demographic of the area also contributed to the rising violence. The city, due to its indigenous labour market, contained a significant number of casual and unskilled workers, with a long history of abrasiveness and confrontation, whose frustrations were reflected in the worst industrial relations record in the country. With football still very much a working class game, in a more aggressive society there was an inevitability that this bitterness would find a new platform on and off the terraces. As the 1964 academic study on Everton support said about crowd trouble: 'It may well be that the standards of behaviour of those supporters reflects the general standard of the city in which the Club has its roots. A certain amount of unseemly behaviour may, therefore, be inevitable.'

With greater mobility there was also a rise in away support, with regular incidents on railways. After Everton's FA Cup defeat at Manchester City in 1956, away fans damaged more than half of their nineteen trains, and twelve months later 200 Everton fans jumped off a stationary train travelling back from Bolton during the journey, causing eight others to stop. Consequently, as early as 1959, British Railways police had developed a so-called 'secret plan' to deal with Everton supporters. Broken windows, smashed lightbulbs and constant stoppages due to the pulling of the emergency cord were a recurring theme of away trips. Moynihan said that 'Everton supporters … liked to break things in the same way that a child likes to break toys.' It was not just Everton. In 1964 British Railways stopped all football specials leaving the city, after similar issues with Liverpool fans. That was off the pitch, on it there was just as much trouble, with newspapers more than happy to paint the club in the worst possible light.[26]

26 British Railways treatment of Everton may also have been influenced by John Moores' ongoing battle with the organisation over their treatment of his Littlewoods mail order goods. Damage whilst in rail transit was a constant problem for the company, so much so that the Everton chairman summoned their Liverpool manager to a meeting. Whilst seated in Moores' office, one of Littlewoods' mail order wardrobes was brought in, accompanied by a large axe. Incredibly, Moores proceeded to smash the wardrobe with the axe in front of his astonished guest and calmly returned to his seat. 'That is how your company is treating our furniture. Do something about it, please.'

'Hooligans, not sportsmen,' Sheffield Wednesday, September 1961

Catterick felt the wrath of the home support for the first time in September 1961, ironically against his previous club. On the first Saturday of the month the visitors handed out a 4-0 hammering, with Tony Kay outstanding for Wednesday. Eric Todd in the *Guardian* said: 'The absence of Collins and a recent crop of injuries could not be held responsible for this sorry display – for the effervescent Collins, like so many of his colleagues is primarily an individualist, and Everton's first requirement is cohesion.' But for some profligate finishing by the visitors the outcome could have been far worse. Kay received a standing ovation from the home supporters, who reserved their ire for Moores and Catterick, verbally abusing both in the stands, while throwing cushions onto the pitch. Two missiles just missed legendary local MP Bessie Braddock, who called the supporters 'Hooligans, not sportsmen. I can see no justification for anybody throwing cushions like that. They might have injured some perfectly innocent person.'

With the abolition of the maximum wage, the players' new inflated contracts were linked inexorably to the money received at the gate, so it was inevitable that supporters demanded higher standards in return, which made conflict inevitable. Shocked by the reaction of supporters to the Sheffield Wednesday performance, the club made an extraordinary admission in the match programme for the next home game against Manchester City:

One cannot escape that Everton's display last Saturday was probably the worst they have given since Arsenal visited Goodison some three years ago and administered a 6-1 defeat ... The players themselves must be forgiven if they are feeling confused. When they trooped off the field after the West Brom game, they received a big ovation from the spectators. Three days later they trooped off to slow handclaps and boos instead. As the players can earn substantial bonuses by your attendance, it is only natural that they are out to please you, the spectator... The spectators have a right to boo and jeer (but not to throw things); that is their prerogative, but will this do any good? That is for you to decide. It is a fact, however, that cheers frequently do more good than jeers when trying to spur a team to greater efforts.

'A game of rugby union', Sheffield United, October 1961

There is no doubting that Catterick instilled a harder edge in his first full campaign in charge. Although supporters welcomed the steelier approach, others felt that on occasions boundaries were crossed. Seven weeks after the Sheffield Wednesday debacle, the BBC radio commentator Bernard Taylor likened the 1-0 home win over their city rivals United at the end of October 1961 to a game of rugby union. 'More than 100,000 have watched Everton in the last four days,' he said, 'but many of them cannot have recognised the game they were watching – perfect low tackles, beautiful hand-offs and plenty of barging in the line-outs, sorry, throw-ins. The referee allowed some of the most glaring fouls to go unpunished and with the home side being the worst offenders it all added up to being a rather dullish performance.'

Catterick took exception to the comments and Leslie Edwards' similar viewpoint in the *Liverpool Echo* about the same game. The journalist said, 'Everton feel it necessary to descend to the tugging and pushing one sees only from the most frustrating of Continental elevens.' There was a feeling amongst rivals that weaker referees let Everton's aggressive tactics go unpunished at Goodison because their big spending had generated a certain amount of influence, whereas away from home it was a different matter. The perceived in-balance in standards perhaps contributed to a moderate away record in Catterick's first full season, with no victories on opponents' grounds for more than six months at one stage. Either way, at Chelsea seven days later a mass brawl ten minutes from time, following an altercation between Roy Vernon and Ken Shellito, was the only noticeable incident of a game full of 'rough stuff' according to the *Daily Mirror*.

'A load of muck', West Ham United, March 1963

The FA Cup fifth-round trip to Upton Park in March 1963 epitomised the changing face of English football. The last time the two teams had met on the ground in the competition, Catterick had scored both goals. On this occasion, there was a malignant undercurrent both on and off the pitch, and it was one of a number of games in the first half of the 1960s that had a negative effect on the club's reputation.

Events at Upton Park did nothing to dispel the gathering belief, particularly in the southern press, that Everton were nothing but rich and overpaid bullyboys whose followers were hired thugs. The only goal of the tie followed a penalty awarded for handball by the visitors' Dennis Stevens, but before Johnny Byrne could successfully convert the kick, Everton supporters threw a mass of bottles onto the pitch, while several invaded the playing area. The grim proceedings had previously led to the experienced referee, Jim Finney, calling both captains together to halt the ruthless tackling as two West Ham players lay flat out on the pitch. The former England cricketer and footballer, Denis Compton, described the game in the *Sunday Express* as 'one of the most brutal and gruelling I have ever seen'.

At the end of the game ground-staff collected crates full of cans and bottles, many with jagged edges, while visiting fans stayed outside the ground for more than an hour afterwards. Given the aggravation, it was no surprise that there was a war of words between the chairmen of the two clubs in the days that followed. Initially, the West Ham chairman Reg Pratt slated the Everton supporters in a memorable outburst. 'They are a load of muck,' Pratt complained, 'these sort of people are bringing sport down to the level of a pig yard. I know this has been a problem for the Everton board for a long time. We object to our players, officials and visitors to our ground being molested by their supporters.'

John Moores snapped back when he heard about the comments. 'If the report is true, this is very unparliamentary language for any club chairman to use. But even if there was any trouble I am far from convinced that the whole of the blame should be laid at Everton's door.' Pratt snapped back, 'Fair enough, but Mr Moores had left when incidents happened outside the ground which led to my calling certain Everton followers "a load of muck."' It was all a bit unedifying and did nothing to enhance the club's standing.

As for events on the pitch, the *Guardian's* Albert Barham made a valid point. 'The great mystery remains why Everton, capable of such superb play, leave their culture in the dressing room and abandon themselves to the baser form of football.' Barham was correct, for forty minutes in London the visitors dominated due to Vernon and Young's interplay and the industry of Morrissey and Stevens. Once they got involved in a kicking match, their inherent superiority was negated. It was a similar theme against Dunfermline earlier in the season in the Fairs Cup. However, Catterick perhaps did not learn the lessons, employing similar tactics in big matches later in the decade, to occasional costly effect.

1962/63 title victory – 'a club gets the crowd it deserves'

Barbed comments about buying success were aimed at Everton even before they had become champions. Over more than two decades Danny Blanchflower's column in the *Sunday Express* was essential reading, but several times the erudite Ulsterman fired a full broadside at the club. In February 1963, Blanchflower accused John Moores of seemingly being desperate to prove he could buy a successful football team, following the signing of Alex Scott from Rangers (ignoring the fact that Spurs also wished to sign the winger). Two months later he wrote, 'Everton must win the league this year. They have created a mood of desperation for themselves.' However, Everton believed his comments publicly damaged the club's reputation and complained to the Football League, whose Management Committee warned Spurs about allowing one of their players to write such provocative pieces in the press.

Taking the lead from Danny Blanchflower's comments, the press reacted in a largely negative manner to Catterick's first title victory. Columnist J.L. Manning wrote in the *Daily Mail*, 'Everton have made sure of winning at least one distinction this season. They will become as unpopular beyond Merseyside as Arsenal were outside London.' Elsewhere Brian James in the same newspaper was hugely critical of the new champions:

This has been a great season for a great club ... but this is the club with a lunatic fringe of fans who have been involved in stoning, bottle throwing, train-wrecking riots. West Ham and Burnley have tasted their savagery this season. Everton have the title now they must grow into champions. But I believe a club gets the crowd it deserves and the clean-up must start on the pitch – and Moores must make sure he does it.[27]

The problem with Everton's title triumph was that outsiders viewed it as being too clinical and one lacking any sort of emotional resonance. Clubs like cash-rich Manchester United and Wolves had dominated the top-flight during the 1950s, but they had been sprinkled with young homegrown players – or in United's case almost the entire team later in the decade – and both had captured the public's imagination with high-profile matches against European opposition. Spurs' double triumph in 1961 had a wider appeal because of their style of play, with a record 2.5 million spectators watching Bill Nicholson's team home and away. Everton held no such attraction so they were ostracised to some extent within the football

27 The joke at the time was that Everton's championship awards were nine medals and two Lonsdale Belts.

world. Brian Glanville covered this point in the *Sunday Times*: 'Everton are not unique and did not pay £99,000 for Greaves [which Spurs did]. Yet, there are ways, and ways of buying, and Everton's, inspired and made possible by Mr John Moores, has been alarming in its cold systematic manner. Players seem to have been bought, less to remove a weakness than as an earnest of ruthless ambition.' Glanville pointed out that Brian Labone was the only player in the starting line-up at the end of the season who had come through the ranks, with the added symbolism that the homegrown Brian Harris had lost his place to the expensive Tony Kay.

There was also a view that the money aspect diluted Catterick's personal achievement of taking his side to the title. When Fred Pickering came to Goodison in March 1964, J.L. Manning – again – attacked clubs for using the transfer system during the season, suggesting the rulebook should forbid them from buying players once the campaign started. 'I tell you why,' Manning concluded, 'under the present system we discover how much money Mr Moores and his directors have to spend. Under the other system we would discover how good a manager is Mr Harry Catterick.' But in Catterick's case, if anything, the money only added another layer of pressure, and it was not as if rival clubs were paupers.[28]

The columnist's opinion ignored the fact that Catterick had displayed his capability before moving to Goodison, as the manager pointed out in a reply contained in Manning's next column in the *Daily Mail*. Catterick started by saying, 'Several of my colleagues regard the concluding paragraph as a barb at myself and my ability as a football manager.' Initially pointing to his work at Crewe and Rochdale – 'I arrived there and found that there was not a single player signed to the club' – Catterick reminded Manning that he had taken relegated Sheffield Wednesday to second in the top-flight having bought just two players, both for less than £15,000. Catterick concluded his reply by saying, 'It was before the Everton cash was behind me and I could challenge other moneyed clubs in the transfer markets that I honestly think I made my mark as a manager.' Everything Catterick said was true of course.

The press may have had a point when they said Everton placed winning above anything else, but that could be said of most teams. What made Everton different, compared to others at the time, was that the fierce ambition came right from the

[28] Apart from Spurs, whose previous outlay matched Everton's, Manchester United spent £170,000 on two players alone in 1962, Denis Law for £115,000 and Paddy Crerand from Celtic for £55,000.

top, not from the manager. This was clear in the years that followed. As Tony Kay said after signing in December 1962, 'I play to win and that is exactly their [Everton's] approach. I think in the same way as our coach Tommy Eggleston, who thinks the same way as the chairman, who thinks the same way as me. How can you go wrong with an outfit like that?'

The negative impact of the national press in the first half of the decade towards Everton undoubtedly caused reputational damage and the mud that was thrown took time clearing – indeed, it remained for a long period. Everton supporters since have consistently felt that the club – and their manager – are airbrushed out of the history of that time. One of the main contributory factors is the widely-held belief that the club was buying success.

'England's most unpopular team'– October 1963

Seven months after their FA Cup defeat on the same ground, Everton travelled to Upton Park as league champions, but in an absorbing afternoon of fast-paced football in the capital, the visitors succumbed to a 4-2 defeat. Absorbing and fast-paced that is to everyone but the watching John Arlott, who was then writing for the *Guardian*. In a blazing critique of Catterick's team under the headline, 'WEST HAM EXPOSE ENGLAND'S MOST UNPOPULAR TEAM', the great cricket writer and commentator said:

Everton set out, primarily, to prevent their opponents scoring. This is a blight on Everton's talent. Their predecessors at the top of English football, Manchester United and Tottenham Hotspur, made friends because they expressed joy in football. Everton are the most unpopular team in England because they play without enjoyment ... once their opponents are in possession they mark and tackle harder than any other team we have seen. Their stop-at-all-cost policy leads them into such shabbiness – and worse – as to alienate them from the sympathy of all but half the population of Liverpool.

Although this was a harsh criticism, there was an element of truth. Virtually all of Catterick's key signings since joining the club – West, Kay, Stevens and Morrissey – aimed to increase the resilience of the side, while Bill Nicholson had spent big money at Spurs on attacking players. Lost on Arlott was that it was Catterick's reaction to the personal pressures arising from managing the richest club in the land, and to the trends within the game. These included a more sophisticated tactical approach, arising primarily from exposure to continental football and the fashion of focusing primarily on stopping the opposition scoring. Catterick would have liked to fill his team with playmakers as mercurial as Inter Milan's Luis Suárez, but such talents were rare, even on the continent.

The net effect was that, as the middle of the decade approached, it was becoming impossible for any team to play with the same joy and freedom of expression as the 'Busby Babes' and the Spurs double-winners. Sides were better organised and defenders were now fitter, stronger and faster, making goal scoring more difficult. A simple glance at the statistics provides all the required evidence: at the start of the 1960s a top-flight team scored an average of eighty league goals a season, but at the end of the decade this had fallen to 55 – a drop of 30 percent in just ten years.

'I could have been blinded' – October 1963

Seven days after the visit to Upton Park came a further incident at Goodison that caused a controversy still remembered today. Everton deservedly defeated Spurs 1-0 thanks to a brilliant strike from Derek Temple but all the talk after the game concerned a dart allegedly thrown at the visiting goalkeeper, Bill Brown. 'I could have been blinded,' said the Scot, 'It just hit the back of my head and I turned round expecting one of the other missiles that the crowd had been throwing at me.' One of his teammates said, 'The Everton crowd are like animals.' Earlier in the month the wrecking of a train by Everton supporters bound for Birmingham had made the front page of the *Daily Express*.

Whether a fan threw a dart at Brown has been subject to speculation over the years, and Catterick poured scorn on the accusation in the week after the game. 'Had Tottenham any complaint, they could have made it to us after the match. But Mr Nicholson [their manager] did not see me, any of our officials, the police, or the referee to make a complaint.' One supporter wrote an open letter to Brown, who had played brilliantly, 'While I do not condone the action of the idiot who threw this missile, you were nowhere near the goal when the dart was thrown. We saw you, after acknowledging the ovation you richly deserved, put your gloves and cap down. Then you noticed the dart at the back of the goal ... I hope you withdraw the accusation.' But as Ken Jones noted in the *Daily Mirror*, 'The facts remain that the dart was in the back of the goal and that marbles landed on the pitch – and no one is denying it.'

'We want the referee', Blackburn Rovers – November 1963

Although there were problems at Goodison, Everton were not the only club with crowd issues – by late 1963 the FA ordered more than fifty of the 92 league clubs to post warning notices following 'hooliganism'. At Anfield there were also concerns. Seven days after Everton faced Spurs, the Spion Kop threw apples, oranges and (bizarrely) a chewed pork chop at Leicester goalkeeper Gordon Banks. However, Everton club officials did little to appease the press. Interviewed about the bad behaviour of their supporters at the time, E. Holland Hughes, the Everton director, attempted to downplay the issue. 'When you get a crowd of 50,000 you are bound to get a little conduct that is not quite parliamentary. It doesn't only happen at Everton of course. At a London match I've seen them throwing toilet rolls.' The club was particularly concerned over the behaviour of younger supporters and at reserve games they allowed them entrance only when accompanied by an adult. Within that rather frenzied atmosphere, on the morning of the home game against Blackburn Rovers on the second Saturday of November 1963, the *Daily Mirror* ran their lead story:

Yeah, yeah, yeah, the new Liverpool Sound may be a baby-faced Beatle telling you that she loves you. But, according to Mr Danny Blanchflower, captain of Spurs, it is: 'A dart whizzing through the air and hitting a goalkeeper's head.' Once again the Merseyside 'terrors' – supporters of Everton and Liverpool – are branded as the roughest, rowdiest rabble who watch British soccer.

However, rather than point an accusing finger at Everton supporters the article claimed that many of the accusations were exaggerated – laughing off Spurs keeper Brown's suggestion that supporters had blown rice from pea-shooters at Goodison – and reporting that police had reported damage to just one train carrying Everton fans all season. Either way, the adverse press coverage was inflicting damage on the club – important even in the pre-commercialised days.

Suffice to say the 50,000 crowd at Goodison was under scrutiny following the Brown incident. The last thing Everton needed was a repeat performance against the Lancashire side, but they got much worse, both on and off the pitch. During the game, the visitors took advantage of Jimmy Gabriel's early injury to run riot against an exposed Labone. The Goodison-bound Fred Pickering scored twice within the opening 23 minutes and then laid on a third for Mike Harrison on the half-hour mark. Although Young pulled one back straightaway, Pickering completed his hat-trick in the second half. By this time, the result of the game had become increasingly irrelevant as referee Ken Stokes incensed the home supporters with a series of contentious decisions against Everton, while failing to punish the visitors for their equally robust approach. In an era when bookings were rare, initially the match official took Gabriel's name for dangerous play and then Vernon's for complaining about the decision. Stokes also booked Tony Kay but there was no option for the referee other than to send-off the fiery midfielder after he appeared to elbow Rovers' Bryan Douglas.

With Gabriel now a passenger and Kay off the pitch, Rovers strolled to a 4-2 victory while the feverish home crowd peppered the players and match officials with a variety of objects, including fruit and coins. At the end of the game, the players of both sides had to cover their heads to protect themselves from the barrage. Referee Stokes, perhaps making a point, stayed on the pitch picking up the last salvos of the assault. After the game a crowd estimated at 2-3,000 gathered outside the main entrance on Goodison Road. The group chanted, 'We want the referee' before being dispersed by mounted police into the surrounding streets. Not surprising the press had a field day and, similar to the Spurs game, the referee reported the incidents in his match report.

The FA investigation into the incidents at Goodison held Everton firmly responsible. Although it was unable to confirm the accusations made by Spurs the governing body accepted the referee's report that during the Blackburn game, 'Missiles were thrown on to the pitch by spectators and that a linesman was spat upon by a spectator whilst he was leaving the field.' The FA fined the club the princely sum of £100, with the threat of ground closure if there was further trouble. Finally, the commission suspended Tony Kay for three weeks.

John Moores had wisely attempted to take the sting out of the report by announcing in advance of publication that, in an unprecedented move in English football, the club would be cordoning off a section of the terracing behind each goal. 'We try to discipline people, so we must accept discipline ourselves. That is why we accept the FA decision with a brave face,' the chairman said afterwards. Strangely, what was intended as a temporary measure lasted more than a decade, the arcs behind the goals becoming a peculiar feature of the ground.

Although the followers of the club were certainly culpable, some keen observers in the game felt that the football authorities were making an example of Everton, as the richest club in the land, and that punishing them did not tackle the wider issue. The *Guardian's* always perceptive Eric Todd said, 'The FA and the Football League are very much mistaken if they think that lunatic fringes are a prerequisite of Merseyside. Has anyone proved that these missile throwers come from Everton? A great pity it is that the spotlight had fallen on Everton when it so easily might have been shared.' Todd's point was valid – on the same day as the Blackburn game, Liverpool supporters had wrecked trains returning from Bolton. One of the reasons why hooliganism remained a blight on the game was the fact the ruling bodies acted in a piecemeal manner, without addressing the wider causes.

Later, Catterick reflected on the reasons for the outbreak of hostility in football. 'The game is being spoiled by ill-temper. Whether it is due to the amount of money successful teams and players are getting, whether the generation now playing has different standards from ours I don't know. Perhaps it is a bit of both … It is possible that some clubs have had too much success; that they haven't learned how to lose.' As much as the Everton manager was correct – and he was – and that he was clearly targeting his own players' lack of discipline, the irony of course was that he was reacting negatively to a set of circumstances to which he and the club, through the injection of the Littlewoods' wealth, had partially contributed.

1964 Report on Supporters' Behaviour

In early 1964, the *Sunday Times* compared the match-day experience at Goodison and Anfield. The article would not have made comfortable reading in the Everton boardroom. 'Why – they might investigate – is the Liverpool crowd so much more humorous and benign than the Everton crowd just across the city,' the paper commented, 'Visiting players say the Everton crowd projects viciousness, which, in turn, evokes ruthless, violent tackling. The Kop, by contrast, has a fine, human generosity.' Whatever the rights and wrongs of the article, it was true that the fall-out from the title victory, plus the unsavoury events at Goodison in the final months of 1963, had turned the press against the club.

John Moores was sufficiently concerned to commission a study from two sociologists and the grandiosely titled *Report on Inquiry into Supporters' Behaviour* landed on his desk in May 1964. The study in many ways is an extraordinary document, shedding light on the attitudes of all those in the club to outsiders (and vice versa) following interviews with stewards, supporters, club officials (including Catterick and secretary Bill Dickinson) and several members of the press. The report begins with a terse introductory paragraph:

The Chairman of the Everton Football Club has expressed his concern at the unfavourable reputation achieved by certain of the Club's supporters. This generally unfavourable view finds its expression in the behaviour of supporters, particularly at away matches. The fact that the Club has been fined by the F.A., has been forced to erect barriers behind the goals, and its supporters directly involved in the decision by British Railways to terminate special football excursions, add weight to the general impression.

Quoting the *Sunday Times* article on the contrast between the Merseyside grounds, the report said the 'difference in attitude by the Press to the supporters of the respective Clubs had become increasingly marked in the second half of the year'. When questioned why Everton received such bad publicity, journalists pointed the finger of blame at one party. According to the authors, 'The attitude of the club's officials in their press dealings leaves something to be desired. Sportswriters do not find Everton Club Officials very co-operative. This is almost entirely a matter of attitude as the Press facilities at Goodison Park are, according to the same Pressmen, above average for Clubs in the country.' The report also claimed that 'There is a strong opinion amongst press representatives that information is difficult to obtain from Everton Football Club Officials.' They pointed to journalists' frustrations at the club's petty behaviour, citing their bizarre refusal to allow press photographs of Fred Pickering in training just after his record transfer.

The journalists' biggest gripe was about the bizarre decision to withdraw the provision of permanent tickets to the press box. This had been a relatively recent development, as previously the club, like most others, had issued permanent press tickets to national newspapers. Journalists now had to apply for games on an individual basis and the report explained this 'often leads to national sportswriters being obliged to queue up with supporters to get their tickets'. The club's reasoning for the change – 'guests' were abusing the system, taking up unused tickets – really did not justify such a draconian reaction. Indeed as the report said, 'If the Club controls the numbers of tickets issued, it is difficult to see what abuses can ensue. The Press can merely substitute one person for another.' Although public relations within football were still very much in its infancy, it was another example of pedantry that did Everton no favours and adverse media coverage was inevitable.

For his part, the Everton manager took an unsurprisingly negative attitude towards the press. 'Mr. Catterick believes that the Press is biased against Everton Football Club and believes this is generally true of any Northern Club outside Manchester,' the report commented. 'His long experience of the game leads him to believe that adverse Press publicity is a hazard faced by a successful club.' However, when told by the report's authors that the press thought Manchester United were more obliging than Everton, the manager provided a typically dogmatic response: 'Mr. Catterick, however, is of the opinion that the "bias" which he believes operates in United's favour, springs only from the fact that the Northern editions of most National papers are printed in Manchester.'

The research also involved consultation with Everton supporters over a variety of issues. Almost all surveyed felt stigmatised, 95 percent admitting that 'generally speaking we are condemned before we set foot on away grounds'. However the authors were fulsome in the praise of the Everton Supporters Club. 'We were impressed by the degree of enthusiasm and interest,' they wrote, 'particularly in their awareness and real concern at the damage being done to the good name of the Club.' The problem was that both Catterick and secretary Bill Dickinson treated the group with a certain amount of suspicion, and consequently the Supporters Club felt ostracised by the Everton hierarchy.

Their findings also included some useful commentary on the links between player and crowd behaviour. 'In the tension of modern football, incidents amongst players are inevitable, but while fans attempt to look like, dress like, walk like their popular idols, it is equally inevitable that any element of aggression will to some, not only seem justified, but even laudable.'

The report concluded by making several recommendations: the appointment of a Press (or PR) Officer; closer working with the Supporters Club; strict treatment of trouble-makers; opening training to the viewing public as well as discussions with the press over how to promote a better image. The club did make some efforts to address the issues – although it took five years to appoint David Exall in a specific PR role. However, the report was only able to tackle the peripheral issues. As the introduction said, 'In endeavouring to investigate this problem, we have recognised that it is a complex and many-sided one, and no single solution can be offered.' Moores was certainly cognisant of the report's findings, which almost certainly influenced his rallying call at the start of the 1964/65 season:

Since we were champions there has been a severe spotlight on Everton. The press are there in great force. They can be extremely critical. If you play attractive and clean football you will get good reports. If you don't you won't. The press last year at times were a little naughty and criticised us, I thought, unfairly. Some games were rough, but if there was any fault it was usually on the other side. Everton are a famous team and we don't want a bad press.

The reputation of Everton supporters was restored to a degree over the following years. 'The mental picture of the average Merseyside supporter has become more than slightly distorted, he has been depicted as a boozing, brawling, semi-literate, bottle-throwing thug,' wrote Frank McGhee before Everton played FC Nürnberg in September 1965. The *Daily Mirror* journalist then added the hand of friendship. 'I can recognise him more readily as someone witty, wise, warm hearted. And, although often biased, he is also appreciative of the other side.'

Opponents also reflected this newly found softer approach to Everton fans from 1965/66 onwards. After their victory at Goodison earlier in that campaign, the West Brom chairman, Jim Gaunt, wrote a letter to the club congratulating Everton on the 'sporting attitude and appreciation' of their supporters. Spurs had lost at Goodison just before the Nürnberg encounter and Bill Nicholson said afterwards, 'This was the best-behaved Everton crowd I have ever known. They were very fair to us.' Why after years of criticism, was there this sudden attempt at rapprochement? To be fair, the positive culture surrounding the city at the time was almost certainly a factor. In addition, the press and other clubs no longer viewed Everton as the dominant force in English football, greedily gobbling up the best players at exorbitant prices in the pursuit of success. Just as importantly, the arrival of a new club in the top-flight from the other side of the Pennines eighteen months before had introduced a new, frighteningly aggressive presence.

The Yorkshire trilogy

Don Revie became Leeds manager just after Catterick came to Goodison, revitalising the Yorkshire side through some astute signings, like Bobby Collins, and the nurturing of a bunch of talented youngsters including Billy Bremner, Terry Cooper, Paul Reaney and Norman Hunter. Revie also swiftly jettisoned their traditional blue and gold kit for the all-white worn by Real Madrid, an outfit at odds with their growing reputation for intimidatory, win-at-all-costs football.

A trio of games with Leeds United – two FA Cup ties at Elland Road separated by a legendary league game at Goodison in November 1964 – symbolised the uncompromising nature of domestic football during the middle of the decade. The first encounter took place when Revie's side were heading towards the second division title, the two teams drawn together in the fourth round of the FA Cup in 1964, with the first game at Elland Road.

FA Cup fourth round, January 1964

There was a curious bit of mind games by Catterick before the game. The Everton manager had let slip that he expected reserve forward Jimmy Hill to play at Leeds, as Young was dropped and Derek Temple injured, and would be sending him to the reserves at Chesterfield in preparation. Don Revie and the press travelled to the Derbyshire town to look at Hill, only to find out that Catterick had kept the player in Liverpool with no intention of playing him in either game.[29]

The crowd of more than 48,000 in west Yorkshire witnessed more than a typical cup encounter; it was a hard-edged brutal affair. With Young and Vernon now restored to the team after being dropped, the visitors went undeservedly behind just before half-time when a clearance from Brian Harris struck Ian Lawson and flew into the net. With another premature departure from the cup on the horizon, the referee handed Everton a deserved lifeline in the final ten minutes. The outstanding Billy Bremner had been walking a disciplinary tightrope all afternoon and it was no surprise when the midfielder clearly felled Alex Scott in the penalty area. One of the most famous spot-kicks in Everton's history followed. In the absence of penalty-king Vernon, Scott had successfully converted twice from the spot in the previous two matches but with the Welshman on the pitch, there was uncertainty on who should take responsibility. It was the winger who stepped up, the Welshman later explaining why, 'Alex was in the groove, he had scored in the last four games, two of them penalties, I thought he was the man.'

29 This was not the last time Catterick would try to fool Revie in this way. Before the 1968 FA Cup semi-final against Leeds, Everton faced Sheffield Wednesday at Hillsborough and Catterick, knowing Revie would be present, played a weakened team again.

Leeds' keeper Gary Sprake had spent a significant part of the previous week facing penalties, and it appeared the practise had paid off as the Welshman saved the winger's kick, only to see the linesman's flag raised to signal that the keeper had clearly moved beforehand. The referee ordered the kick to be retaken, leading to discussions amongst the players about who should take responsibility. Fortunately, common sense prevailed, Vernon stepped up and the 12,000 Everton supporters who had crossed the Pennines watched the forward fire the ball past Sprake's right to keep the Merseyside giants in the competition.

Alex Scott later described the 1-1 draw as 'the dirtiest game I have ever played in. I thought at times it went beyond reasonable limits.' The referee, Mr Langdale, needed a police escort from the ground, having stayed in his dressing room for an hour after the game for his own safety. In the light of such lawlessness on the pitch, it was not surprising that there was vandalism on a number of trains coming back from Leeds, the latest in a line of incidents involving both Merseyside clubs. British Railways responded by cancelling future excursions. 'We can no longer tolerate the disgraceful behaviour of Merseyside maniacs calling themselves football supporters,' they said in a strongly worded statement.

Injury kept Young out of the replay and in his place Catterick selected Jimmy Gabriel at centre-forward, after the young Scot had impressed with his heading ability and tireless work in a trial match at Bellefield. Gabriel later said, 'I had played up front in training sessions, I had put myself about and scored a few goals but never really saw myself playing up there for the first team. After telling me his plan the manager then swore me to secrecy because he didn't want Leeds to get wind of it.' The move allowed the manager the opportunity to see how the team functioned with a more physical presence up front, and Gabriel rewarded Catterick for his gamble on the half-hour mark. Vernon fastened onto a misdirected pass from Norman Hunter and fed the rookie striker, and Gabriel later explained what happened next. 'Paul Madeley seemed to misjudge it and I suddenly found myself racing clear with the ball on my left foot and only Sprake to beat. With my right foot I might have tried to chip the ball or swerve it, but my left foot was for hitting it only. So I hit it and the ball flew into the top corner.' The home side wrapped up the tie, in front of a crowd of more than 66,000, fifteen minutes from the end when Brown's cross somehow found a way through to Vernon who finished easily.

'Spine chilling', First Division, November 1964

On the first day of pre-season in July 1964, John Moores told the press, 'While we want good, strong play we don't want any dirty, spiteful play – no kicking, tripping, pulling shirts and so on.' The chairman then added, 'There is no reason why Everton should not set the highest standards. Robust and vigorous play is not condemned. Petty spite and unnecessary fouling is.' The early part of the campaign had spiteful play and unnecessary fouling in abundance. During the 1-1 draw at Burnley in early September, 78 policemen were required to control the crowd, notably at the Everton end where there were several arrests and numerous objects thrown onto the pitch. Trainers treated nine different players for injury and there was a full-blown fight between Vernon and Burnley's Gordon Harris. The *Guardian* labelled the encounter 'an undignified shambles'.

Much worse was to follow at Old Trafford eleven days later. At the time, it was usual for a pair of teams to face each other twice in close proximity at the start of the campaign or over the holiday period. If the first game was a tough affair, the second usually degenerated as players came prepared to pursue their own vendettas. After a thrilling, if bad-tempered 3-3 draw at Goodison eight days before, the players put their bodies on the line in a brutal contest in Manchester. Trailing 2-1 to United, the game veered out of control spectacularly in the second period. Nobby Stiles struck Temple in the face, so the Everton man sent the midfielder sprawling across the pitch. The home side's Paddy Crerand kicked Fred Pickering across the body with the Everton centre-forward retaliating by brutally charging the United goalkeeper. Sandy Brown flattened Denis Law and the Scottish striker fought back by pushing his compatriot into the crowd. When Jimmy Gabriel cynically took out George Best ten minutes from time to become the fourth player booked, referee Mr J.E. Carr had seen enough. The match official called all twenty outfielders together in the centre of the pitch to 'lay down the law and demand peace' according to Michael Charters in the *Liverpool Echo*.

It was brutal stuff and these merciless contests set the scene for the visit of Leeds United to Goodison on the first Saturday in November 1964. The Yorkshire side had won promotion as second division champions in 1963/64 and during their first season in the top-flight a potent mix of sheer ability and what many regarded as unrestrained malevolence had taken the first division by storm. With twenty points from fifteen games, they were in fourth in the table, while the home side stood eighth. The week before a 17-year-old Johan Cruyff made his Ajax debut, the two teams took part in one of the most infamous league games of all time – the complete antithesis of everything the Dutchman later stood for.

Many accounts since have documented the scenes at Goodison but briefly the highlights (or lowlights) are that the teams drew out their battle lines in the first few seconds, after Billy Bremner brutally fouled Fred Pickering. On four minutes, John Giles shot weakly at Rankin and after the goalkeeper cleared the ball, the Irish international and Sandy Brown clashed outside the box. The Everton man, complaining that Giles had raked his studs down his chest, threw a left-hander at the Leeds man's stomach and was sent-off. 'I wasn't always innocent, but on this occasion I was,' Giles later claimed. To be fair, considering the number of players with spiky natures on both sides, Brown was one of the least likely combatants to depart early.

In an encounter that resembled a cross between professional boxing and rugby union, eleven minutes before half-time Leeds' Willie Bell – who had earlier opened the scoring – brutally fouled Derek Temple by the Paddock, with a two-footed challenge from behind to the kidneys, still cited by those present as the worst foul seen on the ground. The visiting player appeared to feign injury to avoid dismissal, igniting the flames in an already frenzied crowd. When Les Cocker, the Leeds trainer, called for assistance, the ambulance man told him he could 'fetch his own f------ stretcher'. Under a barrage of missiles, referee Ken Stokes took the players off the pitch to protect them from the spectators. For the first time in English league history, a referee had stopped a game for reasons other than the pitch conditions or the weather. The famous picture of captains Brian Labone and Bobby Collins walking off together, with the clock showing 3.40 p.m., remains one of the most celebrated taken on the ground.

Everton's secretary Bill Dickinson announced over the tannoy that 'the game will be resumed in five minutes. I have to warn spectators that if any more missiles are thrown on, the game will be abandoned.' Referee Stokes reportedly wanted to call off proceedings, but changed his mind once in the dressing room, where Catterick showed him Brown's stomach injuries. When combat resumed the mood, on and off the pitch, abated only marginally and in a tense second period, the Yorkshire side held on for a literally hard-fought 1-0 victory. Eight Everton players finished the games with injuries. 'I like my players to play hard but I always tell them the ball must be the first consideration,' said a wounded Catterick. After the game, the referee remained locked in his room for some time while spectators pelted the travelling Leeds coach with missiles.

The newspapers held nothing back in criticism. Jack Archer of the *People* famously portrayed the game as 'spine chilling' while Brian Crowther in the *Guardian* described the players as 'collectively irresponsible' before slamming the Everton supporters. 'The behaviour of the crowd can best be summarised as disgusting,' he wrote. Whatever the legitimacy of his views, the fact is that the situation was symptomatic of wider issues within the game. On the same afternoon at Deepdale, Preston supporters pelted the visiting Manchester City fans with missiles when their team trailed 4-1 and the PA system announced that the referee would abandon the contest if the barrage did not cease.

The subsequent statements by the authorities noticeably focused more on the wider issues rather than the battle of Goodison, which they viewed as a tipping point and not as a one-off. Within 24 hours of the contest, FA secretary Dennis Follows said, 'It is the players and the clubs who must share the responsibility for what is going on. It is all part of the modern trend. Players are no dirtier than they were. It's just that they are no longer able to accept discipline.' Compared to twelve months earlier, when Everton were held up as an example for all that was wrong with the modern game, there was a belated acknowledgement that the problems were more widespread, which is really the point Moores should have been making earlier. For Catterick, he was probably relieved in some respects, as the mayhem had diverted attention away from just two wins in the first eight home games of the season.

But why did this game go so spectacularly out of hand? As a starting point, memories were still fresh of the bloodthirsty FA Cup tie at the start of the year. The Leeds players were ready for the encounter and if not fearful of playing at Goodison, they were certainly conscious that the welcoming committee would not be cordial. John Giles later said, 'Everton were clearly waiting for us on that day in November, to teach us a lesson. They were an experienced side with a number of good, hard players, who were aware of our reputation.' To pour further oil on the troubled waters, abrasive skipper Bobby Collins was returning to Goodison as well, still with a point to prove to Harry Catterick. The midfielder later recalled the events of that grey November day. 'It was diabolical ... it was like a fuse on a bomb being lit ... it really got nasty and brutal. There were a lot of hard challenges that day. But you can't turn the other cheek or they'll kick you.'

On the other side of the barricades, first division sides were also growing aware of Leeds' burgeoning standing for stretching the boundaries of fair play. That the Everton players and crowd were pumped up was no surprise – the season had shown that Leeds' reputation often brought the worst out of the opposition. Brown was the third player dismissed against Revie's side in the league in less than two months, with Spurs having four players booked in a separate encounter. The Yorkshire side were clearly proficient in provoking without being provoked – although equally culpable at Goodison, they had conceded twelve fouls, seven less than Everton. Rob Bagchi and Paul Rogerson said in *The Unforgiven*, 'They knew just how far to wind up the opposition without winding up the referee. It didn't matter if the match statistics exonerated them; they were such perfect villains.'

The referee must also take some responsibility. Although Mr Stokes sent off Brown, the referee had little choice and the problems arose from his failure to take strong enough action on the violent play elsewhere. The players took advantage of his leniency. Before their premature departure, Stokes did not book anyone or call the players together, actions that may have stopped the game from escalating spectacularly. On the same weekend twelve months before, the official had taken charge of the infamous encounter against Blackburn Rovers at Goodison, when there were similar, if slightly less hostile scenes – but only just. This is a key point in the events of the day. Perhaps Stokes just ran out of patience with the Goodison crowd and players, the decision to take everybody off was as much to do with the abuse of a year before as the 38 minutes played against Leeds. Whatever his motives, *The Times* summed up the reasons for the disgrace perfectly, 'Goodison Park has already gained an unsavoury tribal reputation for vandalism. Leeds United, too, more recently have earned black marks for ill temper on the field. The marriage of these two dangerous elements sparked off the explosion.'

Far from wielding a big stick as they had threatened, the FA eventually fined Everton a meagre £250, while suspending Brown for a fortnight. In many ways it was a watershed moment for the club – never again would they be put in the same disciplinary spotlight.

FA Cup fourth round, January 1965

Two months later, the Toffees travelled to Elland Road for both a rematch of their fractious FA Cup encounter and an encore to their wrestling bout in the league game at Goodison. If a crowd of more than 50,000 in west Yorkshire expected something different on the day of the burial of Sir Winston Churchill, they were disappointed, both teams effectively cancelling each other out in a game described as 'A harsh, almost brutal match which jangled on the nerves,' in *The Times*. Catterick had done his homework well, assigning Dennis Stevens to keep control of Bobby Collins and leaving Colin Harvey to keep watch on Billy Bremner.

With Leeds playing, in the words of Michael Charters of the *Liverpool Echo*, 'a fast version of biff-bang-bash football', both Everton players largely succeeded in their tasks, although Stevens let Collins free once on the hour and Jim Storrie converted the skipper's cross. Within eight minutes, Everton were level and like the previous year via the spot. This time the award followed Jackie Charlton punching a Gabriel goal-bound header out from underneath the crossbar. Fred Pickering had replaced Vernon as penalty taker and the record-signing beat Sprake comfortably.

Three days later, a crowd of almost 66,000 jamming the terraces at Goodison saw an equally balanced encounter in a replay that bordered on the epic. The editorial in the match programme acknowledged their previous Goodison encounter in sombre tones:

We hope that our supporters will be happy to let the past bury its dead. Let us not revive the unhappier moments of the League game here, and which to be honest were grossly – exaggerated. Let us live for the future of Everton and forget what happened months ago.

Considering the hangover from their previous visit, Leeds did not exactly endear themselves to the home crowd by refusing to release their line-up until just before the start. 'It has not been possible to find out if there are any changes to the Leeds team,' said secretary Bill Dickinson over the tannoy five minutes before the kick-off.

A high paced, fiercely charged opening half saw plenty of jousting, but no goals, although there were several chances at both ends. It took until twenty minutes from time for the first goal and it was the impressive visitors who delighted their huge support when Jackie Charlton rose superbly to head home John Giles' flighted corner kick. Eleven minutes later Revie's side extended their lead when Bremner's through ball deflected fortuitously into the path of Don Weston, whose shot beat West. The home team replied inside sixty seconds when Pickering fired home from a tight angle. The final eight minutes were frenetic as the visitors, with Bremner and Norman Hunter outstanding, withstood a tremendous barrage, assisted by the bizarre decision of referee Kevin Howley to award an indirect free-kick, and not a penalty, in the Leeds area after Willie Bell floored Alex Scott. Although Everton could count themselves unfortunate, Leeds had exercised more control with Bobby Collins in particular outstanding. 'A wasp constantly stinging the opposition,' said Geoffrey Green in *The Times*.

The other strange by-product was that after this series of brutal contests with Revie's men, games between Everton and Leeds were largely devoid of the intensity of those between other big clubs during the decade. It was if both sides were keen on not re-opening old wounds.

9.
A Rivalry Renewed

ALMOST TO THE EXACT TIME THAT CHELSEA AND EVERTON KICKED-off their first division game at Stamford Bridge on Saturday, 28 October 1961, a young man walked into a record shop in Whitechapel, Liverpool. 'There's a request I want. It's My Bonnie and it was made in Germany. Have you got it?' he asked the man behind the counter, who had never heard of the disc and enquired about who recorded it. 'It's by a group called the Beatles,' came the reply. Although some have doubted the veracity of the story, the significance lies in the fact that the shop worker was a 27-year-old Brian Epstein. By the end of the year, Epstein was the Beatles' manager and the rest is history.[30]

By then Liverpool's music scene had been thriving for two or three years, neatly aligned with Everton's climb out of the dour 1950s and Bill Shankly's arrival at Anfield. Taking their influence from skiffle, a musical genre that mixed traditional and do-it-yourself instruments, the youth of the city also embraced rock 'n' roll – a landmark event being when Gene Vincent and Eddie Cochran played six successive nights at the Liverpool Empire in March 1960. Significantly, the audience included Rory Storm (of the Hurricanes fame), John Lennon, George Harrison, Paul McCartney and Gerry Marsden. Once the Beatles broke through in 1962, the floodgates literally opened. At the height of the so-called *Merseybeat* era,

30 One Everton player not immediately impressed was Jimmy Gabriel. In Liverpool city centre with teammate Andy Rankin, the Scot said that 'I've just been looking at this shop and there's a little postcard in there with the name of a local group called The Beatles. What chance have they got with a name like that?'

of the forty number-one singles in the period 1963-1964 no less than 17 originated in the city. In his seminal documentary, *Beat City*, writer and presenter Daniel Farson summed up those heady days:

Into 1964 Liverpool remained the apple of England's eye, the pride of Great Britain and – increasingly – a source of wonder to the world. The media was infatuated. Everyone was talking about this damp, grubby town that nobody had thought twice about for fifty years... Liverpool, so often out of step with the national mood was now its very model: cheeky and young, un-posh, un-stuffy democratic to the boot heels.

The overpowering sense of excitement at being part of something unique also transmitted itself to visitors, as Alex Young recalled to biographer David France in his 2008 book, *The Golden Vision*: 'I arrived during the early days of Mersey Beat. In addition to the Fab Four there were hundreds of boys strumming guitars and banging drums in local clubs such as The Cavern and Blue Angel. I think the music scene mirrored that of the football (scene).' That was true in some respects yet in reality there was little cross-over between the two,[31] other than the singing of contemporary chart hits, more likely at Anfield than Goodison.

The view is reinforced by the fact that the city's most celebrated quartet had a famously ambivalent attitude to the sport, as Paul Du Noyer noted in his excellent study of the city's musical heritage, *Liverpool – Wondrous Place*, 'It is remarkable that the four most famous Liverpudlian males in the world were almost the only four indifferent to football.' Paul McCartney was the most public about his footballing allegiances, having come from an Everton supporting family and attending the 1968 FA Cup final. In terms of making a choice between the city's two clubs, McCartney told the *Observer* in 2008 that 'if it comes down to a derby match or a crunch or an FA Cup final between the two, I would have to support Everton'. However, the Beatle added a caveat, 'I got a bit of a friendship with Kenny [Dalglish] and I thought "You know what? I am going to support them both."' George Harrison summed up the group's oblique relationship with the game: 'There are three teams in Liverpool and I prefer the other one.'

31 The footballers' venue of choice was The Royal Tiger Club, and worth remembering that, unlike music, football was essentially a male preserve at the time. In truth football and popular music did not really coalesce until the Britpop era of the mid-1990s.

Across the Universe

In May 1965 the American beat poet Allen Ginsberg came to Liverpool and claimed that the city was 'at the centre of consciousness of the human universe'.[32] Whether the statement was accurate is open to debate, but the comment did reflect the significant effect the city was having on popular culture, not only in this country but also across the Atlantic. Even the political world was not free from local influence – newly installed Prime Minister Harold Wilson's home constituency was Huyton.

By the time of Ginsberg's arrival, this prosperity was not just limited to music and the arts. Benefiting from the post-war policy to encourage the location of burgeoning industries in relatively poorer parts of the country, the Mersey conurbation had been classified as a development area in 1949. With shipbuilding booming – Cammell Laird built the Navy's flagship Ark Royal in 1950 – the growing car manufacturing industry seemed a natural fit for the region. Consequently, following significant government influence, Triumph (Speke), Ford (Halewood) and Vauxhall (Ellesmere Port) all planted roots during 1959-1963, creating more than 25,000 jobs following a £65m investment. As well as the omnipresent Littlewoods and Vernons, other local companies like Meccano, Tate and Lyle, BICC cables and Crawford's Biscuits flourished as the wider economy boomed. By the turn of the 1960s, in having close to full-employment Liverpool was enjoying an extended period of affluence not seen since the nineteenth century.

Whilst the area was on the rise both economically and culturally, Liverpool's biggest obsession had fallen behind. If the 1950s sowed the seeds of future prosperity, paradoxically it was undoubtedly the most depressing decade in the city's rich footballing history – in only one season (1950/51) were both clubs in the top-flight. The pivotal campaign during this period came in 1953/54. After three years in the second tier of English football, Everton returned to the top-flight and in doing so swapped divisions with their relegated rivals. It would be eight years before the two teams locked horns in the league again; there was one first-team derby in that time, Liverpool winning a fourth-round FA Cup game at Goodison in 1955. However, the enormous crowds that gathered at both Goodison and Anfield for their regular Liverpool Senior Cup ties pointed to the intensity of the games in

32 Ginsberg had made similar claims about other cities, prompting the Liverpool poet Brian Patten to say that 'Allen believed the centre of human consciousness to be wherever he was at the time.'

the following decade. After several near misses, Liverpool finally returned to the top-flight as second division champions in 1962, re-igniting a rivalry that had existed for nearly seventy years. With the city ready to explode into the wider consciousness, having both teams in the top-flight for the first time in eleven years seemed perfectly in tune with the times.

At the heart of their future battles were two men with many differences debated over the years, linked by the common bond of an unlimited desire to bring success to their respective clubs. When those triumphs happened, then surely Ginsberg would have been convinced that, for supporters at least, it was far more important for the city to be the centre of English football.

Catterick and Shankly – the early years

Harry Catterick and Bill Shankly's rivalry is one of the great reference points of Merseyside football. However, even by the time Liverpool were promoted in 1962 they were familiar foes, having occupied opposing dugouts for more than a decade. Their first managerial encounter had taken place in March 1952, when Catterick was earning his managerial stripes at Crewe and Shankly was at Grimsby, and their two most recent competitive meetings had taken place in 1958/59, when Catterick's Sheffield Wednesday side had beaten Shankly's Huddersfield in both league games on the way to the second division title. After Wednesday had triumphed 4-1 at Hillsborough Shankly was in uncharacteristic complimentary mood. 'That's the first time this season we have been well and truly whacked, but at least we were beaten by a better team,' the Scot told the press. However, Catterick admitted with some satisfaction that after the game Shankly had stormed into his manager's room, complaining about the referee and claimed that 'the better team had lost'. Catterick's team also won 2-1 at Leeds Road late in the season, a crucial result that went some way to Wednesday becoming champions. Before the game, spectators could see both men wandering together pitch-side, when the conversation was all one way – Shankly spending their time together extoling the virtues of Huddersfield's promising forward Les Massie. At the time, both men had little idea of the titanic encounters that lay ahead.

There is no doubt that, by 1962, Catterick was the senior partner, having enjoyed top-flight experience with two established clubs for more than three years. In that time, Shankly, having taken charge of a club that was drifting aimlessly in the old second division in 1959, was very much trying to re-establish the Anfield side in the top-flight. The development of a team that was to become one of the dominant forces of the decade (and beyond) was very much at the embryonic stage. Although Shankly was quite rightly receiving plaudits at the time for engineering such a dramatic change in fortunes, Catterick had shown himself capable of achieving a similar feat – and with scarcer resources – at Sheffield Wednesday. What Catterick had displayed by 1962 was comfort in managing in a completely different state of affairs – one that demanded almost instant success in an environment of boardroom expectations and media scrutiny.

That scenario never applied to Shankly, who was able to build a club, with limited ambitions, in his own image from 1959 onwards. Indeed, whether the charismatic Scot could have performed the same trick if he had walked into Goodison two years later, faced with a demanding owner and a group of 'seen it all, done it all' players – albeit one that had been indulged by Carey – is a moot point. Shankly undoubtedly had the charisma and wherewithal to have pulled it off but it may have been a similar ending to Brian Clough and Leeds United in 1974. In a comparison of the strengths and weaknesses of both men, it is a point that is seldom raised but worth making.

Goodison Park, September 1962

On Friday, 21 September 1962, the *New Musical Express* published a story about two 13-year-old schoolgirls 'Sue' and 'Mary', who were releasing a single on the Decca label, adding as an aside that 'A Liverpool group, the Beatles, have recorded "Love Me Do" for Parlophone Records, set for October 5 release.' For the city's population, 24 hours later there was an infinitely more significant event – the first league derby in eleven years, in front of a crowd of 73,000 at Goodison. For one group it was financially rewarding. Spurs' failure to win at Wolves during the week meant the home side remained in second place and, under the terms of their contracts, the Everton players each received £152 as a crowd-related bonus (equivalent to a month's wages) rather than £26 if they had entered the match in third. The home players, like their opponents, earned every penny in a frenzied atmosphere reflecting the previous frustrations of an audience who had not seen a league fixture between the two clubs for more than a decade.

The drama was soon forthcoming. The theme music for 'Z Cars' was still ringing in the ears of the crowd when the Liverpool goalkeeper Jim Furnell dropped the ball as he ran out of the six-yard box and Vernon pounced to score with just fifty seconds on the clock. The referee, the hugely experienced Kevin Howley, silenced home supporters' celebrations when he blew up for a foul. Many were baffled, including the goal-scorer, who said 48 hours later, 'Whether Furnell was unlucky enough to get a bad bounce, whether the ball struck his foot as he bounced it, or whether he just had a fit of nerves I can't say, but I do know the ball bounced clear of him straight to me. I whipped round and put it into the net. I was staggered when the goal was disallowed because there was never anything approaching a foul.' Five minutes later Vernon and the home crowd's annoyance continued when Stevens beat Furnell but was ruled offside. After Kevin Lewis, replacing the injured Ian St John in the starting line-up, had forced a great save from West, the Toffees went ahead on 27 minutes, the goal a reward for their dominant start to the game. Stevens' harmless chip across the area appeared to strike Gerry Byrne's arm and Howley, to the surprise of many and perhaps wanting to even things up, pointed to the spot and Vernon crashed the ball home.

Eleven minutes later the visitors equalised when Lewis hooked in Ian Callaghan's cross when unmarked in the six-yard box. With wide-men Morrissey and Bingham well shackled by the Liverpool defence, the Toffees struggled to repeat their early pressure and somewhat fortuitously regained the lead after the hour mark. Furnell – who was shaky throughout – failed to gather a cross and the ball fell to Morrissey, whose shot Ronnie Moran blocked on the goal-line. Howley, on his linesman's advice, pointed to the centre-circle despite the protests of the Liverpool team. Examination of the match film five decades later proved inconclusive while years later Moran was still adamant that the ball did not cross the line. Leading 2-1, in terms of both goals and favourable refereeing calls, the home side had enough to see out time but the game ended as it started, with the ball in the net. This time it was Gordon West who was beaten and on this occasion Howley let the goal stand. As the game entered the final sixty seconds Labone allowed Lewis to outjump him and the ball fell to Roger Hunt, who finished clinically. The passionate atmosphere and intense drama set the template for the Merseyside derby for the next decade and beyond.

Goodison Park, March 1964

The Toffees were playing catch-up in the 1963/64 season, but a 3-0 win at Sheffield Wednesday on the first day of February left Catterick's side in eighth place in the table. With 33 points from 28 games, they were six points behind leaders Spurs and three behind second-placed Liverpool, who had two games-in-hand and were next up at Goodison Park.

Two days before 70 million television viewers across the Atlantic watched the Beatles on their historic appearance on the Ed Sullivan Show, an equally passionate audience witnessed a derby masterclass by Everton and Roy Vernon in particular, as Catterick's team played with an adventure rarely seen previously in the campaign. The maverick Welshman was at his razor-sharp best, pulling the Liverpool defence around Goodison Park, scoring twice and striking the upright during a comprehensive 3-1 victory. The skipper may also have saved Ian St John the ignominy of being the first player dismissed in a Goodison derby, asking the referee not to send the Scot off the pitch after he appeared to strike Gordon West near the end.

The Everton forward also showed signs of forming a lively partnership with Gabriel, who scored as a stand-in striker. The Scot later said the main reason for their dominant showing was timely advice from Blackburn's Fred Pickering about Liverpool skipper Ron Yeats before they played in the England-Scotland under-23 game three days before. Gabriel said after the game, 'Fred said Ronnie rarely leaves the middle and he is such a fine centre-half that it is a waste of time trying to play him straight on. I tried to wander away a bit and it paid off with Vernon and myself doing a shuffle and dart act.'

Anfield, September 1964

After a sluggish start to the 1964/65 season, Anfield was probably the last place where Catterick's side wished to play, after five games without a win. But the trip across Stanley Park in the middle of September provided him with one of the most satisfying afternoons of his managerial career. Deprived of five internationals – Parker, Wilson, Young, Vernon and Kay – his team ran out 4-0 victors. With the respective England and Scotland managers, Alf Ramsey and Ian McColl, watching in the stands, the visitors went ahead on 54 seconds when Ron Yeats deflected Morrissey's cross into the path of Derek Temple, who scored with aplomb past Tommy Lawrence. The die was cast, after Roger Hunt had struck the crossbar and seen a shot cleared off the line Pickering broke out from Stevens' measured pass, beat two defenders and saw his shot from twenty yards deflect past a startled Lawrence.

Six minutes later, the game was effectively over – Colin Harvey scoring on his derby debut, for his only goal in the fixture. 'The ball came to me on the edge of the box, I chested it and as it bounced I just lobbed it into the top corner,' the midfielder later said. With Andy Rankin – having usurped West as number one – outstanding, Everton moved swiftly from defence to attack throughout and completed the rout when the outstanding Morrissey cut inside from the left and fired home in the second half. It was also a satisfying day for the visiting fans, faced with taunts about 'Purple Hearts' from the Kop (following accusations over drug use by Everton players) their chants of 'Easy, easy, easy' at the end were the loudest of the day. 'Even Everton themselves, shorn of artists such as Vernon, Young and Parker, could scarcely have hoped to contain Liverpool, let alone administer such a hiding,' said *The Times*. After the game Catterick said tactically his side played it brilliantly. 'We set out to play it tight, very tight, defensively and strike when Liverpool's attacking broke down.'

Between Blue and Red

By 1964 Everton's poor reputation compared to their local rivals was not necessarily restricted to the press, it also extended elsewhere in the game. As one Ipswich supporter wrote in the *Liverpool Echo*, 'Fan support at Goodison Park is fanatic and desperate and seems to suffer nothing save success. Fan support at Anfield is just as fanatic, but the atmosphere is more down-to-earth.'

However, the reputation of the Kop placed a protective blanket over the excesses of the more sinister element of the Liverpool support, which could be as menacing as their rivals from across Stanley Park. As Brian Glanville wrote in a later piece in the *Sunday Times*, 'The mere knowledge that Everton and Liverpool are visiting a town must send shivers down the spine of local shopkeepers and furrow the brows of police superintendents ... Liverpool's own projects the personality of a city rife with mindless violence. There has been enough sentimentality about the Spion Kop. Everton and Liverpool supporters ... must now be regarded as a national menace and treated accordingly.' Yet the general perception was that the real problems lay at Goodison Park.

The reasons why there was a gulf in attitude towards the two clubs in the city were complex. Apart from the press, there was the impact of television and the wider changes in society. The huge popularity of the Beatles put Liverpool on the map and helped make the city the epicentre of youth culture, and it was therefore no surprise the Kop seduced the public in a way similar to the 'Fab Four'. As its cultural significance grew then the city was also going to have a positive impact on the image of any football team, bearing its name, to the outside world. In terms of grabbing attention, Everton were therefore at a disadvantage by not having the club's host city in their name – despite a richer history, this is a drawback with implications today. (There was speculation that one of the reasons why the Abu Dhabi United Group bought Manchester City, and not Everton, in 2008 was because they had their host city in their name, and therefore foreign audiences could place them.)

The other factor was the growth of television, BBC's *Match of the Day* having started at the beginning of the 1964/65 season. On 22 August 1964, the original theme tune 'Drum Majorette' opened the show to a BBC2 viewing audience of just 20,000, restricted to the London area. The only game chosen was Liverpool and Arsenal at Anfield. Although having the reigning champions on the show's opening night was understandable, the standing Kop subsequently proved to be a compelling attraction for the television cameras and watching public. The BBC match director, Alec Weeks, was an avid fan of the ground – if the game was dull, then pointing the cameras at the terracing would liven up the coverage. Even commentator Kenneth Wolstenholme's opening line, 'We are in Beatleville for today's Liverpool v Arsenal match' underlined the link between wider culture and the Anfield side, one Paul du Noyer expanded upon in *Liverpool – Wondrous Place*:

When Bill Shankly led Liverpool Football Club from years of obscurity to the start of unparalleled success ... the Kop became a national symbol. By an extraordinary coincidence, the team's resurgence occurred precisely at the time of the Beatles' rise and Merseybeat's supremacy. And it was the Kop, that swaying mass of humanity at one end of the Anfield ground, which symbolised the two phenomena. In everyday discourse 'the Liverpool sound' was freely used to embrace the music of the terraces as well as the groups.

Suddenly Everton, the senior club and one that had attracted a certain amount of reverence as an original member of football's aristocracy, seemed almost antiquated in comparison. Furthermore, the Goodison hierarchy's thinking continued to be anachronistic. While the electrifying noise and fanaticism generated by packed standing terraces was a magnet for television cameras for the remainder of the decade, Everton persisted in the empty space behind both goals at Goodison Park – undoubtedly affecting the ground's passionate atmosphere.

The perceived different outlook towards television across Stanley Park is cited as one reason why the media viewed both clubs and the two managers differently. The received wisdom was that Catterick did not like television whereas Shankly welcomed the cameras. The truth, as ever, was somewhere in between. Everton's scepticism towards the small screen was entrenched even before Catterick came to Goodison. As early as 1960 Everton were one of only four league clubs to oppose the live screening of games. Catterick's view, expressed in his *Liverpool Echo* column, was that television was a threat to football as an alternative source of entertainment. Alternatively, history says that Liverpool (and Shankly) embraced the small screen, using television's growing popularity to raise the profile of the club, at Everton and Catterick's expense. That is not necessarily the case; in the summer of 1966 Liverpool joined their city rivals in banning coverage of home matches, for a period of several months, sharing Everton's concerns on the effect on attendances. Shankly did not necessarily turn television away – but it is true that the cameras needed him more than the Scot wanted them. Football on the small screen during the decade was in its infancy and needed characters in order to, using modern parlance, 'sell the product'. The Liverpool manager, with his penchant for one-liners (not all original and whether he actually said some of them is doubtful)[33] was an ideal candidate for television to promote. To what extent is also open to debate, as televised football during the decade was limited to *Match of the Day* and regional highlights shows, with little in the way of magazine-style programming.

Having said that, television did raise the visibility of managers and the Liverpool manager made the transition better than his rival did across the Park, however not to the extent that people believe. The myths and legends surrounding Shankly consequently grew over time, unfairly pushing Catterick further and further into the background. As Jonathan Wilson pointed out about Shankly in his biography of Brian Clough, *Nobody Ever Says Thank You*, 'the anecdotes are often good to start with but have been polished to greatness by manipulations over time ... the legend has supplanted the facts.'

---

33 Shankly's famous 1981 statement on Granada TV, 'Somebody said that "football is a matter of life and death to you", I said "Listen, it's more important than that,"' was paraphrasing a quote by the American Football coach Henry Saunders made in 1949. 'Football is not just a matter of life and death; it's much more important than that,' Saunders had said.

10.
The People's Club

LIKE MANY OF THESE THINGS, IT BEGAN WITH A SIMPLE TELEPHONE call. In August 1960 the Stoke City and former Everton goalkeeper, Jimmy O'Neill, received a request via a telegram to ring a particular number. When he did, the man who answered asked him to ensure Stoke City lost their upcoming home game with Norwich City. In return, O'Neill would receive a significant sum of money. O'Neill reported the matter to the Football League, but the press soon got wind of the conversation and within months, newspapers were full of sordid tales of illegal approaches and payments to fix games, which gambling syndicates then bet on.

The revelations had all but disappeared by October 1961, but when bookmakers noted heavy fixed-odds betting on a 'double' for two unexpected away wins, Tranmere Rovers at York and Bradford City at Mansfield Town, suspicions were aroused again. Subsequent Football League enquiries identified that one of the punters had been the Mansfield player, Jimmy Gauld. Although Gauld admitted to fixed odds betting, their investigations missed the important link that as a former Everton player the Scot had once been a teammate of O'Neill, and it was he who made the 1960 approach.

Around this time, the *People* newspaper commenced their own inquiry. A 27-year-old journalist, Michael Gabbert,[34] who had no particular football background, led their investigations and in August 1963, to nobody's surprise, the *People* subsequently exposed the Aberdeen-born Gauld as the leader of the bribes

34 Gabbert had an interesting journalistic career. A Londoner who weighed close to seventeen stone, wore owl-like glasses and smoked six-inch cigars, he later moved to the *News of the World*, being behind the story of the Rolling Stones drugs bust in 1967 and later editing the *Sunday Sport*.

ring. The Scot told the paper how the system worked. The syndicate bet on up to five matches on a fixed-odds coupon, to obtain better odds. In each of those fixtures, there were a number of players who had been paid to throw the game – Gauld said any team could have up to four players 'on the inside'. The conspirators also had to place the same bet on the match, as a form of immoral commitment to the result. A network of go-betweens and intermediaries ensured that the players were unaware of the bigger picture. Gauld told the newspaper that the syndicate of players was earning £1,000 a week in 1961, but associated professional gamblers and bookmakers were earning much more. One betting coup brought in £50,000 – an enormous sum for the time. The scale of the corruption was unknown, although there were estimates of 100 players involved in the north, with claims of similar numbers in other regions.

After exposure as the ringleader, Gauld started working for the *People*, gathering evidence and supplying information on his web of contacts. One story he passed on originated in an evening match at Mansfield. Gauld was in the crowd and started talking to David 'Bronco' Layne of Sheffield Wednesday, the outcome being the striker agreed to the Scot's suggestion that he should attempt to 'fix' a game played by the Yorkshire club by bringing two teammates on board. The match was their visit to champions Ipswich Town in December 1962 and the two players in question were promising centre-half Peter Swan – and Tony Kay. Each of the players staked £50 on the outcome of the game, which was an easy victory for the home team, on a day when the syndicate's other two matches came up. The winnings were far less than expected, as some bookmakers did not pay out due to suspicious betting patterns. The three players received £100 each on top of their stake money. When the newspaper confronted a distressed Layne, he admitted guilt straightaway, as did Swan. 'It was money for jam,' the defender told the *People*. The paper went into print with the story on 12 April 1964 under the banner headline, 'THE BIGGEST SPORTS SCANDAL OF THE CENTURY.' Ironically, during the entire four-year investigation into match-fixing the Ipswich-Sheffield Wednesday fixture was the only top-flight game under suspicion. For his part, nearly forty years later, Kay later explained the events leading up to the infamous encounter:

A few days before the game I was talking with David Layne and Peter Swan. We were good friends: Swanny used to come and stay at my parents' house when we were kids but Layney had only recently arrived at the club. 'How do you fancy our chances on Saturday,' he [Layne] asked. 'We've got no chance,' I said. 'We always get beat at Ipswich.' So he asked if I fancied a bet on it - he could get us odds of 2-1.

The midfielder thought no more of it until nearly eighteen months later. Kay later told the *Evertonian* magazine, 'By the time it broke I was at Everton. I was at the Royal Tiger Club in Liverpool, where we used to hang out because it was kind of private. A friend of mine, a journalist, came up to me. "You're not going to like tomorrow's *People*, You're all over the front page." The following morning there we all were: me, Swan and Layne. As soon as you are on the front page of the newspaper, you know that it's serious.' Following Sheffield Wednesday's example with Layne and Swan, Everton suspended Kay from first-team duties immediately after the breaking of the story. Catterick said very little, apart from 'This is very disturbing. The image of professional football in the public mind is damaged by these reports of bribes.' Although the Everton manager told Kay that 'We'll do everything we can for you,' the fact it was now a criminal enquiry minimised his influence.

The investigations into Kay, Gauld and eight others dragged on until they appeared at Nottingham Assizes in January 1965. During the interim period, the club paid the player £45 a week to work as a steward. In court, his defence – Kay was advised not to enter the witness box – claimed that although it was unsporting to bet on your own team 'the point was whether Kay agreed to ensure his team would lose'. If that meant playing badly, his defence argued, then 'the prosecution would have said that was the corroboration they needed. The only trouble is that he played extremely well.'[35] In addition, when he spoke to the Everton player, Gabbert did not have all the transcriptions of their conversations, in a manner similar to a police interview. Even though it was not necessarily a verbatim record, the court accepted it as evidence of similar quality. But it meant any of Kay's statements to Gabbert offered as evidence for prosecution were potentially biased and taken out of their full context.

Nevertheless, the jury found the players guilty and the judge sentenced the Everton player and his former colleagues to four months in prison. This was harsh

35 *The Daily Telegraph* match report had the headline 'Kay on the Ball – Lesson for the champions' saying, 'Kay got through a pile of work, and his quickness on the ball should have taught Ipswich a lesson.'

and the fact that Kay and Swan were the last defendants to go before the court certainly influenced the term – it is highly likely that the weight of evidence in the preceding cases influenced the judge and jury, rather than their circumstances in isolation. Eighteen months before three players had escaped a custodial sentence for both fixing and betting on games and the suspicion remains that the authorities made an example of Kay in particular.

Justice Lawton even acknowledged the shortcomings of the prosecution's case in his summing up. 'It had been suggested that Mr Gabbert's evidence was unreliable ... but the jury had to do their best with what they had.' Although the evidence to convict them was limited, the judge said that, by betting on their own team, they compromised the principle that a 'football match is a game of uncertainty and that is part of the attraction'. The judge poured scorn on those who claimed that by not playing noticeably badly, the players had somehow protected their innocence, noting, 'would it really be necessary for either of these two [Kay and Swan] to do much to bring about the defeat of Sheffield Wednesday?' In other words, an undetected marginal drop in performance would have been enough to give the opposition the chance to win. By betting on their own team to lose, they had allowed the possibility that they would deliberately play badly, having had a stake in the result. This, after all, was a condition of the Gauld syndicate.

Kay went to jail almost two years to the day after his Toffees debut. Lawton said, 'For £100 Kay has finished what is probably one of the greatest careers in football. He is virtually finished in this country, and I am told in any other.' Although Lawton accepted the Sheffield Wednesday players were involved 'really by chance' and on 'one isolated occasion' he left them with a parting shot. 'Honours, rewards almost beyond a footballer's dreams, hero worship and success in abundance have been tossed aside in unguarded and unworthy moments,' he told the court. Kay eventually served eleven weeks in Thorp Arch open prison in Yorkshire but the most damaging punishment came on release. An FA Commission banned the Everton player for life from all forms of football. It was a crushing blow to Kay. 'I never cried so much in my life,' he later admitted.

Many have pointed out since that the custodial sentence was unfair compared to the more lenient punishment for similar offences in the twenty-first century.[36]

[36] In 2009 a number of Accrington players were fined and banned for up to a year for all betting on their team to lose their game against Bury in May 2008. Once again there were familiar claims that incidents of this nature were rife.

At the time betting shops had been legal for four years and gambling was still held in a certain amount of ill-repute, unlike today, and that was probably reflected in the sentence. Also the players were not operating in isolation. They were, knowingly or not, part of a criminal conspiracy and punished as such. In Kay's case, a *life* ban following a harsh prison sentence was surely zealous; although the argument was the courts were punishing the players for conspiracy, whilst the footballing authorities were doing the same for breaching betting rules. Either way the authorities were effectively punishing the player twice for the same offence, and like anybody else who had served their term, he should have been free to continue his rehabilitation in his chosen profession. Eighteen months later, a number of notable sporting figures, including Everton chairman E. Holland Hughes, Matt Busby, Joe Mercer and Denis Compton wrote an open letter to *The Times*, requesting that the FA review the players' bans. 'They were quite properly punished for these practices by sentences of imprisonment of varying lengths,' the letter stated, going on to request a review of the suspensions, 'to give at least some of these young men some hope that they will be permitted, perhaps on terms of probation, to re-enter their profession before it is too late to do so.' Although there was an FA review in 1968, the life bans effectively remained.

Afterwards Kay followed a nomadic existence. Three years after his release, Arthur Hopcraft interviewed the now former player in his masterpiece study of the game *The Football Man*. The author argued that any criminal conviction for 'fixing' football 'is not just a nasty blotch on the wall, but a jagged hole in the fabric. Two or three more like that and the whole structure falls to rubble.' Hopcraft was correct, if a number of players behaved similarly to those sent down at Nottingham then the game had serious problems – those found guilty deserved punishment. Exhibiting some sympathy though, Hopcraft concluded, 'Professional sport made him, tested him and broke him. He is one of football's tragic casualties because he was so strongly equipped in nearly all his aspects.' But it was an earlier answer that revealed the torment of survival following a ban from the trade that had brought him fame. Five years after Roy Peskett said in the *Daily Mail* that 'Kay of Everton is now touching the greatness he always promised,' Hopcraft asked what the former Everton man had been doing since prison, 'Just going round in circles,' he replied, 'getting nowhere.'[37]

Banned from the game for life, the FA's vigilance in ensuring Kay complied with their diktat went to ridiculous levels – in December 1968 they warned him against playing charity matches. Apart from Kay, the other victims were his employers. Everton lost a key figure at the peak of his powers, less than eighteen months after signing him for a substantial fee. A player he had nurtured at Sheffield Wednesday, Catterick later said Kay was the best he had managed. 'He had an awful lot of skill and it didn't matter who the opposition was, he always thought he could do better. His loss was a great blow to the club,' his former manager said.

To exacerbate the blow to both Kay and Everton, the likelihood was that those imprisoned were only the tip of the iceberg. One senior police officer said after the trial, 'Only the cream of the conspiracies had been skimmed.' To add substance to the claims that the convicted players were only a small part of a wider operation, the hugely respected journalist, Ken Jones, later told an intriguing tale. Then with the *Daily Mirror*, Jones recalled in his book *Jules Rimet Still Gleaming* attending an FA press conference held at Lancaster Gate during the height of the scandal. Sitting alone in the room at the end of the conference, Jones was alarmed at what happened next, as he later wrote: 'I casually turned over a crested tablemat to discover a sheet of FA notepaper carelessly left by a member of the committee that had met to discuss the most sensational revelations British football had ever known. Written on it were names of players equal in prominence to Kay, Swan and Layne.' Jones took the paper away with him back to the newspaper's office but, having effectively stolen it, the journalist could do little and burned the evidence.

If what Jones surmised was true – that the authorities had evidence linking further big-name players with match-fixing activities – then perhaps those at the top of the game knew more about the issue than first thought, which would not be surprising given that stories of match-fixing during the decade are legion. Former Manchester United keeper Harry Gregg claimed in his 2002 autobiography that players from the club conspired to throw games in the very season that the *People* had published their damaging accusations and that the

[37] Kay gave a memorable interview to Hugh McIlvanney in the *Observer* in January 1966, after a 30,000-strong petition for the re-instatement of the banned footballers was presented to the FA. The great Scottish journalist described Kay in typical colourful prose. 'His hair is an unfiery red, his nose is long, narrow and prominently boned and he has a rather jutting chin. He has a habit of turning down the corners of his mouth in a caricature of disapproval, which gives him a faintly Punch-like appearance.' Kay ended the interview with a regrettable warning: 'Something very big has gone out of my life and I'd give anything to get it back. After what I've been through there isn't enough money in the country to make professional footballers ever to take the risk again.' Unfortunately they did.

practice continued into the second half of the decade.[38] As Denis Cowley, who was representing Peter Swan, said in court, 'There could well be two hundred people in the dock, there are only ten and in each sense they could represent twenty players.'

Although the incident involving Kay occurred during his time at Sheffield Wednesday, the *People* published their revelations after his transfer to Goodison. Unfairly perhaps, the disclosure provided yet more unwanted negative publicity to the club. Their reputation would take an even bigger blow as the Kay saga played out, Everton themselves being the subject of further revelations from Michael Gabbert and his cohorts.

Did leading Everton players take pep drugs?

Unlike other sports, the impact of using performance-enhancing drugs within football is not clear. The myriad influences on any game means there is no guarantee that using illegal substances will bring success. That said, this has not stopped their acknowledged use going back nearly a century – the journalist and former Arsenal player, Bernard Joy, admitted in 1952 that his club had provided 'pep pills' to the team before an FA Cup tie against West Ham in 1925. One of the greatest English footballers, Sir Stanley Matthews, claimed in his autobiography that he used amphetamines before an FA Cup game in 1946. During a BBC Radio 4 documentary in 2004, former Manchester United players, Albert Scanlon and Harry Gregg, admitted using amphetamines whilst part of the 'Busby Babes' side of the 1950s.

After investigations by the Council of Europe in 1963 concluded that football in Great Britain had issues with drug use it was inevitable that at some point the press would provide some sort of exposé. With the world of football now clouded with intrigue, following the *People* breaking the bribes scandal story, the same newspaper now introduced the phenomenon of drug taking to its expanding

38 Gregg was repeating allegations that first surfaced in Eamon Dunphy's brilliant 1991 biography of Sir Matt Busby *A Strange Kind of Glory*. Dunphy, who spent five years at Old Trafford in the first half of the 1960s, recalled the tale of two *Daily Mail* journalists confronting several United players, including Gregg, during a stay at Blackpool. When informed of the match-fixing allegations, a shocked Busby persuaded the newspaper not to publish the story. Dunphy later went on to say, 'There is no doubt in my mind that Manchester United players did conspire to fix the result of at least three games during the '60/ '63 period. It is widely accepted within the game that those convicted in the ensuing (Sheffield Wednesday) scandal were not the only prominent players involved in the match-rigging conspiracy.' This also confirms the Ken Jones story. The point here is the court effectively tried the players for the crimes of others and made an example of them. This is especially true of Kay, the highest profile player of those in the dock.

readership. That Everton – the northern oppressors with perceived low moral standards – were the subject made it even more newsworthy. So on the first Sunday of September 1964, the *People* ran with the following headline, 'Did leading Everton players take pep drugs before matches in the 1962/63 season, when the team won the League Championship? The answer is "Yes" and the *People* can and will prove it.' The source of the allegations was the former Everton goalkeeper, Albert Dunlop, who had first approached the newspaper in the May of that year. The player's testimony ran to some 39 foolscap pages. His initial claim was that players took the drug Benzedrine, a powerful stimulant banned from open sale, to help them win matches. His published testimony said, 'Many of the players started taking Benzedrine tablets regularly early in 1961. I cannot remember how they first came to be offered to us. They were used throughout the 1961/62 season and the championship season which followed it ... soon some of the players could not do without the drugs.' Dunlop specifically named four teammates – Alex Young, Roy Vernon, Alex Parker and George Thomson – as well as himself, who were regular users.

Once again Mike Gabbert was the chief investigator and the journalist tracked down the source of the Benzedrine to the 'Spellow Drug Stores' in County Road, near Goodison Park. Although they claimed to supply the drug on prescription to Everton, Gabbert failed to find the doctor who prescribed them, if indeed there was one. The club doctor, whose surgery was nearby, said he had never prescribed the drug to Everton, although he may have done so for an individual player.

The Everton hierarchy took a sceptical stance initially. Chairman John Moores said within 24 hours of the accusations, 'I knew of these rumours some time ago, investigations are being made and a definite statement about it all is likely to be made later this week when they are completed.' Publication of the club's findings, from director E. Holland Hughes, came two days before the next edition of the newspaper, with rumours that the *People* were publishing further accusations. Rather than completely deny the story, to an extent it confirmed some of the basic facts in Dunlop's claims. The club admitted that, unknown to the Everton board, some years before the 1962/63 season any player who wanted it could, before a match, obtain a single pill containing 'a mild stimulant'.[39] However, the statement

[39] Holland Hughes briefed the press that this was Benzedrine, which was consistent with Dunlop's statements, although the director said usage ceased at the end of the 1961/62 season. Nevertheless, it is worth pointing out that the drug was not on the banned list and thus legally, if perhaps not morally, acceptable for use within the laws of the game.

concluded that 'we are satisfied that allegations of wholesale drug-taking are without foundation.'

As expected, Dunlop then provided more salacious tales, stating that Drinamyl, or 'purple hearts' had also been the drug of choice. The goalkeeper claimed that in March 1962, whilst under the influence of the drug, the players destroyed Chelsea 4-0. 'You have never seen anything like it. The boys literally ran the opposition into the ground,' he said about the game. Now also claiming to be an addict, Dunlop described a game at Wolves when he was in a drug-induced stupor and staggered off the pitch at the end.

Of these additional drug accusations made since their initial statement, club officials provided further comments: 'Everton have been unable to find any evidence that there has ever been any general use of a pill, as has been alleged ... the stimulants are mild and were originally prescribed by our doctor. If there is any suggestion they were given in unlimited quantities it is quite contrary to the evidence.' Catterick, who had said little in public beforehand, denied the latest allegations: 'To say that these stimulants have been laid out as part of the players' equipment before a match is complete nonsense. And to further add that they have been given out before training sessions is rubbish.' However, long-serving staff such as Brian Harris and trainer Gordon Watson also told the club that stimulants were available to players as long as they could remember. As part of their investigations, Everton officials listened to the newspaper's tapes in Wardour Street, London, and later received transcripts. Summing up, Holland Hughes insisted: 'I have travelled hundreds of miles in my investigations, but it has been a worthwhile job to clear the club. As far as I am concerned, the club has nothing to fear whatsoever.' Although three players served writs against the *People*, talk of legal action eventually came to nothing.

In a Fix

As well as the allegations of widespread drug taking, Dunlop introduced the spectre of match fixing during the final games of the previous title-winning campaign, after returning to the first-team for the injured West. There were two alleged incidents; the first took place on the coach travelling to the Hawthorns for the vital league encounter in May 1963, when four points were needed from the last two games of the season to clinch the title. Dunlop told the *People* that several players put money into a collection on the coach, the goalkeeper explaining why:

While the Everton team were travelling to Birmingham for the West Bromwich match most of us were approached by Roy Vernon. Roy asked me for £10. And when I handed it over he explained that he wanted it for a bribes 'kitty' to which most of the Everton players were contributing. He said the money would be used to bribe certain West Bromwich players to play badly to lose the match.

The newspaper claimed that Alex Young and Alex Parker, plus a further unnamed teammate, also put money into the collection. The *People* also provided extracts of taped conversations of Dunlop made with a number of Everton players about the alleged incident, without their knowledge. The first was between Dunlop and Vernon, in July 1964. According to the article, when the supposed bribery plot was discussed, the club skipper was quoted on tape as saying, 'There's nothing that can be done about that one [the plot]. They'll never get nobody to say nothing about that.' The Welshman also said, on tape, to have already approached a West Brom player and 'warned him to keep quiet' according to the newspaper. Dunlop also spoke to Young, who when told that Gabbert was investigating the bribery accusations, reportedly said 'If he's been to West Bromwich we're really snookered.' Likewise, Alex Parker said, 'Well that's us in the s---' when also informed that the *People* were on their trail. Everton then took the unusual step of installing microphones and tape recorders in the houses of those under scrutiny. Gabbert subsequently spoke to three players, two in their homes. Both Vernon and Young now appeared to change their stance, both denying the accusations while Parker said that 'I have been advised not to say a word.'

Understandably, after their own investigations, club officials provided a robust response to the allegations of match fixing. Concerning the West Brom game the statement read, 'We have investigated the story ourselves with Everton players and with the opposing player alleged to have been concerned ... we are quite sure that there was no bribery or attempted bribery.' The West Brom chairman, Jim Gaunt, also denied that any of his players had been involved in bribery activities.

However, that was not the end of the matter. A week later, Dunlop, in another exclusive, claimed that prior to the Fulham game in May 1963, the Everton trainer Tommy Eggleston asked the visitors' centre-forward Maurice Cook – whom he had coached at Watford – whether his side were prepared to lose the match for £10 a man. Dunlop claimed to have witnessed the conversation in the trainers' room at Goodison before the game. The Everton keeper alleged Eggleston told young reserve Roy Parnell to fetch Cook from the visitors' dressing room and on his arrival made the offer. Apart from the Everton goalkeeper, the others present in the room were Parnell[40] and Roy Vernon. Made aware of the accusation by the newspaper, the club subsequently made a further statement:

We know that in a conversation about tickets and other matters of personal interest, Tom Eggleston jokingly made some reference which he himself cannot remember to a payment for losing the game. The figure of £10 was mentioned…it is quite clear to us that whatever may have been said was said jokingly, and was taken as a joke by Maurice Cook.

Holland Hughes then added that 'the board are quite satisfied that an idle remark … has been magnified out of all proportion.' After the Fulham player's accusation took the form of a signed affidavit, the *People* took a different view unsurprisingly. 'It is certain that Eggleston's "jest" was not made in a casual encounter with Maurice Cook, the Fulham centre-forward,' claimed Gabbert.

Summing Up

More than fifty years later, this strange sequence of events still leaves much for discussion. Regarding the drug-taking allegations, what is beyond dispute is that Everton did offer stimulants to players as Dunlop alleged – they admitted as much publicly. Having said that, they were undoubtedly not the only club doing so at the time and there was no law against such practice, even for Benzedrine.

However, Dunlop subsequently told the *People* that 'A number of other Everton stars had become so dependent on stimulant drugs that the Benzedrine supplied by the Everton trainers was no longer sufficient to give them the required boost. So they turned to outside sources of supply. And the drug they obtained was Drinamyl, in the form of "purple hearts" tablets…but they, too, can have long-term side effects of a damaging kind.'

This picture of alleged systematic doping of players is questionable. Such a practice would have been highly dangerous to playing staff under the supervision of a club doctor. It is therefore hard to align Dunlop's statement of a team filled

40 The *People* did make clear that Parnell was an innocent party and 'had no hand in the offer of money, and did not know this was what Eggleston wanted to see Cook about when he was sent to fetch him'.

with drug-damaged players with a side capable of finishing fourth and first in successive seasons. As Holland Hughes said reasonably at the time, 'Our players are far too valuable to give them anything that would be harmful in any way. This team has been assembled at considerable cost. How absurd to do anything to undermine it.' Regarding Dunlop's accusations concerning the systematic doping of players, Holland Hughes was correct. However, PFA chairman Cliff Lloyd was against any sort of drug use, warning, 'Anyone who takes stimulants or any form of pills is laying himself open to all sorts of unknown dangers.'

Whether the drugs had the effects that Dunlop claimed cannot be substantiated. An American Medical Association study at the time established that the use of amphetamines could improve the performance of runners and swimmers by approximately 1 percent. However, Dunlop claimed the drugs used by Everton, like in the match against Chelsea, had a much more dramatic physical impact, which may not have been possible based on the types of stimulants involved.

Coincidentally, the one match where Dunlop claimed to have been heavily affected, at Wolves in 1961, was fog-bound, where nobody could see the impact. The goalkeeper told the *People* that he was unaware the game had finished and required assistance off the pitch. However, at least one supporter behind Dunlop's goal later recalled witnessing Brian Labone arrive out of the gloom to tell the goalkeeper the match had ended, before the pair trooped off. Like many of Dunlop's wider allegations, the story was murky and ambiguous.

Dunlop's assertion that on two occasions Everton players and officials conspired to fix games at the end of the 1962/63 campaign are similarly open to debate. On the one hand there is the entrapment of several Everton players who, on face value, made a series of statements supporting the allegation of the bribery of their West Brom counterparts. Although what was printed supported some of the goalkeeper's claims, the *People* published them out of context and, as the betting trial demonstrated, gathering evidence to support an accusation does not support any neutral assessment.

Furthermore, there is no evidence that any bribery actually took place. As Dunlop admitted: 'I have found no proof that any of the West Brom players actually accepted the bribe, but that money collected for that purpose is fully proved.' But there is no evidence of that, other than Dunlop's word. A number of club officials and at least one journalist were travelling with the team on the coach to West Brom and reported nothing suspicious. The only other witness on the coach to come forward told the *People* that he saw Vernon going up the coach with a handful of pound notes. 'I did not know what the money was for,' he said – which is circumstantial evidence at best. It seems strange that players, with opportunity to do so elsewhere, chose a travelling coach to organise the bribery of the opposition, in full view of club officials and the press.

The claims made against Tommy Eggleston are similar in nature, and again there is no evidence that any money changed hands. The sums involved – £10 per man in the Fulham game and possibly something similar at West Brom – seem an unfeasibly low offer to throw a match, when set against the risk of discovery and compared to the much larger figures associated with the first betting scandal reported by the *People*. Everton's investigation into Eggleston claimed that the comment was made as a joke. Maurice Cook's signed statement that 'Because of the smallness of the sum and my reputation for being a completely "straight" player I could hardly believe that Eggleston was serious,' perhaps provides some evidence to support this.

Although the independence of any internal investigation could by questioned by cynics, in their defence Everton did hand the dossier containing their findings on both the drugs and bribery allegations to both the Football League and FA. Missing from their submission were the transcripts of the tape recordings, which they added later.

The authorities could have undertaken their own enquiries, but the fact that they did not in relation to drug use, in public at least, was probably due to the fact there was nothing in the laws of the English game to prevent the use of the types involved. 'Unlike the Italian League and the British Boxing Board of Control, who prohibit the use of stimulants, the League and the FA have not included even an indirect reference to the subject in their rule books,' the *Daily Telegraph* admitted. Regarding the allegations of fixing matches, on face value the conclusion is that the ruling bodies felt they could add little to the club's findings. Some concerned members of the Shareholders' Association felt however that Everton did not go far enough with their investigation and wished to put forward a resolution complaining of the approach taken. A meeting with Holland Hughes, which assuaged their concerns, ended their plans. Four months later Denis Follows, secretary of the FA, said 'the Everton matter is now closed'.

There is another aspect to this investigation that has roots in the Littlewoods organisation. A former director of the company once said that 'The Littlewoods way was certainly that you had to have character, and you certainly had to have morals.' Given Moores was still the Everton chairman who used the wider principles of 'the Littlewoods way' in running the club, it is fair to assume that any employee found to have transgressed would have been dealt with. The fact that does not appear to be the case indicates that the club's dossier reflects Holland Hughes' assertions.

With regard to the allegations, Albert Dunlop's motives also require consideration. The goalkeeper was frustrated that the £1,500 'talent money' awarded to the champions was distributed to the squad based on their appearances during the season. Dunlop, who played just four games, later admitted: 'I was annoyed at this because I stood to gain very little financially from Everton winning the championship.' After retirement, Dunlop lead a troubled existence and whatever his motives – and worth recalling that the club confirmed some of his allegations – the possibility exists that the former goalkeeper did genuinely misinterpret some events happening around him. However, Dunlop took them to his grave when he died aged just 57 in 1990.

'The tragedy of Everton'

When Everton sacked Billy Bingham in 1977, Colin Malam of the *Sunday Telegraph* wrote that the club 'may want success too badly for their own good'. That was undoubtedly true and the desire was at its most intense in the early years of the Moores regime. Whatever the rights and wrongs of the *People* investigations, there was an inevitability that the almost maniacal craving for success from chairman downwards would attract media scrutiny. Any story about the club was therefore bound to be newsworthy, especially if there was potential chicanery involved.

Setting aside the inflammatory accusations, in his closing comments on the bribery scandal Michael Gabbert made a perfectly valid point about Everton, which provided an insight into why they were so unpopular:

They had got to the top after a season [1962/63] in which determination to win, in the case of certain players and Tommy Eggleston had gone to extremes. Such was the tragedy of Everton, the team of football aristocrats. But the urge to win had done grave damage to Goodison Park even before pep drugs were taken, a bribe "kitty" was collected and the head trainer played his extraordinary "joke".

11.
Blackpool

CATTERICK USED 21 PLAYERS IN THE 1964/65 CAMPAIGN, THE growing number of youngsters an indication that a new Everton was emerging. Colin Harvey and Tommy Wright were now established first-team players while Gerry Glover and Jimmy Husband made their debuts late in the season, with John Hurst in the wings. The latter three were part of a truly magnificent team that won the FA Youth Cup in the May, scoring seventeen goals and conceding none in the run to the final, including a 5-0 semi-final aggregate win over a Sunderland side coached by Brian Clough.

Before the pre-season trip to Scandinavia in August 1965, Catterick spoke glowingly about the junior players coming through the ranks. 'We now have some of the finest young players in the country,' he said. 'In the next eighteen months or so the further development of these players should put the club in the position were huge transfer fees will be a thing of the past. This youth policy is one which will bear fruit over the years to come and I think this is something which must be pursued at all times.'

Although time proved him correct, the first half of the 1965/66 season was the lowest point of Catterick's top-flight career at that time. After falling in Europe at the second hurdle, when a George Best inspired Manchester United inflicted a damaging 3-0 defeat at Old Trafford in mid-December, Catterick's side were in the bottom-half of the table, just five points above the drop zone having conceded forty goals in 22 games. Earlier in the season they had lost 5-0 at Anfield in the biggest derby loss for thirty years. 'I never believed that modern Everton could be subjected to such indignities,' said Horace Yates in the *Liverpool Daily Post* after the game. Once again, supporters and press questioned team tactics – Catterick's newly installed 4-2-4 was morphing into 4-5-1 with Pickering playing alone up front, the long balls fired up to him useless if the forward had no support. In addition, the team was still struggling with four men at the back and the need to move the ball quickly through the two 'link' men in midfield, with movement more likely to be across the pitch than towards the strikers. By the time the ball reached the penalty area, the other team had pulled their players back. With that in mind, one supporter made his feelings known on the pages of the *Liverpool Echo*, 'This is the poorest team we have ever had at Goodison. The manager has been quoted as saying it is a transitional period and Everton will be good in two or three years' time. What good is that to an Evertonian? Is transitional a new word invented for mediocre?'

The problem was not just the changing personnel but in deploying players. With Alex Young dropped before Christmas – and the Scot had done nothing in the reserves to justify a recall – the need to integrate Pickering and the attempted switch to 4-2-4 had produced too many square pegs in round holes. Playing Harris in a deeper, defensive role stifled the creativity he would have supplied further up the pitch. Conversely, Gabriel (who was struggling with injury) and Harvey had been playing further forward when they were more suited in more withdrawn roles. Although there were some promising youngsters, they were still subject to a difficult time from the Goodison crowd. This annoyed Catterick greatly, who fired a broadside at supporters, 'I am doing my best to develop local boys, but some of our fans are too impatient. They are apt to vent their displeasure on some youngster who is having a bad time. These lads need encouragement not barracking. Not all players who have an off game are targets for the critics on the terraces. The crowd, or a few of them, seem to pick on only one man.' Elsewhere, some of the reserve strength that had been a feature of the early part of the decade had disappeared and accusations that some players were too complacent had some foundation. Supporters were voting with their feet. Home gates that had topped 50,000 during the title year had now fallen to below 30,000. The crowd of 20,670 for the 2-0 win over Fulham on the weekend before Christmas 1965 was the lowest of the decade for a league game on the ground.

However, with a three-game unbeaten start to the year, 1966 brought an upturn in fortunes for the side – before the now infamous trip to Blackpool in the middle of the month. The aftermath of the match on the Fylde coast is now ingrained within the folklore of the club, hugely symbolic in the way it crystallised the supporters' ambivalence towards Catterick, a man who less than three years before had brought them the title.

Alex Young had returned to the side beforehand but with the Scot's form still significantly below his capabilities, Catterick surprised everybody by selecting the 16-year-old Joe Royle in his place. Although the ground was near frozen, the game took place in slippery conditions. The Everton line-up included John Hurst, playing at centre-half, and goalkeeper Geoff Barnett, his teammate from the victorious FA Youth Cup side. With Gordon West injured, Barnett had replaced the out-of-form Andy Rankin before Christmas. The rookie keeper had a nightmare game, primarily due to a remarkable error in the first half, when he allowed a straightforward Colin Harvey back-pass from the edge of the box to slip through his hands and between his legs for a goal unjustly credited to the midfielder. 'I had turned around to look up the field to see where he was kicking it. The next thing I could hear boos and ah's and the ball was just bobbling into the back of the net,' Harvey later told *bluekipper.com*. With Blackpool's 20-year-old Alan Ball making a mockery of conditions to run riot through the middle, the home side fully deserved their 2-0 win. The midfielder's performance certainly impressed the young debutant, as Royle later recalled to Brian Glanville. 'Bally destroyed us on his own. One of my most vivid memories is of this cheeky little red-headed fellow sitting on the ball in his own penalty area.'

The aftermath of the game is of course notorious for the incident involving the Everton manager and a number of visiting supporters chanting, 'Catterick must go, sack Catterick,' in the coach park after the game. There are many differing accounts of subsequent events that are well worth revisiting. Firstly, E. Holland Hughes, by now the club chairman, said after the game:

We were met by a hostile crowd numbering anything between forty or fifty chanting 'Catterick, Catterick.' Mr Catterick was just ahead of me in the crowd when he appeared to be swept off his feet. The next thing I saw was him staggering towards the coach. I boarded the coach without any great difficulty ... this attack on Mr Catterick, who was in no position to defend himself was a cowardly and brutal action.

Michael Charters added in the *Liverpool Echo*, 'Everton supporters really plumbed the depths on Saturday with an outrageous assault on unsuspecting manager Harry Catterick ... kicked, hacked and knocked to the ground he received a sprained ankle and numerous bruises.' Meanwhile, the local police understandably played down the incident: 'Two officers escorted Mr Catterick towards the waiting team coach because a section of the crowd were showing some animosity and hostility. Someone came from behind and tripped him and the officers carried on helping him into the coach ... the incident was very quickly over.' Holland Hughes disputed the police's version of events, pointing to the presence of a number of uniformed men and plain-clothes detectives mixed in with Everton fans, in such numbers that they obviously feared some sort of disturbance. The chairman complained they did not warn him that 'an ugly situation was likely to arise'. Catterick reportedly had his ankle strapped by the team trainer and was treated for various cuts and bruises. For his part, the Everton manager wisely played down the incident in the immediate aftermath, his main concern at the time being whether any injury would affect the recovery from a recent abdominal operation. Catterick later recounted his role in the day's events:

At the time we had little or no chance of winning any trophies and there were a number of youngsters in the reserves I thought would make the grade. Joe Royle was one of them and I put him in the team instead of Young, deciding to rest a player who was coming towards the twilight of his career. The fact that we lost the game caused a couple of dozen so-called supporters to be disgruntled ... they closed in on me and I was quite deliberately kicked to the ground. It was a nasty business and it was all so stupid because the selection I made for that match was in the best interests of the club.

Amongst the theories advanced since is that the club and Catterick deliberately exacerbated the incident to mask a desperately poor away performance and the problems on the pitch at the time. Royle himself told James Lawton in the *Daily Express* almost thirty years later, 'Things aren't always what they seem and there's no doubt Harry used the situation to his advantage. There was a bit of jostling, but nothing serious, I saw it, but the controversy deflected attention from the defeat.' Catterick always maintained it was more serious than that and earlier had told Colin Wood in the *Daily Mail* that he would have considered prosecutions if the assailants could be identified. The manager also hinted that he would have had no compunction in fighting back in normal circumstances, saying 'My only regret when I was set on was that I was only two or three weeks out of hospital after a major operation and I was unable to do anything about it.' Regardless of what version of events was true – and accounts differ only due to scale – yet again the incident outside Bloomfield Road brought more bad publicity to the club and their fans.

The confrontation posed some serious questions about the relationship, if there was one, between the manager and the team's supporters. Catterick distrusted a number of factions within the game and this undoubtedly contributed to becoming a target of some. The manager was particularly wary of the Everton Supporters Club and continually made his feelings known at board level that the group, in his opinion, meddled in club affairs and had far too much influence. Yet, at the time of the Blackpool incident, there were also purely football reasons for supporters' unrest. Although any Everton history of the decade usually paints a picture of School of Science football and consistent success, this generalisation is somewhat wide of the mark. For some periods, particularly during the middle of the decade, this was not necessarily the case – negative tactics combined with an unbalanced squad of players filling the wrong positions bred poor results. Whereas subsequent accounts claim that supporters assaulted the manager due to the dropping of Young, the two events were merely coincidental. The skirmish was purely the result of a frustration that had seen a title-winning side become effectively also-rans within the space of eighteen months. The charges against Catterick at the time being that he had disturbed a good team and had brought in too many youngsters too early. That said there was no excuse for the fans' behaviour. Although there was widespread support for Catterick, old foe Danny Blanchflower was not so compassionate. 'I wasn't blind with sympathy for him,' he wrote in his *Sunday Express* column, 'I could see that he done a lot to bring it on himself. He skipped across a lot of sacred ground in doing it and he was bound to anger the gods.'

There was another casualty of the Blackpool affair. Geoff Barnett played only once more for the Toffees and eventually joined Arsenal, where strangely for a talented keeper he was quite happy to be understudy to Bob Wilson and Jimmy Rimmer. The Cheshire-born stopper did however replace the injured Wilson in the Arsenal line-up for the 1972 FA Cup final. Catterick held the opinion that Barnett felt guilty about his performance, his error indirectly contributing to the events after the game. In a self-penned article for the *Liverpool Daily Post* in 1971, the manager admitted that 'Barnett was always terribly disturbed about this [fracas] and his future in football and I always felt Everton lost a player because of it.'

12.
Wembley 1966

IF EVER A SEASON NEEDED A CUP RUN, THEN 1965/66 REQUIRED ONE. Setting aside the defeat at Blackpool, there were signs that some parts of the team were returning to normal service in early 1966. Alex Scott was showing his best form since joining the club while Jimmy Gabriel had returned from injury. Catterick had bought the unheralded Mike Trebilcock from Plymouth Argyle on the final day of 1965 and the forward netted his first goal in the home win over Aston Villa.

The Everton board were also conscious of the psychological impact on the players following the alleged attack on Catterick. With that in mind chairman Holland Hughes spoke to the squad before their third-round FA Cup tie against Sunderland, remarkably delivering what was effectively the public utterance every manager dreads, 'The incidents at Blackpool last Saturday have in no way affected the confidence of the Board in Mr Catterick.' Although questionable whether the directors would have sacked their manager if they were to lose to the Wearsiders, given Catterick had the security of a new contract, a cup defeat followed by no improvement in league form would have resulted in some serious questions about his ability to manage the club. The demanding Everton board would also have also noted his increasing unpopularity with supporters, with a prolonged run in the cup now essential.

Sunderland (home), third round

With Liverpool having won the title and the FA Cup since Everton last tasted success, and Shankly's side now on the way to regaining their league crown, the balance of power had shifted inexorably to the red half of the city by the start of 1966. Although not to the same degree, Catterick was in a place similar to Howard Kendall eighteen years later. Had the Everton manager left at that point it would be interesting to hypothesise on his replacement in the Goodison hot seat. The one obvious choice would have been Don Revie at Leeds United. As it happens, history shows the board did not have the opportunity to make that decision.

Under pressure, Catterick played it safe against Sunderland, recalling the now-fit Gabriel and Young to the team at the expense of Hurst and Royle, in one of the biggest games of his managerial career to date. In goal, the fit West was back as Barnett's replacement. After the Blackpool debacle, the players produced their best performance for nearly twelve months. 'There was a masterful serenity and control in their play,' said the *Observer*. Temple and Scott were unstoppable on the flanks and Young had one of those inspired afternoons that justified the loyalty of the thousands who worshipped him. Temple opened the scoring, heading a Scott cross in off the post just before the break. In the second period, Pickering added a second with a fierce shot from just outside the box before Young wrapped up the scoring near the end. Everton spirits lifted with the news that across the Park Tommy Docherty's Chelsea had removed the cup holders via a 2-1 victory. With odds of winning the FA Cup now down to 9/1, Everton had a favourable draw for the next round against Southern League side Bedford Town.

Bedford Town (away), fourth round

For the first time since the autumn, Catterick was able to deploy a full-strength team and this produced an upturn in results. After the Sunderland game Everton went on an eight-game unbeaten run in the league, with five victories. Gabriel's return to the side was key, the Scot forming an impressive midfield partnership with Colin Harvey as the 4-2-4 formation bedded in. Alex Young was also producing his best form since the title-winning season, with the Glaswegian reacting positively to the long-awaited extended run in the team.

After watching Bedford defeat Worcester City, Catterick said, 'They are a good side, they play intelligently. There is no big boot about them, no kick and rush.' Before the game, Catterick fashioned another cunning plan. Conscious that Bedford would also be watching his team before their fourth-round encounter, the manager swapped Gabriel and Harris in the line-up in the victories over Northampton and Stoke, with Gabriel now playing in the back-line and Harris in midfield. On the day of their meeting, in front of an 18,000 sell-out crowd at The Eyrie, the two reverted to their normal roles. With some of their pre-match plans redundant, at one stage one of the Bedford players turned to Harris and said, 'What the f--- are you doing here?'

Catterick would have realised that the subterfuge was not required, as the first division outfit completely outplayed the gallant non-league team. With Colin Harvey in particular having a tremendous game, the visitors had ten corners in the opening thirty minutes before striking two crucial blows prior to the break. Both goals came from Temple, with the source again crosses from Alex Scott. On 37 minutes the future Wembley hero headed home firmly from the Scot's centre and five minutes later the winger got to the bye-line and pulled the ball back for Temple to finish easily. The second half was disappointing, enlightened only by a Pickering headed goal near the end, one beautifully crafted from a Tommy Wright cross. After their easy 3-0 win, at 11/2 Catterick's side was third-placed in the FA Cup betting, behind Chelsea and Manchester United.

Coventry City (home), fifth round

The fifth round pitted Everton against Jimmy Hill's Coventry City side. The future television presenter was in the middle of a brilliant three-year period as manager of the Sky Blues, taking the team from the third division to the top-flight before departing to develop his then fledgling media career. The draw kindly sent Everton back to Goodison and on the first Saturday in March they produced another virtuoso display in recording a third successive 3-0 victory in the competition.

The good form arising from a settled side was clearly apparent in their crisp and purposeful attacking play, the home side overrunning a disappointingly defensive team that were well-placed for promotion from the second division. Once again it was the attacking quartet of Temple, Pickering, Scott and Young who were the arch destroyers. In a desperately one-sided contest in front of 60,000 spectators, Young opened the scoring on thirteen minutes from Scott, his shot going in off the post. With Gabriel and Harvey dominant in the middle of the park, Everton continued their assault but had to wait until twenty minutes from time for a second. All afternoon, Fred Pickering had the beating in the air of George Curtis – whose own managerial partnership with John Sillett would bring cup glory to Coventry two decades later – and Temple picked up his flick and slipped the ball past the keeper. The provider of the second goal became the scorer of the third,

Scott picking up a clearance direct from the goalkeeper and returning it to the area where Pickering almost broke the back of the net with a powerful finish.

Manchester City (away), quarter-final

One feature of the upturn in form after the damaging defeat at Blackpool was the vastly improved defensive shield. The return of West certainly helped, although Catterick was without Rankin for the early months of the year, after the deposed number one fractured a cheekbone when laying lino on the floor and a door opened unexpectedly in his face.

One league match during this period had far-reaching implications not apparent at the time. Having won their two league games after defeating Coventry, the Toffees faced Liverpool at Goodison, determined to get their revenge for the 5-0 drubbing at Anfield. The game was a tepid goalless affair, both teams accused of having other priorities with Everton due to face Manchester City at Maine Road in the FA Cup seven days later, while Liverpool were still in the European Cup Winners' Cup and with a healthy advantage at the top of the table were content for a point. Most importantly, both teams wanted to avoid injuries. Just before the half-hour mark, Fred Pickering took a pass from Brian Labone, then according to the forward, 'As I turned quickly to try and shake off Ron Yeats my leg went from underneath me.' The prognosis was a damaged muscle to the left knee, keeping the player out of the Manchester City game. Apart from Pickering, the other group to look back at the game with regret were the spectators perched atop of St Luke's Church, who were arrested on their return to ground level.

Before the cup trip, Catterick received a further blow when Jimmy Gabriel was declared unfit following a training injury. The home team were still in the second division but in the early days of their stunning revival under Everton legend Joe Mercer. Already in their line-up were some of the players that would take them to the title two years later – Glyn Pardoe, Alan Oakes, Mike Summerbee, Neil Young and Mike Doyle. In addition there was the former Everton defender George Heslop and Dave Connor, a player who would have some interesting encounters with Everton both on and off the pitch in the rest of the decade. Nevertheless, on Grand National day they were firm outsiders.

A crowd of more than 63,000 gathered at a damp Moss Side for the quarter-final tie, in the first sell-out at Maine Road for eleven years. An untidy, bruising contest produced a dull stalemate, with the home team's tactics the main cause.

'Nothing could dampen the enthusiasm at Maine Road – not even City's play, which was as dour and depressing as the day,' said Tony Pawson in the *Observer*. The home team created just one clear-cut opportunity before the visitors staged a late rally, laying siege to the City goal. Young, Morrissey and Harris all wasted good chances as the game ended goalless. It was a typical cup-tie, with City aiming to unsettle their more experienced opponents with some robust tackling. 'These lads are a bit rough,' said Labone after the game, in a masterpiece of understatement.

Three days later, the two sides reconvened at Goodison. The game was similarly hard-fought but far more even than the battle in Manchester. With a clearly unfit Pickering back in the side, the visitors more than held their own. Heslop was outstanding but the real star was Summerbee, whose hard running and powerful shooting were a foretaste of the style that would make him one of the club's greatest ever players. There was a further 120 minutes of goalless action, with chances at both ends, but the biggest opportunity was self-inflicted by the home side, when Labone's over-hit back-pass was skilfully palmed away by West from underneath the bar. There was only partial mitigation for the home team in the fact that Everton had not conceded a goal for more than eight hours in the competition – a new FA Cup record.

City were far more adventurous in the third game, at the neutral Molineux, on the following Monday. The underdogs created three good chances in the opening half-hour and saw a shot strike the crossbar. Against the run of the play, Catterick's side opened the scoring, with the first goal of the tie after more than four hours playing time. It came from a familiar combination – Scott's free-kick met with a fine volley from Temple. On half-time Everton made the game safe, Pickering joining the winger in scoring in every round by shooting home fiercely off the underside of the bar after Harris had put the striker through. The hard-earned victory set up a semi-final at Burnden Park against champions Manchester United.

Manchester United, semi-final

The biggest test on the road to Wembley was the semi-final against the Old Trafford side. Seven days before there had been a controversial diversion, Catterick fielding what was essentially a reserve team in a televised 4-1 defeat at Elland Road. Despite supplying extensive medical evidence in support of his decision, a Football League commission fined Everton a record £2,000, double the previous largest amount. The decision produced a storm of controversy, club officials understandably complaining there was little point in employing expensively paid medical professionals if governing bodies rejected their opinion.

The team stayed in Burnley before the big encounter against Matt Busby's side, the first semi-final at Burnden Park since the fateful game between Stoke City and Derby County in 1946 when overcrowding killed 33 people. The big doubt concerned Fred Pickering and when the forward was declared unfit, Mike Trebilcock – with two goals in his five club games – stepped into the side. Catterick's team had a number of advantages going into the semi-final. First of all Everton won the toss to wear their first-choice blue shirts and Catterick was also relieved to see George Best, now the best player in the country, sit out the game through injury. Furthermore, three days before United suffered a physical and psychological blow when they went out of the European Cup after a draining second-leg in Yugoslavia against Partizan Belgrade.

A crowd of 60,000 witnessed a typical semi-final. Compared to their opponents, Everton were understandably sharper and fresher. With Gabriel shackling Bobby Charlton and Denis Law struggling to get into the game, only Nobby Styles showed anything like his best form for the Mancunians. In a curious way, initially the game resembled the encounter between the two teams at the same stage 43 years later, Everton being overcautious when in a position to press home the advantage against a weakened team. On this occasion though, Catterick's tactics worked to perfection. Sensing that his opponents would tire out on a muddy pitch – one that deteriorated quickly following the ludicrous decision to allow a marching band on before the game – the Everton manager kept it tight with a view to striking late. The semi-final played out in exactly that fashion.

Following a conservative opening period, which featured a crucial save by West from John Connelly, in the second half the underdogs grew into the game as United 'faltered like a car running out of petrol' according to Hugh McIlvanney in the *Observer*. Everton got the rewards their diligence deserved with the crucial goal twelve minutes from time. Temple left Bill Foulkes behind following a Young back-header and Colin Harvey turned home his pass inside from twelve yards out. United collapsed after the goal, Young striking the post and Gregg saved superbly from Trebilcock. Although the league champions staged a late rally, Everton dug in for a well-deserved victory and their first cup final appearance for 33 years. Their opponents were Sheffield Wednesday, who had spoilt the romantics' dreams of a Chelsea-United final by defeating the London club 2-0 at Villa Park.

There were scenes of uncontrolled joy in the Everton dressing room after the game as the champagne flowed freely. 'I am sure the players hardly knew whether to laugh or cry,' said Horace Yates in the *Liverpool Daily Post*. Catterick was a delighted and proud manager at the end, giving full credit to his side. 'They were magnificent to a man,' he proclaimed, 'I was delighted with the way they played the game. It went exactly the way we had planned. We realised they were a strong attacking side and it was our plan to get them coming at us into forward positions and then strike from defence. Harvey took his goal brilliantly.' The goalscorer himself said, 'When I hit the ball I knew it was going in and yet I hardly dared look.'

Sheffield Wednesday, FA Cup final

For the club's first appearance at Wembley since 1933, the manager named a 14-man squad before the game. There were two places up for grabs. At right-back it was a choice between Sandy Brown and Tommy Wright, with the manager admitting beforehand, 'I have an open mind on that. Brown has been playing well recently.' His other problem was the same as the semi-final – the fitness of Fred Pickering. Seven days before the game, Catterick did not inspire confidence in the selection of his most expensive player. 'Fred has had three league games since missing the Cup semi-final,' he said, 'There has been no reaction from his injury but I feel he is not playing with the confidence he was showing in his play before being injured.' The conjecture around the selection for these two places dominated the week before the game. Twenty-four hours before the big kick-off the *Daily Mirror* reported Pickering would be in the starting line-up. Catterick though had other ideas as the former Blackburn striker later admitted, 'After training on the Friday morning Mike Trebilcock, Sandy Brown, Tommy Wright and I were called in to see the manager. Mr Catterick told us that only two of the four could play and the two left out would be terribly disappointed. Then he announced his decision and said that he preferred Tommy and Mike. I was very upset.' In truth, as Pickering later freely admitted, the forward was not fit in any case.

Catterick told Leslie Edwards of the *Liverpool Echo* before the game that 'these decisions were the most difficult I have had to make in my fifteen years of management. Both Pickering and Brown are excellent club men and I have had a particularly difficult duty to inform them of these decisions.' Catterick later explained the rationale behind his choice, 'Pickering was recovering from a knee injury and my problem was whether he would do justice to a Cup final.

He appeared to have enough fitness in training, but in view of the playing conditions I chose Mike Trebilcock.' If Catterick had shown one thing during the campaign, it was the courage of his convictions, reflected in his old ally Eric Todd's tribute to him before the game, in the *Guardian*:

It does not seem so long ago that disgruntled supporters were demanding the head of Mr H. Catterick, of Everton. Some of them expressed their opinion by assaulting him physically. In spite of all of this – or maybe because of it – Mr Catterick defied all outside hostility, ignored any inside, real or imagined, and trod his chosen path. He made whatever adjustments he thought necessary and he brought his team to Wembley. How better could his critics have been answered?

A glance at the TV schedule for the day is a reminder of the time when the FA Cup final was the most important sporting day in the national calendar. On BBC, at 11:15 am, the great David Coleman 'talks to Bobby Moore, England's captain'. Then the regular features: 'meet the fans', 'how the finalists reached Wembley' and the obligatory 'meet the finalists'. Wednesday were dangerous opponents, having won all five games on the road to the final at the first time of asking, scoring eleven goals and conceding five. As well as Chelsea, they had also beaten first division Newcastle and Blackburn away from home.

Catterick's critics were sharpening their knives after an hour of the game; such was Wednesday's superiority and the disappointing showing of the favourites that the cup was surely heading for south Yorkshire. Nothing went right for Catterick's team from the fifth minute when Peter Eustace's throw caught the Everton defence asleep and Wilson deflected Jim McCalliog's shot past West. It was the first goal conceded by Everton in the competition in more than eleven hours' play. Alex Young then had a goal disallowed when he anticipated Gabriel's header but referee Jack Taylor gave offside, a decision that more than fifty years later suspiciously looks the wrong call. The future 1974 World Cup final referee incurred the wrath of Everton supporters even further in not awarding a penalty when goalkeeper Ron Springett appeared to sweep Young's feet from under him. A goal down, Catterick tried to rally the team at half-time, as he later admitted:

I have never known a dressing room so quiet. The players were slumped on the benches – they couldn't believe what had happened to them. I remember saying, 'I'm looking round this dressing room and I can't see many people who are going to be coming back here. This must be your last chance of winning a cup winners medal at Wembley. What are you going to do about it? Go out there and roll your sleeves up. I'm not asking for more ability, you've got that. I'm just asking for a bit more determination.'

The manager's attempts at inspiring his team appeared to be in vain. After the break, Springett saved from Young and on 57 minutes came the killer blow – or so it seemed. After Johnny Fantham pounced on West's poor throw out to Alex Young, the Wednesday player slalomed through the Everton ranks, and when West fumbled his shot, David Ford pounced to finish. 'That should about clinch it, it's Wednesday's cup,' said commentator Kenneth Wolstenholme on the BBC. Only once – in the famous Matthews final of 1953 – had a team come from two goals down at Wembley to lift the trophy.

Yet the two-goal cushion lasted just ninety seconds. From a free-kick, Young nodded down for Mike Trebilcock to fire home. Everton smelt blood. The 4-2-4 formation that had hamstrung the team all season had left big gaps in midfield and left no support for the forwards. But with Gabriel driving forward and Wilson playing a more advanced role, the pressure was now on Wednesday. Six minutes later Everton equalised, as Trebilcock later recalled:

We started to play then and we got a free-kick on the right hand side when Alex Scott was fouled...the big boys went to the far post and told me to get out the way. Sam Ellis was marking Brian Labone and I stood on the edge of the box, thinking that when they challenged for the cross I'd sprint towards the penalty spot and if it comes it comes. It came...it was right in my stride and it was the most beautiful half volley I've ever hit in my life. I kept my head down and just tried to hit the target.

Now level, one of the greatest moments in Everton history duly arrived after 73 minutes. Wednesday's Gerry Young allowed the ball to slip under his foot on the half-way line, leaving Temple a clear route to goal – a situation that rarely happens in Wembley finals. The local-born star ran through and finished brilliantly, as you would expect from a top-class player, although as he later admitted, 'Forwards will tell you that's the worst situation to be in – left with a clear run on goal – because everybody expects you to score. If I had missed I wouldn't have been able to show my face on Merseyside.' With Wednesday floundering at the back, Trebilcock should have completed a hat-trick but hesitated when set up by Young and, although the Yorkshire side rallied, Everton remained in control as they won the most treasured of domestic trophies – at the time anyway – for the third occasion. Geoffrey Green in *The Times* summed up the day perfectly, 'Here was a match were there was no loser and where the game of football itself was the winner.'

After one of the greatest Wembley finals, players and officials celebrated in the evening at the official banquet with special guests from the last cup final victory in 1933. Dixie Dean was there and he paid tribute to the goalscorers. 'All three of them were brilliantly taken,' the great man said. Also in attendance was the referee, who later admitted that the Everton manager was still unhappy over his display. 'In those days the officials attended the winning club's banquet and that night Harry Catterick was still maintaining I had made a mistake. If Everton hadn't won perhaps there would have been even more made of it,' Taylor later said.

For two players the celebrations were not the first time they had touched alcohol on that weekend. At their hotel on the night before the Sunderland game in January, Brian Harris and Jimmy Gabriel cracked open two bottles of wine to wind down. Everton strolled to a 3-0 win and Harris later recalled:

I know it's against the ethics of fitness and athleticism, but footballers are quite superstitious. We both slept like a log and ended up repeating the ritual before every round. The night before Wembley, we sat in our room again and Gabby said: 'I'm not drinking that wine, tomorrow is the biggest day of my life.' I decided to stick with the old routine, he soon cracked and followed suit and the next day when we were 2-0 down he turned to me and shouted 'F--- that Beaujolais'. I said 'Come on, we can battle back' and the rest is cup history.

Catterick would undoubtedly have disapproved of such behaviour. However, the triumph vindicated his key decisions made during the campaign including the return to tried and trusted players after the Blackpool game in January. Before his testimonial at Goodison in 1978, he made it clear where it ranked amongst his many achievements. 'That was my greatest moment. The cup hadn't been to Everton for many years and it was wonderful to bring it back to Merseyside and receive the acclaim of the crowds as we returned to the city.'

13.
Completing the Trinity

THE SUMMER OF 1966 WAS ALL ABOUT ENGLAND AND THE WINNING of the World Cup. But at Everton, major changes were taking place off the field, with Bellefield officially opened on the day after the opening game of the tournament. The club had used the grounds in West Derby for training since 1946 and previously played junior games at the venue. In 1964, Everton made the decision to buy the land for £25,000 in order to make it their permanent training base. The club demolished the existing buildings to put up a completely new complex. Catterick claimed credit for the design, as he told Dudley Doust in an enlightening interview in the *Sunday Times* in 1970. 'I drew up the plans,' he told the American journalist at the venue, and as an example he pointed towards to the fieldhouse, 'the architects didn't want to put in those big ventilation gaps. I told them to follow my sketches.' To Everton's credit there were regular visits from other clubs to the facility, including Manchester United, and Matt Busby was sufficiently impressed to copy the indoor complex at The Cliff. The Anfield hierarchy (minus Bill Shankly) also came in 1968.

Catterick's relatively small office in the corner of the property allowed him a full view of the training arena. In the room was a desk with the plan of a pitch on the top, which remained there for many years after. Players ventured in at their peril. 'You always seemed to be looking at the Cat with the sun in your eyes … the blinds were open and the sun was in your eyes and you were immediately off guard,' said Joe Royle many years later.

On the pitch, Liverpool exposed their deficiencies, masked by the cup final victory, in the Charity Shield game at Goodison in August 1966. Shankly's side overran the home team, having 22 attempts on goal to Everton's five, with thirteen on target against the cup holder's paltry one. Luckily the score did not reflect the humiliation – the visitors netting only once through a Roger Hunt strike on nine minutes. With their close rivals clearly operating on a different level, it was clear the team required an injection of new blood. However, in a shrinking marketplace, even for a club of Everton's stature and wealth it was proving difficult to add to the squad. Before the start of the 1966/67 season, chairman Holland Hughes reflected on the club's transfer strategy. 'We have the resources available, but if we move into the market it will be for someone better than a man we have in a particular position we want to strengthen,' he said, before adding 'we cannot see anyone at the moment to meet that requirement.' However, they had someone in their sights, a World Cup winner plying his trade on the Fylde coast.

Moving the Ball around

Alan Ball was born was Farnworth, Bolton just four days after VE Day in May 1945. The history books document his early struggles in establishing a foothold in the game, as well as a fiery, competitive nature. The rise to the top was difficult; including a first sending-off aged twelve for abusing his teacher who was also the referee. The youngster was then taken off after ten minutes of a Lancashire Schools trial as the coaches thought he was too small. Despite his temperament and size, under the tutelage of his father, Alan Ball senior, the youngster excelled in his early years. Ball senior was a typical demanding father, who thought nothing of teaching his son heading by throwing the ball so often at him that blood ran down his cheeks.

Despite those problems, Ball joined Wolves as a junior in his teens. The Molineux club rejected a permanent deal because of his size, as did his hometown side – whose manager Bill Ridding sent the youngster away with the advice, 'The only apprenticeship you'll get, lad, is as an apprentice jockey.' Nevertheless, Blackpool took him on the ground staff in 1961 and such was his progress in a moderate side that by 1965 he was an England international. His reaction to Alf Ramsey notifying him of his debut in Yugoslavia tells you everything of the self-confidence that flowed freely through his veins. The England manager asked him if he was ready. 'Too f------ right I am' was the reply.

By that time, Ball was on the radar of most of the top clubs in the country, especially as Blackpool were struggling. Catterick was certainly interested, Tony

Kay having alerted him to the embryonic talents of the future Everton legend two years earlier, as the manager later recalled, 'We were playing at Blackpool, and Kay was left-hand side midfield, opposite Ball, then very young. Both carrot-head and they had a ding-dong battle. Tony said "I've clobbered him a couple of times, but the little so-and-so keeps coming back – and he can play."' Roy Vernon featured in the game, a poor 1-1 draw, and the Welshman also paid tribute to the young Blackpool player in his weekly newspaper column, 'I would like to give a pat on the back to Blackpool's young forward Ball. He is a lad of ability and great courage.' The youngster would show more than bravery at Goodison later in the decade.

The press had linked the Everton manager with the flame-haired midfield dynamo since the beginning of 1965, but Catterick showed little interest. Asked in the summer of that year whether the signing was a possibility to improve his forward ranks, the Everton manager was clear, 'He's a good player, but he plays a similar role to Colin Harvey. I don't see him as a striker at all. I would prefer a man who scores goals. There would be no point in paying all that money for a man and then have to change his style.' During the following season the speculation continued, and at one stage news leaked out that Blackpool were open to offers for a swap involving cash plus Jimmy Gabriel in exchange for their prize asset. When asked about the speculation, Catterick gave his default reply, 'All this business is news to me.' The 20-year-old however was adamant that he was leaving Bloomfield Road. Interviewed in February 1966 Ball indicated his future lay elsewhere, admitting to the press, 'I want to get into a winning team and to become a better player.' Rumours of a move to Chelsea floundered when Tommy Docherty declined to bid.

Nevertheless, one manager above anyone else prized the rising star. Leeds boss Don Revie had been watching the midfielder since he was a teenager in Blackpool reserves. After the Fylde club turned down a £60,000 bid from Leeds in August 1965, how Revie cultivated Ball's interest complements the betting scandal of earlier in the decade in portraying the seedier side of the English game in the 1960s. It was a tale of strange phone calls, bags of cash, secret meetings on bleak moors and ultimately leading to FA charges thirteen years after the fact. The saga commenced when an anonymous go-between started calling the Blackpool player at home, maintaining that Revie still wanted him at Leeds to join Bremner and Giles in a midfield that would make the Yorkshire side the best in Europe. The caller told Ball to meet Revie on desolate moorland above Saddleworth.

The midfielder did so, and according to Richard Stott's celebrated 1977 *Daily Mirror* exposé of Revie's unscrupulous methods, the Leeds manager paid him £100 as a 'retainer', something he repeated on their subsequent meetings at the same place. Ball also covered the tale in his 1978 autobiography. To add further confusion to the plot, the England international later changed his story, the World Cup winner admitting, 'I was aware of his interest. Don Revie himself never ever gave me money, ever. There was always somebody else who did. There would be a knock on my door and invariably it will be a man, in rain or sunshine. He would say "an investment for Mr Ball", which I took.'

'I was a World Cup winner, but I was still only a boy'

While this was going (or not going) on, Catterick was watching from afar. To draw Leeds out, he put an implausibly low bid to Blackpool, telling the Tangerines' manager, Ron Suart, 'Don't let anyone know, but this bid is not our final word. I shall want a second chance at Ball.' The Everton boss was convinced Leeds would not raise their £100,000 offer. Catterick then got word – probably from Suart – that the Yorkshire club had set their limit at £105,000 and with Leeds prevaricating – 'Give me time, Alan,' Revie would continually tell the Blackpool player – Everton lodged a bid of £110,000, a record fee for a transfer between British clubs. Over two-and-a-half hours of telephone negotiations, Leeds matched Catterick's fee but with Everton in first Blackpool accepted their offer.

Ball was having coffee in the town centre when his chairman told him to return to Bloomfield Road, where he met Catterick and Holland Hughes for the first time. Catterick told Ball, 'You've got to sign before six o'clock, because that's the deadline for the Cup Winners' Cup. There can't be any days to consider it. If you don't sign by six, then it's all off.' It was a shrewd tactic by the Everton manager, forcing the club and Ball into a corner. The England star spent the next two hours talking to his father, before declaring that he was happy to move, convinced by Alan Ball senior's words, 'I would advise you to go to Everton. It's the type of club for you. It's almost on the doorstep and they don't suffer fools.' Ball's father was correct, as his son was soon to find out. 'Ron Suart had been a lovely man; Catterick ruled by fear,' Ball later admitted, 'The smiling man who signed me for Everton turned out to be the toughest boss of all. The dressing room was tough and the manager was a fearful dictator.' Even for a man of Catterick's standing in the game, the signing of Ball broke new ground. 'This is our biggest transfer since I have been in the manager's chair,' he told the waiting press after his first visit to Bloomfield Road since the regrettable incident with supporters seven months before. One fan calculated that at 9 stone 10 pounds, Ball was worth £50 an ounce, or four times the price of gold.

Ball later spoke in deferential terms of moving to Everton. 'I walked into the dressing room and saw so many great players – Alex Young, Fred Pickering, Brian Labone, Ray Wilson, Alex Scott,' he later said. 'It was awe-inspiring to me because I'd been brought up by my father to respect great players. I was a World Cup winner, but I was still only a boy. These were great players in my eyes – and I was amongst them.' Although they later fell out with dramatic effect, Ball was initially attracted to his new manager's ambition. 'Harry Catterick was the most like me,' the ginger-haired maestro told the *Guardian* in 1977 when asked about his managers. 'He was an out-and-out winner; he wanted to win just that little bit more.'

In 1978 there was a strange sequel to the saga: alerted to Ball's statements in the *Daily Mirror* and his autobiography, the FA fined the England player £3,000 for accepting money as an inducement for moving clubs.[41] Like the recruitment of Alex Scott, it was a classic Catterick transfer coup. The manager later admitted to feeding the press disinformation, sensing they were fishing on behalf of Leeds, as he later recalled:

One newspaperman asked me point blank whether or not we were interested. I felt sure he was asking on behalf of another club, to try to get some ideas of my plans. I told him I found so many faults with Alan Ball it was unbelievable. I think the journalist went back and told whoever was interested that Catterick didn't fancy Ball and so far as Everton were concerned the road was clear. Then I went over the next afternoon and signed him.

While signing Ball was not exactly a gamble, it was comforting for Everton fans that they knew there was a top-class player operating at Goodison, one possessing almost unlimited reserves of strength, stamina and courage. The World Cup winner scored the only goal on debut on the opening day of

[41] Ball's hearing took place on 18 December 1978, in a startling coincidence the case that followed on the same day involved Revie, who was accused of bringing the game into disrepute following his controversial departure from the England manager's post eighteen months before.

the league season at Fulham, just three weeks after the great day at Wembley. Ball then built the foundations for his legendary status on his derby debut at Goodison seven days later. The new signing took just ten minutes to score his first goal on the ground. Morrissey's shot struck a Liverpool defender and deflected towards Ball, who otherwise was standing in an offside position. The England international finished easily. Seven minutes later Ball added a second, taking advantage of uncertainty between Ron Yeats – who endured a nightmare afternoon – and Gordon Milne to crash the ball into the roof of the net. The game degenerated into a kicking match thereafter, a dirty game in a decade of dirty games. Liverpool pulled a goal back just before the break when Tommy Smith fired home after a free-kick had rebounded to him from the Everton wall, but substitute Brown headed a third near the end. Such was the absence of goodwill in a game of more than forty fouls, many players refused to shake hands at the death.

Strangely, although Everton won, like the Charity Shield the visitors held the upper hand in terms of chances – 23 attempts on goal to twelve by the home team. This time Everton carried a new weapon, the new signing the difference between the two fixtures. 'Yesterday was most decidedly Alan Ball's derby,' said the *Daily Express*, 'he won the match with two first half goals and made the champions of Liverpool look like novices.'

Tactical changes

The arrival of Ball allowed Catterick to make the tactical changes to generate the fluid football associated with his side in the second half of the decade. When Ball first played for England, Alf Ramsey had used the youngster as a wide man in a 4-2-4 formation, although the national team manager was keen to use 4-3-3. In his masterful dissection of football tactics, *Inverting the Pyramid*, author Jonathan Wilson said Ball, 'Whose tremendous energy meant he could operate both as a winger and as an auxiliary midfielder,' was the key figure in successfully making that change happen for the national team.

At club level, Catterick found the personnel available to him in the 1965/66 campaign were unable to do both. The Everton manager had tinkered with 4-3-3 and was alive to the possibilities that Ball could do for Everton what he done for his country. The hunch proved correct – the former Blackpool player, with his endless supply of energy, was an ideal player to use in the middle three within the system. Not only that but it allowed Alex Young far greater access, in his preferred role, to the ball in a deeper role in a 4-3-3 system, rather than as a centre-forward in a 4-2-4.

For the first time since Tony Kay's departure, Everton had a player capable of imprinting his personality on the game, no more apparent than in the 3-2 win at West Ham in early October 1966. At Upton Park, Colin Harvey had the best game of his Everton career, but even the homegrown talent had to bow to the virtuosity of the record signing, who did not put a foot wrong all afternoon and in one brilliant piece of skill, the World Cup winner waltzed past five players before seeing his shot cleared off the line. 'Ball stormed through the game as though he was six foot five inches rather than five foot six,' said Maurice Smith in the *People*. Twelve months later, Ball was outstanding in a 4-2 home win over Wolves, drawing this tribute from Horace Yates in the *Liverpool Daily Post*, 'Players of Ball's breed are rare indeed and if he is not the most valuable commodity in football today, it is hard to think of his superior.'

However, there were still teething problems in moving from 4-4-2 to 4-3-3. In the first half of the 1966/67 season, Catterick allowed Ball a roving role, but it was only in the New Year after just three wins in fourteen games that the England man was instructed to play more as a striker. The impact of these changes was a baffling set of shirt numbers – John Hurst wore seven as a central defender in the Anfield derby on New Year's Eve yet Gabriel took the same shirt as a centre-forward against West Brom three weeks later, when Young wore nine as a right-winger and Hurst a number ten, again as a centre-half.

The effect of playing Ball further up the pitch was immediate, the team losing just five times in the last 22 games, as the 1966/67 campaign proved pivotal in the story of Everton during the decade. The arrival of the World Cup winner had galvanised the side, Ball scoring fifteen goals in 41 league games. As David Lacey pointed out in the *Guardian*, 'For a long time Everton seemed a side without a soul. They had a side without a heart. They had wealth and talent, a lot of individual skill but, at times, lacked purpose as a team. But this season, with the arrival of Alan Ball, they have found both heart and soul.' After finishing in mid-table in the cup-winning season, the Toffees rose five places to sixth by the campaign's end. During that time, a man whose contribution to the club remains immeasurable had joined Harvey and Ball in the Everton side.

Kendall takes his marriage vows

Born in Ryton, County Durham in 1946, Howard Kendall joined Preston as an apprentice in 1961. Three years later the skilled midfielder became the then youngest player to appear in an FA Cup final at Wembley, aged 17 years 345 days. Such was his progress that by the middle of the decade, Kendall was one of the most promising players in the country, coveted by many, but not necessarily at Goodison. Indeed as early as May 1966 up to six clubs were linked with the youngster, with Everton a notable omission. Catterick's primary transfer target at the time was actually the outstanding Rangers midfielder John Greig, a player courted via his friendship with the Ibrox boss Scott Symon. When Symon completely ruled out any chance of Greig moving, Catterick turned his attention to the Preston youngster.

However the belief at the end of 1966 was Preston had given Chelsea first refusal on their starlet, with Stamford Bridge manager Tommy Docherty in dispute with their equally promising midfielder John Hollins. When the two patched up their differences Docherty's interest cooled with Liverpool or Spurs now the likely destination. The Anfield club had begun negotiations in October 1966 over the signing of Kendall, offering £75,000, but the deal fell through, with the only assurance Preston providing that they would inform Liverpool when he was available for release. 'We think people in soccer are as good as their word and Preston are among them,' said the Liverpool chairman Sidney Reakes afterwards, whether he thought that was the case five months later is debatable. The future Everton manager then handed two transfer requests in the space of ten days in November, but Preston rejected both.

The time for releasing the midfielder was in the week leading up to Everton's FA Cup clash against Liverpool in March 1967, when the Deepdale club accepted Kendall's third transfer request. Like his closest rivals, for some time Catterick had also told Preston to inform him of any developments, although his interest was not widely known – indeed the likely destination of the young midfielder was still expected to be either Anfield or White Hart Lane. When informed of their intention to sell Kendall on the Thursday before the derby encounter, he moved quickly and brought the youngster to Goodison for a fee of £80,000, a record for a British player under the age of 21, breaking the previous mark of £65,000 paid by Liverpool to Blackpool for Emlyn Hughes just eleven days before. 'Welcome to the big time,' Catterick told his new boy in the car park outside Deepdale. Bill

Shankly had also contacted Preston, and they told the Anfield boss that his £75,000 proposal was not enough. 'Another club had made a bigger offer,' they told him; Shankly had no inkling it was Everton. Keen to raise Liverpool's bid, the manager wanted to speak to the Preston chairman, but the selling club did not return his calls as they concluded the deal.

When Shankly found out the identity of the other club he was livid, and contacted Jimmy Milne, the wily Preston boss, who later recalled, 'Shanks rang me and went right up the wall, "Why didn't you tell me?" he raged. "But you didn't come in, Bill did you?"' Caught out by Catterick, the Scot cut a frustrated figure, curtly saying that 'for nine months we sought to sign Kendall and now he has signed for another club'. Rather than take the matter into his own hands like his opposite number and travel to Deepdale, the Scot's failure to do so had cost Liverpool. Clearly annoyed, Shankly infamously typed out a letter of resignation, which remained unopened in club secretary Peter Robinson's desk.

The next day the Everton boss drily spoke of pinching the player from under the noses of his managerial rival. 'My first inquiry for Kendall was about twelve months ago, and I knew I could trust Preston to keep me informed. I received notification of the figure Preston wanted yesterday and the deal was clinched in the evening. We are delighted to have the boy. I have been keen to do so for a long time, because he has always shown himself a great young prospect from his earliest days in the game.' With expectations that Kendall was going to Anfield, two decades later Jimmy Milne explained why his player went across Stanley Park. 'Harry Catterick at Everton kept on having a go, having a go. When Catterick came in at £80,000, the board said we have to sell. And we did.' As Catterick admitted in the *Liverpool Daily Post* in 1971, Milne was the key figure in the transfer:

He gave me the opportunity of discussing matters with Howard and his parents and they both come from the same part of the world I come from – in the North East – and we had a bit in common. It seemed to me he was keen to join Everton. In fact, this was one of my easiest deals. There was some talk at the time of there being some unwritten agreement between Everton and Liverpool that they would never compete for the same player. I have never known of any such understanding.

The Kendall signing was another classic Catterick transfer assignment, silently staying in the slipstream of the leaders before winning the race with a sprint finish. That result, of course, was possible thanks to the financial muscle of the club, but in this case, it does Catterick a disservice. Whereas Shankly, for example, largely delegated scouting missions to his staff, the Everton manager's quest for new players bordered on the manic and certainly contributed to his subsequent health problems. Several years before the Kendall move, Catterick outlined his scouting strategy. 'I take in three of four other matches every week. In five years I've used five cars at the rate of 60,000 miles a year. It's not enough for me to know that a player is available. I want to know him, particularly away from home. There are a lot of heroes at home.' Catterick admitted to the *Liverpool Echo's* Michael Charters that he had watched Kendall incognito for a long time. 'I have had practically a season ticket for Preston's games in the last twelve months,' he told Charters, 'I went to see Kendall play at every opportunity so that there was never any doubt in my mind when I knew he was available.' The favoured option for scouting was standing on the terraces, as it brought anonymity, Catterick usually disguising himself with a cloth cap, a scarf and glasses, with the collars of his coat pulled up to cover his face. There was another advantage, as he admitted, 'The average fan knows more than most pros credit and they can be a big help. I was once thinking of buying a player when I heard a supporter say, "That's the first good game he's had this season" and I thought again.'

Catterick liked to keep transfers secret – apart from with the selling club of course. The Machiavellian image of the Everton manager as some sort of mystical figure appearing magically, with no warning, to snatch a player from the arms of a competing club – the so-called 'Catterick swoop' – is not correct. BBC Radio Merseyside's Bob Azurdia once asked Catterick about his reputation for secrecy in the transfer market and then suddenly pouncing. The Everton manager replied brusquely, 'This question of swooping isn't really on because I never move quickly. The point is that I negotiate for quite some time. But I always feel that transfer business is essentially between the two clubs until it becomes an established fact and then it's time to release it to the public.' This happened in all of Catterick's big transfer battles during the 1960s to varying degrees – but especially with Ball and Kendall. Yet, although he did not realise it at the time, signing the man who would later succeed him as the most successful manager in Everton history was the last significant purchase in his time at Goodison.

Birth of the Trinity

After Kendall signed, the first outing for the celebrated midfield triumvirate was the 1-0 home defeat to Southampton in March 1967. It was a difficult afternoon for the youngster that raised more questions than answers. 'The arrival of Howard Kendall seems more likely to cause short-terms problems for Everton,' mused Ian Hargraves in the *Liverpool Echo*, who speculated that it would take six months for the midfielder to settle, which proved to be true. Remarkably, there were even doubts amongst his teammates about his ability, as Alan Ball later recalled, 'He was only a kid and he didn't hit it off right away. I can still remember the nudges and winks amongst the rest of us when he made a boob. Someone would be sure to mutter "What a pass. How much did he cost?"' Injured shortly after joining the club, the future Goodison boss spent most of the summer of 1967 training alone to gain fitness.

Elsewhere, Catterick used the remaining fixtures in 1966/67 to experiment. Joe Royle had continued to develop in the reserves and when given a chance to impress, the 18-year-old scored twice at Goodison in a 3-1 home win over Chelsea and three days later the striker scored the only goal of the game in a 1-0 victory at Blackpool, ironically. The side finished strongly, winning four and drawing three of the last eight games. There was a foretaste of the stylish football to come in the final game of the campaign, a 4-1 victory over Sunderland featuring a delightful display of attacking football, including a hat-trick from Johnny Morrissey. 'The Everton future looks bright and I expect the sort of competition we will have at Goodison Park from now on can only make it brighter,' Catterick said optimistically.

But the legend of the Holy Trinity of Ball, Harvey and Kendall really begins on a sunny Saturday afternoon at Goodison in August 1967. The visitors were the league champions, Manchester United, and Everton destroyed the side that would become the European Cup winners nine months later with a brilliant display. The home team submerged United under a flood of relentless pressure for ninety minutes. Kendall and Harvey were magnificent in midfield, their dominance complemented by Ball's industry and forward threat. Everton opened the scoring after thirteen minutes, when Royle, whose strength and maturity belied his lack of experience, met Morrissey's cross and Ball scored from close in. The England international added a second on 65 minutes from a rebound, after Alex Stepney in the United goal turned Harvey's shot against a post. Alex Young was in imperious form, and the Scot added a third, beautifully shimmying past the United defence to fire into the roof of the net at the Park End. The subsequent slow motion film of the goal captured the Scot in all his glory. 'I have no hesitation in suggesting that Everton are on the threshold of real greatness,' claimed Eric Todd in the *Guardian*, 'they may not cross it this season or even next. But cross it they will.'

14.
So Near and Yet so Far

AFTER LIFTING THE FA CUP FOR A THIRD TIME IN 1966, HOPES WERE high that the Toffees could add a fourth with a side very much on the up. The next three years in the competition were a heady mixture of triumph and heroic failure as Catterick's team very nearly did just that after a series of tense and memorable encounters.

1966/67 – lost in the Forest
Wolves (away), fourth round

In defence of the trophy, Everton were drawn against Burnley in the third round. The encounter at Turf Moor was a drab and petulant affair in front of more than 42,000 spectators – 15,000 of whom had travelled from Merseyside. In a match of forty fouls the visitors created only a couple of chances, the best of which fell to Ball in the second half, but the England international saw his shot blocked on the line. Everton won the replay 2-1 thanks to an inspired Alex Young.

The reward for the victors was a trip to second tier Wolverhampton Wanderers, Catterick considering their hosts as the best he had seen at that level for several years, one superior to many in the top-flight. His fears proved well founded at Molineux. The home side boasted first-class attacking talent in wingers Dave Wagstaffe and Terry Wharton, plus Ernie Hunt and Hugh McIlmoyle, and the visitors had Gordon West to thank for surviving the trip and returning to Goodison with a 1-1 draw. Wharton opened the scoring but Everton equalised late on when Ball fell theatrically in the area and scored from the resulting penalty. But it was West that the vast travelling army of Everton supporters had to thank, his diving save from a stinging Hunt volley near the end probably the best of his Everton career.

With a home tie against Liverpool up for grabs, at Goodison the 62,000 crowd – several thousand were locked out – gave West a fantastic reception but it was Jimmy Husband who announced himself in the replay as an Everton player. The home team produced one of their best performances for several years, with Husband, Ball and Young again all outstanding. Young set up the lively young Geordie with a superb 30-yard through ball for the opener before Temple struck a second after 35 minutes. Although the visitors pulled one back before the break, after fifty minutes Ball produced a brilliant pass, releasing Young on the right and when his cross produced chaos in the Wolves defence, Husband nipped in to wrap up the game. Catterick was effusive in his praise of the greenhorn winger after the 3-1 victory, saying, 'He is one of the finest prospects in the British Isles today. The sky is the limit for Jimmy.' Sir Alf Ramsey had earlier shared the same views of the Everton manager. After watching Husband at West Brom in January, the England boss proclaimed that 'the young man will become a great player'. Unfortunately for a number of reasons that was not to happen, but Husband was to provide very good service over several years.

Liverpool (home), fifth round

Howard Kendall had moved to Goodison in the week before the game but the transfer was merely a sideshow to a fifth-round tie that is still the greatest derby occasion outside Wembley. To add spice the seismic encounter pitted the reigning league champions against the cup holders. The interest was staggering and to ensure as many supporters could watch the game as possible, there were eight huge screens placed at Anfield, taking the total audience to 105,000 – 64,500 at Goodison and 40,500 across the Park – to make the attendance the biggest for any domestic game outside of Wembley.

More than 40,000 fans queued for up to 24 hours at Goodison Park – some collapsed with exhaustion – for tickets that sold out in three hours, supporters paying £34,350 in total for the privilege of watching a piece of cup history. The search for the prized possessions produced desperate measures, including famously a Ford Consul car in exchange for a place in the ground. Asked about the game against the local rivals, Catterick quipped, 'At least it will save Bill Shankly and I a lot of time and trouble spying on the other fellows, I think we know a little bit about each other.' Nevertheless, the Everton boss was quietly confident, claiming, 'I believe we can win this game and win at Goodison. We are the more skilful side. We have a wonderful spirit right through the team. Liverpool, as long as I can remember, have always been big and powerful … Everton may be smaller, but they are quicker and I think that this can make its contribution.'

To ensure the best conditions for viewing the screens, the game kicked off at 7 p.m. on the Saturday evening. Kendall was cup-tied and as he watched the game, the future Everton manger was probably relieved. The atmosphere was electric, but the windy conditions, combined with an overwhelming fear of defeat on both sides, turned the game into a niggling, unpleasant contest, with the gales blowing paper and thick smoke around the arena. 'A parody of what a great match should be,' said the legendary Peter Wilson in the *Daily Mirror*. Michael Charters in the *Liverpool Echo* concluded that 'the vast crowd deserved better than this'. Asked what he thought of the game at half-time, one spectator summed up the thoughts of many. 'It's alright, but it will never replace football.'

Everton were clearly the better side, busier in attack with masterful performances by Harvey, Husband and Hurst laying the foundation for a narrow victory, the only goal arriving two minutes into added time at the end of a thunderous but poor-quality opening half. Following Ron Yeats' fluffed clearance, Gordon Milne's[42] back pass from twenty yards out to Tommy Lawrence fell short and, as Jimmy Husband moved in at the edge of the box, the ball appeared to rebound off the Liverpool keeper and shoot towards the bye-line. As the players converged, Alan Ball got there first and the England international fired home from what seemed an impossibly tight angle. Although the visitors staged a second-half rally, Everton kept Liverpool at arm's length and fully deserved their victory, although it did not stop Shankly typically growling that 'it was a travesty of justice'. A triumphant Catterick told the press: 'Once I saw the conditions I realised that good football was virtually impossible. Defensively we played it very tight and of course we have a very good defensive record. It was a good game to win.' The match-winner later recalled his strike. 'The wind had taken it away from the goal, and I just gambled and went after it,' Ball said, 'I smacked the volley from an acute angle right in the other corner. I've never hit a volley as sweetly in my life.' The reward was a trip to the Trent.

42 The second member of the Milne family to have a significant impact on Everton that week, for it was his father Jimmy who sold Howard Kendall to Everton.

Nottingham Forest (away), quarter-final

A big injury blow at Spurs severely dented Everton's hopes of defending the trophy, when Gordon West broke a bone in his hand, the loss damaging as the keeper was enjoying the best season of his career. Reserve keeper Andy Rankin had once been first choice and although the local-born stopper could still put in top-class performances, his glaring weakness was a lack of judgement when coming off his line. Even though Rankin had not developed as expected, Catterick had turned down several approaches from other clubs.

If the clash against Liverpool had shown the worst side of football during the decade, the quarter-final showdown at the City Ground displayed the best. It was arguably the most dramatic game of the Catterick era. Although Fred Pickering had returned from injury, in the merry-go-round of selecting Everton's centre-forward during the season, it was Sandy Brown's turn against Nottingham Forest, a team chasing the domestic double, lying second in the league table and having lost just once in 26 matches. With the cultured Welsh international Terry Hennessy marshalling a strong defence and Henry Newton acting as the midfield lynchpin, Forest's strength was in attack, featuring one-time Everton target, Joe Baker, and Frank Wignall, who had progressed rapidly since leaving Goodison four years before. The main threat came from Ian Storey-Moore, a hugely gifted winger or centre-forward who would have won more than one England cap but for injury. However, the identity of the opposing manager made the tie fascinating: Johnny Carey, who had taken charge four years earlier. The Irishman had reached a settlement with Everton nine months after his dismissal, the matter being settled out of court. Their history therefore added spice to the encounter.

Although a compelling contest in front of more than 47,000, one of the biggest ever gates at the City Ground, the first hour gave no indication of the drama to follow.[43] Everton, playing with fluency and flair, were in almost total command against one of the best teams in the country. By that stage the cup holders were one goal up – coming ten minutes before half-time, when Ball's perfectly weighted ball freed Husband in the inside-left channel and the winger slid the ball under Peter Grummitt in the Forest goal. Just before the goal came one of those unforeseen incidents that unexpectedly change a game. Catterick had told Brian Labone to keep a close eye on Joe Baker and shortly after kick-off

[43] Unlike the Grand National at Aintree, which took place during the game, where Foinavon memorably won at 100-1.

his skipper was guilty of an uncharacteristically heavy challenge on the striker, who was left with an injured thigh. Baker puzzlingly stayed on the pitch until limping off just before Husband's goal, replaced by the probing winger Alan Hinton, with Storey-Moore moving to a central role. The twist of fate would ultimately turn the tie. Midway through the second half, Labone's poor clearance eventually fell to Wignall, Rankin could only parry the former Everton player's strike, and Storey-Moore pounced to equalise. A fit West would probably have saved the shot cleanly.

The goal transformed the game. Within two minutes Forest were ahead. Wignall's pass fell to Storey-Moore and the replacement centre-forward fired past Rankin from the edge of the penalty area. 'We're going to see something sensational in this match!' screamed commentator Kenneth Wolstenholme on *Match of the Day*, his words almost drowned in the cacophony of noise. After twice going close to restoring parity, the visitors equalised ten minutes from time. Brown's shimmy took him clear of Hennessy and when the ball arrived Husband finished coolly with a first-time shot. Two minutes later, Colin Harvey cleared a Wignall effort off the line, before Grummitt saved brilliantly from Morrissey's fearsome drive and then John Hurst's header went into the side netting, fooling those present into believing it was a goal.

With the exhilarated crowd now resigned to a replay at Goodison three days later, there was a sting in the tale in the final minute. Wignall headed down and after Storey-Moore's shot from eight yards out initially hit Hurst, Rankin stopped a second attempt before the Forest player headed a third effort against the underside of the bar. With time appearing to freeze and Rankin prone, the ball bounced down and the Forest man was the first to react and headed the winner in front of the ecstatic home fans at the fourth attempt. The holders went out on their shields, 3-2 in an absolute classic, many of those present maintaining for years after they had witnessed the best ever game on the ground. 'Everton dragged themselves from the field,' wrote David Lacey in the *Guardian*, 'dazed by defeat after they had played so well and realising, for the first time probably, just how Sheffield Wednesday had felt when they saw a 2-0 lead whittled away to nothing at Wembley.' The referee Jimmy Finney also summed up the feelings of everyone present, 'It was a great game to referee … it was a match fit to grace Wembley.' For the vanquished, there was no consolation in playing a part in such a memorable game, as one Everton player admitted afterwards. 'You don't mind losing when you've played badly, but you feel sick, physically sick, when you go out after playing well.'

1967/68 – Wembley woe

Southport (away), third round

After an inconsistent first half of the league season, per the previous three campaigns the FA Cup was the best option of a trophy. At 14/1 Everton were sixth favourites. The third round brought a visit up the coast to Southport, where there were 80,000 ticket applications for the 19,000 capacity Haig Avenue. The championship winner from 1962/63, Billy Bingham, was manager of the third division outfit and they too had profited from Catterick's youth policy, with six first-team players having come through the ranks at Everton.

Ironically, having turned down an opportunity to swell their coffers by moving the tie to Goodison, to improve their chances, Bingham's side then spent the encounter trying to do just that. In a rugged encounter on a poor pitch, the home side had just three shots to their opponents' eighteen and forced not a single corner. The only goal of the game arrived ten minutes from time, Husband broke in the middle and when the ball reached Kendall on the right, his centre found Royle, who rose powerfully to head the ball into the corner of the net. One unhappy man was the mayor of the coastal town, Alderman John Simms Mitchell. 'What spoiled the day was the way in which the referee allowed himself to be addressed by [Alan] Ball on a number of occasions. His performance, allowing for his unquestionable ability, was a disgrace to our national sport.' The statement could perhaps be put down to a bit of sour grapes.

Tranmere Rovers (home), fifth round

The fourth round of the FA Cup took Everton up the north-west coast again, this time to Carlisle. The improvements to the team since Christmas were visible. The opposing sides started the game a division apart but by the end the gap looked far wider. Speedier in thought and execution, the visitors eased to a 2-0 win, but it should have been far more. Jimmy Husband scored the first fortuitously, the goalkeeper failing to hold Harvey's cross-shot and the ball rebounding in off the onrushing Geordie youngster. Royle put the game to bed with a brilliant goal following a surging 40-yard run. Everton created numerous other chances and saw both Morrissey and Husband hit the bar. The reward was a fifth-round tie against Tranmere Rovers, who had shocked first division Coventry City in the fourth round in a replay, 2-0 at Prenton Park.

There was credence to the belief that this could be Everton's year with the news that Tranmere's George Yardley – the country's top-scorer with 27 goals in 37 games – would miss the game with a ruptured kidney. Despite a computer programme forecasting a 9-0 win for the visitors, Everton were hot favourites when the two sides met at Goodison on the second Saturday in March, in front of a crowd of 62,634. Everton were without Colin Harvey and Alan Ball, but there was a further blow to the third division side when forward George Hudson left the pitch after ten minutes. In the end the departure of Tranmere's fourth-round hero made little difference, the home side putting in a professional performance against a side featuring the former Everton players Johnny King, Graham Williams and Dennis Stevens.

Tranmere keeper Jimmy Cumbes was the man-of-the-match as the Rovers goal was under continuous siege – in the opening six minutes Everton went close on five occasions. The goal the Toffees promised came on the half-hour, when Royle headed home from Wright's long cross, the ball spinning wildly after bouncing, a familiar occurrence for county cricketer Cumbes. Just before the break it was effectively game over when Young broke into the Rovers box and stabbed the ball into the middle, where Morrissey reacted first and fired home. Tranmere were not in the game at any stage and only Cumbes' magnificence prevented any further goals.

Leicester City (away), quarter-final

As an offensive force, the team was developing at pace at this time, Ball's work ethic and ingenuity complementing Husband's mobility and clever use of space, while Joe Royle's hours spent on the practice pitch were repaid with more clinical finishing. Everton therefore travelled to Filbert Street for their FA Cup quarter-final tie in confident mood and rewarded their large following in a 43,519 crowd with a terrific display. Composed and dominant for most of the game, the visitors were ahead on 33 minutes when Alan Woollett headed a centre dangerously across his own area towards Ball, whose cross-shot was skilfully turned in by Husband at the edge of the six-yard box. Criminally, having gained control, Catterick's almost ceded the initiative in first-half stoppage time, when Davie Gibson's corner from the left found its way to David Nish, who fired home an equaliser. A year before Everton had failed when tested at Nottingham Forest but twelve months later they were in no mood to do the same.

Quickly re-establishing the ascendancy, the visitors regained the lead midway through the second period with a quite stunning goal. John Hurst (replacing the injured Colin Harvey) moved diagonally towards the inside-right position and Kendall met his reverse cross to the far post with a perfect volley, the ball crashing into the net in front of the packed away end. Leicester were now committed to attack and, with the visitors breaking dangerously, Husband put the tie out of their reach, picking up Tommy Wright's delicious through ball and finishing sweetly past an onrushing Peter Shilton. A year earlier, there was heartbreak for Husband when his two goals were not enough at the City Ground. This year not even an ankle injury could prevent the Geordie leaving the ground with 'a grin as wide as a lad is entitled to wear when he has scored two goals and sent his team into the semi-finals', according to Michael Charters in the *Liverpool Echo*.

Leeds United, semi-final

By the time Everton played Leeds United at Old Trafford in the semi-final, there were fitness doubts over Howard Kendall, Colin Harvey, Jimmy Husband and Tommy Wright, but all were pronounced available. However, John Hurst had contracted jaundice, a condition that brought the pre-match training camp into turmoil, with the risks of infection to other players. For their opponents, Revie's team were now in familiar territory, the climax of the season promising the bounty of silverware. Leeds had just won their first major trophy, following a 1-0 victory over Arsenal at Wembley in the League Cup final. As well as another trip to the twin towers, they still had designs on the league title and the Fairs Cup. The Yorkshire side had lost just nine times in sixty games in all competitions during the season.

Catterick anticipated a dour contest and in front of a crowd paying record receipts outside Wembley of £51,000, that is what the Everton manager and the 63,000 spectators got. It took just three minutes for the trainer to appear for the first time, as the first 25 minutes brought thirteen fouls in a grim, hopeless midfield battle. The makeshift Leeds attack of Paul Madeley and Mick Jones helped the 19-year-old Roger Kenyon step seamlessly in for the missing Hurst while the new signing from Glentoran, Tommy Jackson, coolly replaced Ball as the underdogs started to gain control of an under-par and unfit John Giles and Billy Bremner in the middle of the park. One incident summed up the dour stalemate, after 26 minutes Norman Hunter cruelly scythed down Joe Royle with the ball *ten yards* away. As the watching Hugh McIlvanney said in the *Observer*, 'Anyone foolish enough to imagine that he would be allowed to use his skills to beat an opponent was liable to find himself turning somersaults or waiting for the trainer to establish that he still had two legs.' Only Jimmy Husband from either side showed any imagination or drive and, unlike the game at Leicester, his efforts were largely wasted as teammates failed to respond to the winger's promptings.

The crucial moment of the tie arrived after 42 minutes. Don Revie's persistence with vulnerable goalkeeper Gary Sprake still baffles five decades on. Although talented, the Welshman was prone to horrific and costly errors, especially in the big games – four months before the stopper had famously conceded a ludicrous own goal by throwing the ball into the net at the Kop end at Anfield. Catterick had instructed Joe Royle to pay close attention to Sprake and in the first half the burly striker had twice charged the goalkeeper, the second crucially resulting in a badly damaged right shoulder. Three minutes before the break and unable to use his throwing arm, the Leeds keeper tried to evade the prowling Everton forward and his weak kick went straight to Jimmy Husband on the right. The winger instinctively lobbed the ball back towards the goal and Jack Charlton handled before it crossed the line, although it looked like the backtracking Paul Reaney could have blocked the ball legitimately. With Alan Ball absent, Johnny Morrissey had responsibility for the penalty, having taken only one previously for the club. The winger later recalled the crucial kick:

Bally was our main penalty taker – well he took everything, corners, free-kicks, the lot! – and during our final workout on the Friday morning, the boss, Harry Catterick, asked which one of us was going to take over. None of the other lads were all that keen. So, because I didn't suffer from nerves, I decided to volunteer and during practice that morning I had ten or a dozen spot kicks. Despite the noise I didn't panic. I took about a 12-yard run and side-footed it with my right foot to Sprake's left. He dived the right way but it went just inside the post.

A goal behind, before the break Leeds almost levelled when Terry Cooper followed a brilliant 30-yard run with a powerful shot that thudded against West's crossbar. Revie's side continued to press but their attacks floundered on the Everton defence, as the magnificent Labone looked a class apart from his England rival Jackie Charlton. Earlier in the season, Tommy Jackson had smothered the great Eusébio in a European Cup tie for Glentoran and, in only his second game for the club, the Ulsterman performed a similar role with John Giles. 'He eliminated Giles in midfield, reducing him to a fussy non-entity,' said Geoffrey Green in *The Times*. At the other end Catterick's side continued to threaten with Kendall, Royle and Husband all spurning opportunities to add a second. Leeds looked a tired side as their traditional power game deserted them and Everton hung on for a thoroughly well-deserved victory and a seventh FA Cup final.

The Everton manager was delighted after the match. 'The greatest win in my years of management,' he declared. His skipper added, 'What little football came from Everton. Any clear-cut chances which were made came from us.' That was true. After playing enterprising, attacking football at Leicester in the quarter-final, Everton had shown they could grind out results by playing Leeds at their own game. While Everton were dismantling Revie's side, at Villa Park in the other semi-final West Brom defeated Birmingham City 2-0, ending Fred Pickering's chance to make amends for his heartbreak two years before.

West Brom, FA Cup final

Their opponents at Wembley had already played nine games, against Everton's five, in reaching the final. Liverpool were amongst the Baggies' victims, Alan Ashman's side ruining any aspirations of a first derby FA Cup final in the last eight, with a 2-1 victory in a second replay at Maine Road. Before the final, the focus understandably was on the fact that Everton had completed a league double over the Midlands side; their 6-2 win at the Hawthorns followed a 2-0 victory at Goodison earlier in the campaign. The result at West Brom made Everton the firm favourites for many, including the bookmakers, who had the Toffees at 6-4 on, with their opponents 5-4.

In retrospect too much has been made of the thrashing of West Brom in the March, for the Midlands team were a dangerously unpredictable outfit. During the season Ashman's side had completed a league double over eventual champions Manchester City, stuck six goals at the Hawthorns past title-holders Manchester United and hammered Burnley 8-1. In his *Sunday Times* preview Brian Glanville described them as 'a side of mysterious capacity, baffling resource, a high potential ceiling of performance'.

In the powerful Jeff Astle they also had a striker who had scored in every round, while players like the skilful Bobby Hope and Tony Brown would not have looked out of place in the Everton line-up. The difference was in defence where West Brom were clearly inferior to their opponents, who had conceded just one goal in their five matches. Catterick's side had West and Labone in the form of their lives, with a defensive midfield shield of Kendall and Harvey augmenting the impassable rearguard. Consequently they were favourites, their form since the new year leaving their manager brimming with confidence: 'I thought Everton's team would be too young to win honours this season,' Catterick admitted, 'but around Christmas they began to blend and develop fine team work. I think we can win this final by one goal.' However, a number of observers felt that the more experienced Midlands side, who had skirted with elimination a number of times, had their name engraved on the trophy. They were not wrong.

Catterick fielded a full strength side, with Hurst having recovered spectacularly from his illness. With Albion wearing their 'lucky' all white away strip and Everton donning their classic second kit of amber shirts and blue shorts, ironically the first FA Cup final shown on colour television proved to be a dull, monochrome affair played out on a treacherous pitch, which absorbed both the players' energies and the hopes of a classic encounter. Before the game Catterick said, 'The fact that we won the Cup in 1966 means I personally do not feel the pressure. No doubt some of the team may feel different.' Unfortunately, that was the case as the favourites, with a far superior line-up to the one that lifted the trophy two years before, failed to do themselves justice in a typically nervous finale to the domestic season. Everton were reliant on Ball to provide inspiration and although the England international ran relentlessly, passed incisively, and covered every blade of grass, his teammates failed to offer the same quality. A vicious first half was full of bad tackles and injured players, with the 100,000 spectators (paying record receipts of £110,000) chanting the familiar refrain, 'We want football, we want football.'

Those present in the stadium and a 150 million worldwide TV audience witnessed a bit more action in the second period. Although West Brom displayed greater defensive obduracy than expected, Everton attacked with vigour in the last quarter and should have got their reward just five minutes from time. Johnny Morrissey – one of the better Everton players – arced the ball perfectly to an unmarked Husband standing just outside the six-yard box in the centre of the goal,

Alex Young – known as the Golden Vision to his adoring fans – was key to Harry Catterick's Everton throughout the 1960s, even if the two didn't always see eye to eye. [GETTY]

Harry Catterick joins his players in the Goodison stands after securing his first league title as Everton manager, following a 4-1 win over Fulham on the last day of the 1962/63 season. [MIRRORPIX]

Everton chairman John Moores pours champagne for Roy Vernon in the dressing room following the win over Fulham. The Welshman was the biggest influence on the pitch in Catterick's early years. [ALAMY]

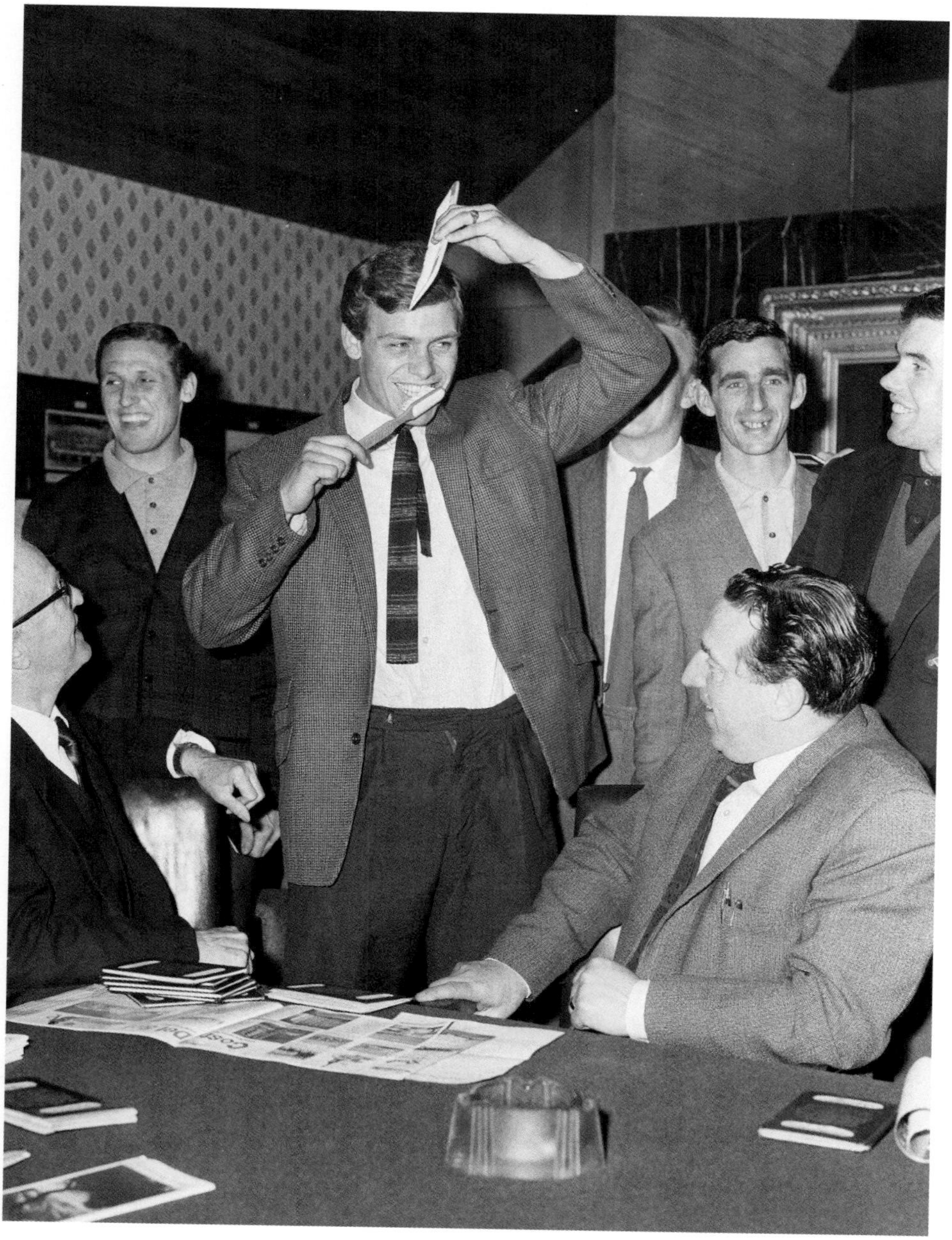

Gordon West may be joking as the players hand their passports to John Moores before an end of season trip to Spain following the title win, but the keeper was a notoriously nervous character in the dressing room. [MIRRORPIX]

Moores and Catterick wander around an empty Goodison Park in the summer of 1963, admiring the new roof on the Bullens Road Stand. Three years later the ground was used for a World Cup semi-final. [ALAMY]

Catterick may have been against the filming of matches, but has no trouble operating the camera ahead of Everton's game with the mighty Inter Milan in the 1963/64 European Cup, a tie they would lose narrowly. [GETTY]

Everton's midfield enforcer Tony Kay arrives at Mansfield Magistrates Court after the *People* newspaper's match-fixing exposé implicated him. Ultimately found guilty, his subsequent lifetime ban was unfair on the player, Catterick and the club. [PA]

In a separate story the *People* also alleged drug taking among members of the Everton squad – pictured here in the paper are Roy Vernon, Alex Parker and Alex Young. The newspaper's allegations, via former goalkeeper Albert Dunlop, proved explosive. [ALAMY]

The Battle of Goodison: captains Brian Labone and Bobby Collins leave the field midway through the game as referee Ken Stokes makes league history by temporarily stopping proceedings during Everton v Leeds, November 1964. [ALAMY]

Colin Harvey fires home the only goal of the game in Everton's FA Cup semi-final win over Manchester United in April 1966. Such was the midfielder's subsequent development that several of the game's key figures rated him the best of the Holy Trinity by the end of the decade. [MIRRORPIX]

Tommy Eggleston and Harry Catterick look on from the bench during the 1966 FA Cup final, accompanied by Fred Pickering and Sandy Brown, who painfully missed out on selection, and reserve keeper Andy Rankin. [COLORSPORT]

Everton fans hoist aloft an Alex Young banner in their half of the ground at Wembley before the final. [ALAMY]

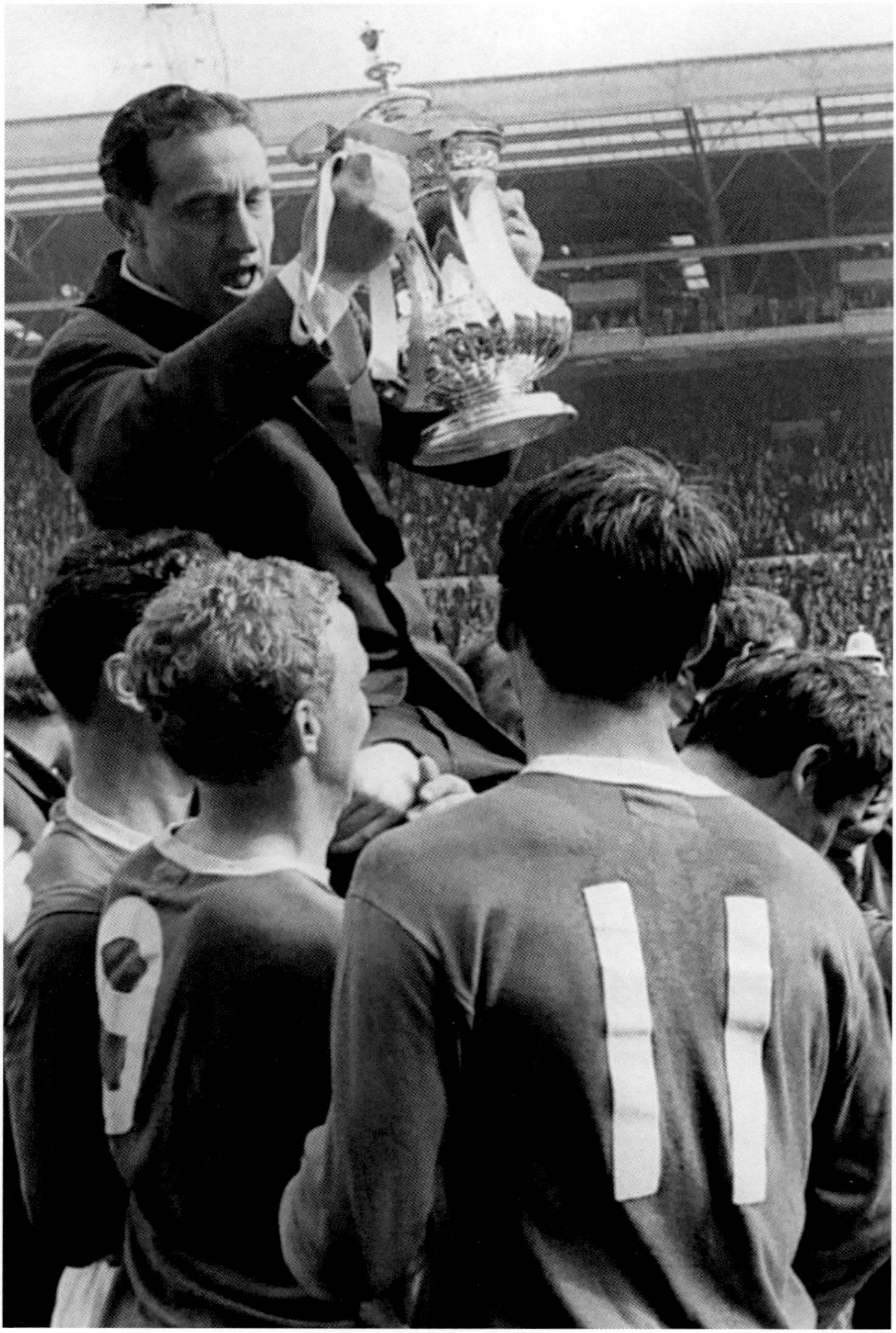

Catterick is hoisted aloft by his players on the Wembley pitch after Everton come from behind to record a 3-2 victory over Sheffield Wednesday to secure their third FA Cup crown. It was a triumphant end to a difficult campaign. [MIRRORPIX]

Mike Trebilcock and Derek Temple, who both scored in the comeback, glug champagne from the trophy in the dressing room following full time. [PA]

Alan Ball, Colin Harvey, Howard Kendall, Joe Royle and Alan Whittle do a lap of honour around Goodison after securing the league title against West Brom in April 1970. [COLORSPORT]

Catterick and his trainer Wilf Dixon emerge from the dugout after the title is secured – it was the second championship triumph in Catterick's reign and his third and last major trophy with the club. [COLORSPORT]

Then club skipper Brian Labone and Alan Ball, teammates for both club and country, toast to success with the trophy between them following the West Brom game. For many, Ball's subsequent ascent to the captaincy unsettled the equilibrium of the team. [GETTY]

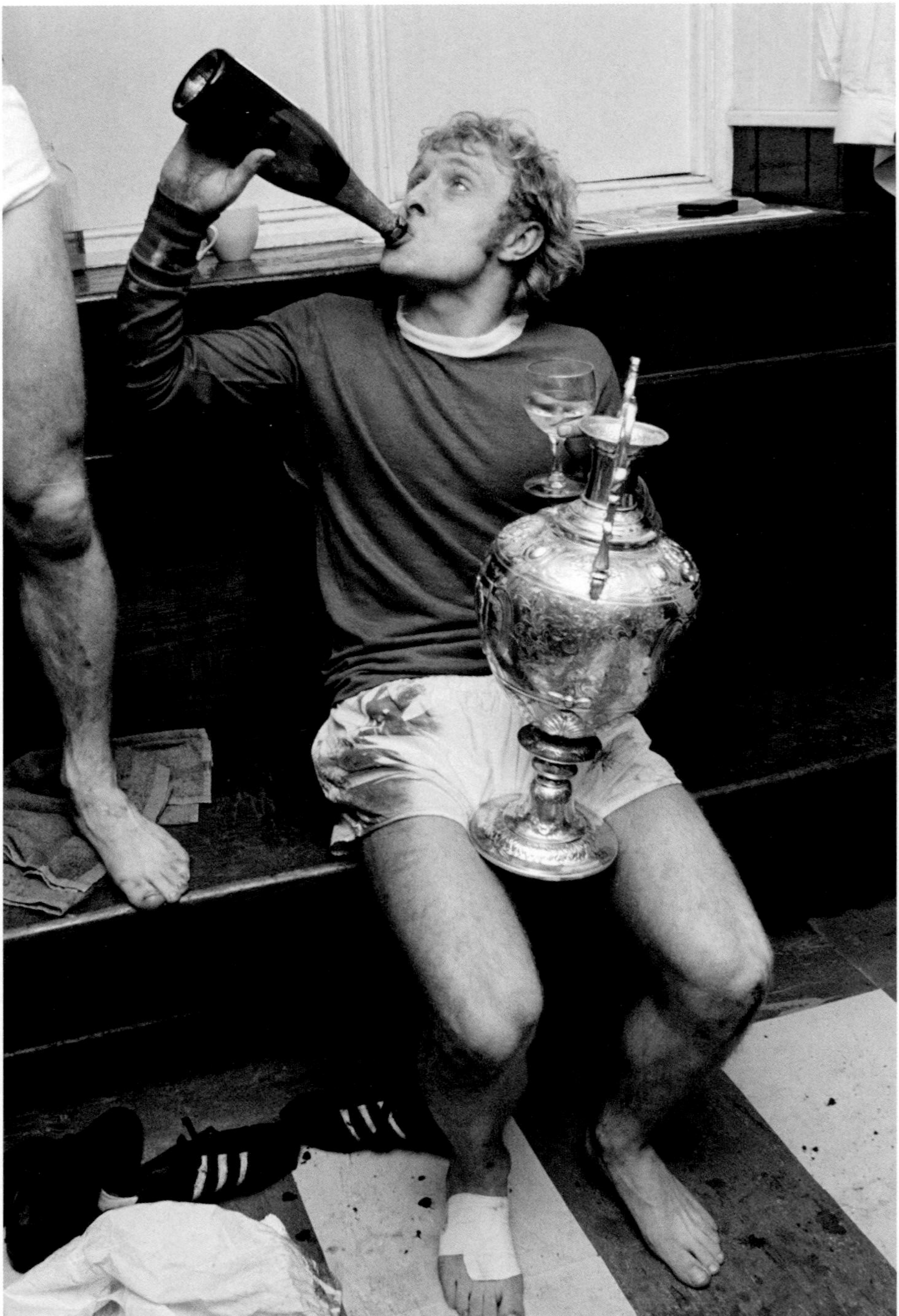

Alan Whittle, so crucial in the run-in, celebrates in slightly less measured fashion in the dressing room. However, like several of his teammates, the striker's form deteriorated in the years that immediately followed. [GETTY]

John Moores was no stranger to the dressing room, and here the chairman joins the Everton squad to celebrate the league title victory in 1963. [PA]

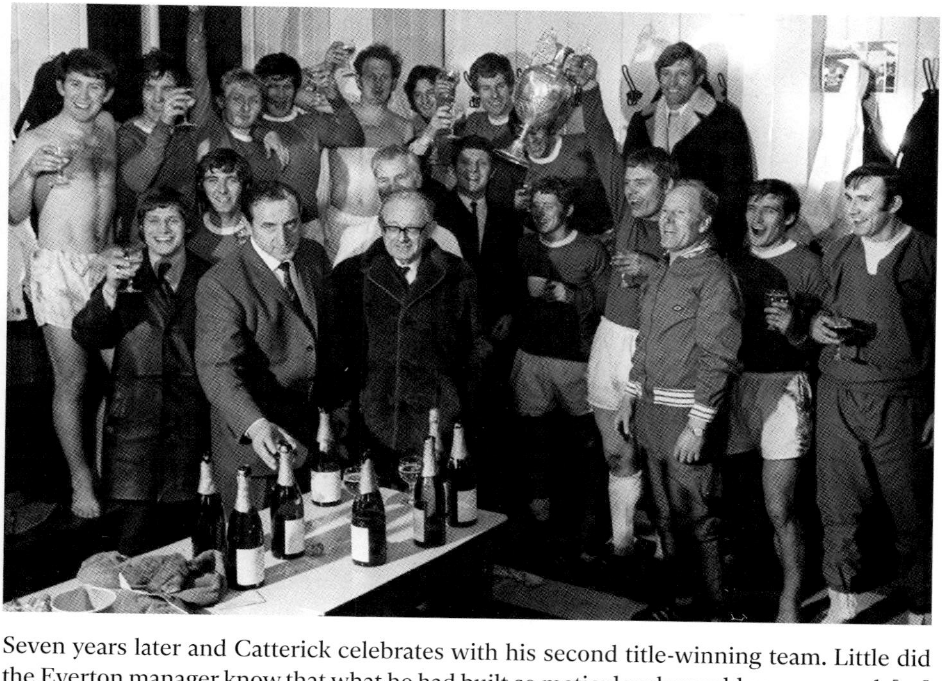

Seven years later and Catterick celebrates with his second title-winning team. Little did the Everton manager know that what he had built so meticulously would soon unravel. [PA]

Takis Ikonomopoulos punches the ball away from his own goal as Panathinaikos frustrate Everton in the first leg of their European Cup quarter-final in March 1971. [PA]

Ferenc Puskás watches on from the sidelines in the second leg as his side progress to the semi-finals at Everton's expense. The brutal tactics of the Greek side was at odds with his reputation as a gloriously gifted player. [OFFSIDE]

Alan Ball celebrates giving his side the lead against Liverpool in the 1971 FA Cup semi-final, but the 2-1 defeat ended a miserable week for Catterick's side as the balance of power on Merseyside shifted towards the red half. [ALAMY]

Ball and Catterick shake hands at Bellefield on the day his shock sale to Arsenal is announced, 22 December 1971. The forced smiles reflect the fact their relationship had deteriorated to a damaging degree. [MIRRORPIX]

Bill Shankly and Harry Catterick, the two managers who defined football on Merseyside during the 1960s, enjoy a chat after retirement at the iconic Adelphi Hotel in Liverpool, October 1975. [ALAMY]

but with Ball standing right behind, the 20-year-old got underneath the ball and headed over. The forward's chance to put his name in the history books had gone. 'It was a lamentable miss,' said the *Observer*'s Hugh McIlvanney. After the game, the Geordie gave his side of events. 'The ball came across perfectly. It could not have been better and I certainly should have scored. Behind me was Alan Ball and as I waited Alan shouted, but in that split second I must have been distracted. Just for the moment I was caught in two minds. I didn't know whether to leave it or go for it and the ball hit me on the top of the head. I got completely underneath it, it was a nightmare.' Interviewed many years later the miss still rankled with Husband. 'It was my mistake. It was the biggest mistake I ever made and I had to do it at Wembley.'

With ninety minutes producing no goals, at the start of extra time there were short odds on the match-up producing the first FA Cup final replay of the Wembley era. With socks rolled down to most players' ankles, as the heavy ground took a toll, the teams had barely begun the exhausting extra period when the underdogs struck an unexpected killer blow. Astle skipped past Kendall's tackle and when his initial weak shot rebounded back off Graham Lovett and then Harvey, the forward swung at the ball with his left foot and this time a perfect strike from fifteen yards out flew above West's left shoulder and into the corner of the net. With defender Hurst now pushed up, Catterick's men strove for an equaliser, but fatigue meant their threat weakened and Everton's best effort was Royle's fine strike that John Osborne in the Albion goal caught at the second attempt. When referee Leo Callaghan blew the whistle for full time, Catterick's attempt to record two FA Cup final wins in three years had failed. Although his side had most of the game's better players and led on goal attempts 23-14, West Brom's robust approach – they committed 32 of the game's 49 fouls – unsettled the rhythm of the favourites. After the game Catterick claimed his team had done well:

I feel that for a young side, these boys played very creditably. They're only failing was their finishing. We had the bulk of the game and the better chances. I think the tension I had feared did show through in the play of one or two of our younger players, but nobody could have tried harder. They will return to Wembley again, all the better for the experience they have gained today.

This continual reference to the youth of the side was a curious feature of his reign after 1966. Catterick's blinkered belief that the team was on a continuous upward curve, with their best days ahead of them, was one of the reasons he failed to rebuild the squad when needed by the end of the decade. His 1968 side was therefore not a greenhorn outfit filled with promising youth players. Wilson and Ball had appeared in the World Cup final and, as well as the England full-back, there were four other survivors from the Sheffield Wednesday game. Although lacking performers at their absolute peak in age terms, Everton were a well-balanced unit with an experienced goalkeeper and defence plus a midfield that may have been relatively young, but still had sufficient big-game expertise. Unfortunately, on the day it proved insufficient.[44]

1968/69 – 'We were just shadows'

Everton's quest for a third Wembley final in four seasons began with a home draw against Ipswich Town at Goodison, and the tie produced a comfortable 2-1 victory, with goals from Joe Royle and John Hurst. (Two weeks later the two teams drew 2-2 on the same ground, referee Maurice Fussey notoriously failing to spot the visitor's Ray Crawford scoring with his arm, a decision so bad it remains in the memory of those who were present.) Royle and Hurst were again on the scoresheet when Coventry City were beaten 2-0 at Goodison in the fourth round. The victory set up a fifth-round tie against Bristol Rovers.

Bristol Rovers (home), fifth round

By the time Everton faced the third division outfit at Goodison, the small squad was showing signs of wear and tear. Although Harvey had returned, Kendall had picked up a season-threatening injury in the 1-0 win at QPR in early February. The favourites for the trophy made hard work of despatching their feisty opponents, with future Liverpool centre-half Larry Lloyd putting in a typically combative display. The only goal of the game in front of a 55,294 crowd came on 33 minutes, when Ball charged down a defensive clearance and fed Royle, who took a couple of steps before unleashing a left-footed shot that went in off the upright. In the second half Everton uncharacteristically lost control of the game and although

[44] The result was obviously too much for one young Everton supporter, who broke into a Watford brewery to ease the pain on the way home. Discovered by police 'lying on the floor...very inebriated,' the fan was fined £10 following a court appearance.

Rovers had only one real attempt that Sandy Brown cleared off the line, the visitors still posed a real threat in an enterprising display.

Manchester United (away), quarter-final

Everton travelled to Old Trafford in the FA Cup on the first day of March as 11/2 favourites for the competition. History favoured Catterick. It was his fourth FA Cup encounter against Manchester United as a manager, and the Everton boss had won all three previous ties – two at Old Trafford with Sheffield Wednesday and the 1966 semi-final. Like three years before, Everton were playing Manchester United immediately following a European Cup match and for Matt Busby, after announcing his retirement two months before, it was a last opportunity to add to his two managerial FA Cup triumphs.

On a bitterly cold afternoon there was an even frostier atmosphere on the pitch – it was a typical cup-tie of the decade, full of fouls and stoppages. Although Nobby Stiles nullified his World Cup winning colleague Alan Ball, Everton were the more organised and resilient team. With Labone yet again an immovable rock at the centre of the Everton defence and the young United centre-half Steve James snuffing out the threat of Royle, a goal seemed a remote possibility. Then twelve minutes from time Morrissey forced John Fitzpatrick to concede a corner and, from the resulting cross, Jimmy Husband flicked on and Royle forced the ball home with his knee, thus keeping up his record of scoring in every round. The game continued to have a flinty edge: George Best's bravery was one of the great man's many qualities but, close to full time, even the Irishman was taking liberties by engaging in a punch-up with Johnny Morrissey after the Everton player had fouled the winger. Having already been booked, it was a miracle that Best remained on the pitch. Despite the expected barrage, Catterick's side held firm for their hard-fought victory and a semi-final showdown with Manchester City at the end of March. The omens were good, Everton had defeated both United and City on their road to glory in 1966.

Manchester City, semi-final

City had enjoyed a fitful campaign, tamely surrendering their title while Turkish side Fenerbahçe had inflicted a shock European Cup defeat at the first hurdle. Although they stood mid-table before the Villa Park clash, the bookmakers made both teams 11/8 to reach the final, even if Everton had completed a league double over Joe Mercer's outfit. The odds reflected that in their famous trio of Colin Bell, Mike Summerbee and Francis Lee, City still had match-winners. Meanwhile, for their third semi-final in four years, with Kendall and Harvey back Catterick could pick a first choice starting line-up for the first time in three months.

Hopes were high that with two good football teams the occasion would be different from the usual mediocre fayre served at this stage of the competition. Those expectations were realised. The anti-football was even worse. Joe Mercer had noted that in both their previous semi-final victories, the Toffees had eschewed their natural attacking style for a more pragmatic, defensive game, forcing their opponents into making mistakes. The former Everton player was keen not to go the same way as Manchester United and Leeds. With Colin Bell and Mike Doyle both playing with injuries, coach Allison deployed Dave Connor in his usual man-marking role on Alan Ball, following the England international around every part of the pitch. City then compressed the play into the middle of the park, denying Catterick's midfield trio the space to weave their magical patterns. With play forced sideways, rather than forwards, the *Sunday Telegraph's* David Miller said it was an afternoon of 'blunt, often artless, football', played in a freezing, biting wind before a 63,025 crowd paying ground record receipts of £38,929.

Nevertheless, for an hour, City were easily the better and more enterprising of the two teams as, not for the first or last time, Catterick's side failed to do themselves justice on the big occasion. Ball, who had not scored for four months, in particular influenced the game only sporadically. Although the presence of Connor offers partial mitigation, the England international was off form, although still clearly remaining his side's biggest threat, as young Tommy Booth competently dominated Joe Royle. Elsewhere, the decision to play Kendall backfired and the future manager of both clubs went off on the hour mark. The introduction of Tommy Jackson at least gave Everton some energy and in their best spell of the game Ball twice went close to opening the scoring.

The crucial moment of the tie came with less than two minutes to go. Bell found Francis Lee and the forward's clever reverse pass set up the onrushing Neil Young in the inside-left position, but West's right shoulder blocked the striker's shot as the ball flew out for a corner. It proved only a temporary respite. Young's kick arced to the left of the Everton goal and Summerbee's neat touch set up Booth six yards out for a deserved winner for the Manchester side. 'Lucky City? Unlucky Everton? Not really,' was Eric Todd's view in the *Guardian*. In truth Everton may have been fortunate to have forced a replay but that was no consolation to the shattered players after the game. 'Don't go in there. They are all upset, terribly upset,' said John Moores to waiting journalists outside the losers' dressing room. A clearly emotional Gordon West sought solace with the victors. 'We never really started, we were just shadows,' admitted a devastated Catterick.

After the game supporters were critical of the manager's plans, seemingly having instructed his players to employ cautious, stifling tactics, at odds with the expansive game successfully used in the league. His skipper defended Catterick. 'We were not told to play a defensive game. It would be ludicrous to play that way in an FA Cup semi-final … we were told by the manager to go out an attack,' said Brian Labone. 'As a result of our loss of form, the players had a subconscious feeling, as the game developed, not to take risks, not to open out and be more adventurous in attack.' With relegation threatened Leicester City winning the other semi-final, it was a big opportunity squandered.

15.
Born in Blue

LOCAL BORN PLAYERS SHOULD BE THE LIFEBLOOD OF ANY CLUB AND during the late 1950s and 1960s Everton were fortunately blessed with a flowering of talent that eventually led to Harry Catterick putting the chequebook back in the drawer. Some players' achievements are woven into the club's history, whilst others whose contribution were just as important have remained in the background.

One such player was full-back Tommy Wright. Joining the club as an apprentice forward, the local-born player replaced the injured Alex Parker during the 1964/65 season, eventually making 374 appearances, all but three at full-back, a club record for the position that was only broken by Leighton Baines in 2017. Wright was very much an athletic modern full-back, accomplished both as a defender and as an attacking threat, providing a stream of crosses for Joe Royle in particular. Wright, with Ray Wilson, formed possibly the club's most accomplished full-back pairing, as well as winning eleven caps for England from 1968-70 when competition for places in the national team was at its peak. Strong – but fair – in the tackle, the defender hardly missed a game until, like others, injuries started to strike after the 1970 title victory and a knee problem ended his Everton career at the age of just 29 in 1973. One of Wright's defensive partners in the first-team is quite simply one the greatest Everton players and Evertonians of all time.

'Every inch a born footballer'

Brian Labone's reputation as chief supporter and ambassador for Everton perhaps overshadows his illustrious playing career as a centre-half of international class and noble leader of Catterick's team. An Evertonian from birth, the former grammar schoolboy joined the club in 1957 and made rapid progress, an early turning point being an encounter with a club legend when he was still in the 'A' team. 'We had some practice matches at Bellefield and I then got the job of marking Dave Hickson at Goodison,' he later recalled. 'I must have done a pretty good job as after that I was in the reserves at seventeen and after about eighteen months I went into the first team.' [45] The *Liverpool Echo* faithfully reported on his debut at Birmingham in March 1958 that 'a feature of his work in the early stages had been his obvious desire to find a colleague with his clearances. There was no question of getting the ball away haphazardly.' Such a scientific manner was not exactly in keeping with the defensive standards of the time, but Labone maintained that style throughout his career. It was no surprise, therefore, that by the time Catterick arrived he was the defensive lynchpin.

International recognition was just a question of time and in early 1962 came an incident that cemented the partnership between Labone and his manager. Selected for duty with England under-23s for a game against Scotland, the defender withdrew from the international squad to join an injury-stricken Everton for a fixture at Arsenal on the same night. Catterick, hugely impressed by the unselfish act, said, 'It is one of the greatest sporting gestures I have known and it is purely voluntary.' Ironically the league game was postponed but to help ensure that the young centre-half's international options were not limited in the future, Catterick brought down the former 6 feet 2 inch former guardsman George Heslop from Newcastle as his reserve. Catterick was impressed with Heslop when he had snuffed out Ian St John at Anfield earlier in the campaign, but the manager was clear that the new signing was nothing more than a back-up for Labone. 'We hope that when Brian is chosen for international matches we are in a position to release him. It embarrasses us that we cannot do so in existing circumstances,' the manager said.

Eight months later, in October 1962, Labone duly became the first Everton player capped by England in a full international during the post-war era, recognition for his startling progress since Catterick had taken the managerial reins. The manager had instructed Labone to lose a stone during the previous close season; consequently, the centre-half became a far more mobile and

[45] The game in question was the traditional curtain raiser to the season, a friendly between the first- and reserve-teams at Goodison. The *Liverpool Echo* confirms Labone's recollections from the August 1957 game. 'Labone was coming out of his duels with Hickson with considerable credit. The former grammar school boy looked every inch a born footballer.'

combative figure. His international debut was one of 26 caps for his country; in truth it should have been more. At under-23 level, the centre-half initially struggled with the 4-2-4 played by England against the three-man defence Everton employed at the time and this delayed his entry to the national side. Labone had certainly impressed a great Evertonian in his time as captain of the young England team. 'This fellow has everything,' said team manager Joe Mercer. At senior level, Labone was certainly a more capable centre-half than others who were capped on a regular basis in the first half of the decade, while later Alf Ramsey understandably preferred the more vocal and domineering Jack Charlton as a more natural partner for Bobby Moore, whose leadership qualities and playing style had more in common with the Everton player. It did not help Labone's prospects that Moore filled his usual role on the left-hand side of the defence.

Labone famously withdrew from the England squad in the summer of 1966 prior to the World Cup to get married, although not from the final selection of 22 players as is sometimes reported. Having not played for his country for three years, Labone was not included in Ramsey's original preliminary 40-man squad (from which he selected the final 22 players) but the manager brought the defender in as a replacement in early May for Chelsea's Marvin Hinton. Shortly afterwards Labone reportedly asked the England manager not to be included in England's Scandinavian tour during June as it clashed with his impending nuptials, effectively removing any outside chance of selection for the final party. Although later cited as an example of Labone's unselfish nature that was not his attitude at the time, which was purely pragmatic. 'I never expected to be picked for the final twenty-two,' he told Brian Glanville about his wedding plans in the *Sunday Times* in 1968, 'and if I'd thought I was going to be, I'd probably have put it back a bit.'

By the time England were world champions, Labone had already lifted a trophy at Wembley, in that year's FA Cup final, having become skipper during the previous campaign, almost by accident. Catterick had made Alex Parker captain in succession to Roy Vernon, an unusual appointment given the Scot's peak years had passed and he had become injury prone. With Parker injured and vice-captain Brian Harris dropped for the visit to Blackpool in October 1964, Catterick required a new leader. In many ways, it was an easy choice. Labone had developed into a centre-half of substance over the previous two years and as a player with blue blood running through his veins, he was a natural. The defender did not see it that way. With typical modesty a few years later, Labone admitted his surprise at the choice. 'There were so many other players in the team who had more experience and who I thought more worthy of succeeding Alex Parker. Perhaps Mr Catterick thought that my more tranquil nature might get the best out of some of our more flamboyant characters.' Labone was correct, although the original appointment of Parker was a strange one, the pair were both placid characters and possibly Catterick hoped that a more responsible skipper would take some of the scrutiny off the team's darker side.

The only crisis of Labone's Everton career had been earlier in the cup-winning campaign. With the defence struggling to adapt to the new 4-2-4 formation, the skipper suffered an uncomfortable evening in a 3-2 home defeat to West Brom, and in a shock move the defender found himself out of the side, for the visit to Chelsea, for the first time since making his debut seven years before. His replacement, George Heslop, fared no better at Stamford Bridge in a 3-1 defeat. Linked with a move for Blackburn's hugely accomplished Mike England, Catterick tossed aside the new formation for the trip to the Hawthorns in the next match and with the team playing with a more familiar back three, Everton returned with a well-deserved 1-1 draw. More importantly, Catterick took Labone to one side in the dressing room before the game to reassure his skipper he regarded the rumours over England as unfounded speculation and, as far as his manager was concerned, the club skipper now had an opportunity to re-establish himself in the Everton team. Labone, typically, responded with his best performance of the season and never looked back.

Having developed into one of the best defenders in the country, in September 1967 Labone rocked the football world by announcing his retirement at the end of his contract, which had eighteen months to run. Although nominally for business reasons, his leaving was primarily due to struggles on the pitch. 'For some time I just didn't think I was doing myself justice,' he later told Brian Glanville, 'I was doing things that were foreign to me, I was doing them like a robot. The pressure had got so much I was getting the ball away from the danger area; I'd always tried to play a bit of football from centre-half. I felt I was playing to about half my form. I thought if it's going to be like this, it's time to say bye-bye.' Not for the first time with a player, releasing the pressure brought immediate benefits, as Labone later confessed: 'It seemed to lift a weight off my shoulders ... I started to play well again. I got back into the England team.' Amongst several fine displays on returning to the national side, one in particular stood out –

a tremendous performance in front of 120,000 at the Bernabéu against Spain in a 2-1 victory in May 1968. 'Brian is starting to make the transition from a very good player to a great player,' observed the now Sir Alf Ramsey in tribute. The centre-half was also runner-up to George Best as 1968 Footballer of the Year.

Ramsey also sent a warning to Labone about retiring prematurely. 'Obviously he has much more football in him than one more year and when he goes, he should remember he will have a long time ahead to spend in business.' Behind the fatherly words, Ramsey was cognisant that Bobby Moore would probably need a new centre-half partner in the Mexico World Cup, with Jackie Charlton ageing, so it was in his own interest to keep the Everton skipper in the game. The England manager therefore continued to court Labone in the months following his surprise announcement. 'I can promise him nothing, any more than any other,' he obliquely said about the Everton player's international prospects, 'but the situation is there for him to create his opportunity.'

Whether Ramsey's words struck a chord with Labone are unknown but having been selected for his country during the interim, in January 1969 the Everton skipper had a change of heart, after confiding in one other leading manager, who told him that he had now become a great player and would regret retiring early. The apparent apathy of his own manager in comparison puzzled Labone, and he did not discuss the issue with Catterick, only publicly announcing his plans to continue after the Everton boss asked him to reconsider his decision. 'Mr Catterick felt that my experience is necessary to the present youthful side,' Labone admitted, before adding tellingly, 'and it would also appear that I may be required for international duty at a later date.' Ramsey and Catterick saw eye-to-eye over virtually nothing, but perhaps the Everton manager had good reason to thank the World Cup winner for keeping his first lieutenant in the game. The England manager was nothing if not bloody-minded though. A week after Labone's announcement, England played Romania at Wembley and in Bobby Moore's absence Ramsey indicated to Catterick that Labone would not only start, but would captain the side. Typically, Ramsey left Labone out the line-up completely, an action that did little to defuse the difficult relationship between the two managers.

Catterick and Labone worked in tandem until his skipper retired in 1972. Labone later paid tribute to his manager, 'He could keep you at arm's length, but at the same time he was a good communicator with his players. He could let his hair down, too. He was a lover of fine wines and fine cigars. He was tough. He didn't hesitate to let you know if he thought you weren't playing well enough. But by the same token he would reward you by inviting you for a game of golf.' The skipper, who sadly died in 2006, also appreciated Catterick's man-management. 'Obviously I liked him because he picked me all the time, but I always found him very straight in all my dealings with him as captain. I very rarely saw him blow his top in the dressing room. He'd perhaps pull an individual to one side, but he'd never belittle you in front of others. And that counts for a lot with players.' Probably the greatest tribute to Brian Labone is that it is hard to imagine him ever giving Catterick that opportunity.

'You haven't a hope'

Derek Temple has two strikes against him in any retrospective view of his Goodison career. The first was the adulation and attention given understandably to contemporaries and fellow forwards Roy Vernon and Alex Young. The second was probably more welcome: his association with the 1966 FA Cup final. Consequently, there is not enough consideration to his undoubted natural ability and achievements over a decade of service. In the early 1960s when top Italian clubs would only poach the elite of British footballers such as Jimmy Greaves and Denis Law, there is no greater tribute to his accomplished talent than the two failed attempts to take Temple to Serie A.

The local-born player's goal ratio of one in every three games at Goodison is noteworthy for somebody who was nominally a winger – a record of 83 goals in 275 games more than adequately compares to Young's 87 goals in 273 appearances, although even the Scot was not an orthodox striker. Additionally, of all the players who appeared for Everton in the old-fashioned line-up that featured five forwards, only Temple was able to play effectively in all those roles. (In 275 games, Temple played 175 as a winger on both flanks, 81 in the two inside-forward roles with the rest as a centre-forward.) This versatility was often counter-productive; if injuries hit one of the forwards then Catterick would usually call on Temple to fill the gap.

After setting a number of scoring records for Liverpool Schoolboys as a centre-forward, Temple joined the ground staff in 1954, the club beating off competition from a host of other sides, amongst them Liverpool, Manchester United and Wolves. Temple failed to develop the upper body strength needed to remain as the main striker after making his first-team debut in 1957. Progress slowed following national service, as he later explained, 'I came out of the army in 1960 but, having been involved in a lesser standard, and playing 7,000 feet above sea level, I had lost my pace. But it was not until the following season I managed to get into the senior side, then when Harry Catterick arrived things took off for me.'

The manager certainly had to thank Temple for relieving some of the pressure placed on him at the start of the 1961/62 campaign. After five defeats in the opening seven games, newly promoted Ipswich arrived at Goodison, on a day when a future Wembley hero enjoyed one of his finest hours in an Everton shirt. Against Alf Ramsey's side, Temple was inspired, opening the scoring after beating three players before firing home from 25 yards, and then adding another before half-time. Temple completed his hat-trick near the end, scoring the final goal from a neat pass from Frank Wignall in a 5-2 win over the eventual league champions. At the end of that season a director of Sampdoria visited Goodison for the Liverpool Senior Cup final to 'assess' Alex Young and Ian St John for the Italian club. As it happened, the official was only interested in Temple, and approached Catterick afterwards over a transfer. The manager ensured a proposed deal (and a £100 a week wage for the player) did not get off the ground – which was the Italians' loss, as with his deceptive change of pace and powerful ball-striking Temple would have been a significant asset to Serie A.

Due to injury, Temple played only five games in the 1962/63 championship-winning season before reaching peak form in late 1963, scoring seven goals in eleven games. Two strikes typified the scope of his talents. There was an astonishing goal in the 4-1 win over Sheffield United at Goodison, Temple cutting through five players from out wide before slipping the ball past the keeper. In the next home game there was a 30-yard howitzer to win a tight encounter against Spurs. The winger was consistently effective, ending the season with fourteen goals in 51 games. Such was Temple's form that there was more interest from Italy. In April (ironically 24 hours before the Tony Kay story broke) the English-based Italian agent and 'fixer' Gigi Peronace visited Goodison to watch Temple again, specifically on behalf of the leading Serie A clubs. Speaking to Catterick, he asked about a deal for the Everton player. 'You haven't a hope,' said the manager. Temple scored another fourteen goals in 1964/65, winning his only senior cap for England in May 1965, creating Terry Paine's winner against Germany in Nuremberg. The forward's best season was twelve months later, when he netted in every round of the FA Cup apart from the semi-final.

Temple's versatility in the 1966/67 campaign resulted in him playing a more central role, allowing Johnny Morrissey to take his place on the left-flank in Catterick's favoured 4-3-3 formation. This key move in personnel helped create an important piece of the jigsaw in the building of the 1970 championship-winning side and with the arrival of Joe Royle now restricting opportunities through the middle, Temple departed for Preston in September 1967, following some typical Catterick double-speak. After Temple initially said he was not interested in a move to Deepdale, Catterick replied ambiguously, 'Fair enough, I don't want to lose you, but you might as well go and have a word.' As Temple admitted later, 'I knew the writing was on the wall and I went to have a word with Jimmy Milne.' It was inevitable that the FA Cup hero would be on his way – for a £33,000 fee, but his Wembley winner was priceless.

'Rocketing his way to stardom'

Long-serving Everton trainer Gordon Watson nominated Colin Harvey as the finest post-war Everton player, and there is an argument to say that there were few, if any, that were better. After signing as an apprentice in 1962 progress was such that his debut quite rightly has gone down in the rich folklore of the club. In September 1963, with Jimmy Gabriel absent for the second leg of the European Cup tie against Inter Milan, Harvey travelled to Italy with the expectation that another youngster, Barrie Rees, would fill the Scotsman's boots. In Italy the rumours abounded that Harvey would make the team and so it proved as he later recalled:

You always remember your first game and to play in the San Siro was unbelievable. I wasn't told I was playing until late in the afternoon. I just went out there thinking not a great deal was expected of me and I would just do my best. It was a great team performance and I really enjoyed the occasion ... afterwards Harry Catterick said 'well done' and if you got that out of him you had played well. Then for the next game I was back in the reserves. That was the way he was.

The newcomer produced a wonderfully composed performance and the biggest tribute is that Catterick likened the experience of playing Inter as a reserve side moving up to play the first-team. For the debutant to prove himself by effectively moving up two levels was indeed something special. However, it took twelve months for the midfielder to become a first-team regular but like many local-born players at any club, in his early days the man famously dubbed the 'White Pele' was a primary target for terrace abuse. This was never more apparent than during a difficult afternoon for the 19-year-old in a 3-2 home defeat by Blackburn at the end of October 1964. The criticism clearly affected Harvey, and Catterick was furious with the supporters afterwards, claiming the barracking had a negative impact on the young midfielder. The Everton manager admitted after the game, 'He was failing to do things which I know he can do with his eyes closed at other times,' before adding, 'when I saw Colin Harvey in the dressing room after he was shattered – absolutely shattered.' After he left Goodison, Catterick's mood hardly improved when he found a fan had scratched 'Drop Harvey' into the bodywork of his car – although such was his status as Everton manager, a policeman offered to repair the damage.

To his great credit, one of Everton's most beloved sons put the difficult days behind him and began to flourish, the midfield craftsman progressing rapidly in a deeper wing-half role. The local-born star was outstanding in the 2-1 home victory over Burnley just ten weeks later, drawing praise from Leslie Edwards in the *Liverpool Echo*, 'Harvey is now a favourite. The way he turned defenders one way and slipped the ball the other and the extremely good judgement of the through passes shows that manager Catterick knows his real potential.' The *Liverpool Daily Post* banner headline was equally effusive: 'Colin Harvey is rocketing his way to stardom.' Harvey continued to progress and was outstanding as Everton lifted the FA Cup in the following campaign, but it was the arrival of Alan Ball that fired his imagination. 'He was unbelievable,' Harvey later admitted, 'he was a ball of fire. Fantastic. It rubbed off on the rest of us and raised everyone's game. You wanted to be as good as him.' Many informed supporters would say that as a technically adroit, box-to-box midfielder with an endless supply of stamina, Harvey was just that by the end of the decade.

During 1968 the midfielder was reaching his absolute peak, having speeded up in all aspects of his play, in both swiftness of thought and in clearly gaining a yard of pace. Catterick was a huge fan at this time,[46] proclaiming 'Harvey is a players' player, whose worth is recognised specifically within the elite circle of professional

46 When Harvey scored a magnificent goal in the 4-0 home win over QPR on his 24th birthday in November 1968, to cap a top-class display, Catterick appeared with a gift of two bottles of sherry in the dressing room afterwards to crack open with his teammates. The Everton manager then toasted the player's health with the comment, 'And here's to your England cap.' One would eventually follow in 1971, but there should have been many more.

men who would go for Harvey above most others in the Everton team.' To back his view, both Don Revie and Joe Mercer felt that Harvey was the best of the vaunted midfield trio. Catterick can also take the credit for the local born player's progress. 'He was a demanding manager,' Harvey later admitted, 'one of the first things he said to me was that it was my job to run from box to box, tackle and create things. He did not expect you to do anything less.'

With such a punishing workload, it was inevitable that injuries would follow. Having hardly missed a game after breaking into the first-team, Harvey sat out the middle of the 1969/70 season with a mysterious eye infection and was then troubled by a long-term hip injury. In December 1972 Harvey was dropped by Everton for the first time, taking a berth on the substitute's bench as the 19-year-old Mick Buckley filled his place in the midfield engine room for the trip to Coventry. The *Liverpool Echo* reflected on his decade in the Everton team, and provided a perfect insight into the qualities of one of the club's greatest servants:

At his best – and he maintained this level year after year – Harvey was the perfect wing half, the ideal midfield player by contemporary standards. Although slightly built, he could win the ball in the tackle with the power and timing of his challenge. He could use it and pass with immense skill and precision. He could dribble, beat men, shoot, score goals and his work-rate was phenomenal. His sharpness on and off the ball was remarkable. To this abundance of footballing talent he added enthusiasm, a competitive spirit and a whole-hearted dedication which forced him, in every match and training session, to give everything he'd got. He does not know how to play any other way.

That was not the end of the road though. Harvey played a further 24 league games in the next two years, but the niggling injuries and the arrival of Martin Dobson prefaced his departure to Sheffield Wednesday in a £70,000 deal in September 1974. That signalled the end of the first half of his Everton career, but the second would be just as successful and action-packed.

'This boy must be given the chance to make the grade now'

Like Colin Harvey, Joe Royle is one of Everton's favourite sons, his association with the club dating back more than 50 years as both a player and FA Cup winning manager. Royle had joined Everton after leaving Quarry Bank High School –

where he became the first high school pupil to represent Liverpool Schools – with Catterick beating Manchester United to his signature.[47] Liverpool and Chelsea had also showed an interest, with the future Everton manager also meeting Bill Shankly. At thirteen stone and at just over six feet in height, the 16-year-old had physical maturity way beyond his years. After playing in the 'B' team during the 1964/65 season, such was his startling physical development that Royle missed out promotion to the 'A' team and went straight to the reserves where, playing in the inside-right position, he had scored five times in fourteen games by January 1966.

By that stage, Catterick was looking for new options in attack and chose one that was completely left-field, selecting Royle for the notorious away game at Blackpool. Catterick told the youngster of his decision on the Friday before the game. In his autobiography, Royle recalled walking into the office to see his manager surprisingly on the telephone. 'I'm just telling your dad that provided there's no worsening of the weather, you will be in the team tomorrow,' the Everton manager said. The press soon got wind of the change, making Royle, at the age of 16 years 282 days, the youngest player at the time to appear in the Everton first-team. Catterick was unusually brash to the waiting journalists. 'This boy is a natural. He can shoot with either foot and is the best header of a ball at the club. His progress has been remarkable. I don't care how he plays tomorrow or even this season. I have complete faith in him having the ability to become a first-class player. This boy must be given the chance to make the grade now.' Wearing the number 8 shirt, Royle had a quiet game. 'I was in a spin going into the match and I remained in a daze throughout our 2-0 defeat on a frozen pitch,' he later said.

Understandably, Royle was placed back in the reserves, making one just one more appearance that season, and four more at the end of the 1966/67 campaign. During the following season, Royle established himself in the team, after Catterick took the youngster out of the firing line following just one goal in the opening seven league matches. Nevertheless, fearing his physical presence was being wasted in the reserves, Catterick recalled the striker as a substitute for the Manchester City game at home in November 1967 and Royle was an ever-present over the next five years. During the next two campaigns, the young striker developed quickly. 'Not so long ago Royle was just another football

[47] Catterick had actually decided to move for Royle after seeing him play for Lancashire Boys against Cheshire Boys in 1964. Roger Kenyon appeared in the same game and did enough for Catterick to pursue the future club skipper.

commoner, just another player. To the purists he seemed a bit slow in his reactions, a bit too raw and lazy-looking,' said Alan Hoby in the *Sunday Express*, 'then came the astonishing advance.'

The credit for Royle's progress was down to his manager, who realised his protégé needed firm direction. 'The reason Joe has improved, has sharpened up, is that he's being made to work harder at the game,' Catterick said. 'Some players like training. Joe likes playing in matches. He needs to be pushed.' Particularly, Catterick ensured that Royle tackled his biggest weakness, shooting, in three extra afternoon sessions per week. The development continued throughout the 1969/70 championship-winning season, the striker showing more consistency in scoring 23 goals. 'He has stepped up his work rate remarkably, and this is showing in his ninety minute performances these days,' said Catterick. Another big fan was the journalist Brian Glanville. 'He has in abundance the qualities of imagination, anticipation and courage so vital if you're going to score goals against the modern, massed defence,' was Glanville's description of Royle in the *Sunday Times*.

Royle scored a further 23 goals in all competitions in 1970/71, despite a dip in form, but began to feel the strain as Alan Ball's deeper role reduced support. Now effectively acting as a lone presence up front, the 22-year-old needed the all-action game of the World Cup winner, the two players having struck up a natural understanding on the pitch. 'I think more than anyone I have a contact with him [Ball], in the game,' Royle said in 1968, 'I can't really pay high enough tribute to Bally, he's easily the best player of his kind in the world.' Fashioned on the training pitch at Bellefield, an example of their footballing empathy came at Elland Road in November 1968. On face value Ball's delivery from the right to the near post looked harmless, but Royle had anticipated the cross perfectly and, having sprinted diagonally at speed from the far side, dived full length to divert the ball past Gary Sprake.

Three years later and the burden of largely becoming the team's sole threat was becoming too much, especially true away from home where the future Toffees boss was isolated and suffered from a lack of protection from tough tackling opponents. By the summer of 1971, the striker had missed only four out of 187 games in three-and-a-half years and the physical burden understandably placed a strain, leading to a loss of form and a chronic back injury within two years.[48]

---

[48] Royle made his 200th Everton appearance at the age of just 22 years 4 months in August 1971, the youngest player to reach that mark.

During this time, the Everton manager periodically had to deny rumours that he was offloading the striker, with Bill Shankly and Brian Clough whispered to be amongst the suitors. In November 1971 Catterick said, 'It has been rumoured for some time Everton would be prepared to sell Royle if the right offer came along. Nothing could be further from the truth. Admittedly, Royle has not been playing in top form, but he has suffered a number of injuries over the last twelve months.' That afternoon the future Everton boss scored four times in the victory over Southampton.

After recovering from his back condition, which laid him off for a year following a starring performance for England against Yugoslavia in October 1972, Royle returned to the team under Billy Bingham, but a series of further injuries hampered his rehabilitation and the striker only fleetingly showed the powerhouse form of the Catterick years. Frequently linked with a move away from Goodison, many believed Royle's departure was perhaps inevitable after the signing of Bob Latchford in February 1974, although several observers and the former Birmingham player himself thought they could play together. Instead it was the striker's physical decline that lead Bingham to believe that the 25-year-old was considered surplus to requirements and he eventually left Goodison for Manchester City in a £200,000 deal in December 1974, his 119 goals (in 276 games) a club post-war record at the time. But like Colin Harvey, Royle would return for more success.

16.
The Real School of Science

THERE IS SOMETHING INTANGIBLE ABOUT DESCRIBING EVERTON AS 'The School of Science'. Although it is the phrase supporters most associate with the club, putting a time and a place to justify the description often proves elusive. But if there was a single period worthy of the depiction then it was the first half of the 1968/69 season when the team undoubtedly played the best and most attractive football of the Catterick era.

This period was part of an upward curve, which lasted the best part of three years after Royle returned to the team in early November 1967. At that stage, the striker was eighteen years of age and the youngest member of a team that, although experienced to a point, was still a work-in-progress. Jimmy Husband and John Hurst were 20, while Howard Kendall was 21 years of age; Alan Ball was aged 22, while Colin Harvey and Tommy Wright had both just turned 23. When Roger Kenyon played against Burnley at the end of December, there were seven homegrown players in the line-up. This was no accident; on arriving Catterick had completely revised the scouting system for young players and then their subsequent development following recruitment. His view was that any youth policy had a five-year cycle – youngsters arrived at fifteen years of age and became first-team players by twenty – and those who broke into the squad in the second half of the decade were a product of this revolution.

Catterick argued that the team was not good enough to sustain a title bid, lacking the maturity that breeds consistency. The other regular outfielders –

Labone, Morrissey, Brown, Young and Wilson – were all in the 27-32 age bracket. Although the average age of the side was around 24-25, the team lacked players at their peak, which at the time was probably around 24-28 years of age. Having just signed a new seven-year deal, Catterick was still optimistic though. 'Our young team is learning all the time to play together as a team. Everton fans can be assured that they have not seen anything like the best of this combination,' he told the press at the end of 1967. The contract award shows both the complete faith of the Everton board in their manager but also the comparative lack of pressure to bring in trophies, compared to today. After all, since his only championship in 1963, both Liverpool and Manchester United had won two titles while Everton, despite being possibly the richest club in the country, had brought in one FA Cup and failed in Europe.

At the same time, Catterick was backing his own judgement in an era of unprecedented domestic competitiveness. Keeping faith with so many players with their best years ahead of them may have been a gamble, but most were already proven performers in the top-flight. By the turn of 1968, it looked like his loyalty was bearing fruit. With West and Labone in peak form at the back and Royle and Husband developing an understanding up front, the team had won six out of their previous nine league games before a 2-0 defeat at Elland Road, when Everton fielded an all-English line-up for the first time in fourteen years. The loss in Yorkshire left Catterick's side seventh in the table, with 28 points from 26 games – but with only three wins in fourteen away matches.

Howard Kendall made his first significant mark in the Everton history books during the Merseyside derby at Goodison two weeks after the loss at Leeds. In a typically hard-fought war of attrition, Kendall scored the only goal against the run of play after 31 minutes. A challenge from goalkeeper Tommy Lawrence forced Jimmy Husband out of the penalty area and the wide-man pushed the ball back to Alan Ball who crossed. Kendall timed his run to meet the centre perfectly and the midfielder drilled home his shot at the Gwladys Street end. In a match of more than forty fouls, it took the home team 72 minutes to force their first corner, but the Everton defence held tight and they may have added to their tally when Wright's free-kick struck the crossbar. With the reserves winning the mini-derby at Anfield, Catterick jubilantly recycled his arch-rival's taunt. 'I see the two best teams in Liverpool won today,' he said.

Seven days after defeating Tranmere to reach the quarter-final of the FA Cup in early March, Everton ran riot in the Midlands, this time winning 6-2 at West Brom, with Alan Ball scoring four times in a game that carried far more significance in the light of what followed. Blonde-haired Alan Whittle had an outstanding debut, thoughts turning immediately to comparisons with Denis Law, one that would haunt the youngster for years. The 18-year-old was outstanding in a confident and almost arrogant display, impressing the watching Sir Alf Ramsey, who cornered Catterick after the game. 'Where did you find him?' said the shocked England manager. 'He's a natural. He can't miss,' came the reply. Ball was back down to earth the following Saturday, when he was sent-off for the only time in his Everton career, for dissent in a 1-0 home win over Newcastle, when the wounds from the clash at St James Park earlier in the season were re-opened. Ball's punishment was a fine and a fortnight's suspension, a somewhat draconian ruling given the authorities had only fined Ian St John after two dismissals.

Not only were Everton in the FA Cup semi-final against Leeds United but also their upsurge in league form had taken them to the fringes of the title race. A 2-1 victory over Chelsea on Easter Saturday took the points tally to 25 from a possible 32 since just before Christmas and left Everton seven off the top with two games in hand on the leaders, Manchester United. Setting aside the importance of the semi-final, Catterick's team selection for league games at this time was perplexing. Just before Easter, conscious that Leeds manager Don Revie would be watching, Catterick fielded a weakened side at Sheffield Wednesday. Included in the line-up were the untried Frank D'Arcy and there was a debut for Terry Owen, father of Michael. The game ended goalless.

On Easter Monday, five days before the Leeds game, Catterick put out five reserves at Nottingham Forest, in a 1-0 defeat. For one player his non-selection signalled the end of a glorious Goodison career. Alex Young was named in the party to travel to the City Ground and, considering the absence of several senior players, the Scot expected to start but was in for a shock. 'Just before the game came the bombshell,' Young later said, 'I was named as a substitute. Several youngsters were playing, some of them making their first-team debuts … I felt that I could at least have been some help with my experience. Everton lost and I knew I was finished with first team football at Goodison Park.'

At the time Everton were only three points behind the eventual champions, Manchester City, then in third, with a game in hand and a visit to Maine Road to come. Although the manager played the percentages, such was the momentum there was surely a case for fielding a full side (minus the suspended Ball) against Sheffield Wednesday and Nottingham Forest, especially as the opposition had nothing at stake in either game. The gamble may have been worthwhile. The top two, Manchester United and Leeds United, both having cup commitments, fell away and Joe Mercer's City eventually won the title with 58 points. Everton would have been champions if they had taken maximum points at Sheffield Wednesday and Nottingham Forest and drawn at Maine Road. As it happens, Everton lost in Manchester and drew at West Ham, ending the season in fifth place with 52 points. Catterick's side had been the best in the country since the turn of the year and he could be genuinely criticised for not making an effort to win the title.

The season ended on a high though. Three days after the FA Cup final defeat to West Brom, in the last league game of the season against relegated Fulham (managed by Bobby Robson) the losers treated the 38,000 crowd, who had defied a bus strike, to a sumptuous display of attacking football in a 5-1 victory. Those in attendance stayed after the game to offer 'their team the most emotional and heart-rending reception it is possible to give', according to Chris James in the *Liverpool Echo*. Talking via the PA system to the crowd after the game, Catterick promised the supporters they had seen the shape of things to come. He was as good as his word.

'Everton must be the most exciting side in the Football League'

Before the start of the 1968/69 campaign, the manager set out his stall for the season ahead. 'Everton's hopes,' he said, 'continue to be based on skill. This is our tradition. We have no room for the strong-arm type of player and we believe we can succeed with skill.'[49] *The Times* shared his optimism. 'Everton are young enough and skilful enough to beat the whole field,' said Geoffrey Green before the campaign started.

A tough opening day clash at Old Trafford put those sentiments to test, against the team crowned European Cup winners at an emotional Wembley in May. On the most beautiful summer's day imaginable, the wayward finishing that haunted Everton in the FA Cup final returned. The away side shocked the 63,000 crowd by

49 The players were certainly strong-armed in the traditional Blues (first-team) against Ambers (reserves) pre-season friendly at Goodison. In front of 12,000 spectators, first Alan Ball and Tommy Jackson squared up after a bad foul by the England midfielder. The game then descended into an ugly farce, with petty feuds between teammates – Jimmy Husband was helped off the pitch following a foul by Aiden Maher whilst reserve Harry Bennett was carried-off following a Joe Royle challenge.

making a powerful start as Joe Royle, Alan Ball and Colin Harvey all squandered chances to put Everton ahead. After United took the lead against the run of play, Ball quickly equalised, before Bobby Charlton scored again before the interval. The visitors held the upper hand for the rest of the game, with only wayward finishing and United goalkeeper Alex Stepney keeping Everton at bay. The home team held on for a lucky 2-1 victory against an Everton side that had only themselves to blame. 'It is going to be a shocking waste of approach, talent and drive if we are going to have the same old story of wasted opportunities,' wrote Jack Rowe in the *Liverpool Daily Post*.

Three days later Catterick's side put Burnley to the sword, 3-0 at Goodison. The home team started at a frantic pace and maintained the momentum over the ninety minutes, although as at Old Trafford the score masked a plethora of missed opportunities. A week later, a brilliant performance of 'restless speed' according to *The Times* produced a stunning 4-1 victory at West Ham. By mid-September Everton were reaching peak form, and in destroying Sheffield Wednesday 3-0 with a mouth-watering exhibition, they produced a performance of such brilliance that talk of the title was inevitable. After the game Catterick said it was the best club display he had seen in many years, adding 'that is the sort of football entertainment I've always thought the team was capable of producing. It is what I have been aiming to get.' Nevertheless, the manager dampened expectations of the title. 'The physical nature of the game is such that it is not always pure football that wins championships,' Catterick said.

After the Wednesday display, the team's irresistible form continued, a decent Luton side were overwhelmed 5-1 in the League Cup before West Brom were hammered 4-0 at Goodison. Revenge for the cup final defeat brought another standing ovation at the end from the home crowd as well as kind words from Paul Wilcox in the *Guardian*. 'At the moment Everton must be the most exciting side in the Football League. To watch them is a pleasure.' On the first Saturday in October, Everton defeated champions Manchester City 2-0 at home, in another superb display. The team was gelling in a wonderful fashion, the ball moving sweetly from man to man with intelligent movement throughout the side. *The Times*' Tom German summed up the real driving force behind the startling improvement over the previous twelve months, 'If there is a more effective, more talented trio than Ball, Kendall and Harvey, they do not spring readily to mind.'

Although the three players had always blended well, they were now performing at a significantly higher level than before. There were a couple of reasons for the upgrade. Colin Harvey had clearly gone up a level, and against West Brom the midfielder had scored a brilliant goal, carrying the ball more than thirty yards, dribbling past three Albion defenders before producing a cool finish. Secondly, the manager had instigated a slight tactical shift in the midfield formation. Whereas previously the tendency had been to play Ball in an advanced role in turning a 4-3-3 system into a 4-2-4 formation, Catterick encouraged the World Cup winner to act as a decoy, allowing Kendall and Harvey to progress higher up the pitch and add further options to the attack.

These subtle changes were never more effective than in the visit to Southampton seven days after the City victory. Four days before, Everton dominated the Merseyside derby at Anfield but only came away with a 1-1 draw, after Tommy Smith had cancelled out Alan Ball's opener. Notably, Howard Kendall had half of the away team's ten shots on goal, seeing one strike the bar and another unluckily disallowed when Ball had strayed into an offside position. At the Dell, Everton were far more ruthless after a slow start, having a dozen attempts before they equalised a Ron Davies goal for the home team. Thereafter Catterick's side purred during a 5-2 win in front of 21,688 privileged spectators. 'They turned on a display of such exciting, skilful, classical attacking football that the local fans gave them a standing ovation at the end,' wrote Michael Charters in the *Liverpool Echo*. Watching also was John Arlott, who in the *Guardian* noted the transformation in the team's set-up:

Everton have made a steady transition from the muscular to the nimble so that they now muster four or five forwards and two wing half backs [Kendall and Harvey], all of light build and high speed who are completely grounded in the skills of the game and capable, as soon as one attack breaks down, of creating a fresh and different one before the opposing defence can remuster. The perception and control of their movement is such that they produce a remarkably high rate of shots at goal.

Rather than chase success, by 1968/69 Catterick's views indicated a manager more interested in playing good, rather than winning, football. 'Our main objective is to entertain. We set out to play a lot of attractive football, the kind that wins friends,' he said later in the season. 'From what our friends say and people from other clubs we have played have told me, I know we have achieved this objective.

We have had some fair results with this football, too. We are very happy that we are third in the table. It would please me more if we finished second and entertained than if we won the title by any other means.' Compared to his views in the early days about being about only being interested in success, it was a startling about-turn. The resignation of John Moores as chairman and then the death of his replacement, Edward Holland Hughes, undoubtedly enhanced Catterick's power within the club, as had a seven-year contract in 1967. Although Moores retained more than a passing interest, it is hard to imagine Catterick making such statements six years before.

To be fair, there was a measure of truth in what the Everton manager was saying. Whereas the perceived greed and their ruthless pursuit of success made them enemies in the early part of the decade, by the end of the 1960s critics viewed the club in a more positive light. The desire to play good football in an era of work-rate, of teams filled with 'cloggers' as Catterick called them, succeeded in wiping out the previous damaging publicity. After an unlucky 3-1 defeat at Arsenal in December 1968, when defensive lapses cost the side dearly, Catterick told the waiting press, 'It's all very well to play attractively, but it doesn't win championships. We were not ruthless enough.' But the *Daily Mail's* Brian James, a critic of the team earlier in the decade, replied in print, 'Nothing I have heard in a long time saddened me more than a statement like this, coming after a match like this, from the manager of a team like this. Because I remember another Everton side. The team that won the title in 1963. That, too, was Catterick's team – but it is a side remembered with little affection. It lacked the adventure and enterprise of the Everton side of Saturday.'

Two weeks before the Arsenal game, Everton's 16-game unbeaten league run had ended unluckily in a 2-1 defeat at old foes Leeds United. At that point, Catterick's outfit had played like title winners in both style and results. In their 37 league games thus far in 1968, Everton had won 23 times and drew eight, with just six defeats. In a stirring contest across the Pennines both sides displayed championship form. Having trailed to an early John Giles penalty, the visitors equalised and remained in control for long periods, mainly thanks to their midfield trio. 'They are the deep well of the side's inspiration,' said Geoffrey Green in *The Times*. 'In close harness, doing things almost with their eyes closed, linked by an instinctive awareness of each other.' The efforts of the richly talented threesome proved in vain as Leeds clinched the points in the second half when Paul Madeley beat Sandy Brown in the air and Eddie Gray volleyed home.

Seven days later, the side returned to form with a 7-1 home victory over Leicester City at Goodison as Catterick's side treated the 42,000 crowd to an afternoon filled with extravagant attacking football. Joe Royle's hat-trick was the highlight as Everton took their goal tally to 48 in just 21 league games. It was one of only three occasions in a thirty-year professional career that Peter Shilton conceded seven goals, and the goalkeeper was so shocked he asked for a transfer a week later. Royle's treble was a landmark in a campaign when he developed into a striker who bore comparison to Everton's great centre-forwards of the past, his goals contributing to a season where the team's football, as players and supporters have since argued, was superior to that of twelve months later. Although not the case over the whole campaign, it was certainly true that the standards displayed by Catterick's side in the autumn of 1968, during a run of eleven league games (in which they scored 32 goals and conceded ten) culminating in the thrashing of the Filbert Street side exceeded anything they achieved afterwards. Indeed, there is an argument that no Everton side has ever played better, with only two other comparable periods in the post-war era. The first is the 10-game winning run in October-November 1984, which included the famous 5-0 win over Manchester United. The other is a brilliant sequence of ten games in late 1986 and early 1987 that yielded 31 goals, with just six conceded, when the football played was certainly superior to anything from two years before.

After that victory over Leicester, Everton stood second on thirty points from 21 games, the same tally as Leeds, who had played a game less. Both sides trailed Liverpool by two points. By the end of the year, with two further victories and a single defeat in four matches, Everton stood four points behind, with Leeds still sandwiched between the Merseyside giants. The final victory of the year was noteworthy – a 3-1 win over league champions Manchester City at Maine Road in front of a 54,000 crowd. After Joe Royle's header put the visitors ahead in the opening minute, Everton adapted far better to the treacherous conditions than City, who had scored sixteen goals in their previous three home games. Within eight minutes, Jimmy Husband had added a second and the winger's header near the end wrapped up a comfortable win.

Everton continued their pre-Christmas form into the new year, a 3-1 league victory against Sunderland at Roker Park featuring another thrilling display of high quality football of imagination and pace. Newcastle United legend Jackie

Milburn was on Wearside and said presciently, 'They're great now, but they're going to be even better in two years' time.' However, a more accurate reflection of their rapid progress came in the home win over Wolves at Goodison at the end of January. Against a dangerous and capable Midlands outfit, who also played attractive football, they ran out 4-0 victors, with two goals from Joe Royle, who took his career tally to 38 in 65 games for the Toffees. In attendance was Bristol Rovers chairman Freddie Ford, on a scouting mission before their FA Cup tie. 'Everton are the finest team I've seen in years on this display. If you want quality football this is the side,' Ford said. His counterpart at Wolves, John Ireland, echoed those thoughts. 'That was the finest club performance I've seen for years.'

The victory over Wolves signalled the end of a golden period for Catterick's side, the harsh winter and FA Cup run meaning Everton featured in little top-flight football in the new year, playing only four league games in ten weeks after Boxing Day. Understandably, with a backlog of fixtures to fulfil – including nine games in April – the finesse and style of the early part of the campaign diluted as the team struggled to score goals, Ball netting only three times in 22 matches after Christmas while Royle ended the season with two goals in twelve games. The campaign concluded with a 1-1 draw at Leicester in early May, the 1968/69 season bringing 57 points and just six defeats in 42 league games, for a fine third-placed finish. The 77 goals were the highest in the top-flight that season, a campaign in which for four months no Catterick side had played better.

17.
'I Don't Buy Cloggers'

ALTHOUGH CATTERICK HAD ADDED THE STELLAR TALENTS OF ALAN Ball and Howard Kendall, the first-team squad reduced to a worrying extent in the late 1960s. The departures included Jimmy Gabriel, Alex Scott, Derek Temple, George Heslop, Gerry Glover, Mike Trebilcock, Alex Young, Brian Harris, Dennis Stevens and Fred Pickering. The arrival of new talent from Bellefield had partially bridged the gap but unlike earlier in the decade there was a shortage of experienced support.

Outside the regular starting eleven, only Sandy Brown had any real experience. Tommy Jackson was relatively new to English football while the others were also inexperienced products of the youth system: Alan Whittle, Roger Kenyon, Terry Darracott, Gerry Humphreys and Frank D'Arcy. In the 1962/63 title-winning season, Catterick had a large squad of experienced and battle-hardened players. If any lost form or were injured there was always a capable replacement. That was not the case by later in the decade.

To be fair, Catterick realised these problems at this time, acknowledging that there were choices in replenishing the playing staff through relying on the next batch of Bellefield graduates to match the achievements of their illustrious predecessors, or by recruitment from outside. Speaking to Michael Charters in the *Liverpool Echo* in October 1968, Catterick explained that 'no major club can exist solely on a youth policy. It always needs to go into the transfer market to build up the playing staff.'

Attempts to strengthen the squad in the years that followed were hindered because Catterick was facing a completely different market to the one he had played so effectively nearly a decade before. The days of bullying clubs into selling players had long gone. The lifting of the maximum wage and the increased wealth within the game, primarily on the back of the World Cup win, had allowed clubs to offer longer, and significantly more lucrative, contracts to their star players. With the commercial opportunities and media exposure as we know today in their embryonic stage, players were now becoming assets in their own right, worth more to clubs than money in the bank. Chairmen were now just as likely to spend spare cash on new stands, as a means of generating further revenue. Added to that, Catterick's filter of only purchasing players who could play – 'I don't buy cloggers,' he once told Tony Stevens of the *Liverpool Weekly News* – also brought its own difficulties.

The other by-product, that bigger wages naturally produced smaller squads, also meant managers were reticent to let their top players go, with no guarantee of bringing in replacements. There were also other factors to consider. Scotland had long been a fertile ground for English clubs, but the pool of talent north of the border was beginning to diminish by the end of the decade. The failure to land striker Colin Stein in 1968 showed the two Glasgow giants were also now just as powerful as their counterparts from south of the border. That said, the one player Catterick coveted more than any other in his time at Goodison was Celtic's gifted midfielder Bobby Murdoch, but the manager did not even trouble Jock Stein with a bid, as it would have been a waste of time.

The net effect was a dramatic slump in spending: in 1969/70 English clubs collectively paid £2.6m on players compared to £3.9m in the twelve months before. 'The transfer of star football players, once known as Soccer's Slave Market, is grinding to a halt,' wrote Frank Taylor in the *Daily Mirror*. Catterick concurred, 'I think the transfer market is dying on its feet,' he said. Power was also now moving ever so slowly from club to player, as agents and advisors became more prominent. A case in point was the on-off-on-off move for Manchester City's Dave Connor, just before the FA Cup quarter-final tie with Manchester United in March 1969. The Everton manager was a keen admirer of the utility player, especially in the way he had competed against his midfield triumvirate over the previous seasons. Although Connor was not a first choice in the City line-up, his versatility, experience, and combative style would have been very useful for a small squad. At first, the deal appeared straightforward. Everton offered £40,000, with City accepting the bid. However, Connor had recently turned down a move to Spurs and, having just signed a four-year deal at Maine Road, he did the same to Catterick. Within 24 hours, Connor performed an about-turn and the move was back on – yet the next day the deal broke down again, when the City player expressed a desire to stay in Manchester, where he just moved into a new house. It would not be the last time that the changing face of the transfer market would make negotiations increasingly protracted and uncertain.

Ernie Hunt – the donkey's kick back

A genial and colourful character, Ernie Hunt – famously christened Roger Patrick Hunt before changing his name to avoid confusion with the Liverpool striker – first impressed Catterick when playing against Everton for his hometown club Swindon in the FA Cup in 1963. After moving to Wolves, Hunt scored twenty goals in 37 goals as the Midlands side achieved promotion to the top flight in the 1966/67 season, before Catterick paid £70,000 for his services in September 1967.

The transfer was baffling in some respects. With Fred Pickering sold and the teenaged Joe Royle still finding his way, the team was crying out for an experienced, powerful centre-forward. After a failed bid to bring back Frank Wignall from Nottingham Forest, Catterick's targets were rumoured to be Southampton's Ron Davies, scorer of 37 top-flight goals in 1966/67, and Bolton's sought-after Francis Lee, who had recently been transfer listed. Davies stayed put while Lee went to City shortly after, for £60,000, or £10,000 less than Catterick paid for Hunt. In Manchester, the barrel-chested forward would be the catalyst for City's most successful era at the time. Two weeks later Don Revie paid £100,000 to bring the selfless England international Mick Jones to Leeds from Sheffield United, another player who would have been a meaningful purchase. Meanwhile, at just under 5 foot 8 inches, Hunt was never going to add any height or weight to the attack with Alan Ball or Jimmy Husband also filling his natural place on the pitch. After the signing, Catterick said, 'Everton now have all the players I want and we are not looking for anyone.' The statement drew bemusement from fans, desperate for a big striker.

The new man lasted just six months, before moving to Coventry City, scoring a famous 'donkey kick' free-kick against Everton in front of the *Match of the Day* cameras in October 1970. It was the first time a Catterick big money move had not worked out and, in retrospect, the Hunt deal proved a tipping point in his transfer activity, as much for the players the manager could have bought rather than the one he did.

'I could not agree to Stein's excessive demands over salary'

Like Joe Baker before him, and Mark Hughes during the 1990s, Colin Stein always seemed destined for a move to Goodison. A classic feisty Scottish striker of the time, who mixed aggression and goal-scoring potency in equal measure, Stein was eventually the subject of three failed transfer attempts made by two Everton managers over a six-year period. The first was one of the more interesting tales of the Catterick era, providing proof of the changes in the transfer market. Notwithstanding the requirement for a more expansive game plan, one of the lessons of the 1968 FA Cup final defeat was Everton needed greater penetration in attack. It was an open secret that Catterick was on the lookout for another striker. The general feeling was that Joe Royle, despite scoring twenty goals in the previous campaign, was not the finished article, particularly with regard to shooting and finishing.

In October 1968, the search for a target-man took Catterick to familiar territory north of the border, where Stein, then at Hibernian, was establishing a reputation as a deadly striker of rare potential. Having followed his usual practice of watching a player from the terraces on several occasions, the Everton manager had first registered an interest at the start of the campaign. Hibernian accepted an offer of £90,000 and Catterick travelled north to seal the deal. The Everton manager, used to hunting down his quarry, was in for a shock as Stein later told the *Scotsman*:

One day I had to go to a big Edinburgh hotel for signing talks, only the Hibs chairman William Harrower wouldn't tell me who with. What he did say, just as we were going in the door, was that he'd never sell me to another Scottish club. It was Everton. Their manager Harry Catterick even got a car to fetch Linda [his girlfriend] from her work but I wouldn't sign.

Despite the money offered of £100 per week and a signing-on fee of £4,500, Stein had surprisingly refused the club's personal terms. 'The money's not good enough. I knew what I wanted and Mr Catterick's offer did not come up to it,' Stein said afterwards. The Everton manager countered by saying, 'The terms we offered him were as good, if not better, than any he could get in Britain. He has refused a good deal of money.' Within days, Stein had gone to Glasgow Rangers – his preferred choice in any case – in a £100,000 deal, the first six-figure transfer between Scottish clubs, where he took Alex Ferguson's number nine shirt and scored six goals in his first two games.

Following the flawed move for Ernie Hunt, the failure to land Stein was another indication that Catterick was perhaps losing his Midas touch in the transfer market. More importantly, unlike earlier in the decade, there was now a wider number of clubs with money to spend. However, a furious Catterick was keen to have the last word and did so in one of the more memorable and cutting remarks of his Everton managerial career. 'I could not agree to Stein's excessive demands over salary,' he said, 'and in the interests of my club I refused to meet his requirements.'

Whether Stein, whose notorious ill-discipline resulted in a sending-off count that reached double figures, may have disturbed the dressing room equilibrium is a good point. That said, when Stein and Royle were on opposing teams in an English League and Scottish League clash five months later, to most observers the Scot looked a more dangerous and complete player. Undeterred by his initial failure, Catterick tried to sign the striker again four years later and then in 1974 Billy Bingham attempted to bring Stein to the club after he had moved to Coventry. Back in 1968 though, the Everton manager's hard-line stance drew support from Eric Todd in the *Guardian*. 'Football could do with more men of Catterick's breed and sanity,' he opined, 'it is a very good thing to show these precocious young men that they will not always get what they want or what they think they are worth.' Nevertheless, a year later Catterick still had regrets over the failure to land the Scot. 'What an asset he would have been at Everton, he would have fitted in perfectly with our style and I am very sorry he decided not to join us,' he confessed to the *Liverpool Echo*.

'The £150,000 Question'

With the side struggling for form in the autumn of 1970, Catterick spoke again about the problems of signing players in his weekly column in the *Liverpool Echo*: 'England's top clubs have more than one million pounds available to buy players. There's only one snag. The players they want can't be bought. The transfer market is dying, for clubs are holding onto their best players. Clubs who sell their best players end up relegated. The great clubs of the future will be forced to rely primarily on home produced players.'

That may have been true but for several years Catterick's mantra to supporters about buying players was that there was no interest 'unless they were better than those already at the club'. Such was the dip in fortunes after lifting the title in 1970 that there was now a fair number scattered about the country. One, infamously, was the young Preston midfield player, Archie Gemmill. Catterick had been tracking Gemmill for a while from his Southport base, as the Scot later revealed in his autobiography. 'In September 1970 I was definitely going to Everton. Months earlier the men at Goodison Park had been crowned champions of England and here was their manager, Harry Catterick, generously offering me a four-year contract with a £5,000 signing-on fee and wages starting at £225 a week, rising to £250, £275 and then £300.'

However, Derby County and, more specifically, Brian Clough got wind of the deal and the charismatic manager travelled to Preston in an attempt to steal the promising Scot from under Catterick's nose. With Alan Ball senior, the North End manager, having encouraged Gemmill to speak to Clough, the Derby boss eventually turned up at his house. Telling the player he would wait in the car overnight if it meant changing his mind, Gemmill's wife took pity and offered Clough the spare room. Catterick twice tried to get in touch with Gemmill when Clough was in the house – via a neighbour's phone, who told the young midfielder that it was 'his mother' in a comical subterfuge – but on Monday morning, over breakfast, the Scot agreed to go to Derby.

At 10 a.m. that day, Alan Ball senior had expected Gemmill at Deepdale to talk to Everton. There was no sign of the player. Ninety minutes later the 23-year-old turned up with Clough, telling Ball senior about his wish to join the Midlands side, subject to the clubs agreeing a fee. At 3 p.m. a £65,000 deal was done, with Everton matching the terms ninety minutes later – but it was too little too late. In his book, Gemmill explained how Clough had sweet-talked him. Offered more than £10,000 a year by Everton, 'I joined Derby for seventy pounds a week,' he wrote, 'no signing-on fee, a colour television and the promise I'd get my front room re-carpeted.'

Catterick claimed that Ball senior had broken a written agreement to sell Gemmill to Everton and later told Michael Charters in the *Liverpool Echo* his thoughts about the failed deal. 'He would have suited us, but I put a price on him which I thought to be right and would not go above that when Derby

County signed him.' Gemmill would have been a tremendous acquisition; the industrious and clever midfielder capable of filling any of the roles performed by Catterick's trio, as he proved in a brilliant club career with Derby and Nottingham Forest.

Nevertheless, having told supporters over a period of years that he was only interested in players who could improve the side, once identifying those in question, the Everton manager was duty bound to deliver. If Gemmill was the answer – and by bidding that appeared to be the case – then Catterick should simply have offered more money than Derby, employing the same strategy as in the Alan Ball or Howard Kendall deals. The manager failed to do so, but still defended his position to Michael Charters in the *Liverpool Echo*, 'If I had wanted another midfield player urgently, I would have gone for higher. But it was not necessary and that is why I pulled out of the Gemmill transfer.' Yet within a fortnight Catterick spent £150,000 – on a midfielder.

Everton paid the fee to Nottingham Forest for Henry Newton, an accomplished player Catterick had previously tried to prise away two years before. Strong in the tackle and a more than decent passer of the ball, with a shot known as 'Enry's 'Ammer,' in many ways the 26-year-old spoiler was a strong addition to a team short of midfield defensive cover. Like previous target Dave Connor, the Forest man was equally adept in a man-marking role. Satisfying for Catterick was that he beat Brian Clough for the player's signature as well. However the Everton manager was probably unaware that Newton himself wanted a move to the Baseball Ground, as the player admitted on leaving the club in 1973. 'I was very disappointed that Derby didn't succeed in signing me three years ago,' Newton claimed, 'They were the club I really wanted to join, and for a long time I had regrets on moving to Everton.'

The problem for supporters nonetheless was that Newton was not the adored Ball, Harvey or Kendall – whose places were now mysteriously under threat. (This was a not an unusual state of affairs, Terry Yorath had the same problem later at Leeds, supporters at Elland Road failing to accept the Welshman on the basis he was not Billy Bremner or John Giles.) Yet what Catterick was doing made sense in some respects. In the previous two league seasons at least one of the midfield trio was missing in 35 of 84 league games – almost a complete campaign. During 1968/69 Kendall's injury after Christmas was a significant contribution to a failing title challenge whilst twelve months later the enforced absence of Ball and

Harvey in the middle months of the campaign threatened to have a similar effect. During that time, Catterick used either Tommy Jackson or Sandy Brown as their replacements, both proficient players but not in the same class. With the demands of a European campaign, the manager could easily justify the purchase of the more capable and versatile Newton. Catterick's argument to Michael Charters was compelling. 'It is no use saying that at the moment I didn't need him,' he told Charters, 'You'd look a fool if in a few weeks' time if I had Ball, Kendall or Harvey off injured for a spell and I did not have Newton available as a class replacement. Then people would say "Why didn't you sign Newton when he was available?"'

However, the purchase of Newton ran contrary to what he had told Dudley Doust in the *Sunday Times* earlier in the year. In the interview Catterick said the days of buying to bolster the squad, as he once had done, were also over, for economic reasons as much as anything else. 'I won't buy reserve players,' he told the American, 'it's not a good policy. You can't go along to a boy and say "We'll pay sixty thousand pounds for you if we need you."' With the money in the game now empowering players, convincing them second-string football was a good thing was also obsolete. 'Players of top quality... would they be content to stay in reserve football?' Catterick rhetorically told Doust.

On that basis then, Catterick did not intend to play Newton as a reserve so, with a tough away game at Arsenal coming up, the issue was where the new signing fitted in. The consensus was that, on a like-for-like basis, the out-of-form Kendall's place in the side was the one under threat. Indeed, other clubs were aware of this and immediately Derby County and Manchester United were rumoured to be preparing bids. The Everton manager, infamously, did swap Kendall with Newton at Highbury, only to play the man who replaced him as the club's most successful manager at centre-half – 'a position I'd never played in my life' as he later admitted in his autobiography. In reality, the easier option was to play the new signing there on the day. To magnify the problem, instead of playing the experienced Hurst as Kendall's partner, Labone's understudy Roger Kenyon paired up with the rookie centre-half.

The omens were not good at Highbury. Newton had been there with Forest a fortnight before and had been on the wrong end of a 4-0 thrashing. On a sunny autumn afternoon, it was a case of *déjà vu* for the man from the East Midlands. Apart from the selection of Kendall at centre-half, the other *faux pas* was goalkeeper Andy Rankin's garish cap. It looked 'both in colour and style,' according to David Tossell in *Seventy One Guns: The Year of the first Arsenal Double*, 'frighteningly like something Donny Osmond would wear to trill out "Puppy Love" to a nation of screaming teenaged girls.'

BBC *Match of the Day* viewers saw a shambolic Everton display against a side that would displace them as champions. The team's historic weakness to the high ball across the goal only magnified the mistake of playing Kendall against John Radford and Ray Kennedy, strikers whose main strengths were in the air. In midfield the new signing's passing was out of tune with Ball and Harvey. 'The £150,000 question – Why have Everton bought Henry Newton? – remains unanswered,' Brian Glanville wrote in the *Sunday Times* of the defeat, 'He clearly, if unwittingly, was a source of confusion rather than inspiration. His transfer may reflect the evident crisis of confidence in the team as a whole.' *The Times* headline ran 'Everton like eleven captains with no ship.'

After the humiliating defeat, Newton said, 'Where you could say I ran the show with Forest, Everton play it much closer. They're a tighter side. At Forest we would swing the ball round a lot more. It's obvious I'm going to need more time to settle with Everton.' Although a fine player, Newton was probably in the right place at the wrong time and palpably failed to fill his potential in three injury-filled years, his time at Goodison cruelly defined by that nightmare opening ninety minutes. The rationale behind his purchase remained a mystery to most, although David Lacey in the *Guardian* had one theory. 'One suspects,' he wrote, 'he was signed for the same reason that men climb mountains – he was there.'

18.
Seventh Heaven

OMINOUSLY, DON REVIE'S MAGNIFICENT LEEDS UNITED HAD romped to the title in 1968/69 with a league record 67 points, having conceded just 26 goals. At the end of the season, Catterick noted the parsimony of the Leeds back-line as heralding a new era. 'This points to the development of defensive football and how it can win honours. It is the modern trend and I would like to see clubs trying to break away from it. Spectators want attractive, open, attacking football,' he said. They were laudable sentiments, but Everton fans also wished to see winning football, and at the cusp of a new decade could his side deliver the trophy their loyal support deserved?

'Everton reach for greatness'

The 1969/70 season was an unusually scheduled campaign. With England's defence of the World Cup due to start in early June 1970, and Sir Alf Ramsey demanding a month's preparation for the champions, the Football League truncated the season by four weeks. The net effect was to compress the already hectic schedule even further, with seven league games in August alone.

The summer of 1969 was notable for Neil Armstrong becoming the first man to walk on the moon, the death of the Rolling Stones' Brian Jones and the 'Football War' between Honduras and El Salvador, the latter invading the former after rioting following a World Cup game between the two teams. Just twenty-four hours after the Beatles were photographed crossing Abbey Road, Everton travelled to Highbury on the opening day for a tough start, against a rapidly improving side that had just finished fourth. Missing was Alan Ball, the midfielder carrying over a suspension due to three bookings from the previous season. The England international had signed a new six-year deal in the summer, the basic wage of £10,000 making him reputedly the highest paid player in the country.

On the eve of the visit to Highbury, Catterick re-emphasised his concerns over the modern game. 'I think this season will produce more physical play than ever before. Unlike some other teams, Everton are not equipped in this department.' The rugged encounter proved him right to a degree. It was 'tight, unadventurous and very boring,' according to Michael Parkinson in the *Sunday Times*, 'both sides ventured nothing and played like misers.' Others noted a harder edge to the side, something missing in previous years and contradicting one of Catterick's claims about his team. Whatever the press complaints about the lack of entertainment, Everton got their rewards when, five minutes from time, the Arsenal defence failed to clear Morrissey's free-kick and the excellent John Hurst scooped the ball home.

Four days later Everton produced a much more cohesive display at Old Trafford. Twelve months earlier the side had played superbly but were let down by weak finishing and a soft underbelly. Bobby Charlton had earlier written in his weekly *Goal* magazine column that Everton 'must be the best starters of all-time. They just seem to click into gear straightaway, while some of us are still struggling to find our feet.' They proved him right on a warm August evening when the side staked a real claim to be title contenders. The visitors won 2-0 with two beautifully created goals: on 38 minutes Hurst fed Ball, continued his run, and from the return pass scored past Jimmy Rimmer. Then twenty minutes from time the World Cup winner struck himself with a header, after Royle had outfoxed two United players before crafting a beautifully placed cross direct to the midfielder. In the return fixture, a week later, it was even easier. The new United manager, Wilf McGuinness, dropped Denis Law and Charlton, but it made little difference as Everton strolled into a three-goal lead in the opening half-hour. 'Everton declare after 26 minutes,' proclaimed the *Liverpool Echo* as the Blues quite clearly took the foot off the gas against outclassed opponents. Four wins from four matched the start of the 1962/63 title-winning campaign, the *Liverpool Echo's* Michael Charters noting that, even at this premature stage of the season, the opening day win was the turning point. 'This was the game that Everton grew up,' he said of the triumph at Arsenal, 'adding a new-found professionalism and maturity which was lacking last season in crucial matches against top opposition.'

With three points taken from the next two matches, Everton were top with eleven points from six games when mighty Leeds United visited Goodison on the last Saturday in August. The Yorkshire side had not lost for a record 34 league games, a sequence stretching back to the previous October. Having just won the title for the first time, Revie's side were also in the process of removing some of the shackles imposed previously during the decade. The addition of the dangerous goal-poacher Allan Clarke from Leicester City in the summer – a player Catterick rejected at the time, for not being physical enough – increased their firepower substantially. The impact was to produce a team at the peak of their powers over the next three years – one good enough to rank with any produced in England and a side that simply did not do 'off' days. Teams literally had to chisel out a victory over the champions. The Toffees were also battling history, mustering just one league win against the Yorkshire side since their return to the top flight five years before.

Brian Labone had described Leeds' performance during the goalless draw at Goodison in the previous April as the best by a visiting side in his time at the club. At the end of a gloriously sunny August afternoon, the Everton skipper could have used a similar phrase, but this time in respect of the home team. Everton tore into their opponents from the start, going ahead as early as the fourth minute, Jimmy Husband stabbing a loose ball home from near to the penalty spot after Sandy Brown's free-kick. On 21 minutes Joe Royle headed home Morrissey's cross on the rebound after the striker's initial effort had struck the bar and just after half-time the forward made it 3-0, his shot skewering in from the edge of the box after good work from John Hurst and then Husband. The sight of Leeds players arguing amongst themselves was evidence of how much the home team's display had them uncharacteristically rattled. Johnny Morrissey's performance was the best of his ten years at Goodison, reducing the usually excellent Paul Reaney to a nervous wreck. '[Reaney] did not know what day it was,' wrote Eric Todd in the *Guardian*. Another player producing arguably his best Everton display was Joe Royle, who dominated big Jack Charlton from start to finish.

It was only in the final quarter that the Elland Road outfit got any sort of a grip on the game, pulling a goal back when West allowed John Giles' corner to drift over his head and Billy Bremner chested the ball home on the goal line. Then Clarke volleyed home in the six-yard box from Peter Lorimer's knock down to set up a tense finale, before referee Gordon Hill blew for full time, the 51,797 spectators leaving the ground believing they had seen the new power in English football. David Miller in the *Sunday Telegraph* was full of praise for both teams: 'This was one of the finest league matches I can recall since the birth of this newspaper [1961], an outstanding spectacle of continuous excitement, unflinching application and occasional brilliance.' Catterick said after the game 'Leeds could not have been beaten by a better side,' while the *Observer* remarked 'Everton reach for greatness.'

Seven days later the unbeaten opening ended when the central defensive vulnerabilities apparent at the end of the Leeds game re-appeared. Brian Clough's Derby County were also enjoying a great start, standing third before their encounter at the Baseball Ground. Despite a brilliant consolation strike from Howard Kendall, the damage came from two corner kicks, the first West failed to gather and John O'Hare headed home, and then Kevin Hector's neat flick-on looped over the keeper's head to give the Rams an insurmountable two-goal lead. Everton won the following two games – at home to West Ham and away to Newcastle – before a visit to East Anglia and Bobby Robson's Ipswich Town. In the early autumn sunshine, they produced arguably their most complete performance of the season. Catterick's side strolled to a 3-0 victory, hardly giving the home team the privilege of a kick. Having had two goals disallowed for offside, Ball opened the scoring just before the break, with Royle adding a second. The third goal summed up the style of the class of 1969/70. Taking possession in the centre-circle, Colin Harvey found Ball on the wing, swiftly took a return pass then played a slick one-two with Joe Royle that split the Ipswich defence before shooting past David Best. 'They are a grand side,' said Robson after the game, 'thank goodness we've only to meet them twice in a season.'

Fed to the Wolves

Hooliganism and the associated trouble on the pitch continued to grow during the 1960s. Visiting fans now saw the match as a 'day out' and for the first time it was apparent that there was a minority, intent on causing trouble, who possessed only tenuous links with the club they 'supported'. Inevitably, as football violence increased, in an era of wider civil disorder the media was quick to tie the two together. Consequently, there was increased coverage in the press and television and for the first time the problem entered the political arena. James Callaghan, then Home Secretary, said, 'We hear of these young men who, after the final whistle, rove the streets and terrorise passers-by. I agree that the wanton destruction is perpetrated by a relatively small number of people who call themselves football fans. They are nothing of the sort and I think the clubs would be glad to be well rid of them.' Catterick though felt that the growth in hooliganism was a result of younger people wanting more excitement and thrills from a football match. 'The ordinary cut-and-thrust of a game, the incidents, the tackling, the tactics aren't enough,' he admitted to Alan Hoby of the *Sunday Express* in 1967. 'The hooligan element wants to see action, flare-ups, the more rugged the better. They want to see a punch-up. In other words – violence.'

Removing the perpetrators would prove problematical in the decades that followed and unfortunately Everton were not immune to its effect, no more than on the trip to Newcastle in October 1967. In a game full of controversy, the referee dismissed Gordon West for striking Newcastle's Albert Bennett[50] near the end, the goalkeeper responding by throwing dirt at the home team's dugout. Earlier in the match the police warned Johnny Morrissey, who had gone off injured, for continuous use of foul language from the side-lines. This may seem tame by later standards, but the game made back-page headlines and the press unfairly viewed the visitors' provocative behaviour as the cause of clashes between fans outside the ground.

The fall-out from the game in the north-east pales in comparison with Everton's visit to Wolves on the first Saturday of October 1969. On face value the visit to Molineux for a game shown on BBC's *Match of the Day* looks straight forward enough, Everton easing to a 3-2 victory with goals from Joe Royle, Johnny Morrissey and Colin Harvey, all of which have been broadcast many times since. However, the battle-zone also featured 84 injured spectators, more than 20 arrests, 41 fouls, a player sent-off, two penalties and a policeman punched while escorting the referee from the pitch. 'The scene was not Cagliari, nor the occasion of a European Cup-tie, but Molineux on a mellow autumn afternoon for a First Division match,' said a disbelieving Albert Barham in the *Guardian*.

---

50 Bennett was also involved in one of two notorious reserve games at St James' Park involving Everton during the decade. In the first, in March 1966, there was a rare, simultaneous, triple sending-off. The referee dismissed Bennett and the visitors' Gerry Glover for fighting after a dreadful John Craggs tackle on Everton's Aiden Maher, with the original miscreant also sent-off. Three years later there was more controversy. Newcastle reserves scored from the spot but the referee disallowed the goal for encroaching, did not order a retake but instead awarded a free-kick in Everton's favour, with complete disregard to the laws of the game. With ill-feeling abounding the second period saw continuous arguments between the Everton bench and spectators, and just before the hour mark the police were called to the ground. Arthur Proudler, the Everton trainer, was ordered to the tunnel where he was met by the local constabulary and escorted away from St James' Park for his own safety. To complete the surreal afternoon, the game ended in a 20-man brawl.

The violence erupted when referee Keith Walker dismissed home favourite Derek Dougan for dissent after the controversial Northern Ireland international disputed the award of a free-kick on the hour mark. Fights broke out and youngsters were injured as the crowd surged forward to try to attack the man in black, play held up as hundreds spilled onto the pitch. Although police restored a modicum of control, there was still some trouble on the terraces when Wolves were awarded a penalty late in the game, commentator Barry Davies saying on *Match of the Day*, 'How on earth anyone can take a penalty with that cauldron behind the goal is beyond me?'

Referee Walker, escorted from the pitch for the second successive Saturday, was forced to move home, while the events of the day were subject to a summit meeting between both the Football League and FA. Len Shipman, president of the Football League, said, 'We must do something or else we shall have the Home Office asking us what we are doing about trouble at our grounds. I am very concerned that unless we act we shall have a major crowd disaster on our hands.' Even the Minister for Sport, Denis Howell, got involved, the former referee publicly supporting Walker for booking Alan Ball for not retreating at a free-kick. Meanwhile, the outspoken Dougan was eventually suspended for eight weeks, despite the support of Sandy Brown and Colin Harvey as character witnesses.

One week later a 3-1 home victory over Sunderland left Everton with twelve wins and two draws from their opening fifteen league games, keeping them five points clear of sole conquerors Derby County. Then in the 6-2 victory over Stoke at Goodison there were further signs that luck was on their side. Deprived of first-choice keeper Gordon Banks, replacement John Farmer lasted 19 minutes for the visitors before leaving the pitch with a suspected fractured rib, defender Denis Smith taking the gloves. Although the final score-line sounds convincing, at the hour mark there was only a single goal between the sides and Everton needed three late strikes to make the game safe. Defensive frailties still existed, typified by Brian Labone's atrocious mistake for the visitors' second goal. Brian Glanville said in the *Sunday Times*, 'Everton are top, Everton are talented, yet there's still something about them which doesn't quite convince. The parts are somehow greater than the whole.' The manager was convinced though. After several years of preaching caution about a team that was not yet capable of competing for honours, Catterick proclaimed afterwards, 'Everton can win something this season. We played as well as this last season but this time the ball seems to be running for us.

It makes such a difference.'

The rise of the spoilers

When Matt Busby retired as manager of Manchester United in early 1969, he spoke chillingly about the degeneration of English football. 'The way things are going alarms me deeply,' the Scot admitted, 'what is new and frightening about the game is that you now have sides whose main assets are physical hardness and the ability to smother fluid, expansive football. They use strength and fitness in the name of professionalism to neutralize skill, and the unfortunate truth is that all too often it can be done.' Busby, to be fair, highlighted Everton as one of the teams 'who believe the game is about skill, talent, technique and imagination'. But Busby warned that 'for any one [skilled team] in the Football League, you'll now find ten who rely solely on runners, hard men and a smothering midfield and defence'.

Catterick's assertion that luck was making a difference to the progress of the team was perhaps true, but in reality the side was now more experienced and had developed a resolve to fight back, in physical terms, during difficult games, even if it blunted their natural style. Everton had previously found it difficult breaking down massed defences – witness their poor European record – but on the training ground, Catterick had preached the importance of maintaining their pattern of play against defensive sides, without resorting to the usual long ball tactics. Draws in previous years were now turning into wins, and that was the big difference. That said Paul Wilcox in the *Guardian* picked up the price of this change of style following the home win over Stoke: 'Everton have talent and skill in abundance: yet they do not seem to be using their gifts with the same majestic attractiveness as last season. They seem to have sacrificed some of their ability to entertain in reaching their pinnacle. Perhaps they have come to the conclusion that being thought of as value for money is no substitute for trophies.'

Also making a difference were the changes in the game. The rapid development of formations and tactics over the previous decade, combined with greater mobility and fitness, had resulted in an increasing emphasis on midfield power. Geoffrey Green covered this in *The Times* during the early part of the campaign. Noting that it was essential for every top team to have at least two quality midfield players, their esteemed football correspondent looked no further than the league leaders for proof: 'It is borne out in the present alignment of the league table. Everton are top because in Ball, Harvey and Kendall they possess probably the most effective, sophisticated central three-cornered partnership in the country.'

There was a downside to the growing dominance of Everton. Taking their lead from the way Manchester City had nullified the midfield trio in the FA Cup semi-final, sides – especially the weaker ones – sought to halt the Toffees in the style abhorred by Busby, via any means imaginable in some cases. The visit to Coventry City's Highfield Road at the end of October was a case in point, on an afternoon when there was further proof that Everton had all the tools to lift the title. Following the game, the home manager Noel Cantwell – ironically a protégé of Busby – was explicit in his tactical plan sketched out beforehand. 'We aimed to knock Everton out of their stride by stamping out their midfield trio of Alan Ball, Howard Kendall and Colin Harvey.' Two years earlier, Catterick had echoed Busby's later fears about opponents' strong-armed treatment to Alan Hoby in the *Sunday Express*:

More and more emphasis is laid on the physical side of the game…upon destroying… wrecking. Today, when clubs send scouts along before a game to watch the opposition's key player – or players – they really put them under the microscope. Unfortunately, after the scouts have reported back, instructions often go out to stop and destroy a particular player on the other side early in the game.

At Highfield Road, Cantwell had been literally true to his word of planning to eliminate the midfield triumvirate, and in doing so realised Catterick's worries. In the first four minutes, the Everton trainer was called into action on no less than five occasions, with Royle and Ball singled out as targets. The foul play continued throughout a first half extended by six minutes, a total unheard of at the time.

The second period continued in a less vigorous vein, but just when it looked like the home team would escape with a draw, three minutes from time one of the 24 Coventry fouls of the afternoon proved fatal. Dietmar Bruck tackled Jimmy Husband heavily and when Tommy Wright tapped the ball to the forward, Joe Royle met his long, arching centre perfectly under the slate grey skies to head home the winner. Five years later Royle told the *Liverpool Echo* that the goal was his most important for the club. 'The goal was a far post header from a Jimmy Husband cross,' he said, 'It was a very closely fought game. It could have gone either way. But if you're going to win the championship you tend to have a bit of luck and we won 1-0. That was a turning point.'

The hard-earned victory was the team's sixth away win of the season and their turbocharged start now left them six points ahead of the chasing pack. Nevertheless, Catterick was fuming after final whistle. 'I was disgusted with Coventry's tactics,' he said, 'but I was proud of my players that they kept their heads in the face of intimidation and always tried to play football.' Busby would have been a happy man.

Leeds take the lead

With several of the squad undergoing daily medical treatment, Everton then went down to a 2-0 defeat at West Brom, only their second league loss of the campaign, on an unhappy afternoon for the defence and West, who performed erratically throughout. Seven days later, Catterick was encouraged by a 1-1 draw at rapidly improving Chelsea, a side who themselves had lost just once in seventeen league games. The visitors took the lead early via Husband but West's feeble clearance from a corner led to Peter Osgood equalising within five minutes. The away game at Spurs at the end of November was fortunately postponed due to bad weather when there was no Labone, Harvey and Husband through injury. In Harvey's case, an eye condition caused genuine fear for his career at one stage. The scheduling of the fixture at White Hart Lane would develop into a saga that had some influence on the destination of the title.

By the beginning of December, the Toffees still topped the table with 35 points from 21 games, Leeds were three behind from one game more with Liverpool trailing a distant third on 28 points. Shankly's side were the next opponents, for the first derby of the season, at Goodison where the Toffees had won all ten league matches, scoring 28 goals in the process. Even more comforting, Liverpool had not won on the ground since returning to the top flight seven years before, and the unfancied Portuguese side, Vitoria Setubal, had just knocked them out of Europe. Although Everton were missing Husband and Harvey, replaced by derby debutants Alan Whittle and Tommy Jackson, they were still clear favourites going into the fixture.

Nevertheless, not for the first time the game did not go with the form guide. The visitors ruthlessly exposed the lack of balance in the team and the defensive frailties apparent in the earlier home matches of the season, particularly to crosses placed deep into the Everton box. Taking the game plan patented by Manchester City in the semi-final, Shankly brought in Ian Ross to perform a man-to-man marking job on Alan Ball and, with Ian St John and Emlyn Hughes, the Scot neutralized the Everton midfield. After a dull opening half, the visitors then went ahead when Hughes bundled the ball home at the far post from Ian Callaghan's cross. Six minutes later came one of the most famous of all derby moments – Sandy Brown's memorable diving header past his own goalkeeper from Peter Thompson's cross. The full-back later explained the traumatic sequence of events, 'I thought I was going to head it over the bar. At the last minute, the ball dipped and I didn't get the contact I intended. I was shouting at Gordon West to come for it, but it was too late.' The cameras captured perfectly the shocked Scot, on his knees inside the goal, staring at the ball in the back of the net. When Bobby Graham went through to complete a crushing 3-0 victory, the miserable afternoon for the home team was complete.

At one stage holding an eight-point lead in the title race, Everton were now just one ahead of Leeds United as they faced a trip to Upton Park seven days later. On a nerve-shredding afternoon, Everton produced their best defensive display of the season thus far, while Ball's restrained performance in the face of intense provocation was exemplary. The aggression was not entirely one way. 'Everton defended their lead in the league with physical determination rather than graceful skills,' said the watching Hugh McIlvanney in the *Observer*, adding that '[Frank] D'Arcy, the second-half substitute, behaved like a runaway bulldozer and Royle, descending to uncharacteristic depths, put Stephenson off the field with a dreadful foul.' The visitors got the break their resilience deserved on the half-hour, when Bobby Moore's ill-judged cross-field pass went straight to Alan Whittle, who ran forty yards to score past Bobby Ferguson. The Hammers laid siege to West's goal for the rest of the game, Geoff Hurst twice struck the woodwork while there was sweet irony when Sandy Brown headed off the line from the big Bermudian striker, Clyde Best, in the final minute. As one observer noted after the game, it was an afternoon when Everton showed the stuff of champions.

The pressure continued when they faced an excellent Derby County side at Goodison on the following Saturday, with Leeds' 4-1 victory over the Hammers during the week taking them top of the table for the first time. The Yorkshire side had played two games more than their rivals, partially due to the abandonment of Everton's game at Spurs on the same night due to floodlight failure, much to Catterick's frustration when it was mooted the game would be replayed at the end of the season. 'We could be without key players. We might even be without five players after 15 April because of England's World Cup defence. It's a real choker,' he complained. Against Derby, Brian Clough's side displayed the obduracy that characterised his Nottingham Forest side a decade later. Like Forest, they could also play and on a snow-bound pitch, Everton – and Ball in particular – needed to be at their best against a visiting team whose goalkeeper Les Green was magnificent. Elsewhere the Liverpool-born Roy McFarland showed the folly of both Catterick and Shankly allowing the best English centre-half of his era to leave Tranmere Rovers for the Midlands. After Green had saved a Royle penalty, the home side got the break their persistence deserved five minutes from time, Ball evading a number of challenges in the Derby penalty area to slide the ball past the keeper. Three days later, the home game against Manchester City followed an almost identical pattern in an equally memorable encounter, constant Everton pressure and a missed Royle penalty – this time the forward shooting against the post. There was also a late goal, this time one that was beautifully constructed; Royle headed Tommy Jackson's cross back into the middle of the box and a jubilant Whittle fired home.

Everton had scored more than one goal only once in nine games, but a trio of successive 1-0 victories had taken Catterick's side three points ahead of Leeds, from the same number of matches. It was a useful lead before the biggest league game of the season – the trip to Elland Road two days after Christmas. Whilst critics acknowledged Revie's side as by far the best team in England on a bad pitch, Everton had long been condemned for dropping from their high standards on heavy grounds. Catterick denied this on BBC's *Sportsnight with Coleman* earlier that month. 'We are not going to retreat from skilful football for heavy grounds or anything else, we have possibly the best cup record of any side over the past four seasons – and most cup football is played from December to March.'

The Everton manager had an opportunity to prove his point in a frozen west Yorkshire, having struck a minor psychological blow before the game. Everton and Manchester City had brought their match forward to give a free Boxing Day and avoid two fixtures inside 24 hours. Don Revie had tried to do the same with their game at Newcastle, but the Magpies quite correctly refused, citing the impact of losing the receipts from a full house at St. James' Park. As it happened they were proved correct, a crowd of 54,000 saw Leeds lose 2-1, their first league defeat since the loss at Goodison. Now three points ahead with a game in hand, Catterick missed a great opportunity to turn the screw in the battle of the dreadnoughts at Elland Road. Still without Harvey, whose eye condition was a continuing cause for concern, once again in a big game the manager eschewed the stylish play associated with his side. Figuring that Leeds, having played the day before, would tire late in the game, Catterick was keen to drag Revie's side into a war of attrition in the early stages but provoking their ruthless opponents into a physical battle proved to be a big mistake. 'It was Everton who set out on some wild vendetta and that it in itself was highly significant of their mounting anxiety,' said Geoffrey Green in *The Times*, adding 'the first quarter of an hour of this match was little short of mayhem. The stage seemed clear at Everton's behest for a bar room brawl devoid of Queensberry Rules.'

With such blatant, uncharacteristic machismo – 'From the kick off they charged like Highlanders – and most of them were swinging something more deadly than a kilt,' Hugh McIlvanney dutifully acknowledged in the *Observer* – Everton players committed seven of the first eight fouls of the game, Howard Kendall being the unlikely hatchet man. After that unusual beginning, Leeds established clear supremacy with Billy Bremner completely overshadowing a subdued Alan Ball and the home side were two goals up by the half-hour mark, when once again the weakness to high crosses proved to be Everton's undoing. First Peter Lorimer headed Bremner's centre into the six-yard box, with the excellent grafter Mick Jones finishing untidily. Lorimer also provided the assist for the second, his cross from the right touchline soaring a vast distance to the far post, where Jones out-jumped Hurst for his second of the afternoon. It took an hour for Everton to respond, when against the run of play Royle met Wright's free-kick from the right and from his nod-down Whittle bundled the ball home. Despite a late rally when Morrissey hit Gary Sprake's post, Leeds were comfortable winners, striking a huge blow to Everton's title aspirations. Indeed, as the 46,770 spectators left Elland Road, the feeling was that improving Chelsea – impressive 5-1 winners at Crystal Palace – in third place were the biggest threat to retaining their crown. A week later, a survey of fourteen top-flight managers in the *Sunday Times* found all but one thought Leeds would defend their title, with the other believing it would go to goal average. The bookmakers agreed: Leeds were now 4/7 with Everton pushed out to 2/1.

'Simply, the present team is not good enough'

Accusations that Everton lacked the resilience for a season-long challenge then re-appeared when they lost 2-1 at second division Sheffield United in the third-round of the FA Cup. Having gone behind to a Ball penalty, the underdogs overpowered Everton with direct, accurate football, unsurprisingly scoring both their goals from crosses that the visitors' defence failed to clear. Thankfully, with confidence low, an attempt to play the away game at Spurs failed for a third time on the following Wednesday, as Tottenham needed a cup replay. Twenty-four hours later there was further bad news. With three cautions during the campaign Alan Ball was summoned to an FA disciplinary commission in Derby. The result was a five-week ban and a £100 fine. With Colin Harvey still out with an eye problem, the verdict was hugely damaging. 'For Everton, this suspension is little short of a disaster,' wrote Donald Saunders in the *Daily Telegraph*, 'it could well cost them the championship.'

There were two positive developments on the following Saturday – a 3-0 win over Ipswich restored some lost confidence, with Royle scoring his first goals since November, a period in which the returning Jimmy Husband had been out of the team with injury. The fact was not lost on Catterick, who was a huge admirer of the Newcastle-born forward. 'He is a professionals' player,' the manager told Michael Charters in the *Liverpool Echo*, 'the professionals in the game know what he can do. No defence can afford to relax for a moment when he gets the ball.' Husband had an unusual style, although nominally a wide-man his tendency was to move inside on the diagonal. This was natural, as Catterick explained, 'Probably, Husband's best position is at inside left. He has never said a word about being asked to play on the right but just gone out and done a wonderful job for me.' Despite the victory over Ipswich, Billy Bremner did not share any of the renewed optimism. 'I think Everton are overrated,' the Leeds skipper told BBC's *Match of the Day*. As well as Husband's return, in another encouraging development, Colin Harvey successfully played for the 'A' team on the same day, having recovered from his eye condition, diagnosed as inflammation on an optic nerve. The midfielder elaborated on his return to the *Liverpool Echo*:

When it cleared Harry Catterick decided to ease me back with a game in the A team at Bellefield. That very morning, a paper ran a story that I was losing the sight of my eye. The reason Catterick barred the Press from Bellefield that day was that he didn't want me distracted, he just wanted me to measure my game again. I didn't even know the gates were locked and then we had those pictures of photographers up telephone poles trying to take a picture of me.

On the following Saturday the midfielder returned for the trip to Southampton, a calamitous encounter on the south coast against a side that had not tasted victory in twenty league matches. The familiar defensive shortcomings were all too apparent when the young Mick Channon scored from a cross in the first half and, after Morrissey equalised four minutes from the end, the future England international and successful racehorse trainer netted the damaging winner in injury-time. Recent signing Keith Newton failed to clear a cross and when Joe Kirkup's return came in, Channon headed home. Of the last nine goals conceded by Everton, eight had been via crosses from deep. With Leeds defeating Coventry on the same day to leapfrog Everton at the top, the performance and the setup of the team concerned the watching John Arlott in the *Guardian*: 'Everton are clearly alarmed, disturbed like a front runner whose lead is cut down and finally taken by an opponent of unmistakeable strength. They muster immense talent, yet they went into this game, against a team which had not won a league match since August, with two defensive players – Brown and Hurst – wearing inside forwards' shirts.'

Some years earlier Brian Labone commented about Gordon West that 'He takes defeat badly, too. He's bathed, dressed and gone within ten minutes every time we lose.' So when teammates targeted the Everton keeper for criticism in the away dressing room after the game, there was always going to be consequences. True to his skipper's words, West left the ground ten minutes before his colleagues. 'I will ask for a move on Monday,' the goalkeeper told the waiting press, who also heard the clearly distressed England international mutter 'this is the end for me.'

Although West had tempered his excitable and nervous nature over recent seasons, there was still the odd flashpoint and the keeper then went missing, a search establishing that he travelled to Southampton station alone. Arriving in London the goalkeeper went privately across the capital to Euston by taxi. On the train home to Merseyside, a visibly angry West sat alone in a compartment and did not have a meal with the others, reiterating he was putting in a transfer request. However, the expectation of a public showdown with Catterick on the Monday failed to materialise when the *Liverpool Daily Post*'s Jack Rowe advised West to take a step back and not act rashly. Whatever manager and player discussed, they did so privately, the goalkeeper subsequently denying newspaper reports of his discontent to end any transfer speculation. In the aftermath, Catterick was unhappy with the local press and made them *persona non grata*. The manager told

Dudley Doust in the *Sunday Times* that it was down to their behaviour on the journey home from London. 'On the train back, they went into West's compartment when they should have been eating with us in the dining room,' he said, 'Besides it was a matter between West and the club.'

The fallout from the West affair acted as a distraction from the second-half collapse of the side at the Dell, and a manager who tactically had lost his way, playing an extra full-back against a team with the worst home record in the division, while leaving Whittle on the sidelines. One angry correspondent to the *Liverpool Echo* wrote a week later, 'I was disgusted to see the selected Everton team at Southampton. For a manager who has gone on record as saying, "we play attractive, attacking football," Mr Catterick must have seen, with eight defensive players in his line-up, something which has eluded me and fellow supporters.'

The three remaining games of Ball's ban were all at home, the Toffees taking three points from the first two, a goalless draw against Newcastle United followed by a tight 1-0 victory over Wolves on the final day of January, when Royle's eighteenth goal of the campaign proved decisive. An argument over the banning television cameras then diverted attention away from the crucial fixture against Arsenal at Goodison. Once again that game highlighted a recurring weakness. 'The uncertainty of the defence must be a major concern to manager Harry Catterick at a crucial stage of Everton's championship challenge,' said the *Daily Mirror's* Derek Wallis as the home team conceded two sloppy goals to the Gunners and had to be thankful that Alan Whittle produced a pair of equalisers to snatch an undeserved draw. The following week the two-goal hero made way for the returning Ball,[51] but the result was another goalless draw at home, this time against Coventry City, for whom goalkeeper Bill Glazier had an inspired afternoon.

The final game of the month was a crucial trip to Nottingham Forest, against a side that had lost just once – to Leeds – in fifteen home league games that season. It was a bruising encounter. 'We want football,' chanted the crowd in the second half. Displaying nothing of the rhythm that had laid waste to the top-flight earlier in the campaign, the visitors went a goal down in the seventeenth minute when Keith Newton misread a cross-field pass from namesake, Henry, and from Barry Lyons' cross the Scot Alex Ingram headed home. Despite Ball being well shackled

51 When Ball wore his famous white boots for the first time, not against Chelsea in the Charity Shield in August 1970 as usually reported.

in midfield, showing aggravation 'like the postman who is having his legs attacked by a snapping terrier', according to the *Guardian*, Everton netted an important equaliser just after the break. A harmless cross from Wright confused the whole of the Forest defence and Royle scored with a header. Although it was a crucial goal, with Leeds winning 2-0 at home to Crystal Palace the Elland Road side now had a two-point lead at the top. Despite having played a game less, but with a significantly inferior goal average, for the first time the championship was out of Catterick's hands. 'The title may already have passed Everton by,' admitted the *Liverpool Daily Post*.

What had gone wrong with the side? One problem had been scoring goals, just seventeen in the same number of games. Joe Royle had netted just five in that time. Fellow forwards Husband and Morrissey had scored fourteen goals between them all season. Whereas the side had played with scientific precision in the early part of the campaign, Michael Charters in the *Liverpool Echo* commented that since December 'an insidious form of frenzy has developed' and 'that desire to succeed has become so frantic now that it is reflected in their play'. Catterick had simpler explanations. 'We've had too many players below their best,' he said, 'as many as four or five in one game. It is a question of getting a higher percentage of players in top form again. There's no logical reason for the dip in form.' There was a more specific reason though, as he later revealed to Dudley Doust in the *Sunday Times*. 'The loss of Ball was crucial, without Harvey for eight or nine matches, we were even worse off.'

Although Catterick was still cautiously optimistic on their title chances, others were not so. Leeds had become so battle-hardened that supporters saw no way back in the title-race, notwithstanding the Yorkshire side had the pressure of fighting across three fronts, in the hunt for a remarkable treble of the league, FA Cup and European Cup. However, they showed no signs of letting up, Leeds 'gave the impression they could climb Everest without oxygen', according to the *Observer*. In contrast, Catterick's side were stumbling up the rock face. 'Everton must be feeling they get punished for every mistake they make,' said Billy Bremner in a 1970 attempt at mind games. One supporter's views vented to the *Liverpool Echo* painted an angry picture of a team revisiting old habits:

Despite the excuses, the reason for Everton's recent poor performances is the same old story of disintegration when real pressure is put on them. I remember their poor finishing against West Bromwich at Wembley, their poor display at Villa Park [in the 1969 FA Cup semi-final] and a complete inability to win vital League games both this season and last. Simply, the present team is not good enough.

Turning the tide in March

Despite such hard words, there were still nine games to redress the balance. The first was at the start of March when Everton travelled to Burnley, while Leeds had a tough fixture at Anfield. With Jimmy Husband out injured, Whittle was back in the side. The belief beforehand was the snow-covered pitch would make conditions unplayable, so Gordon West and Brian Labone consumed extra-large breakfasts at the team hotel. Without their knowledge, an army of volunteers helped clear most of the snow and the game, to their horror, went ahead. Nobody knows whether the additional portions limited their mobility, but when West rushed from his line in the first half, the goalkeeper collided with his colleague and Labone's damaged kidney ruled the defender out for the remainder of the season. The club skipper later recalled the incident to BBC Radio Merseyside:

The ball was going back to Westie and Steve Kindon was about to overtake me. As I wasn't as quick as him, Westie was forced to come out and we collided at a combined speed of forty miles per hour. I was badly winded and was getting worse and worse before the end of the game. In the toilet afterwards I was passing blood and ended up two weeks in Lourdes Hospital with ruptured kidneys. From that double breakfast we had I was in hospital for two weeks.

It was the only black spot on a good day for the Toffees. A suspiciously offside Alan Ball put the visitors ahead, only to see Burnley equalise within sixty seconds, but when the ball ran loose in the Clarets' penalty box before the break, John Hurst was on hand to score the winner and a season-changing goal. Leeds drew 0-0 at Anfield, when Everton had to thank Leo Callaghan for a huge slice of luck, the referee blowing for full time just before the visitors' Paul Madeley put the ball in the net. Partially thanks to Callaghan, a reinvigorated Everton's destiny was again in their own hands, with a deficit of a single point having played a game less.

Four days later came the visit to Spurs, for the fourth attempt at playing the fixture, in rain-sodden conditions. 'I should have a season ticket for this place, I've been here so often,' joked Catterick. It would have been another aborted attempt, but for the Herculean efforts of the ground staff to make the pitch playable after snow threatened to produce a further postponement. Roger Kenyon replaced the injured Labone and with the midfield triumvirate showing signs of recovering their form, the visitors scored the only goal of the game on nineteen minutes when Newton's cross from the left swerved across the face of the Spurs goal and Alan Whittle fired home. Catterick took great satisfaction from the performance of Ball, the stand-in skipper producing one of his best displays of the season, the only player to retain his poise and touch on a surface 'resembling Blackpool beach with the tide going out', according to *The Times*. Everton were now a point ahead of Leeds, with seven games left apiece. 'They have rediscovered heart, drive and purpose just when it can do them most good,' wrote Horace Yates in the *Liverpool Daily Post*.

Everton played Spurs in their next game too, with referee Danny Lyden the centre of attention on a dramatic afternoon of three penalties at Goodison Park. The game stood evenly balanced at 1-1 when opposition centre-half Mike England conceded the first of the afternoon, needlessly fouling Royle by the dead ball line, with Ball converting easily. Then the defender repeated the offence, this time pushing Royle in the back. Pat Jennings saved Ball's kick, although the referee ignored his linesman's flag, signalling the keeper had moved beforehand. Spurs then brought parity with the third penalty of the afternoon, twenty minutes from time. Thankfully for most of the 53,000 crowd, Royle netted again four minutes later. The four points taken off Spurs in as many days took them three clear of Leeds, who on the same afternoon drew the first of three magnificent, but draining, FA Cup semi-final games against Manchester United, four days before facing Standard Liege in the second leg of their European Cup quarter-final.

Seven days later came the game Evertonians had been waiting three months for – a chance for revenge at Anfield. Liverpool had tailed off after a strong start to the season and four weeks before had lost at Watford in the FA Cup, a watershed match in the Anfield side's history, signalling the end of several senior players' careers. The large band of Everton supporters spread around the ground knew that any league title would taste sweeter if Catterick's side could avenge the Goodison debacle. Their wishes came true in the best way possible. Eleven minutes into the game came the opening goal for the visitors, which highlighted perfectly the renewed confidence of the side and the primacy of the midfield trio.

Ball, near the right touchline, made Hurst's awkward pass look straightforward and his second touch fed Kendall. Taking a few strides infield, the future Goodison boss slipped the ball to Harvey, who without seemingly looking played a reverse pass to Morrissey on the left flank. Moving inside, the winger's cross was met by the trio of Joe Royle, Liverpool goalkeeper Ray Clemence and Ron Yeats, the Everton striker's head appearing to get the final touch as the ball looped into the goal at the Kop end.

Four minutes after half-time the visitors clinched the game. Royle's header from Sandy Brown's free-kick ended up with Whittle glancing home Harvey's shot off his knee. Gordon West had enjoyed a famously tempestuous but good-humoured relationship with the Kop end, but as he told Gerald Sinstadt and Brian Barwick for their book *Everton v Liverpool: A celebration of the Merseyside derby*, the second goal brought sweet satisfaction, one that was captured memorably on camera:

It happened when I ran down to the Kop goal for the first time. I suddenly realised that the whole crowd there was putting two fingers up. I'd no idea what it was all about. I looked over my shoulder to see who it was meant for – and there was no one there. Then I realised they were doing it to me. But it all came right for me in 1970. After we'd lost 3-0 at Goodison, there we were at Anfield where I'd been taking all this stick. We were 1-0 up at half-time and that was good, but it wasn't good enough for me. Then we went 2-0 up and I remember being on my hands and knees looking up at the Kop – and they were all silent. It was just lovely.

It was an equally pleasant feeling for all the Everton fans as their team swept aside their local rivals with imperious ease. The midfield trio 'were now indisputable masters,' according to David Miller in the *Sunday Telegraph*, 'evading and absorbing Liverpool's renowned physical challenge with swift switching of position, which consistently found the opposition arrive just as the train was pulling out'. The visitors comfortably kept the game under their command until full time, when their supporters' chants of 'Champions! Champions!' echoed around the home of their enemy. Max Marquis in the *Sunday Times* had no doubts who the star turns were, 'Nearly all the Everton players did well, but Ball, the self-possessed man of the match, Harvey and Kendall were quite devastating … Liverpool, unhappily, were a bunch of journeymen against the Everton artists.'

After the game, the press asked Catterick whether the team had come out of their slump. 'What slump? We have won twenty-five games. Nobody has won more than twenty,' he replied bullishly. For Alan Ball it was one of the most memorable games of his club career, the midfielder relishing the closing stages with victory secured. 'Those last five minutes I'll always savour from my football life,' he later recalled with some pride, 'there wasn't another feeling like that one in the world.'[52] The only downside of a memorable afternoon was the news from Molineux, where a patched-up Leeds side had resiliently ground out a 2-1 win.

Revie's side were still three points behind, with a game in hand, and it was clear that the following Easter weekend was crucial, Everton entertaining Chelsea on the Saturday with a trip to Stoke on the Monday, with Leeds' corresponding fixtures against Southampton at Elland Road and a difficult visit to Derby County. Just as crucially in the interim Don Revie's side had two further titanic FA Cup semi-final matches against Manchester United, winning the second 1-0 to reach Wembley. In front of a Goodison crowd of more than 57,000 – wound up no doubt about Catterick's recent claim that 'at times this season I felt our support was not what it should be' – Everton had an opportunity to take a major step towards a seventh league title against Chelsea. Those supporters with radios heard before the game that Leeds, with Revie resting several players following urgent medical advice, had put out five reserves for the visit of Southampton. (Their substitute was Jimmy Lumsden, who later worked with David Moyes at Everton.) Don Revie, still chasing two cups, appeared to be waving the white flag.

On paper, the London side, having lost just twice in 28 games, should have been formidable opposition but with goalkeeper Peter Bonetti and Ron Harris out injured – and minds on the FA Cup final three weeks later – they proved to be feeble adversaries, with deputy stopper Tommy Hughes having a nightmare afternoon.[53] Howard Kendall opened the scoring after just fourteen seconds (the fastest goal scored by an Everton player on the ground) and, with the clock at the

52 Ball enjoyed a tremendous record at Anfield. In a 20-year period when Liverpool were dominant at home, for a visitor the England international uniquely enjoyed a winning record on the ground, six victories – for Blackpool, Everton, Arsenal (3) and Southampton – against five defeats. That mirrored his entire club-playing career against the Anfield side, 12 wins against 10 losses in 33 matches, with 11 goals scored.

53 Hughes had replaced the flu-ridden Bonetti in Chelsea's 5-2 home defeat to Leeds in January. His hapless display did not go unnoticed by the *Observer*. 'It would take a holiday in Afghanistan to protect him from the aftermath of a performance that brought back memories of the Scottish eccentric Frank Haffey.' The Scot of course once let in nine at Wembley for his country. Chelsea's performance at Goodison was also affected by the breaking of a club curfew by central defenders David Webb and John Dempsey on the night before the game.

corner of the Gwladys Street end barely showing five minutes past three, Alan Ball met Morrissey's cross at the far post to head home unopposed. After that it was a procession, Royle scored with a header before the break and added a fourth immediately after, while Alan Whittle completed the scoring from Morrissey's cross before the hour mark. Not even two late Chelsea goals could spoil the party atmosphere. 'This was the superb Everton of last September,' said Derek Hodgson in the *Daily Telegraph*.[54]

Celebrations increased after the game when news filtered through from Elland Road. Having gone ahead through Peter Lorimer on the hour, Leeds' weakened team collapsed in almost comical fashion. Revie's side, usually so sound defensively, conceded two own goals and a penalty on their way to a shock 3-1 defeat. Everton were now five points ahead and needed six from four games to become champions. Arthur Hopcraft summed up the prevailing mood in the *Observer*: 'With this ebullient win Everton seem to have claimed the championship. In any case, the game will be cherished in recollection for a long time by Everton supporters as the one in which the team made all their promises blossom.'

By Easter Monday evening, Everton needed just two points. On an afternoon when Alan Whittle's early goal settled the game against Stoke, Catterick's side showed the hallmark of champions – winning despite not playing well. Gordon West, in particular, was outstanding, the keeper having his best game of the season. Down the road, Leeds United, two days before a European Cup semi-final date against Celtic, fielded an entire reserve side at Derby County and were soundly beaten 4-1. Their defeat made the mathematics of the title chase easy: if Everton defeated West Brom at Goodison two days later, they were champions.

Apart from the promise of seeing the potential champions, the 58,000 Everton supporters travelling to Goodison on Wednesday 1 April would have been talking about the inclement weather. The temperature hovered just above freezing all day after an overnight snowfall and there was still a damp chill remaining in the air as a packed ground saw their team line up against a West Brom side featuring four teenagers. Catterick's side laid siege to the visitors' goal from the start but had to wait twenty minutes for the breakthrough, Whittle killing Harvey's shot with the outside of his foot before turning neatly and firing past John Osborne. The cool

[54] Everton created top-flight history with the victory over Chelsea, becoming the first team since the expansion to 22 clubs in 1919 to defeat all their opponents at least once in the league during the season. It was only achieved once more before the reduction to 20 clubs in the Premier League era – by Everton again in 1984/85.

finish was his eleventh goal in fourteen games. The second goal on 65 minutes was a beauty. Man-of-the-match Colin Harvey picked up a loose ball, beat two men and from the inside-left channel struck a ferocious shot past Osborne. The rest of the game was played out in scenes of mounting excitement, large numbers of spectators invading the pitch (and the press-box) when referee Leo Callaghan blew for full time. Afterwards, Manchester United chairman and member of the League Management Committee, Louis Edwards, presented stand-in skipper Alan Ball with the championship trophy. It was a wholly satisfying achievement. Not surprisingly, Catterick opened up to the press afterwards:

They wanted me to predict this success weeks ago, but I have learned to be patient. Now I regard this as a triumph for the players, the reward for genuine teamwork. I rate it a tremendous achievement to score twenty-eight wins in this, the toughest competition in the world. Every player has played his part splendidly, and I am proud of them.

Everton won the title because they were the best league team in England that season. Fortunately, their bad spell came during the middle of the campaign, meaning they had time to regroup before forging ahead in the final six weeks. As Brian Labone admitted, 'We won the Championship, lost it and won it again in the end. We have had to withstand a lot of criticism, but it has all worked out well.' Although the skipper's old joke that the midfield trio of Ball, Harvey and Kendall was 'the only three man team to win the title', this was not the case. The three players – David Miller in the *Sunday Telegraph* described them as 'possibly the most valuable midfield combination in European soccer' – appeared together in only 24 of the 42 league games that season. Curiously, there was little difference between the team's win percentage when all were available and if one of the trio was out. That said it was impossible to underplay their contribution. In the words of Colin Wood in the *Daily Mail*, 'Until another club can find the means to subdue the astonishing invention, stamina and scoring power of the midfield trio of Harvey, Kendall and Ball, Everton will remain among the leaders.' Ball, for his part, reflected on their role in the campaign for the *Liverpool Echo* in January 1974:

We played complete and utter football. We didn't have an anchor man, all three of us went forward and went back as well as scoring goals – and we got a lot in that season. We played together as one man. We were utterly dedicated to playing football, to going at teams and taking them apart. That one season, we were out of this world.

Although the vaunted midfield trio took the plaudits, the title triumph was a real team effort where fortunately any injuries or suspensions happened to players with ready-made replacements. Ulsterman Tommy Jackson effectively filled in for one of the midfield stars, Roger Kenyon appeared to be the natural successor for Brian Labone and, famously, Alan Whittle's goals were pivotal. Four of those came in 1-0 victories, which numbered ten in total – the same as the two previous seasons combined. Greater patience and resilience had transmitted into the art of winning games, but the graceful play of Catterick's team was a welcome antidote to the relentlessly uncompromising style of Leeds and Liverpool. Malcolm Winton noted these points in the *Sunday Times*, 'Everyone who likes stylish football will be grateful that Everton are the new champions. To their elegance they have added heart. They used to give up too easily but after that terrific fight-back against Leeds in the championship nobody can accuse them of that now.' Nevertheless, Eric Todd in the *Guardian* summed up the campaign in the most comprehensive fashion:

Rich in resources, prolific in talent and ambition, Everton made it clear from the start that they meant to win something. They were an exceptional team and they played like one showing a fine contempt of crises when they were denuded of the services of such stalwarts as Harvey, Labone and the incredible Ball. Above all, perhaps, they have confirmed that money can buy success although that statement on its own fails to take into account the work put in to make the success possible.

Everton won, somewhat fortuitously, three days later at Sheffield Wednesday before concluding the campaign with a goalless draw at Sunderland. Their total of 66 points was a club record and one less than the highest ever in the division, achieved by Leeds twelve months before. Everton scored 72 goals and, despite the odd alarm, only 34 were conceded, West keeping a club-record 21 clean sheets. A major factor in the defence was the calming presence of John Hurst at centre-half, who had joined the club as a schoolboy forward in 1962. Although not the quickest, Hurst was a great reader of the game, could push up and the link-up with his skipper effectively became Everton's first established central defensive partnership. Labone later paid tribute to his colleague: 'He originally came to us as an inside forward but lacked a bit of pace for the position and dropped back alongside me. I attacked the ball and he was in the sweeper role. He had more skill on the ball than me and was a good reader of play who was very cool and unflappable.'

Supporters expected it to be the start of a golden period. For Alan Ball, a World Cup winner, it was the first (and last) domestic winner's medal of his career.[55] The midfielder proclaimed after the game, 'I honestly believe we are the best team in the country. I can see five great seasons ahead. This team is certain to go better. We have lots of skill and every player works hard for each other. With that behind us how can we fail?' The Everton manager agreed. 'They have a long way to go before they reach their peak,' proclaimed Catterick. Whether they would depended on Everton repeating their form of the golden autumn and early spring, rather than the vulnerable side they had exhibited in the winter months. That aside, in all respects, winning the league title in such a dominant fashion was a hugely impressive achievement, but somehow it is almost a forgotten championship outside of Goodison.

In the shadows

In his review of Rob Sawyer's excellent biography of Harry Catterick in November 2014, the *Guardian's* Daniel Taylor remarked that the former Everton manager 'occupies a strange place in football's annals, embraced by few, rarely mentioned when the sport drifts into nostalgia and the stories of his era are regaled'. A key factor in this assessment is the circumstances surrounding the winning of the 1969/70 title. The compressed nature of the campaign deprived spectators of the excitement of a prolonged duel for the crown between Everton and Leeds, by some distance the two best teams in the country. The contest should have captured both the headlines and the imagination of the wider public. On the first Saturday in March, each side had one hand on the championship trophy, but while Everton played seven league games in the next 25 days, Leeds appeared in only four whilst also engaging in six draining cup matches. With Catterick's side winning all their games and Leeds dropping points, instead of the contest being similar to two golfers going head-to-head on the closing holes of a major

55 Once when challenged about his lack of career medals, Ball, referring to 1966, replied 'just the big one son.'

championship, it produced an anti-climax where Everton posted a score in the clubhouse their exhausted opponents could not match. This mismatch in fixtures and the suddenness of the triumph therefore deprived fans of a memorable finale to the season.

The contest for the league title was merely a third of the campaign's plot, which for some time had distilled to Leeds' quest for the treble. Consequently when the title was clinched on April Fools' Day, Everton were in the margins as the 'Battle of Britain' – the first leg of the Leeds and Celtic European Cup semi-final, taking place on the same night – dominated the back page headlines. Leeds' journey ultimately resulted in failure across all three fronts – runners-up in the league, Don Revie's side lost the tie against Celtic and then the FA Cup final to Chelsea. The Yorkshire club therefore cast a shadow over everybody else in the closing months of the 1969/70 season, primarily Everton of course, who became one of a number of bit-part actors as Leeds took the starring role.

A glance at the 'Review of the Season' in the first of the famous *Rothmans Football Yearbooks*, published that summer, also highlights this point. Beginning with the story of Leeds' season – 'they had a fantastic campaign' the editorial said – the review pauses to talk about Manchester City's continued progress under Joe Mercer (who ended the season with the League Cup and European Cup Winners' Cup) and Arsenal's Fairs Cup triumph. Only at the bottom of the first page does the annual mention the title victory, beginning by saying that 'Everton's performance in winning the League title was, unfortunately, overshadowed by Leeds' efforts.' However, the review does go on to say that 'it was a first class, and eminently worthy performance.' In the *Sun*, Peter Batt summed it up in similar fashion, 'Unfortunately they have won the title in a year when their own consistency has been overshadowed by the rest of the country's obsession with Leeds' assault on the treble.'

There was also the theory that Everton did not deserve to be champions anyway. Leeds, by fielding weakened teams near the end of the campaign, had handed the title to Catterick's side. On face value, the argument has some merit; as several publications about Leeds have pointed out the gap between the two sides of nine points was exactly the number they dropped in those last six games. That ignores two salient facts: Leeds would have needed to win all those matches, and that Everton took only a point from their last game at already relegated Sunderland, a match they would surely have won had the need arose. However, as

Alan Ball pointed out at the time it would have been interesting to see how Everton would have reacted if Leeds had kept the pressure up to the end of the season. But there are always various narratives to any title campaign, and the fact remains Everton finished well clear of the chasing pack, their perfectly executed sprint finish literally forcing Leeds into submission.

Added to that, in a perfect world Everton should also have lifted the championship trophy at Goodison on a warm May Saturday afternoon, broadcast – if permitted by the club – in glorious technicolour for more than 10 million viewers on BBC's *Match of the Day* that night, the audience presented with a chance to appreciate the excellence of Catterick's side. Instead, the celebration took place on a freezing cold April evening, recorded for posterity on a few rolls of grainy black and white news film. Supporters could argue, with some justification, that there is no bad time to become champions, but the nature of the climax to the league season contributed to the lack of wider public recognition. It was very much an insular triumph.

To rub further salt into the wounds, the Manager of the Year award did not go to Catterick. In 1970 the 24 British sports writers making up the panel broke from tradition and gave the award to Don Revie ahead of the Everton boss, by just two votes, to the surprise of their managerial peers. Previously they had given the honour to the manager of the league champions or of the European Cup winners. Catterick seemed nonplussed about his failure to land the award. 'Of course I am disappointed,' he admitted, 'in fact it is one of the most disappointing things ever to happen to me in football. The voting shows that you don't have to win something to win the award.' Even his closest rival exhibited some sympathy several years later. 'It must have been a terrible blow for a fellow like Harry, who had just won his second championship,' Bill Shankly wrote in his autobiography.

Catterick also admitted in the aftermath of the title triumph to receiving tempting offers from other clubs during his time in the Goodison hot seat. As well as one big club who offered 'a lovely house with its own swimming pool' he also told Horace Yates in the *Liverpool Daily Post* of an offer received following the notorious incident at Blackpool in 1966. Catterick said, 'Within a week of the assault, a big club had moved in, feeling this was the time to strike, the time when I would be receptive to an offer.'

Two years before that, having not renewed his contract, Catterick held preliminary discussions with the Italian agent, Gigi Peronace, about a possible move to manage in Serie A. (It was probably no coincidence that a new deal at Goodison was agreed shortly afterwards.) Then in 1965 there was an offer of £10,000 a year to manage Wolves, which he turned down. In December 1968, Catterick also rejected approaches from both Nottingham Forest and Leicester City. According to informed sources in February 1970, he was also the target for a number of big clubs on the Iberian Peninsula. Nevertheless, this reply to Yates on why he remained Everton manager summed up his reasons for staying:

It is simply that I am very much an Evertonian. I have spent most of my life here. As far as I am concerned this club is a way of life. I like to feel I have another ten years to give to the game. I would like to think I will be an Evertonian to the end of my managerial days.

19. Strained Relations

DURING THE 1960S AND EARLY 1970S, THE FIRST SEEDS WERE SOWN of football's growth into the sporting, business and cultural phenomenon it is today. Clubs (and the national team) faced pressures not really witnessed before via the intense desire for success and media scrutiny, especially so with the growth of television. Everton's reaction to those changes were largely viewed as hostile. At a shareholder's meeting during that period, one attendee accused the Everton board of being 'anti-everything'. A harsh accusation perhaps but there was an element truth in the description, acknowledged in chairman George Watts' reply that the club had 'a hell of a lot more to do to overcome this apparent bad image we have'. The question of how much of this was down to the board and how much was Catterick's wishes was a debatable point. Although when it came to releasing players for international duty there was no doubt whose views took precedence.

Club versus country

When Catterick took over at Goodison in 1961, Walter Winterbottom was the England manager and at that point, remarkably, no Everton player had been capped for the national team in the post-war era. Brian Labone broke that sequence when selected for the 3-1 victory over Northern Ireland in October 1962. The defender later appeared in Alf Ramsey's first game in charge, a 5-2 loss against France four months later, but it was four years before his next appearance. However, with other internationals on the books, there was the age-old question of priorities. There were no designated international weeks and also some Saturday games that clashed with the league programme, when the rules only allowed clubs to postpone matches if they had at least two players called up for duty simultaneously.[56] There was a perpetual club versus country battle.

In the 1962/63 season, with a squad full of internationals now at Goodison, it was inevitable that there would be conflict. Although the club was able to postpone the game against Nottingham Forest in October with three players on international duty, Catterick was criticised for not releasing Roy Vernon for Wales' crucial European Championship qualifying game against Hungary in March 1963. There was also a dispute following Tony Kay's selection for his England debut against Brazil in the first week of May, coming 24 hours after Everton's crucial visit to West Brom. Catterick asked the FA if they could release Kay but they told him, 'No. Impossible. Out of the question.' Frustratingly for Everton, the FA had released both Bobby Charlton and Ray Wilson for important games for their clubs. Then before the international, Everton withdrew Kay from the squad without warning. England manager Ramsey took an uncharacteristically diplomatic stance. 'I am disappointed of course, because Kay is an important player for England,' Ramsey said, 'but he is important to Everton too. And this match could decide the title.' Kay quite rightly was keen not to jeopardise his future chances, telling the *Daily Mirror*, 'It was the club's decision – not mine.'

For others it was a typical short-sighted action. 'This club has always bent over backwards to put themselves first,' noted a disapproving Brian James in the *Daily Mail*, adding that 'Scots and Welshmen have been refused permission to play for their country.' James had a point; the club took the unusual step of refusing to release players for international duty for a period at the start of the 1961/62 season as it dealt with an injury crisis. However, Catterick defended his actions in a *News of the World* interview during the summer of 1963. 'Everton must come before any national or domestic consideration. If I were England's team manager, I would want clubs to put England first. Employed by Everton I must be strictly professional. Results count more than even the style of play,' the manager said.

As the decade wore on there were increasing international calls on Catterick's side, with the usual nervous wait for news on casualties – the Everton manager particularly abhorred midweek games, which gave little recovery time. In the

56 Some cynics claimed that the strange signing of the Northern Ireland international Jimmy Hill from Norwich City in September 1963 was to further protect the club from this rule, the winger making just seven appearances in two years.

1967/68 season, Ray Wilson (twice) and Alan Ball both missed games through injuries sustained whilst playing for England. Matters came to a head in November 1968, when England travelled to Romania for a friendly while seven days later there was a separate game for the under-23 side, captained by John Hurst, at Birmingham. Tommy Wright sustained an injury in Bucharest after ten minutes and nobody from the FA contacted Catterick. The first the manager knew about the knock was when the full-back arrived home some 36 hours after the match. To make matters worse Howard Kendall then pulled a hamstring in the under-23 side, one described by Sir Alf Ramsey as 'not too serious'. The England manager's comments annoyed Catterick in the aftermath:

It's all right for Sir Alf to say after the game in Birmingham this week that he did not think Kendall's injury in that game was not too serious. It's serious for Everton if he misses one game and I'm sure it concerns our season ticket holders that one of the club's players will be missing because of an injury received in what was, after all, a friendly game. Where will it end, this one-way traffic in co-operation? I am all for country against club when important issues are at stake. But I cannot see the worth of international games of no consequence being played when vital European contests and the championships are in dispute.

Catterick later boycotted a get-together organised by Ramsey four weeks later, to coincide with the home match against Bulgaria. Twelve months later there was further rancour. Catterick withdrew Labone and Ball from the squad to face Holland in November 1969, so before the Wembley international against Portugal four weeks later, Ramsey wanted all the selected squad to attend beforehand, for a full medical from two doctors and two trainers. Unsurprisingly, Catterick had issues, refusing to send the selected Harvey and Labone to London. Although Harvey's eye injury was serious, Catterick said Labone had a 'toe in plaster' but the defender played in both league games either side of the England contest.

Commenting on press criticism that Everton had refused half of the sixteen requests for international duty that season, Catterick told Robert Oxby in the *Daily Telegraph*: 'In the last three years I have had seven or eight players returning injured from England duty. It has meant doing without them the following Saturday. Nobody has the right to criticize me for putting the interests of my employers first. If we reach the end of the season without winning anything and I have a shareholders meeting, it won't help me to say players were unavailable because of England calls.'

Such a stance was understandable, but it did little to enhance the reputation of Catterick and the club, and by default damaged the prospects of his stars. No Everton player who made their England debut under Ramsey had a lengthy international career – Wilson and Ball were established in the side before joining and Labone started under Winterbottom – and, notoriously, Howard Kendall was not capped at all.[57] Although not alone in his concerns, Catterick was regarded as the most outspoken critic of the international set-up but it was the lack of communication between the parties that was damaging. As Brian James said in the *Daily Mail*, 'The whole thing has become a little childish. A straight talk between Sir Alf and those who think like Catterick would be the place to start.' That did not happen.

On (and off) the small screen

The received wisdom surrounding Harry Catterick was that he did not like Everton matches televised as it gave rivals an opportunity to study playing styles and tactics. There was perhaps an element of truth in that. However, as early as 1961 the Everton manager aired his suspicions on the growth of television and the threat the small screen posed to football as an alternative source of entertainment. Consequently, the manager was against televised football on the basis that he felt the authorities consistently undervalued the product and gave it away too cheaply to a direct rival. His stance was pay the going rate and there were no issues televising football.

That said, when Catterick entered Goodison Park in 1961 he was pushing at an open door with regards to distrusting television. In fact, the Board's suspicions were even more entrenched than their manager's. Having twelve months earlier fought against the screening of live games, in 1966 Everton banned the cameras for a period, not because of the manager's wishes but over a point of principle of the Football League negotiating a television contract without consulting with the clubs. It was Everton, and not just necessarily Catterick, who did not want

57 Having said that Ramsey's loyalty to the old guard and the plethora of talent in English football restricted opportunities generally. A good example is West Brom's Tony Brown, scorer of more than 200 league goals as a Frank Lampard type attacking midfielder, who won just one cap in 1971.

television coverage during the decade.[58] Thereafter the club's suspicions of the small screen remained, but they were certainly not alone.

However, a combination of the 1966 World Cup win and the advent of colour television made football on the box a compelling attraction. At the start of the new decade the sport enjoyed massive audiences – ITV's *Big Match* covering the London area alone used to get upwards of nine million viewers – as the game became a mainstay of popular culture. With Everton challenging for the title, in 1969/70 it was no surprise that the cameras were a regular feature at Goodison Park. By the time of the home game against Arsenal in February 1970, Everton had featured on the small screen in fifteen out of the 25 weekends in the campaign, leading to the Goodison hierarchy making a decision that people cite regularly as symbolising Everton's distrust of television under Catterick. Mindful that the team had received too much exposure in their opinion, chairman Jack Sharp told the BBC that the club would not allow the cameras for the visit of the London side. Sharp explained, 'The board felt that Everton have had a surfeit of television this season and thought that some other clubs should have the opportunity of having the games televised. Everton have no bias against it in any way.' Sharp was correct. Although the history books say that the club (and Catterick) generally distrusted television, the occasional banning of cameras was an exception, not the general rule. During the three years prior to 1970 the cameras visited Goodison twelve times for league matches – exactly the same amount as at Anfield, where Liverpool enjoyed a more 'media friendly' reputation.[59]

But the burgeoning interest in the sport across newspapers and television meant Everton's stance on coverage at the time was outmoded. Having support in some quarters for banning the cameras, Sharp put the club under the further spotlight in an interview with the *Daily Mail*: 'This is certainly no crusade against television. Basically, we are not against it. Our manager, Harry Catterick, feels that every tactical move we make is open to scrutiny. Clubs who may be playing

---

58 Everton took their ban on cameras to ludicrous lengths. In the home game against Stoke in February 1966, chairman E. Holland Hughes said he had turned away a BBC cameraman who wanted to film the game. This was news to the BBC, who said 'we had no plans to film this match'. The mystery was solved when it turned out the man was a freelance seeking background shots for the television serial 'United!' The lack of co-operation also manifested itself in having no permanent platform for cameras near the halfway line: until 1970 they were placed incongruously in the Main Stand on a line with the edge of the Park End penalty box.

59 Prior to the 1970/71 season, *Match of the Day* featured highlights of just one game per show, as did regional programmes on commercial television. When Everton supporters bemoan the absence of televised footage of, say, Alex Young or Alan Ball, it is due to the lack of footage generally, not Everton's dislike of the cameras.

us only a short time after these TV games may be able to profit by a close study of methods.'

Whether Catterick welcomed the chairman bringing his name into the issue is not known, but either way critics disparaged Sharp's view on the basis that opposition scouts watching from the stands had the same view as the cameras and the televised ban could not extend to away games. Equally perplexing was that Catterick had previously appeared in front of the BBC cameras in December 1969, admitting to the team's vulnerability to high balls from wide, while giving a detailed summary of the individual strengths and weaknesses of his players. Sharp then denied the allegation that there were playing reasons for turning the cameras away. 'Our decision is not concerned with exposure of tactical moves on the TV screens,' he told the *Liverpool Daily Post*. The Everton manager, though, got some unlikely support from old foe Danny Blanchflower in his always-readable *Sunday Express* column, although the former Spurs player thought it was also a sign of pressure:

Harry Catterick is right. It takes an expert eye to see it in the heat of the game but any mug can see it when the TV camera slows it down or repeats it again and again as they are inclined to do with the goals ... If TV has visited Goodison 15 times this season, that is too much. Obviously, they wanted to be there as often as possible because you are in the forefront of the race. They have been greedy and they have brought the ban upon themselves.

Blanchflower then went on to surmise whether the ban reflected the pressures of the title-race on the Everton manager. 'What a pity you did not limit it earlier rather than ban it now. Your move now is rather like shutting the gate after the horse has bolted. If some managers have not already got wise to your tactical moves, then your action will bring their attention to them,' Blanchflower claimed, 'I am worried about your chances now, Harry, because you are worried about them yourself ... I think you have played into Leeds' hands.' History would show that regardless of Catterick's beliefs, ultimately the ban did not influence the destiny of the championship.

However, having welcomed the cameras back at the start of the 1970/71 season, with ten of their matches already televised across the networks, for the second time in less than twelve months the directors barred BBC cameras from showing the Leeds game at Goodison just before Christmas. Like many, the board felt that there was over-exposure and this was contributing to a decline in attendances. Catterick concurred about the impact on gates, but the manager's primary belief about television was that broadcasters got football on the cheap, which was also true. *Match of the Day* paid just £750 a game to the home side for coverage, while commercial television could pay a paltry £30 upwards for screening regional matches. When Everton faced Borussia Mönchengladbach in their 1970 European Cup tie, the manager noted their opponents received £11,000 from German TV for the rights to screen the home leg, while ITV paid Everton just £2,500 for the match at Goodison. 'Football and television are both in the entertainment business. We are rivals for crowd support,' Catterick told the *Liverpool Echo*. 'We should not allow TV to have easy use of football. The pull of TV is strong enough for many people to keep them from active watching. We must not help to make it stronger.' [60]

With the televised ban still in operation, when it was suggested after the impressive 3-0 win over Chelsea in January 1971 that the club had passed up a good promotional opportunity, Catterick responded bluntly. 'My heart bleeds for television,' he said. However, when asked whether he would revise those objections if Everton received £4,000 per game, rather than the standard £750, he changed his tune. 'I certainly would,' Catterick admitted.

The Everton manager received surprising support from his managerial rival from across the Park, who was not as welcoming to television as people suggest. Shankly wanted to stop the Saturday lunchtime preview shows and television providing score updates while games were in progress.[61] The Liverpool manager also agreed with his Goodison counterpart about the wider issues. 'The money the

60 Catterick may have been sceptical about the relationship between football and television but that did not stop him appearing for the Everton team in BBC's *Quizball* in 1970. A rather convoluted programme where players scored goals by answering questions, Everton – consisting of Catterick, Brian Labone, Joe Royle and guest supporter, disc-jockey Ed Stewart – lost to Celtic in the final. The big game was the semi-final against a Falkirk outfit lead by Alex Ferguson. Trailing with one question remaining Ferguson's teammate, future Scotland boss Andy Roxburgh, was struggling to name the winning rider of the previous year's Grand National. With Ferguson whispering the answer at the other end of the table, a wavering Roxburgh incorrectly blurted out the world's most famous flat-jockey, Lester Piggott. A visibly angry Ferguson uttered 'Jesus Christ' in the first public viewing of what was later known as the 'hairdryer' treatment.

61 Everton were never against the televised of football games *per se*. Like the Liverpool manager they felt that the promotional interviews on the Saturday lunchtime magazine programmes, *Football Preview* and *On the Ball*, made it easy to pinpoint which games were televised that weekend and would affect attendances. In 1971 the Football League banned the interviews following Everton's proposal. As proof that they were not against television, the Everton board also spent £45,000 on new floodlights in 1970 to provide better lighting for colour television in evening games, when less suitable equipment was available at half that cost.

TV people ask for televising football is just a drop in the ocean when you see the thousands of pounds they pay to some entertainers. But TV is having a growing effect on cutting attendances throughout the country,' Shankly said. They may have been polar opposites in some people's eyes when it came to the media, but Catterick and Shankly had more in common than generally realised.

The press

In the early months of 1970, Arthur Hopcraft interviewed the Everton manager for the *Guardian*, his opening paragraph providing a perfect synopsis of the air of mystery that surrounded the Everton boss. 'Harry Catterick's pursuit of secrecy is one of the marvels of modern football,' he wrote, 'like Malcolm Allison's resonance and the length of Jack Charlton's neck. According to the legend, the Everton manager doesn't let his right hand know there's a left one.'

So why the secrecy? Why the mistrust of the media that is an integral part of the Catterick legend? First there was a question of personality. Catterick was a notoriously remote man not prone to flights of fancy. Tony Stevens of the *Liverpool Weekly News* asked the Everton overlord about his reserved manner prior to the start of the 1972/73 season. 'Some managers are always ready to run to the papers and have their names splashed about,' he replied, 'I would describe myself as a quiet type. I just make sure I don't tell lies. People who deal with me have learned I mean what I say.' The only time Catterick became animated after a game was if it had been violent – 'defence by intimidation' as he liked to call it.

Although the comparisons with Bill Shankly largely cast Catterick in a negative light, in his early days at Liverpool the press also regarded the Scot as aloof and his cryptic quotes could baffle. 'He speaks in Morse as it were,' the *Guardian's* Eric Todd once wrote. It was only as the media spotlight brightened during the second half of the decade that the Liverpool manager opened out, his otherworldliness and occasional refusal to accept actuality contrasting with Catterick's hard-nosed realism. But the Everton manager saw through his Anfield counterpart's attitude to the press, feeling that the soundbites were not necessarily a reflection of his extrovert personality, but more an exercise in ego massaging. 'Bill is famous for coming up with football stories,' he told the *News of the World* in October 1972, 'but it might be a mistake to take them all at face value. There is more to Bill than that and I believe he says these things and waits for them to be printed so he can enjoy the fuss he has caused.'

Compounding this dogmatic stance was his belief that club business should remain just that. There were the occasional calculated lapses but Catterick largely remained tight-lipped around the big issues, save for the usual platitudes. Interviewed by Colin Wood of the *Daily Mail* in the days after the (so-called) assault at Blackpool in January 1966, the Everton boss reinforced his view around the need for privacy, for the benefit of both manager and player. 'The unfortunate thing as far as we managers are concerned,' he explained, 'is that the public cannot know all the facts behind the transfers of players and the reasons for players being left out of the side.' This desire for privacy of course extended to keeping the details of the match-day starting line-up from the press. At best this was given as a starting XI in alphabetical order or, as in the home game against Colchester in the FA Cup in 1971, he provided a 15-man squad to the press, refusing to be drawn on the final team selection. 'There are times when Harry Catterick could give lessons in security to the Security Service,' wrote Horace Yates in the next day's *Liverpool Daily Post*.

However, Catterick's suspicious attitude to the media at Goodison probably had their roots in the aftermath of the dreadful 4-0 loss to Sheffield Wednesday at Goodison in September 1961. Several players went public in the press after the game, claiming that the result was directly due to a change in tactics. Catterick was furious when the story was printed, feeling clearly undermined at an early stage in his management tenure. 'I am determined to get to the bottom of the allegations,' the manager said. Whether he did is unknown, but what happened next was a further statement by the players, after a team meeting, in the Sunday newspapers: 'We have no complaint to make about the tactics of the new management and we are confident that when all the players are fit and we recover our form results will come.'

Even though staff had a clause in their contracts forbidding detrimental comments about the club to the press, this watershed episode early in his Goodison managerial career taught Catterick two distinct lessons: keep a tight rein on your players and communications with the media, defining characteristics of his time at the club. Catterick was not alone in the management fraternity in being circumspect with the media – of his rivals, Bill Nicholson[62] had a similar manner

62 Catterick had probably more admiration for the Spurs boss than for any of his contemporaries, particularly in the way he did not court publicity. 'Nicholson is my type of manager,' he said in 1972, 'He only makes public statements when he has something to say – not like some of the managers I could mention who tend to talk unnecessarily.'

– but by the end of the decade this attitude was outmoded. In his academic study *The Football Manager: A History* author Neil Carter argued that by the mid-1960s 'a flair for public relations was a growing requisite for the job [as manager] … clubs became aware of the need to sell themselves and to promote the right image. The advertising of the club therefore, became a function of the manager, and he came to be seen as "the club."' For some this was a natural progression but was clearly beyond Catterick, a conservative who clearly struggled with the extra scrutiny stimulated by the voracious appetite the press and television now had for the game. In the final analysis, it was to prove costly.

20.
Death in the Afternoon

EVEN DISCOUNTING THE IMPACT OF THE 1970 WORLD CUP, THE programme for the campaign following the title victory was daunting, mirroring that of Leeds United in the previous season. To reduce the strain, Everton withdrew from the League Cup to help ensure they could focus on chasing honours on three fronts. The third competition was, of course, the European Cup, Everton making a second appearance having gone out at the preliminary stage seven years earlier. Unlike 1963/64, when they had the toughest draw imaginable against Inter Milan, in 1970/71 the illogical seeding process initially made Everton one of four protected teams, with Cagliari, Spartak Moscow and Borussia Mönchengladbach, at the expense of champions Feyenoord and the rising Ajax. Even after a kind pairing with Icelandic champions Keflavik, Catterick's cynicism towards the continental game showed no sign of abating in the new decade. 'I'm not one who goes overboard about European football,' he said, 'I look on it as a financial arrangement. It enables both sets of supporters to see their team in action, but I'm not a fan of these two-legged affairs. My idea of the game is that it is played over ninety minutes.'

European Cup 1970/71

Keflavik, first round

The quest for a first European trophy began with a 9-2 aggregate victory over Icelandic side Keflavik, the 6-2 first-leg win over the minnows – backed by sixteen supporters – at Goodison featuring one of Gordon West's emotional outbursts that punctuated his Everton career. Whereas the visitors' keeper, Thorsteinn Olafsson, left the field to a standing ovation, the former England international endured a nightmare evening. With the game goalless, West failed to gather the ball and when Keith Newton cleared, it struck the keeper and rebounded into the empty net. The stopper then nearly conceded a second when losing control of a back pass, the Gwladys Street fans needing to alert him to the presence of the Icelandic winger Fridrik Ragnarsson. Facing abuse from the crowd, in front of millions of BBC television viewers West replied with a V-sign. To complete a difficult game, the Everton keeper was clearly at fault for a second goal near the end, badly misjudging a free-kick. While the rest of the side formed a guard of honour for their brave opponents at the final whistle, West beat a hasty retreat. 'It was a stupid thing to do,' the keeper admitted, 'hurrying off to the dressing room as I did. But I felt sick, shocked and shattered.'

West's nerves and volatility were well known, and it was a wonder sometimes how he enjoyed a hugely successful career. The stopper later spoke of the difficulties in controlling his emotions. 'If a forward charged me and I lost the ball I would shout and argue instead of getting the thing cleared,' the keeper admitted. 'If one of my teammates was fouled, I felt I had to get involved and sort out the culprit. When we lost I was cruel to myself. I used to worry myself silly saying it was my fault.'

Teammates were also conscious of West's emotional behaviour. When Alex Young first saw the pallid faced newcomer before his debut, the Scot remarked, 'How can we rely on a goalkeeper in this state?' Even the keeper's great friend Brian Labone acknowledged the anxiety that massively affected West on matchday. 'It happens before every game. Gordon's face goes white, then he rushes off to be sick,' the skipper said in 1968.

Catterick dropped West from the side after the game for his own good, blaming the crowd for making the goalkeeper's notorious nervous disposition worse with their barracking. 'Even before the game started against Keflavik, some of the terrace fans at the Gwladys Street end were shouting obscene abuse at him,' admitted Catterick. 'Now his form has gone. His confidence is shattered because he thinks every mistake he makes is going to cost a goal.'

Borussia Mönchengladbach, second round

Andy Rankin replaced West in goal, and endured a similarly torrid time, including the infamous 4-0 loss at Arsenal. Four days after the Highbury embarrassment, there was a chance to restore confidence in the second round of the European Cup. Typically, the draw was not kind to the Toffees, their opponents being Borussia Mönchengladbach, emerging as a major power in the Bundesliga. The Germans had the reputation of being a fine footballing team, featuring in their ranks ten internationals, including the top-class full-back and future World Cup winner, Berti Vogts, Herbert Wimmer and up front the intelligent and dangerous Jupp Heynckes, who later enjoyed a stellar managerial career. Their star player, though, was the charismatic, opinionated, but prodigiously talented Günter Netzer, undoubtedly one of the best midfield playmakers of all time. The blonde-haired club skipper was at Highbury for the Arsenal game, and the German was uncharacteristically diplomatic afterwards, 'Our players are a little afraid of Everton, they are a fine footballing team.' Against a side that had not lost all season, Catterick was equally wary of the Germans. 'Mönchengladbach are the best team I have seen in Europe,' he admitted, 'they are adaptable, they can change tactics. They have defenders who can score goals and midfield players who can attack and defend.'

With Henry Newton ineligible for the trip to Germany, Catterick recalled John Hurst to the team, with Kendall moving back to the middle of the park, after his nightmare experience at centre-half in north London. The threat from the new signing Newton appeared to galvanise the midfield trio, who collectively produced one of the best displays of the campaign. Ball was in particularly sparkling form and although the Toffees withstood a first-half barrage, they returned home with a creditable 1-1 draw. The German side had gone ahead ten minutes before the break when Rankin, who was otherwise outstanding, failed to reach Netzer's cross and Vogts' shot went in off the unfortunate John Hurst. The Germans were as good as their reputation but the visitors took the sting out of the game and their diligence was rewarded with a superb equaliser, albeit scored in slightly unusual circumstances. There were a number of toilet rolls in the Borussia penalty area and when goalkeeper Wolfgang Kleff was clearing them away, the visitors moved forward and Kendall, seeing the distraction, equalised via a tremendous shot into the angle from twenty yards. 'I scored thirty goals for Everton and I think that was one of my best,' he later said.

The return at Goodison a fortnight later was an absolute classic. A deluge produced testing conditions on an evening when Kleff more than made amends for his first-leg aberration. Although the German keeper was outstanding, the hero in a breathless climax to the tie was his opposite number, Andy Rankin. The drama, played out in front of a rain-soaked crowd of 42,744 paying receipts of more than £31,000, started in the opening twenty seconds. Johnny Morrissey's in-swinging cross from the left aimed for Royle fooled everybody and nestled in the far corner of the net at the Park End of the ground. The home team failed to take further advantage of their early goal and the well-drilled Germans got back in the tie after 34 minutes. Roger Kenyon gave away a needless free-kick and although Rankin parried Herbert Laumen's header from Netzer's cross, the midfielder beat Keith Newton to the rebound and slid the ball home. With parity restored, the Toffees continued to press but found Kleff in magnificent form. Although several saves were typically flamboyant from a foreign keeper, one in particular from Royle's header was truly magnificent.

With the game ending in deadlock, the tie moved into extra time but despite continuous Everton pressure, the Germans remained steadfast and could have nicked the game when Horst Köppel's header from Netzer's cross struck the top of the crossbar. A further thirty minutes combat failed to produce a goal and the two teams, for the first time in a European Cup tie, faced a penalty shoot-out. Previously they had gone to the toss of a coin, if required, but UEFA introduced this solution for any contest before the quarter-finals, thereafter a third game would be needed.

Joe Royle took the first of five kicks for each side and although he struck it well, the ball went straight down the middle and Kleff saved with his body. Strangely, there appeared to be some uncertainty after the stop. One radio commentator, thinking it was sudden death, broadcast, 'That's it, Everton are out,' and attempted to return to the studio, only to be corrected. Kleff also appeared to be confused, wandering around and perhaps thinking that was the end of the game as well. Either way, after both Klaus Sieloff and Ball netted – the Everton skipper wearing the famous white boots with his white socks around his ankles – goalscoring hero Laumen fired wide to level the score. Morrissey, Kendall and substitute Sandy Brown all scored their kicks and with Heynckes and Köppel doing likewise, responsibility for the last penalty before sudden-death fell to Ludwig Müller. The left-back side-footed the ball to Rankin's right but the keeper, who quite blatantly moved before the kick was taken, stopped the ball a good 2-3 feet before the goal-line. This time there was no doubt about the rules and the thousands of home fans celebrated as if it was the final itself. 'The German lad hit the ball well and to be honest, I think I moved about half an hour before he took the kick,' confessed Rankin.

Catterick was a relieved man after the game, saving rare praise for an opponent. 'I have never seen a better goalkeeping display [by Kleff]. The lad had a bit of luck at times but he deserved it. It was a pity one side had to lose after such a great game. I was proud of my boys. I thought they played magnificently – as they did in Germany – and this was one of the great occasions of my life.' The Everton manager was less impressed with the penalty shoot-out. 'A circus act,' he said, 'but I must admit I cannot come up with a better idea. In my opinion it is unfair to put players under so much pressure after two hours' football.'

Panathinaikos, quarter-final first-leg

Although the 1970/71 campaign is not a fondly remembered season, by the end of February 1971 there were several reasons for cautious optimism amongst Evertonians. A sequence of one defeat in twelve games had taken the team to the cusp of European qualification, and the Toffees had progressed smoothly in the FA Cup. Henry Newton had moved to left-back and firmed up the defence, whilst both Jimmy Husband and Alan Ball were getting back to their best.

The European Cup draw had been kind too. In drawing Panathinaikos, Everton had avoided the fancied Ajax, Celtic, Atlético Madrid and Red Star Belgrade, with the opening leg against the Greek outfit scheduled for the second Tuesday in March at Goodison. Their opponents were nothing but well prepared. Whereas the Toffees had played on the Saturday before the game, the Greek football association granted their champions a week off. The fact that their manager was the legendary Hungarian, Ferenc Puskás, also opened a few doors when they arrived in England seven days before the tie. Having trained at Chelsea for three days, the players watched the FA Cup game against Colchester after moving up north. However, there was a bit of needle between both clubs by that point. The Greek's club secretary had publicly accused Everton of providing no welcoming party at Goodison for the Colchester match and not providing training facilities. To accentuate the dispute, the Greeks then trained at Melwood, at the invitation of Bill Shankly. 'A perfectly natural gesture of hospitality … I did not do it to upset Everton,' said the Scot afterwards, with one eye no doubt on scoring psychological points before the FA Cup semi-final three weeks later.

Regarded as the weakest of the last eight teams, having failed to get beyond the first round in their six previous appearances in the European Cup, the Greeks were still a well-drilled and capable unit, with ten internationals. In their gifted skipper, Dimitri Domazos, they had the best performer on either team, a playmaker of genuine world-class talent. Sweeper Aristidis Kamaras was the best defender in the country while centre-forward Antonis Antoniadis (the leading scorer in that season's competition with ten goals) was a major danger in the air. For their part, the Greeks saw their biggest threat as Jimmy Husband, who had been outstanding in the FA Cup game against Colchester.

Both parties saw the first leg as the crucial game, the Greek secretary saying, 'If it is a 2-0 defeat or less, our chances are good. We play much better at home than away.' Catterick agreed with those sentiments at the club's hideaway in Cheshire, 'We will have to go hard for goals. We will have to play well to beat them, because it is going to be difficult for us in Athens. They are much under-rated side, because I found them to have a high degree of skill and they are very strong.' The game in front of a crowd of more than 46,000, including 2,500 away fans, was undoubtedly the most frustrating of Catterick's managerial career and indeed probably in the history of the club.

The match went according the script. The visitors targeted Husband from the start, and a bad foul by Domazos, of all people, lead to the winger going off in the opening ten minutes, replaced by the rookie David Johnson. Although Everton could claim to be unlucky, they were also wasteful to an unbelievable extent against a packed defence that played heroically, albeit with good fortune in a match of more than fifty fouls. The Greeks 'defended with single-minded devotion to duty and added ruthlessness when all else failed,' said Chris James in the *Liverpool Echo*. There was an endless stream of chances. Royle had a header kicked off the line and nodded three further attempts over, Wright's header hit the bar and the full-back missed three other chances. Johnson's shot also struck the bar whilst Ball's free-kick came back off the woodwork. Nevertheless, there was a feeling that the team overdid the continuous stream of lobbed balls into the box from Morrissey and Johnson and something more subtle may have paid dividends.

While Everton were taking profligacy to new levels, at the other end goalkeeper Rankin watched on as an underemployed bystander, waiting 66 minutes to make his first save. That was the only occasion the Everton keeper was required until eight minutes from time. Twenty-four hours after Joe Frazier had defeated

Muhammad Ali in the 'Fight of the Century' in Madison Square Garden, the Greeks delivered their own knockout punch at Goodison with a goal that still resonates today. A free-kick from the halfway line was headed down by Antoniadis to Harilaos Grammos, whose clever return ball took out two defenders and found his teammate in space to the left of the penalty spot. The incongruously red-shirted Rankin could only parry the striker's fierce left-footed strike before the ball nestled in the back of the net for a vital away goal.

The home side, as expected, continued their barrage and in added time came an unexpected equaliser. Royle knocked on Johnson's header from Everton's seventeenth corner kick of the game and when the ball ran loose, the substitute swivelled to fire into the roof of the net. The smart finish – so late spectators were unsure the goal stood as the referee blew for time straightaway – could not detract from a disappointing result. As Albert Barham noted in the *Guardian*, 'Thus from the easiest of easy victories Everton have sentenced themselves to the most difficult task of all: setting out to win in Athens in a fortnight's time.' Catterick summed up the thoughts of the home crowd after the game: 'We played all the football. We created sufficient chances to have won easily – but we didn't stick them in the net,' before adding 'the Greeks had the luck you usually get when you play with a packed defence. There had certainly been a lot of fouls and obstruction typical of European football. I've always said our game in Athens would be hard. I don't see it being any harder just because the score is now 1-1. But the Greeks will have to play more football than they did tonight.'

Puskás claimed afterwards that 'Everton played rather nervously,' with the great Hungarian admitting that his team 'came to defend. It was all we could do against a team like Everton on their own ground.' He also warned Catterick, 'Everton will have the same handicap in Athens as we have had at Goodison of playing away, so it is evenly balanced now.' Both managers were wrong though. The Greeks' away goal gave them the clear advantage, left them no obligation to change their tactics and it was Everton alone who had to go on the attack in Athens.

Panathinaikos, quarter-final second-leg

In 1971, there were many similarities between Leoforos and Goodison Park. Both were traditional venues housed in densely populated areas, with a reputation for being bear-pits. Panathinaikos' home venue was even more intimidating, housing 25,000 partisan spectators literally breathing down the players' necks, with further viewing from the apartments surrounding the ground. The pitch was bumpy and hard. Off the pitch, with the home team being close to bankruptcy, they had been paying their staff with match tickets, rather than money, for several weeks before the game. Nevertheless, their players were on £2,000 a man to progress to the last four.

Everton arrived in Greece to find the interest more akin to an international, sharing the Greek capital with thousands of flag waving locals on the eve of Independence Day. With the country's biggest club in unchartered territory, popular demand meant pressure was successfully placed on the government before the tie to join Eurovision so the population could watch both legs live on television. To add to the sense of history in the making, the Acropolis was floodlit, something only done previously on national holidays. The interest was reflected in the enormous demand for tickets for the game against the English champions; those priced at 50p were fetching £30 on the black market.

Having to score at least once to stay in the tie, the hostile and partisan environment had placed even more demands on the visitors, as did the welcoming party in the city. Geoffrey Green described the scenes outside the team hotel colourfully in *The Times*, 'One might add that all through the dark hours of last night, a calculated cacophony of sound drawn from squads of motor cars being revved up, their horns kept blaring, with chanting from mobs outside the Everton hotel, was another plan to upset the foe. It was enough to waken the dead.' Consequently, there was also a fear in some quarters that Catterick's side were sacrificial lambs. 'Everton were not merely playing Panathinaikos,' Green later commented, 'they were playing the Greek nation.'

As if that was not enough, Catterick also had to contend with an injury crisis. Eight players were receiving treatment before the trip to Greece and although only two – Henry Newton and Jimmy Husband – were absent for the afternoon kick-off, there were fitness doubts over several, notably Alan Ball, who had received a bad knock in a defeat at Newcastle seven days before. Needing a goal desperately, the visitors strangely lacked urgency in another bitterly fought game of more than fifty fouls, most of them in the petty category. 'The whole approach of Everton was one of a lacklustre team playing perhaps with Saturday's FA Cup tie against Liverpool on their minds,' wrote Albert Barham in the *Guardian*.

The bumpy pitch and alien conditions laid waste to the close passing style of Everton's midfield. 'When the ball was not being belted almost over the mountains from one end to the other, it was kicking and bounding high for groups of leaping players,' wrote Green. Although the Greeks showed more attacking intent than at Goodison, the chances for both teams were rare. The French referee Robert Helies allowed some outrageous behaviour from the home side, while the pressure of the crowd certainly influenced his policy of penalising every challenge by an Everton player. When Joe Royle was injured, Helies did not allow trainer Wilf Dixon on the pitch to treat the striker. The worst example of the referee's largesse towards the home team came during the opening half, when Frangiskos Sourpis brutally scythed down Whittle inside the box, yet the referee bafflingly awarded a foul for obstruction in the area. Examination of the colour film more than forty years later shows it was clearly a penalty. To Everton's credit, they did not retaliate despite the fierce provocation.

With the Greek defence keeping the Everton attack in check, only Morrissey had any effect on a game where the home team had most of the ball. Domazos, in particular, was outstanding, although Antoniadis wasted two chances created by the skilful midfielder. In response Catterick's team created little in a moribund performance. The best opportunity arrived after 58 minutes, when Kendall met Royle's knockdown with a fierce volley that the Greek keeper saved at full stretch. To no avail, Catterick introduced Johnson in the hope of repeating his first leg heroics, and in a frantic finish the Greeks came closest to breaking the deadlock when Domazos broke from midfield and saw his well struck shot rebound out from the inside of Rankin's right-hand post. When the referee blew for full time, after securing a semi-final berth against all expectations the home supporters invaded the pitch, carrying the victorious players and Puskás on their shoulders.

The immediate aftermath was one of understandable bitterness, with Catterick not surprisingly complaining about the Greeks' behaviour. 'They were spitting in our faces and gouging at our eyes by sticking their fingers into them,' he claimed afterwards. 'I think every one of my players got a knock of some sort. I was in danger once or twice from some of the tackles and I was on the sidelines.' Puskas for his part defended his side, saying, 'Everton, with their record and tradition, are a better team than us, so we had to play the best way to stop them. It was like a cup final for us.' Later Catterick added his usual refrain over whether European football was worth it. 'This has been a bitter experience,' he said afterwards, 'but in a way it might make us all the more determined to win on Saturday [the FA Cup semi-final]. We are going to make a full report to UEFA, and include in it all the incidents surrounding this match. It would have been better if we had been able to do so having won, otherwise it might sound like sour grapes.'

Included in any report would have been the infamous tale of secretary Bill Dickinson being called away from the breakfast table to take a phone call containing a simple message, 'Everton you die'. Having said that, Everton's experience of the trip – the poor refereeing, vociferous crowds around the hotel and a general atmosphere of intimidation – was not unusual for the time. Liverpool experienced similar in Milan in 1965 as did the national side in Mexico less than twelve months before. Although Catterick summed up the trip by saying it was the 'worst reception we have had in Europe', one member of the party laughed it off as 'good humoured nonsense'.

That proved no consolation as both club and employees counted the financial cost. A final appearance would have been worth anything up to £100,000 in gate money alone, while according to Howard Kendall in his autobiography, Catterick's team-talk afterwards was limited to blaming the players for the £5,000 the defeat had cost him in potential bonuses. The manager was not the only one who suffered financially. Members of the press heard one Everton player say afterwards, 'There goes a big part of my mortgage,' with the realisation of a lost bonus of £1,500. In comparison, Puskás picked up $12,000 for taking his team to the semi-final.

Attention since has also focused on the second-leg performance of the French referee, whose officiating so blatantly favoured the Greeks in the eyes of the Everton party, and whether it pointed to something more sinister going on in the background. Although there have been no specific accusations concerning the Everton visit to Athens, other than the allegations that the referee enjoyed the pre-game hospitality rather too well, the Greeks' semi-final encounter against Red Star Belgrade has been subject to a number of rumours over the years. Like Everton, the visiting players suffered noisy mobs outside their hotel in the days before the game and claimed afterwards that the hosts had tampered with their food and drink. After winning the home leg comfortably 4-1, the impressively strong Red Star outfit surprisingly lost 3-0 in Athens and went out on the away goals rule.

However, just when the match was consigned to the history books, the Red Star tie was back in the news in 2007. Georgios Papadopoulos, Greece's ruling military dictator at the time, had been both a political and financial supporter of the country's biggest club side. In April 2007 his widow, Despina Gaspari, alleged on television that the two teams had conspired to fix the return leg. Gaspari claimed that her husband told her during the game that Red Star 'will let us win and they'll get money for that', and the Yugoslav ambassador confirmed the fact at half-time. In that context, it is interesting to note that the second-leg referee was José María Ortiz de Mendíbil, who was implicated in the 1974 *Sunday Times* investigation into the bribery of match officials in the 1960s, on account of his controversial handling of the European Cup semi-final second leg between Inter Milan and Liverpool in 1965.

It was a strange tale and although there was nothing of substance to support her accusations, it does add to the suspicions of the Everton manager and players surrounding the game. The reality for Everton was that they should have done enough in the first leg to remove the need for any conspiracy theories. As Albert Barham said in the *Guardian*, 'The lesson of European football is to win the tie at home, and that Everton failed to do and so contributed to this Greek tragedy.'

Blue tide turns Red

The championship win in 1970 was Everton's seventh title – bringing them level with Arsenal, Manchester United and Liverpool. Furthermore, the Goodison side had three FA Cup triumphs, the same as the Gunners and United, and two more than Liverpool. As a founder member of the Football League, they were the senior club in the city, possessing historically the biggest support and greater financial resources. On the pitch, with ten major domestic honours, Everton were also the more successful of the two sides in England's most prosperous footballing outpost.

For Liverpool, the first few months of 1970 were also pivotal. The shock 1-0 quarter-final defeat at unfancied Watford[63] in March led to the departures of the core of the side that had won two league titles in the preceding decade. Consequently, when the two teams met in the first derby of 1970/71 campaign, at Anfield in late November, no fewer than six of Shankly's side were making their debut in the fixture. The new Liverpool were the same as the old one and in some ways the antithesis of Catterick's side – a tight rearguard, a functional midfield and hardworking forward-line, not naturally attractive but effective.

The derby proved to be a dramatic afternoon after a disappointing first half punctuated by 25 fouls, obscene chanting from both sets of supporters and several half-chances, mostly for the visitors. The second period, though, was the one of the

63 Watford's goalkeeper was the future Everton boss Mike Walker.

most memorable in derby history. The home team had conceded just thirteen goals in 23 games, but Everton breached the Liverpool defence twice in the space of seven minutes. The drama began just before the hour mark. Tommy Smith won the ball in the right-back position, and pressurised by Morrissey, only succeeded in playing the ball into Alan Whittle's path just outside the box. Spotting Ray Clemence six yards off his line, the blonde-haired striker produced a delightful chip that landed beautifully inside the net, in front of the travelling Blues at the Anfield Road end. It got even better seven minutes later; Ball's return pass to Morrissey on the left took out Smith and Chris Lawler and the winger's cross from the bye-line reached Joe Royle at the far post, who scored with a towering header.

For Everton supporters there was a pleasing sense of *déjà vu*. Eight months earlier the same two men had scored in the 2-0 victory in the title run-in. History would not be repeated. After 69 minutes, Steve Heighway on the left picked up Tommy Smith's long diagonal ball and after Hurst committed himself too early with a sliding challenge, the derby debutant cut inside and scored at Rankin's unguarded near post. It was a dreadful goal to concede, but worse was to come. Seven minutes later Heighway avoided Wright's tackle and Labone should have cleared the Irishman's left-footed cross but the centre-half perplexingly failed to get off the floor and derby newcomer John Toshack headed home in front of the baying Kop, who now smelt blood. The home fans got what they wanted six minutes from time when Toshack flicked on Alec Lindsay's cross and, with substitute Keith Newton static, full-back Lawler appeared at the far post to drive the ball past a despairing Rankin. There was no response from the Toffees as they slipped to a crushing 3-2 defeat.

'Everton never will forgive themselves nor be forgiven for throwing away the game as they did,' wrote Eric Todd in the *Guardian* afterwards. Catterick clearly articulated who was at fault for the dramatic collapse. 'We threw the game away. Liverpool were allowed to score three goals that should have been prevented. We are going to have to do a lot of work to tighten up the defence.' The contest had laid bare the flaws in the team that were apparent in the championship-winning season and beforehand: a chronic weakness defending high balls played from deep and (perhaps unfair) accusations that the side lacked heart under pressure.

What the players and supporters could not realise at the time was that the match was also a watershed moment in Merseyside soccer. Five months earlier Keith Newton, Labone and Ball had all played for England against West Germany in Leon when the world champions had collapsed in a similar style. The result, or more specifically the manner of the defeat, caused irrevocable damage to the psyche of the national side, ending the veneer of invincibility that came with being world champions whilst presaging a period of dominance for the victors. As the fortunes of both England and (West) Germany followed a diverse path following Leon, so too did those of the two clubs in the aftermath of Liverpool's comeback victory. The World Cup victory gave the Germans a psychological stranglehold in the fixture and some would say the same is also true of the Merseyside derby.

Old Trafford, March 1971

As the dark clouds from the stuttering start to the 1970/71 season were disappearing, progress in the FA Cup was providing proof that there could be a glorious ending to the campaign. After easing through to the fifth round with home victories over Blackburn and Middlesbrough, when Derby County visited Goodison for a place in the quarter-finals, Everton had won four out of six games since the start of the year, with the only loss a hugely unlucky defeat at Spurs. At White Hart Lane Labone suffered what most observers thought at the time to be a possible career ending injury, a severe muscle tear following a challenge by Jimmy Neighbour that left a gash to the bone. 'It was frightening wound, the worst injury of its type I have seen in thirty years' experience of football,' said Catterick. Thankfully, the England international returned within six weeks.

As expected, Brian Clough's side proved tough opponents at Goodison, dominating the opening period for long periods. David Miller, in the *Sunday Telegraph*, praised 'the brilliant quality of the midfield play of both teams, first-time passing of marvellous precision under intense physical challenge'. Catterick had made two changes for the game, replacing the injured Andy Rankin and Johnny Morrissey with Gordon West and the 19-year-old David Johnson, who had scored on his only previous appearance at Burnley in early January. The youngster rewarded Catterick with the only goal of the game just before the break; the wind caught Kendall's centre from the right touchline and while others waited for the ball to go out of play, Johnson reacted quickly and headed powerfully home past Colin Boulton. With league leaders Leeds going out 3-2 at Colchester United on the same day, bookmakers installed the Toffees as 2-1 favourites to lift the trophy after the draw for the quarter-final fortuitously produced a home tie against the conquerors of Don Revie's team.

The visit of the fourth division outfit to a sunlit Goodison on the first Saturday in March showed up the respective wealth of both sides: win bonuses of £500 per man for Everton, £10 for their opponents. Before the game Catterick drilled his side for hours on the training pitch to counter the high balls played long to the twin Colchester strikers, Dave Simmons and Ray Crawford, who had both proved so effective against Leeds. The Everton manager also considered their defence was big and immobile, so midfield players and forwards practised first-time passing in and around the box.

The Colchester goalkeeper, Graham Smith, had played in the same Quarry Bank school team as Joe Royle, but Everton put paid to any thoughts of a memorable return to the city in a devastating first-half performance. With cup rules dictating that, in the event of colour clash, each side donned their away strips, the home side ran riot in their classic amber and blue change kit. Catterick's suspicions that swift movement and accurate passing would unsettle the away defence proved accurate, Everton scoring four goals in thirteen minutes during the first half before easing to a 5-0 win, in front of a 53,000 crowd of whom 8,000 had made the trek up north. The reward was a semi-final against Liverpool at Old Trafford on 27 March, three days after their European Cup quarter-final second leg in Athens. The destiny of the season – and indeed, Catterick's legacy – was compressed to a four-day span at the end of March. 'I regard the next week as possibly the most important in the history of the Everton club,' said Michael Charters beforehand in the *Liverpool Echo*. Few disagreed.

But after the goalless draw in the Greek capital sent Everton crashing out of Europe's premier competition, a tired and frustrated group of players and officials landed in Manchester airport on the Wednesday evening, with the semi-final less than 72 hours away. The Football Association had rejected both Everton and Arsenal's request to move the date of the semi-finals, because of proximity to the European games.[64] Having already been on antibiotics, Catterick was ill during the flight, jeopardising the chances of taking his place in the dugout at Old Trafford on the Saturday. In what hopefully was not an omen, the Everton party then had to move from their hotel in Lymm, after it was discovered they had double-booked with Liverpool. Shankly's side had appeared in Europe too, wrapping up a 4-1

[64] Everton's argument was based on the distance they had to travel to Greece and for the rather tenuous rationale that Panathinaikos had their league fixture postponed before the second leg. The FA rejected the request and then, equally unsurprisingly, both Everton and Liverpool turned down their approach to toss for the choice of Goodison Park or Anfield as the venue for the semi-final, to avoid travelling.

aggregate win over Bayern Munich. Their rebuilding job had continued since the derby victory at Anfield, and although his team conceded few goals, they lacked punch up front. The bookmakers viewed Liverpool as 11/10 favourites, with Everton at 7/4.

Catterick was still bedridden come the Saturday, with Wilf Dixon taking over the reins. From his sickbed the Everton manager, unconvincingly, was still positive. 'I think that our defeat in the European Cup – silly and unnecessary defeat that it was – will have just tipped the scales our way.' Crucially for the Toffees, Henry Newton was still unavailable. Now the established left-back, the former Nottingham Forest's settling influence on the defence would be missed. Despite several players carrying knocks, Everton were unchanged from Athens.

In front of 62,188 spectators paying more than £70,000 in gate receipts, the two sides produced a classic FA Cup semi-final of ebbs and flows. 'Often these games are disappointing but this was a marvellous exception to the rule, a vivid full-blooded affair,' wrote Michael Parkinson in the *Sunday Times*. 'Throughout, it maintained a pace, a quality of raw excitement and an uncertainty of outcome that matched the setting and the occasion.' Everton started the game as if their European setback had never happened. Moving the ball crisply and purposefully around the pitch, the Toffees were comfortably the better side and went ahead as early as the tenth minute with a well-worked goal. Harvey's long throw to the bye-line was headed back by Royle to the unmarked Morrissey, the energetic Whittle beat Ray Clemence to the winger's cross and Ball scored with a crisp half-volley at the far post. With the midfield trio in fine form, the side in blue maintained a stranglehold for the rest of the half, without threatening to extend their lead. Horace Yates of the *Liverpool Daily Post* said, 'In the first half they were easily the better, more accomplished side, showing samples of football brilliance that almost seemed out of place in such a nerve-sapping confrontation.' However, there was the unedifying spectacle of a number of Everton players clearly arguing as they left the pitch at the break, captured by the BBC cameras. 'Everton went in at half-time looking like winners, but it was merely an illusion,' wrote Parkinson.

The game changed after the break. Shankly told his side to use the midfield more rather than go long to John Toshack, and with Brian Hall and Emlyn Hughes seeing more of the ball and man-of-the-match Tommy Smith driving the team forward, Liverpool started the second half the stronger side. Four minutes into the period came the incident that many Evertonians still say changed the game. After tweaking his hamstring in the opening period, Brian Labone challenged John Toshack in the penalty area and then fell to floor, having pulled a thigh muscle. 'I just felt something snap at the back of my thigh,' the skipper said later, 'I knew at once what it was, although I had never pulled a hamstring before.' Substitute Sandy Brown was hugely experienced but not a natural centre-half, and the departure of Labone robbed the team of their talisman. The game had already started to turn before the substitution, but the loss only accelerated the change in fortunes. Within minutes, Royle headed Larry Lloyd's header off the line and just before the hour came the equaliser. Smith easily brushed Whittle off the ball and found Steve Heighway wide on the left. Perhaps conscious of his threat at Anfield, Wright and centre-half Hurst converged on the Irishman, as did Brown, showing the natural habits of a full-back. This created an enormous gap in the middle filled by the unmarked Alun Evans, who took Heighway's pass and fired past the exposed Rankin. With their Anfield comeback surely in the minds of both teams, Liverpool now held the psychological upper hand against disheartened opponents.

The mortal blow came on 72 minutes and, once again, Everton were the architects of their own downfall. When Evans picked up the ball on the left touchline it was Hurst, not Brown, who left the middle and the forward's high cross landed by the penalty spot. Rankin (notoriously weak in coming off his line at this stage of his career) fumbled and took out both Brown and Toshack, leaving the unattended Brian Hall to hook the ball home. Had regular centre-half Hurst remained in the middle the story could probably have been different. With the fight knocked out of them, Everton had little to offer and the only question that remained was whether their rivals could add further goals. Thankfully the Everton hordes at the Scoreboard End were spared further suffering. At the final whistle 'the reign of Harvey, Ball and Kendall had long since ended,' said Horace Yates, 'and Everton were left without a rallying point, comprehensively beaten in a match which had seemed wholly theirs'. Michael Parkinson added, 'At the end Liverpool rejoiced and Alan Ball walked from the field looking like a man who has had the prize in his hand and had seen it taken away.' [65]

---

[65] Some would say the cards were stacked against Everton from the start. The game took place close to the twenty first anniversary of Liverpool's 2-0 FA Cup semi-final victory over Everton in 1950, also in Manchester. The two dates were marked by three other sporting coincidences: on both Cambridge easily beat Oxford in the Boat Race and in rugby union Wales defeated France to clinch the Five Nations Grand Slam. In the other semi-finals in 1950 and 1971 Arsenal undeservedly equalised in the final minute to earn replays which they won. The only consolation for Everton supporters was that the Gunners defeated Liverpool in both finals.

Like most of the defeats in the post-championship period, the Old Trafford loss was primarily due to defensive frailties. 'They were two bad goals,' said Brian Labone in an honest appraisal on *Match of the Day* after the game, which won many plaudits – the former skipper admitting that he would not have ventured wide for the first goal, unlike Brown. The frustration of being a helpless bystander still rankled the Everton skipper in the years that followed, as he later told BBC Radio Merseyside: 'It was a bit of *déjà vu*. When we won the cup in 1966, United had come from a defeat in Europe. It was a terrible thing being off the pitch and watching your team being beaten when you're sitting on the bench. I still reckon to this day if I'd been on the pitch I'd have headed those high balls away. Big John Toshack was good in the air but they were two ludicrous goals.' The skipper told the *Liverpool Echo* in 1977 that there were several senior players in tears in the dressing room after the game.

It was a devastating defeat to a technically inferior side but one showing greater resilience and determination when it mattered. 'Everton didn't fight. When we came at them in the second half they just faded,' said Tommy Smith after the game. Catterick understandably said little from his sick-bed, only admitting, 'Liverpool are a strong, physical side who make it difficult for opponents to play against.' As a disconsolate Everton left Old Trafford, chairman George Watts counted the financial cost of the double cup removal. 'This has meant £250,000 to us,' he confessed. But the psychological damage of two crushing cup defeats when well favoured in both could not be quantified in financial terms. It took Manchester City coach Malcolm Allison to sum up the mood of most Evertonians in the *Daily Express* after the game:

Imagine the feelings of Harry Catterick this morning. He has a fine, richly gifted side and less than twelve months ago he knew he could point his men at Europe's top prize. His team had impressed themselves as a force which could dominate the English game and could build themselves a reputation in Europe. But all the grand ambitions, the soaring hopes have dissolved in Athens and Manchester. Two matches, 180 minutes football, have undone the work of years and now he has to build again from ashes.

21. Post-Mortem

THERE WERE STILL EIGHT GAMES LEFT AFTER THE LIVERPOOL DEFEAT, although the players – understandably perhaps – showed little appetite for the fight. The home game against West Ham three days later reflected the declining fortunes of the side. Alan Ball was lucky to escape a dismissal for strangling Billy Bonds while the visitors' winner came via a Howard Kendall own goal, the Everton player tried to clear Harry Redknapp's cross but only succeeded in hooking the ball into his own net. There was just one victory after the semi-final as the team eventually finished fourteenth in the table, acquiring 37 points, 29 less than twelve months before. The 44 goals conceded away from Goodison was the second highest in the division. Writing in the *Liverpool Echo* at the end of season Michael Charters pulled no punches in his review of the campaign, picking six points that contributed towards the club's decline:

- Indifferent form
- Inadequate teamwork
- Lack of fight
- Defensive lapses
- Bad luck with injuries
- No killer punch

Only Howard Kendall, Johnny Morrissey and Henry Newton ('a first class acquisition') were spared individual criticism. West was 'only a shadow of the great goalkeeper who earned England honours', Labone was 'troubled by injuries and loss of form' while John Hurst endured 'a disappointing season, failing to dominate the middle'. Charters was also critical of Joe Royle, who 'would have been dropped if there had been someone challenging for his place' while Alan Ball's 'poor season has had the most effect on Everton's indifferent performances'. The reasons for the fall from grace were many and varied.

Curse of the defending champions

After the 2-0 defeat at Molineux on Boxing Day 1970 had left the team in fourteenth place, thoughts turned to the complete loss of league form, compared to the standards set in the previous four years. Catterick wrote about the issue in the *Liverpool Echo* afterwards:

If it depended on talent, ability and the will-to-win, Everton would be the leaders, but there is more to winning the League Championship than that. The hardest part is getting players who have reached the pinnacle of success to wind themselves up and do it all over again. In years gone by, this was perhaps possible, but such are the pressures today, it is very much harder. I wonder whether fans realised that when this season began my players had to win thirty out of forty-two matches in the world's toughest competition. That's some target, especially as in our case we have European Cup commitments as well ... I am just as proud of my side now as I was a year ago. The talent has left them but not their fighting spirit.

There were some salient points. Retaining the title was becoming increasingly difficult – no side had done so since Wolves in 1959. There was also some truth to back Catterick's argument of the problems of motivating players. Reigning champions Manchester City had finished thirteenth and gone out of the European Cup at the first hurdle in 1968/69. That said, the majority of champions remained competitive: Everton themselves finished third in 1963/64, Manchester United second in 1967/68 and two years later Leeds were runners-up. None had suffered such a dramatic fall from grace as Everton – although on ability alone they were still a top six side.

The crucial point, given Catterick recognised the pressures of the campaign, was the failure to attract new blood in the short-term, even as squad players. Over the previous three years Catterick had showed little inclination to seriously enter the transfer market. Although the manager admitted to having made more than sixty enquiries for players in the previous twelve months, there had been only three definite offers. After the failure to land Manchester City's Dave Connor in early 1969, Catterick tried to lure the utility player Paddy Mulligan to Goodison but the Irishman chose Chelsea instead. The Everton manager did sign Rochdale's Steve Melledew after the striker netted a hat-trick in a 4-3 friendly victory over the Toffees in July 1969, but the £10,000 acquisition failed to progress beyond the reserve team.

A month later, Catterick unsuccessfully tried to hijack Jimmy Greenhoff's £100,000 move to Stoke City from Birmingham City, only becoming aware of his availability at the eleventh hour. Alan Ball actually phoned the striker at home and pleaded with Greenhoff not to sign for Stoke, as Everton wanted him. However, having already shaken hands on the deal, Greenhoff to his credit still signed for the Potteries club. The failure to acquire the blonde-haired forward was a missed opportunity, the talented and hard-working player becoming one of the best and most effective front-men of the following decade.

Apart from Henry Newton, the only major signing Catterick made in the three years prior to 1971 had been namesake full-back Keith Newton, bought in December 1969 for £80,000 from Blackburn Rovers after a protracted six-month period of negotiations. Although a fine, overlapping right-back (who could play on the left if required) there seemed little point paying a significant fee for a 28-year-old when Tommy Wright was the established choice on that flank. By the time Newton departed for Burnley in the summer of 1972, an England international right-back had played in that position in only three out of 56 games for Everton. 'He was not a good tackler,' said Catterick afterwards, 'which we needed.'

The cup defeats – especially at Old Trafford – happened partly because of Catterick's reluctance to make new signings from a position of strength at the turn of the decade. After acquiring Henry Newton in October 1970, Catterick let slip that he wanted two more players to complete the squad. Six months later that had still not happened. At the business end of the 1970/71 campaign, there was a scarcity of established players outside the regular starting line-up to fill in. Catterick alluded to this after the disastrous Liverpool defeat, pointing to the loss of Henry Newton and Jimmy Husband before the game. 'No team can afford at this level of competition to be without such accomplished players,' the manager said afterwards. Correct, but his failure to address the overall weakness of the squad had not helped.

Mexico 1970

Feeling better placed to strengthen the team, Catterick chose to stay at home rather than travel to Mexico for the World Cup in June 1970. Sir Alf Ramsey's England squad – considered possibly their strongest in history – featured four of the title-winners: Brian Labone, Tommy Wright, Keith Newton and Alan Ball. All played their part as the defending champions went out at the quarter-final stage to old foes West Germany. Newton was outstanding in that match, setting up both England's goals in the notorious 3-2 defeat, one that also saw the international swansong of Brian Labone (who, for a player with just two club goals, spurned a great chance at 2-2). In the group match against Romania, Tommy Wright came on as a substitute for Newton – perhaps showing the folly of spending £80,000 on an international right-back, when there was already one at the club.

There has been much discussion on whether the World Cup had a significant impact on the decline after 1970. Some maintain that more than a month away at high-altitude, after an arduous domestic campaign, was always going to have physical effects. The counter-argument is that there was eight weeks between the defeat by West Germany and the Charity Shield game against Chelsea, leaving plenty of time to refresh batteries during the summer. However, there is some evidence of an effect. At the end of 1970 a poll of football writers found that only three of the England squad were performing better than before the World Cup, with thirteen below form, including all four Everton players.[66] As Catterick said himself after the 1-0 home defeat to Manchester City in August 1970: 'It was a wonderful honour for Everton to have four of our players in England's squad. But there is no doubt that this has had an adverse effect on us. They have had too much football, and the strain seems to be telling on them at present. It's a mental rather than physical problem. They've lost a bit of their enthusiasm for the game.' Whether this explained the collective drop in standards for the team is debatable – Newton had become a bit-part player and Labone endured spells out of the side.

So when supporters speak of the links between the Mexico World Cup and the decline of the team, it probably boils down to one person, Alan Ball. At the end of the tournament, Ramsey had said, 'I expect all the players from Mexico to go off like a bomb when the season starts. But I am also certain they will feel the effects of so strenuous a World Cup in the later stages of the season.' The England

[66] A purely subjective assessment by journalists where players were marked below average; average and above average.

manager's prediction was correct as far as Ball was concerned; the skipper displayed some of the best form of his career at the start of the 1970/71 campaign but then fell away dramatically. Substituted in the England match against Greece in April 1971 after a lacklustre display, the World Cup winner uncharacteristically cut a tired, dispirited figure. 'Ball was a worn-out shadow of the player who has given so much in the cause of England and Everton,' said Norman Giller in the *Daily Express*. The last home game of the season – a goalless draw against already relegated Blackpool – provided a famous image that summed up the mood of the England international, the club and supporters at the time – a rain-soaked Ball standing at the near post, looking both bemused and frustrated as another chance goes begging.

From a playing perspective, there is evidence to support Catterick's opinion that the question was more a psychological problem, rather than physical one, of players continually being asked to be at their peak. The backlog of fixtures at the tail-end of the 1968/69 season, and the early finish to the title-winning campaign, meant that 52 league games were played over a twelve-month period prior to the World Cup. In the midst of that, five Everton players – West,[67] Wright, Harvey, Ball and Labone – had travelled with England on a tough four-match South American tour in June 1969. The problem therefore was not actually the World Cup, more the accumulation of games and travelling in the preceding period. Catterick did little to address the issue, particularly in failing to bring in new blood in the summer of 1970. Whereas Don Revie at Leeds kept his England players fresh by giving them extra days off training, the Everton manager did not. Fortunately, or unfortunately, for the Everton manager, the decline of the team after 1970 meant that the club versus country issue disappeared as well.

The changing game

The style of the 1970 championship-winning team came from Harry Catterick's biggest influence as a coach – the Spurs title-winners of 1951, the 'push and run' side of manager Arthur Rowe, one of the most intelligent men in English football history. It was a simple tactic – pass the ball to a teammate and sprint past the

[67] West appeared in the opening match of the tour, before 105,000 spectators in the high humidity of the Azteca Stadium, but had not enjoyed the experience. A notoriously nervous character, the Everton keeper found it difficult to judge the flight of the ball in the high altitude and the speed off the turf. The keeper returned home after the game with a shoulder injury, having played for his country for the third and final time. Before the opening day of the 1969/70 season, the goalkeeper announced that he did not want Ramsey's consideration for the World Cup squad, citing family reasons.

marker to collect the return – but enhanced by a more creative use of space and angles than had been seen previously. From his early days as a manager, Catterick was keen to replicate Rowe's revolutionary methods. 'I always had a great respect for Arthur,' he told Peter Morris for his 1971 book, *The Team Makers*, 'I admired what he did at Tottenham. The Spurs of those days were always entertaining to watch. They were also highly effective. And this, after all, is what the game is all about.'

Like many of his contemporaries, the dominant Hungarian side of the 1950s also greatly influenced Catterick, an outfit whose strength lay in their flexibility as a team and movement around the pitch. In particular, the Everton manager was a disciple of their great football strategist and technician Árpád Csanádi, whose books, in particular his bible, *Soccer*, were a massive influence. Both volumes of the weighty tome were continuously present on his desk at Bellefield. For Catterick, the book provided everything he wanted to know about coaching, training, tactics, and diet. Csanádi's presence on Merseyside training grounds continued long after Catterick left Everton – Rafael Benitez being one of the Hungarian's many students.

The Everton manager's first attempt to adopt these progressive tactics came in his days at Sheffield Wednesday, where he felt under-appreciated, especially after their second place finish in 1960/61. 'No one gave me much credit for that and I did not have at Sheffield the development facilities I have here [at Everton],' he later claimed. Critics may have disagreed, for the general view was that he took a largely negative approach at Hillsborough. Then in his early years at Goodison, operating under the intense pressure of bringing immediate success, the manager deliberately sacrificed a fair share of his football values, by harnessing the strengths of the squad to match the demands of John Moores. Jimmy Gabriel, Brian Harris, Tony Kay and, say, Dennis Stevens, collectively played a power game in the middle of the park. As the decade ended Catterick had diluted and replaced that approach with a more educated and finely tuned style of play, the midfield triumvirate the fulcrum of a fluid 4-3-3 formation.

However, in the early 1970s, more club sides were moving to a 4-4-2 set-up. The extra man in midfield, usually the ball-winner, reflected the need for greater defensive solidity. The two strikers up front remained isolated and operated in tandem – John Radford and Ray Kennedy (Arsenal), Allan Clarke and Mick Jones (Leeds) with John O'Hare and Kevin Hector (Derby County) were examples within successful teams who had made the transformation. Catterick eschewed the change, preferring to retain the 4-3-3 formation that had served the side so well. Specifically the problem with this set-up was that teams were now frequently outnumbering Everton with their four-man midfield, and the opposition were exploiting the vacant space left behind Jimmy Husband as he darted inside.

Additionally, the problem for the manager was that the nuances and precision that characterised the midfield trio was always going to have a limited shelf life. As Ball said himself in 1974, the trio moved forward and back as a unit and played with no holding player, so as the three naturally aged and changed, and opponents devised counter-measures, there was always going to be a revision in tactics required at some point. The signing of Henry Newton in October 1970 provided an ideal opportunity for Catterick to review the make-up of the team. The manager could have deployed the former Nottingham Forest player as a natural ball-winner with the existing trio in a four-man midfield, although this would have probably meant jettisoning Johnny Morrissey and losing some natural width, but occasionally managers have to make those sacrifices to progress.

Alternatively, Newton could have replaced Alan Ball in midfield, with the England international moving further up the pitch in a 4-3-3, perhaps playing off Joe Royle on the right. In one stroke Catterick could have stabilised the rearguard and got the best out of Ball as an attacker, as he did in 1966-69, but this option sadly was never pursued, perhaps because there was an implied criticism of his skipper. Some options were more viable than others, but the fact is Catterick took a strangely passive approach to the decline after 1970, resisting any change. Altering the formation may have resulted in breaking up the championship-winning side, but having made Newton the third most expensive player in English football history surely there was no alternative. As Alan Ball later said of Catterick, 'For me, he felt all along that the same players would all come good again and blind the world for a second time.'

A test of character

By the early 1970s, the key consequence of England's 1966 World Cup victory, the reliance on work-rate and the proliferation of ball-winners, was squeezing the type of football associated with Everton out of the domestic game. When 42 Everton players turned up for pre-season in July 1971, Catterick was asked about the change of scenery. The manager re-iterated his belief in skilful football. 'That is why', he said 'we will have nothing to do with anything physical and why we shall concentrate on the development of basic skills.'

Alan Hoby of the *Sunday Express* once asked if Everton could maintain their style of play against massed, ruthless defences. Catterick shrugged and responded, 'It's a gamble, at a time when the kicking and tackling are getting worse, you could say that I'm going into reverse.' Catterick's comments of going against the grain of the contemporary game paints a picture of a manager who was all too willing to retain his principles at the cost of success. Catterick concluded by telling Hoby, 'I have taken a long, hard look at Everton's approach to the game and decided that we will not alter our style. Someone has got to make a stand against the negative, spoiling play which is ruining English football as a spectacle.' That attitude was perfectly acceptable if it produced winning football, but when that was not the case then changes were required, but Catterick never shifted from this philosophy until it was too late. A blinkered approach to the team's pure playing style, plus parsimony in the transfer market, undoubtedly led to a failure to land a trophy in the years after 1970. The manager admitted as such after the semi-final defeat to Liverpool. 'I am convinced that Everton's refusal to jump on the bandwagon and sacrifice footballing ability for physical power,' he wrote in the *Liverpool Echo*, 'partly explains why we will end the season with nothing.'

Arsène Wenger is an example of a modern manager whose policies are reminiscent of Catterick's stubbornness in the years after 1970. Following Arsenal's 2004 title victory, critics accused the Frenchman of not altering his footballing philosophy to adapt to the changing game, as well as being frugal with transfer funds. In terms of title triumphs, the result was the same for both men, with Wenger's unpopularity with swathes of Gunners' supporters before his departure reminiscent of Catterick's fall from grace after 1970. Furthermore, like Arsenal over the past decade or more, the 1970/71 campaign raised more questions on whether the team had the necessary resilience and character to compete at the top level. 'Everton's stamina has been found wanting before,' wrote Mike Ellis in the *Sun* at the time, 'their failure to lift themselves when things are going wrong has also been evident in the past.' That may not have been completely true – mentally weak sides do not win championships – but the feeling persists that during 1968-1971 the side lacked application in one-off games and failed to impose their undoubted superiority as a result.

Brian Labone later made the point that 'we had a bit more steel in the side in 1962/63, we had Tony Kay and Dennis Stevens in the team and we were a bit of a harder side. We [in 1969/70] were a very lightweight side; we were a pure footballing side with Ball, Harvey and Kendall.' The skipper was correct. Although Everton undoubtedly developed a harder edge, they lost more big league and cup matches than they won. Johnny Morrissey played in both the 1963 title-winning team and the side of later in the decade. His views on the two also carry some weight, 'The [1969/70] side lacked something. The first title team had character and I don't think the later team did to the same extent.'

... And marriage

With Catterick looking for the reasons behind their slow start to the 1970/71 campaign, the Everton manager made the headlines following the successful visit to West Ham in the September. Asked about his team's drop in standards, Catterick came up with an unusual reason that raised the eyebrows of those present:

I am convinced that our poor start can be put down to the fact that four of our players got married during the close-season. I have seen it happen time and again in football – newlywed players losing their form during the first months of marriage. We keep a stopwatch check on them and all the newlyweds are down on the times they were setting last season. They tend to be a little sluggish until they have settled to their new way of life.

To complete a surreal post-match inquest, the slightly puzzled journalists informed Catterick that Brian Labone's horse, Goodison, had won at 20-1. The defender had failed to tip-off his teammates. 'That's him back for extra training every day this week,' quipped the manager.

22.
Joyless Division

ONE OF THE FEATURES OF EVERTON'S RICH HISTORY IS THE RELATIVE absence of world-class or truly famous players, compared to say a club like Spurs. This is a curious anomaly; however, one player, at his peak, who does fit comfortably into both categories is Alan Ball, the best outfielder in Everton's post-war history. As the team's dominant figure, the midfielder personified the varying fortunes of the club far more than any other of his colleagues. During 1966-70 his drive and goal-scoring prowess from the middle of the park reflected the rise of Catterick's side. Thereafter his own struggles for form and injury problems similarly mirrored their sharp decline. Because he was the only Everton player during the period known in every household in the country, the England international was subject to far more column inches and wider media scrutiny than his teammates combined. Consequently, rather than Ball being a subplot, he was a separate story in itself; his tale at Goodison was therefore a curious one.

In some respects the England international was a player of extremes, a brilliantly effective and calculating midfielder but someone who 'at times behaves as if someone had just trodden on his train set', in the words of the *Guardian's* David Lacey. Not surprisingly, Ball's long-standing disciplinary problems were a focus of press attention, not least during the middle of the 1969/70 campaign when there was a real fear that they could seriously damage Everton's title challenge. Going into the derby game against Liverpool in early December, the midfielder had already been booked twice. At Goodison, Ball was well shackled by the young Scot, Ian Ross, brought in especially by Shankly to do just that job. Booked for the third time during the campaign, for a foul on Ian St John, Ball now faced a lengthy suspension at a time when the punishment for the offence was more vigorous than today. In looking for answers to an uncharacteristically poor performance from the league leaders in a 3-0 loss, Eric Todd in the *Guardian* pointed the finger at one man:

Everton's lack of discipline, and of disciplined football, contributed to their downfall. And for that, Ball must accept most of the responsibility. Ball perpetrated two early fouls, and thereafter he appeared to rate destruction above construction. His petulant histrionics impressed nobody, his shouting and gesticulations merely confused and irritated his colleagues.

Five days later, for the fourth time as an Everton player, Ball appeared before an FA disciplinary commission. Apart from three previous suspensions with Everton, Ball had been banned for fourteen days at Blackpool in 1964 and twelve months later received a £100 fine for a sending-off in an England under-23 game in Austria.[68] The commission considered these previous misdemeanours before delivering a devastating, if not unexpected, decision to Catterick and Everton supporters – Ball was banned for five weeks, at a critical stage of an already compressed season. The England international was lucky: at a time when receiving three bookings was a significant disciplinary issue, George Best received a 28-day ban at the same hearing for the far less serious offence of knocking the ball out of the referee's hand. Although appreciating the potential damage to Everton's championship ambitions, Donald Saunders shared that view in the *Daily Telegraph*, noting that 'on leaving the hotel, Ball wore the expression of a man who has just averted a serious accident.'

Nevertheless, the punishment meted out to the Everton midfielder was because he was patently unable to learn lessons. As Ken Jones pointed out in the *Daily Mirror*, 'Ball's temperament shows itself in the tears and the gestures. The years when he has experienced outstanding success have done nothing to help him. He cries when he fails, explodes when things go against him.' Ball could have argued with some justification that some of his outbursts were due to intense provocation and lack of protection from referees. Stud marks on his chest were a

[68] For throwing the ball at the referee, the Hungarian Gyula Gere, who had controversially disallowed Roy Vernon's goal in the European Cup match against Inter Milan at Goodison two years before.

regular feature and he suffered from bad ankles that puffed up after games. His father said at the time, 'At the moment he's the most marked man in football. He takes more stick than even George Best, because Alan Ball is Everton, and Everton are top of the league.'

At the captain's table

Ball returned to the team in February 1970 and, following the injury to Brian Labone, was skipper for the remainder of the campaign as Everton lifted the title. The midfielder's firebrand image had worked against him in the captaincy stakes, having previously skippered a senior team only once, for the Football League against the Scottish League at Hampden Park in March 1969 – and that was because no other World Cup winner was playing.

Catterick had taken a bit of a gamble, but at the end of the season paid tribute to the stand-in captain. 'I cannot speak too highly of the job he has done,' he said, 'He is always a great example as regards work rate and effort, and it is simply wonderful how he has managed to exercise the greatest discipline in face of what has sometimes been terrible provocation.' They were all fair points and having passed the audition, Ball was appointed club skipper on a permanent basis in the following summer, echoing the handing of the armband to Roy Vernon a decade before. No better way to control the excesses of the most important player at the club than by handing out accountability. Ball confirmed this at the time, 'I am not worrying about being captain. I really am hoping it will make me a more mature player – I feel now that I've got responsibility for ten other men, as well as myself.'

Ball's first league game in his permanent role was also Everton's opening match as defending champions in August 1970. Arsenal were the visitors in front of an incongruously half-built main stand where many spectators could not find their allotted seats.[69] A goal up at the break, the home team's defence displayed similar disorganisation in the second period, conceding two sloppy goals in a 2-2 draw as the hosts went off the boil. Michael Charters in the *Liverpool Echo* later believed the stalemate was a pointer to the rest of the campaign. 'The first

69 The Main Stand eventually cost £500,000. The impact on Goodison was noted by Geoffrey Green in *The Times*, '... it has stepped into the demanding seventies with a facelift it scarcely seemed to need compared with some I know. New giant stands in place of old; the latest in dazzling floodlight systems that cast not a shadow. A cathedral of a place indeed, fit for the gods of the game.'

indication of the team's inability to fight back when things went wrong,' he said, 'a failing which cost them during the season.' With the new skipper publicly berating his teammates – 'once or twice they would have been justified in answering back' said Eric Todd in the *Guardian* – the agenda to the champions' early season struggles was set.

Seven days later there was a repeat performance, this time unfortunately at Leeds United. For an hour Everton were more than competitive. Displaying all the virtues of twelve months before, the visitors had moved smoothly into a 2-1 lead when John Giles' cross appeared to be harmlessly passing out of play. Inexplicably, Keith Newton headed the ball back into the danger area to the waiting Billy Bremner, who volleyed home. Immediately the Everton captain turned on his left-back, who replied with a few well-directed verbal volleys of his own. Just as the skirmish appeared ready to escalate into something more serious, Brian Labone stepped in to separate the two parties. It was an unwanted spectacle in front of 47,000 supporters. With the visitors losing control, ten minutes from time Bremner controlled Peter Lorimer's cross brilliantly and turned quickly to side-foot past West. The result was unfair on Ball, who produced one of his greatest displays in an Everton shirt. However, there were growing signs that the very characteristics that made him a truly great player – the enormous self-belief, the total commitment to the very highest standards and the will-to-win – would also hinder his captaincy.

Before the season started Ball had outlined the ground rules Catterick had given for his role, 'I've been given the clear understanding that if I see something needs doing I have authority to get it done – and I'll be given full backing, even if my decision is wrong. Provided I can give a sound reason for that decision.' Giving such an emotional and driven player such carte-blanche instructions was always going to invite trouble. His intolerance on the pitch also extended to opponents, one of whom said, 'He gets on my nerves. He always reminds me of a little boy stamping his feet in a corner because he cannot get his own way.' [70] There were also no signs of lessons learned in the next game at Stamford Bridge. With Labone dropped, Everton once again threw away a lead on two occasions during an

[70] Speaking to the *Daily Mail's* Martin Samuel in 2017, Graeme Souness said Alan Ball was, with the great Brazilian Zico, one of the two players he faced who were impossible to intimidate on the pitch. Of one encounter, the Scottish midfielder said, 'by the second-half, he was so comfortable he was running by me, saying "Woof, woof" and blowing kisses. It drove me mad. He wasn't just a great player — he was the best wind-up merchant I've ever known.'

entertaining 2-2 draw, but there was another flashpoint within the opening minute. When Ball and Kendall argued over the taking of a free-kick, the latter pushed his skipper away and it needed the referee's intervention to split them up.

With both Manchester clubs inflicting further defeats in the next week, by early September Everton stood third from bottom, their championship hopes dead after just six games. With Labone out the team and Hurst playing poorly, the frailties from the turn of the year were reappearing, with eight of the first eleven goals conceded down to defensive or goalkeeping errors. Inevitably, the focus was still on Ball and whether his confrontational approach on the pitch had contributed to the dire start. Captaining a winning side is easier than a struggling one, as the new man in charge was finding out. Michael Charters, writing in the *Liverpool Echo*, pulled no punches: 'As the new captain, in every match this season, Ball has let his teammates know when he thinks they have made a mistake. If his comments cannot be heard by spectators, the manner in which they are delivered leave no doubt about the acid in his remarks.' After his departure Ball confirmed these shortcomings as skipper: 'Looking back, I think I was too harsh. I expected too much from people round me.'

To counter the harsh criticism, Catterick understandably strove to defend the Everton skipper. 'The last thing I want among my players is complacency. I would be disturbed if they accepted mistakes with a shrug of the shoulders. I want the players to be upset about mistakes. It keeps them at concert pitch,' he said. Catterick also made a legitimate point that two of the best skippers of the time, Dave Mackay and Billy Bremner, were also fist-shakers. The Everton manager added that 'if you have an extrovert as a captain, half the work for the manager and coach is already done'. Ball also confirmed that he was merely carrying out Catterick's orders in the *Sunday Mirror* after his bitter exit from the club. 'Mr C begged me to go out on the park and shout my way through a match. "Go out there and make them work," he'd tell me. I did and I continued to dish out orders right through my bleak off-form days. I did it even though I knew I was risking the anger of the fans because of my own form. I didn't mind – and I don't blame the manager for using me that way.'

There is a balance and it was clear that Ball had crossed the line at Elland Road in particular, and the scenes at Leeds and Chelsea reflected badly on the club and were affecting a group of players who, perhaps unfairly, had previously carried a reputation for lacking heart. Before the away game at West Ham in September

1970, Ball naturally received support from his close friend, the England skipper Bobby Moore, 'Alan is a natural for captaincy. He gets himself involved in every game and can lift his teammates.' Man-of-the match at Leeds, he was brilliant again at Upton Park, as the visitors played superbly for a 2-1 win, Ball impressing the watching Ken Jones from the *Daily Mirror*:

There are times when Alan Ball's reputation for industry tends to obscure the marvellous range of his skills. A combination of both makes him a player who seems destined to play an increasingly influential role both for Everton and his country. His close control and willingness to attack defenders with the ball is something which disconcerts the most assured and accomplished opponents. His passes can lure the most experienced defender into trouble. Never still, he seems to cover every inch of the pitch and his marvellous industry has never been more evident than it was at West Ham.

The beginning of the end

Ball, like his teammates, failed to recover the form of the championship season and after the two crushing cup defeats of March 1971 the club – and Catterick – stood at the crossroads in the summer of that year. There was still optimism amongst supporters. A *Liverpool Echo* poll found that more than half of Everton fans were quite happy with the performance of the side during the campaign, whilst a staggering 88 percent voted for Howard Kendall as player of the season. Tellingly three-quarters were not happy with the captaincy of Alan Ball. However, the generally positive response clearly indicated that supporters viewed the 1970/71 season as an aberration and normal service would resume.

There was some optimism consequently at the start of the 1971/72 season, which began with a sterile opening day goalless draw at Ipswich, when the visitors deployed as many as nine men in a blanket rearguard, as Catterick made a belated attempt to reflect the wider defensive changes in the game. Four days later there was a 2-0 loss at West Brom before a visit to Goodison of promoted Sheffield United, on a pivotal afternoon that ultimately led to the skipper's departure from the club. 'Not for the first time an off day for Ball meant an off day for Everton,' wrote Eric Todd in the *Guardian* as the club captain endured a frustrating game, completed by Alan Woodward's winner for the visitors ten minutes from time.

The home team's dressing room was quiet afterwards, but Ball was seething, after a humiliating defeat to a team who should not have had a chance of winning. When Catterick entered the dressing room the skipper exploded. 'Boss,' he said, 'you know who beat us today? A glorified Third Division team and you know where they beat us? At Goodison Park.' Catterick said nothing. Ball continued in front of his teammates, 'They call that team Sheffield United boss. Roll that name round your tongue. Come on boss, you tell us the name of the team that beat us, Everton, today. I want to hear you say it.' Even in the privacy of the dressing room, it was an uncomfortable outburst.

The first goals of the season arrived in a 2-0 home win over Chelsea three days later – Colin Harvey's sole brace in nearly 400 first-team games – before a visit to West Ham. Catterick had quite clearly set out to undermine his skipper, in response to the dressing room flare-up on the preceding Saturday. Ball was poor at Upton Park in a 1-0 defeat, but did not expect the comments from the manager afterwards. In the dressing room Catterick accused the England World Cup winner of not trying, something that sent his skipper into a fury. 'Nobody can make a worse accusation than that to Alan Ball,' the player later admitted.

Ball seethed privately on the journey home, failing to join his teammates for a drink, in order to remain clear-headed for the inevitable confrontation when they returned to Bellefield. As Catterick approached his sports car, Ball chased after him. 'You accused me of not trying today – I will not stand for that!' his skipper shouted. 'If you really believed what you said to me in front of the whole team today. I think it's time you and I parted.' The Everton manager – who now surrounded Ball with his coaching team, a typical policy if faced with a difficult player – seemed nonplussed. 'Why have you taken it so personally?' Catterick said, which only inflamed Ball further. As this was happening, players remained in their cars, listening to the manager and skipper continuing their rather public falling out. The argument ended with Ball admitting to Catterick that he had been hiding a groin injury for several weeks. 'I'll not kick another ball for you until I'm 100 percent fit,' Ball told his manager. But Catterick was a wily operator. Rather than escalate the disagreement, the Everton manager backed off and, with the club in a midst of an injury crisis, told his skipper to take time off but only if he made himself available for the four games in the next fortnight.

The short-term fix appeared to have worked when, with Ball outstanding, David Johnson's goal was enough for a 1-0 home win over Manchester United three days later. The following Saturday then brought a dispiriting 2-0 home defeat at the hands of champions-elect Derby County – to rub salt in the wounds Frank Wignall was a scorer, a player Catterick discarded nearly a decade before. Sections of the crowd abused the players near the end, to the outrage of chairman George Watts, who defended the side. 'I appeal to our fans not to add to our problems by barracking our players. We have enough trouble as it is with our injuries at crisis level.' Although there was some support for his stance, one letter to the *Liverpool Echo* summed up the feelings of many fans, 'How do you encourage a team that turns out each week with half-fit players and others well below form?'

Ball played his final game at Wolves, before his enforced lay off, Joe Royle scoring the club's first away goal of the season on a day when rumours were rife that the striker was leaving for a British record fee, with Birmingham's Trevor Francis, then a hugely talented teenager, moving to Goodison for £220,000. By now, with up to six first-team players missing through injury – Ball, Howard Kendall, Harvey, Royle, Wright and Jimmy Husband were side-lined on various occasions – there were a number of homegrown players in the starting line-up. In the following home game against Arsenal, young full-back Peter Scott, Terry Darracott and midfielder Billy Kenny all featured in an encouraging 2-1 win against the champions. That merely proved to be a false dawn, with four defeats and one draw in the following five games, including a particularly poor display at bottom-of-the-table Crystal Palace described by Donald Saunders in the *Daily Telegraph* as the worst he had seen in more than a decade of watching the club.

During the following week, there was further trouble with the Everton skipper. Forced by the specialist to rest, Ball said later, 'I believe he told the gaffer that I could be in serious trouble if I didn't do as I was told.' So when the back-room staff at Bellefield informed the World Cup winner that, in their opinion, he should miss the home game against Coventry, there were angry scenes. 'I played hell with the physiotherapist, the trainers and even the gaffer,' Ball told the *People*, 'I ended up shouting at Mr Catterick: "Aren't I good enough for this team? I can get fit. Don't you want me to play Saturday?"' The manager's answer was obvious because the skipper, in his own words, 'went berserk and ended up running out of the ground almost in tears because they told me I had to take it easy'. Although Ball later apologised, such behaviour from a senior player and team captain was hardly going to lift the morale of an already struggling squad.

In the bottom four for only the second time in his Goodison career, Catterick welcomed Ball back for the visit to Leeds on the penultimate weekend in October, the midfielder performing creditably and scoring in a 3-2 defeat. A week later in the home game against Newcastle United the England international provided a valedictory flourish to his Everton career, although nobody realised at the time. In the second half, picking up a loose ball in the middle of the pitch, the midfielder struck a magnificent winning goal from thirty yards out that flew past keeper Iam McFaul at the Gladwys Street End. 'The inherent genius of Alan Ball carried Everton to a much needed and well deserved victory,' said the *Guardian*.

Having matched his league goals tally from the previous season in the space of seven days, Ball was back to his confident self when arriving in London for the game against Spurs. 'I am feeling back on my game and in the mood to make a few people eat their words,' said the World Cup winner. 'I've taken a lot of criticism over the past year, though I wasn't really worried about it. You can tell Spurs we expect to beat them.' Twenty-four hours later it was a different story. After a dreadful 3-0 loss, the *Sunday Times* was critical of the skipper, 'Alan Ball, striving to return after injury, had a sad match, he disputed the midfield for 25 minutes and then faded.'

After a narrow derby win over Liverpool at Goodison and a rampant 8-0 victory over Southampton[71] in late November, Catterick's side had reverted to type in the next four games, failing to score in any. The 1971/72 season, despite a brief flourish of three successive home wins in late October and early November, was becoming an increasingly desperate experience. The visit to Derby on the last Saturday before Christmas summed up the campaign in many ways. The team coach broke down on the journey down and the players missed their pre-match meal and ate sandwiches instead. The mechanical failure affecting the Everton players was hugely symbolic. On the pitch the team were poor, producing not a single shot on target in ninety minutes. The dreadful performance prompted Alan Pinch in the *Liverpool Daily Post* to say, 'For Everton fans, travelling to watch away matches has become a grim exercise in soccer masochism.' The 2-0 loss left Catterick's side fifth from bottom, having scored just four times in their eleven away games.

71 On 20 November 1971 expectations of the 26,000 supporters at Goodison were low on a snowy, wintry afternoon against a moderate south coast side. The home side then treated the die-hards to perhaps, in the circumstances, the most freakish game in the club's history. Everton completely threw away the formbook – and then some – in an astonishing 8-0 victory, on an afternoon when Joe Royle scored four times, while David Johnson netted a hat-trick. It was also a fitting stage for Alan Ball to score his final goal for the club.

Monday, 20 December 1971 – Mee time

The final Monday before Christmas 1971 was therefore a dispiriting one if you were an Everton supporter. Over the weekend there were rumours that Catterick was preparing to sell Colin Harvey for £150,000, with two clubs interested. In the morning Arsenal manager Bertie Mee made one of his regular calls to Bellefield, perhaps in reaction to the story, but the Gunners' boss was also a long-time admirer of the Everton skipper, and usually asked Catterick, in hope rather than expectation, of Ball's availability. Three months earlier there were rumours that the Everton skipper would be shortly on the market. Presciently, Arsenal were an interested party.

Such inquiries were not unusual. Manchester United were also devotees of the England international and rumours had been circulating for some time that they were ready to make a move – a swap deal involving Brian Kidd plus cash had been mooted six months before. Catterick had earlier admitted that there had been definite offers for three of his players totalling £600,000, one of them being Ball. Asked once if the Old Trafford side had ever tried to buy the England international, Catterick did not either confirm or deny the story, replying with his own rhetorical question, 'Would United sell us George Best?' The same issue arose at the previous shareholders AGM, forcing chairman George Watts to state publicly, 'Ball is under contract with Everton. I imagine there must be dozens of clubs who would like to sign him.'

Mee was probably unaware that Catterick had been apoplectic with his captain's performance at the Baseball Ground. There was a confrontation in the dressing room afterwards, with a furious argument between manager and skipper that also involved Howard Kendall, after a confrontation on the pitch between the two players. The dispute concluded when Catterick told Ball he would be left out the side for the Huddersfield game two days after Christmas. With the pressures of the current campaign, plus the issues with teammates arising from his leadership, doubtless the thought of jettisoning Ball must have crossed Catterick's mind on the Sunday. Apart from the breakdown of their relationship, why else consider selling now? There were obvious football reasons – his captain was simply not the player of two years before. At that time the Everton manager had described Ball as 'a priceless Everton asset', but after the game in the Midlands, the *Liverpool Echo's* Michael Charters put it to Catterick that his skipper was burnt out at 26 years of age. The manager did not disagree.

Offloading Alan Ball in December 1971 therefore was not the same as moving him on in December 1969, although many Everton supporters would have you believe it was. Four weeks before Mee's approach the perceptive Brian James, who had moved from the *Daily Mail* to the *Sunday Times*, had analysed the Everton captain's performance in England's recent victory over Switzerland. James compared Ball's statistics in the game to the data recorded for the midfielder in three matches in 1965/66. Such comparisons are commonplace in the modern game but more than forty years ago it was highly unusual. James noted that Ball had possession against the Swiss on 66 occasions, which was comparable to the figures from six years before of 67, 68 and eighty in the three games analysed. The midfielder completed 45 of his fifty passes made in the match and enjoyed ten successful dribbles out of eleven attempted. They were the positives, said James, before adding:

Where the doubts begin to grow is in examining Ball's contribution to a frustrated attack. He got the ball forward to them, but he too rarely joined it. Only once was he 'clocked' as having driven onto the Swiss goal-area itself… in those 1965-66 surveys Ball was noticed lurking in the goalmouth 12-20 times a match. Yet this reluctance on the part of the Everton man really to attack for England is not a one-match aberration. Indeed it is part of a strange pattern in his play for club and country.

James explained that this was down to 'Ball's own attitude, his combative nature wants him to be where the work is, which means midfield, yet the fact is that, especially in a [England] team that already fielded two defensive players in its midfield three, Ball is very largely duplicating the job already being done by [Peter] Storey and [Emlyn] Hughes.' With the game becoming increasingly reliant on midfield domination, it was only natural that Ball would appear more in the centre of the park – especially in his role as skipper – but James' comments would have carried a ring of truth with Everton players and supporters. Back at Goodison they could see their skipper increasingly in the company of Harvey and Kendall, both of whom were initially ball-winners who then used possession better than their skipper. Around the same time as James' analysis, Ball described his role at Everton in the *Liverpool Echo*:

I regard 75 percent of my game as winning possession and accurate distribution of the ball. My job is to move through the departments of the side. I must drop back to help out the defence, to do my job in midfield and also move up to take balls knocked on, or centred by the front men. Most of my goals come from close range. I've got to be in position for these half-chances from goalmouth tangles.

Ball was describing a (largely self-imposed) workload that he may have been able to perform admirably when in his early twenties, but the England man was now closer to thirty years of age and, although nominally in his peak years, it was almost a decade since his top-flight debut. As a child, Ball used to do a paper round without a bike, and this obsession with stamina carried through to his later years. 'You make yourself do something your body doesn't want to do because I believe that's the way to play football,' he told the *Guardian* in 1977, but those hard years of graft for both club and country were undoubtedly taking a toll. The World Cup winner could still adequately perform the 75 percent of the role he defined. The other 25 percent was the main problem – the ability to make his presence felt in the opposing box, as Brian James pointed out. After averaging one goal every three games in his league career up until the start of the 1970s (including seventeen in his last campaign with Blackpool), Ball's strike rate had fallen to a trickle. Having said that, due to his own lack of form and the struggles of the team, his strategy was that if it was not working in one part of the pitch, he would simply move to another. (Wayne Rooney was subject to similar accusations after Sir Alex Ferguson departed.) Ball's continuous all-action style ran contrary to the advice of his father, who wanted him to control both his temper and the tempo of his play. As Ball senior once commented to the *Daily Mail* about his son: 'I've scolded him. I've told him not to retaliate…but he wants to do every job on the pitch. He gets as upset about other people's failings as much as his own and sheer anger and frustration at it all builds up.'

Catterick would have known all of this, of course, and concluded that the long-term dip in performances over the previous eighteen months could no longer be put down to the effects of the World Cup. Michael Charters wrote in the *Liverpool Echo*, 'Ball has pushed his slight frame beyond the limits of his physical capacity. He has given 100 per cent so often that now he cannot give 100 per cent, although his body wants him to.' The crunch came in the month before Catterick sanctioned the transfer. After his enforced break, Ball told the manager that his fitness was the best since the title season, only to produce a string of poor performances, culminating in the mediocre display at Derby County. Ball was not playing for a transfer though and still cared deeply about the club. One Sunday night during this period the Everton captain phoned Alan Ball senior and turned up almost in tears at his house, speaking until the early hours over his poor form and the struggles of the club he still loved.

In normal circumstances the Everton manager would have provided a friendly response of 'not for sale' to Mee's inquiry, but perhaps the Derby County game had brought a rethink. Catterick was obviously cognisant of the disputes with his skipper earlier in the season and would have had the noise from the dressing room argument at the Baseball Ground still ringing in his ears. Above all was the corrosive effect of the captaincy on Ball's play and relations with teammates on the pitch. As Ken Jones wrote in the *Daily Mirror*, 'He is easy prey to the pressures of the modern game. When it is coupled with a breakdown of the team's play we see his worst side.' Catterick made a similar admission to the *News of the World* in October 1972: 'Alan set himself such high standards that he became annoyed when others fell short of them. He began shouting at colleagues and some had the impression that he thought they couldn't play. You can't have that sort of thing, can you?'

Combined with the long-term decline in Ball's form, then there was a compelling case for selling his prize asset, albeit for the right price. When Mee made his fateful approach on the Monday, Catterick was open to offers. Thus, to the Arsenal manager's great surprise, this time his rival provided an opening. 'You might be able to buy him,' the Everton manager said, 'at the right price.'[72] Following a quick board meeting, the directors agreed to allow the Everton boss to handle the deal. The England international provided a little-known account of what happened next to the *Sunday Mirror* a fortnight later:

I was in the bath after training when coach Tom Casey said the boss wanted me to go upstairs. Here we go again I thought. I'm due for another rollocking because I played badly in the 2-0 defeat at Derby the previous Saturday. Mr Catterick offered me a seat in his plush office which overlooks the vast training ground at Bellefield. He looked glassy-eyed. But his voice never faltered when he said 'I have some news

72 The generally accepted view of events is that Catterick told Ball on the Monday that the club had received a British record bid and a manager was in a room down the corridor to speak to him. This could not be true, as Mee did not travel up to Bellefield until 24 hours later.

for you. We have had an offer for you and it's too good to turn down.' Mr Catterick didn't tell me which club. I had to ask. 'Arsenal' he said.

Ball sat in silence for a full three minutes, before saying 'what about the fans, what will they think?' Catterick told Ball to think of the cash. At that point, Ball did not intend to leave the club, but the Everton manager still held a trump card. Catterick knew that for a proud player like the Everton skipper and World Cup winner there was one action that would make him reconsider his position. Realising that Ball probably thought that the threat to drop him was a throwaway comment, uttered in the heat of the moment in the Baseball Ground changing room, Catterick reminded his star player that he was not in his plans for the next game against Huddersfield. The ploy worked and a furious Ball snapped, 'You drop me from THIS team and I want to go.' The club captain effectively would rather have moved than suffer the public humiliation of dropping to the bench, especially in a side that was plainly struggling. Told to return by 4 p.m. with a decision over his future at the club, Ball had already made his mind up by the time he went to meet his father, telling him 'after what Harry Catterick said today I'll never kick another ball for Everton.'

Tuesday, 21 December 1971

Mee cancelled a scouting trip to Scotland and travelled up to Merseyside instead for a meeting with Catterick and Ball to refine the details of the deal. The final fee was £220,000; Ball had become the first man to become the most expensive British footballer on two separate occasions. After the title win in 1970 Catterick had said he would only sell Ball 'when he was thirty and for £250,000'. The Everton manager was letting his prize asset go three years before schedule and for £30,000 less. Ball later recalled the meeting with the two men. 'To my face, Harry Catterick told me he thought I could do nothing more for his team. I didn't know that anything could hurt so much. Then I looked across at Bertie Mee and I thought one of these men is wrong. I'll make sure it's not Mr Mee. I'll die for him if I have to.' The news of their skipper's departure came as a shock to the players. 'We always thought he was Harry's favourite,' Joe Royle told Ball's biographer David Tossell, 'It made us all the more surprised when he came out of Harry's office and declared he was going to move.'

Wednesday, 22 December 1971

With his pride piqued, Ball travelled down to Arsenal with his father to discuss a deal 24 hours later. The midfielder's preference was to stay in the north-west for family reasons and Alan Ball senior spoke to both Manchester clubs. Although City were able to match the transfer fee they could not compete with the wages paid by the London club. United feigned no interest and then seemingly changed their mind, telling Ball they would have a representative waiting at Euston. Arsenal got wind of their move and arranged to meet Ball off the train at Watford. Chased by waiting pressmen, they threw off their pursuers and got their man to a hotel in Regent's Park, where he signed for the Gunners, for a reported annual salary of £12,500. Ball was previously quoted as saying, 'I'd have walked all the way to Old Trafford,' but his first choice was Manchester City. The midfielder was a keen admirer of Malcolm Allison and Ball had phoned the charismatic coach when news of the deal broke. Allison told him, 'I will make you the best midfield player in Europe, but for those wages you've been offered, sign for Arsenal.'

Ball understandably remained shocked at the speed of the career-changing move. Returning to Bellefield the following day for training, he went to see Catterick again. Ball found the manager sitting in his office, his head in his hands. 'What shall I do,' said Catterick, before admitting that 'someday I will tell you the whole story of your transfer.' His manager never did. Whether he, or the club, had an ulterior motive for selling the skipper has never materialised. Ball left Bellefield a desperately sad man, as he admitted less than a fortnight later. 'I say goodbye to Merseyside ... feeling completely choked. Tears and me have never been far apart since the shock hit me between the eyes. My pride – and I have tons of that – has been deeply hurt. That mountain of money at the moment of departure didn't offer a shred of compensation.'

Catterick, of course, initially remained tight-lipped about whole affair. 'We had this fantastic offer from Arsenal and I talked it over in great detail with my directors,' he said. 'We decided after great length that it was in the best interests of the club and player that we should part. He is still a very fine player – don't forget I bought him so I know all his qualities.' What those best interests were, Catterick never explained, indeed as Danny Blanchflower said in the *Sunday Express* about the oblique comments, 'that is pretty smooth business talk, hiding more than it reveals'. In August 1972, the manager merely added to the uncertainty. 'If the public could have been made aware of the facts, they would have agreed with it,' he told Michael Charters. There were rumours that Ball had gambling debts and therefore welcomed a move, but if that were the case, why to everybody did the club skipper appear so genuinely shocked and upset at the transfer?

Saturday, 1 January 1972

The problem with the sale of Alan Ball is that it was a story that did not go away. Fate dictated that the midfielder's Highbury debut would be against his former club on New Year's Day, less than a fortnight after Mee's speculative call. Before then Catterick had the first game of the new era against Huddersfield at Goodison five days before the trip to London. Any unrealistic expectations in the 40,000 crowd that the sale of Ball could possibly act as a catalyst for a change in fortunes were not fulfilled, as the home team struggled to contain one of the poorest sides to play in the top-flight during the decade. A goal down after six minutes, Everton laboured to a 2-2 draw. Catterick replaced the out-of-sorts Joe Royle with Mick Lyons just after the hour mark, the former protesting by going straight to the dressing room. The big striker had a paranoid fear of being replaced. 'It's the most humiliating, sick-making walk in sport when you're called off and substituted,' he admitted ten months later, before adding about the Huddersfield incident, 'Even now, that feeling of shame sickens me.' Elsewhere the press saw little change from the days before Ball left. 'Everton on the evidence of this match,' said the *Guardian*, 'are in dire trouble.'

Catterick initially saw the transfer as the beginning of a new era, after criticising his failing players. 'I have been extremely patient, giving them every chance to regain their form and attitude to the game,' the manager said, 'now my patience has ended. I've given them every chance. If they don't achieve what I want, changes will be made.' The manager was as good as his word for the first meeting against his now former captain. Sixth from bottom, there were six changes to the line-up at Derby just a fortnight before. The result was a largely anonymous first-team, unrecognisable from the title side less than two years before: *West; Scott, McLaughlin, Kenyon, Lyons; Jones, Darracott, Kendall; Royle, Whittle, Johnson.*

Only four of the starting line-up had appeared in the European Cup second leg against Panathinaikos just nine months before and, of the ten outfield players, only Kenyon and Kendall were more than 23 years of age. The amount of youngsters brought some unexpected issues, several having a clause in their contracts preventing them from wearing their hair fashionably long.[73] Catterick had also appointed Kendall as skipper on an interim basis, the accepted wisdom being Henry Newton would be the next club captain after recovering from injury. (As it was Everton's most successful manager would get the job on a full time basis.)

With the eyes of the football world on north London, Catterick had obviously wound up his players. 'He motivated them as never before,' said Ball later. With no away victory for fifteen months, his plan was effectively to crudely kick Arsenal out of the game, a complete *volte-face* from the School of Science principles of only a few years before. Even that benign gentleman of the game, Bob Wilson, was sufficiently rattled to menacingly confront Joe Royle after being kicked by the Everton striker. Despite their negative approach, Everton went ahead on twenty minutes, stand-in skipper Kendall striking a perfect volley from Pat Rice's poor headed clearance. The determined visitors withheld a mighty second-half onslaught until eight minutes from time, when Peter Simpson equalised with a superb cross-shot. It was a decent point in the circumstances, but their deterioration over the previous eighteen months was reflected in a contribution to an encounter that 'was never a game', according to Alan Hoby of the *Sunday Express*, 'it was more like a martial trumpet call to arms, a mockery of football, bitter, bruising and bristling with hostility.'

A young Terry Darracott effectively shadowed Ball throughout the game, and the frustrated new signing commented on Everton's change of style afterwards. 'What did surprise me, though, was that everybody-back, all-defensive whack-into-them system they used,' he provocatively told the *Daily Mirror*. 'That never happened all the time I was at Everton, although there were occasions when I wished it had. The fans won't like it because they have been reared on quality.' The remarks clearly irked Catterick, who was also upset with Alan Ball senior leaking details, to the press, of the Everton manager's private conversations with his son on the day he left. In addition, Ball senior's comment that Catterick 'cracked under the pressure built up by injuries and poor results until he reached the stage where he desperately had to do something' was also likely to draw a response. In retrospect perhaps the fallout from the failed bid to sign Archie Gemmill when the Scot was at Alan Ball senior's Preston

73 The actual wording said, 'Hair is to be as short as deemed suitable for the player to carry out his duties with the club.'

may have been somehow part of the decision to sell his son. [74]

Monday, 3 January 1972

The tit-for-tat continued in the press, a huge gulf quickly appearing between the club and their former star. It was traditional for a recently transferred player to visit his former teammates in the dressing room before the game, but that did not happen at Highbury. Mindful of Ball's comments to the Sunday press, 24 hours later Catterick told journalists, 'The spirit among the players has been lifted 200 per cent since Ball has gone.' [75]

The club had also banned players from talking to the press, but one anonymously told Michael Charters that 'Ball was always critical, telling them they couldn't play. Now it has all changed. I've never known spirit on the field change for the better so much and so quickly.' That may have been true, but the feeling persists that some players (and their manager) were making Ball a scapegoat for their own shortcomings. As captain, his role was to point out things that were going wrong; perhaps he did not use the right methods but then again his teammates gave him plenty of opportunities to voice displeasure at their poor form.

Tuesday, 4 January 1972

To add further intrigue, 24 hours later Ball attended an FA disciplinary hearing to appeal a booking received playing for Everton against Liverpool six weeks before.[76] Typically, it became another cause célèbre. Before Ball departed, Everton requested that Bill Shankly and Ian Callaghan appear as witnesses

---

[74] Conspiracy theorists could read something into this. Alan Ball senior and junior had an extremely close relationship. Ball senior had a clear conflict of interest in selling Archie Gemmill to Everton in 1970, as a player who could pose a threat to his son in both roles of midfielder and skipper. In fact, it would be safe to assume that both father and son had conversations about the deal without Catterick's knowledge. Whether the Everton manager felt this contributed to the failure to land Gemmill and led to a lack of trust in his skipper is only speculation, although worth remembering that Catterick accused Ball's father of reneging on a written agreement to sell the Scot to Everton.

[75] This was in stark contrast to his statement after the midfielder's arrival five-and-a-half years before. 'What has made the difference,' Catterick said then, 'is that Ball's incoming has lifted the standard of the others by 10 per cent.'

[76] To help clean up the game, at the start of the 1971/72 season the Football League tightened down on foul play. Consequently bookings multiplied, with the resulting appeals causing a backlog. Colin Harvey's appearance in front of the FA panel in October 1971, following a booking for a tackle from behind on West Ham's John Ayris, typified the chaos. Harry Catterick and secretary Bill Dickinson were called as witnesses for the defence, as was Bobby Moore. But on the day Moore was delayed in traffic plus Catterick and Dickinson were grounded by fog at Manchester airport – and they possessed the photograph from *Goal* magazine of the tackle that could potentially clear Harvey. Bizarrely, during the hearing a motorcycle courier was sent to the *Goal* offices to pick up a second copy of the magazine, which showed the tackle was clearly from the side and Harvey was subsequently cleared. Moore eventually turned up after the hearing. 'Sorry I'm late,' he said, 'the traffic was awful and I couldn't come any earlier because of training. We've got a big game against Liverpool on Wednesday.'

on his behalf. On the day, they were the England international's only representatives. After the hearing cleared Ball, Shankly launched a broadside at his rivals. 'It is unbelievable that Everton should have left Alan Ball stranded today. He got his booking when he was an Everton player and they have washed their hands of the whole affair.' Equally frustrating for the Liverpool manager was that, although Callaghan turned up to represent Ball, he claimed that Everton's Gary Jones failed to arrive to support Chris Lawler, who was booked in the same game.

Everton officials quickly refuted Shankly's comments, pointing out they would have supported the player if told about the hearing but no contact was made – indeed Catterick had originally offered to help Ball. A furious Everton board made an official complaint to the Football League about Shankly's behaviour before the Liverpool boss promptly withdrew his claims, admitting that he had actually turned down Everton's offer to help Lawler. The story did not end there. Ball went into print to defend Shankly's attendance at the hearing and criticized Everton for interfering in a matter that was no longer in their interest. George Watts, the club chairman, quite rightly answered Ball's claims, pointing out that their complaint was not over Shankly's presence, but his comments afterwards. 'We must refute Alan Ball's statement that Everton objected to Mr Shankly appearing at his hearing. This is complete nonsense,' said Watts. Ball then reacted to Catterick's comments about the improved team spirit after his departure: 'Such an outburst only twelve days after I had left Everton is a slur on my character.' It was proving to be a messy divorce.

Summing up

The subsequent years provided no evidence to suggest that selling Ball was a mistake, especially given the record fee. The England international enjoyed some early success with the Gunners, with an FA Cup final appearance at the end of the campaign and a league runners-up medal the following season. The midfielder was not afraid to comment publicly on how his former manager had made a mistake. 'I've proved myself with Arsenal,' he told *Shoot* magazine in 1973, 'I feel I'm producing the sort of form that helped Everton win the League Championship in 1970. I don't apologise if this is a bit of personal drum beating. Imagine how you'd feel in the same situation.'

Seven years later though, in the same publication, Ball was more conciliatory towards Catterick. 'Nowadays you'd say it was good for business. He'd had five years out of me and was doubling the fee he'd paid to Blackpool. I didn't understand his logic but I do now. I must admit, I like a man who makes decisions. Whether they were right or wrong, Catterick certainly made them.' Ball's career at Highbury fizzled out as the club went into decline in the middle of the decade – by demanding to be the focal point of the team he was disrupting the usual direct playing style of Mee's side. After old nemesis Don Revie ruthlessly discarded the midfielder from the England team in 1975, Ball left Arsenal for Southampton exactly five years after his Everton departure. The earlier brushes with authority came back to haunt him. Remarkably, for a World Cup winner, the Football League twice refused applications for a testimonial. Having said that, in two spells on the south coast, Ball enjoyed an Indian summer, appropriately playing his last top-flight game against the club he loved in October 1982.

However, whatever the reasons for selling his skipper, there is no denying that Catterick treated one of his senior players with a certain amount of contempt. As one of the best three Everton players – with only Dixie Dean and, arguably, Neville Southall being above him in the all-time list – Ball deserved so much better. It is hard to imagine Catterick selling, say, Howard Kendall or Joe Royle, at the time in the same manner. Nevertheless, it is clear now that the growing disunion between two influenced the almost callous way Catterick offloaded his biggest star. As the old saying goes, revenge is a dish best served cold. In spite of the conspiracy theories over the years, a combination of good business and broken relations forced the sale. Indeed as Ball said himself of his public argument with Catterick in the Bellefield car park three months before, 'On reflection I think that row could have been the beginning of the end of me at Everton.'

There is another possible scenario though – that Catterick never really wanted to sell Ball. It is easy to speculate with the benefit of hindsight that the sanctioning of the transfer was simply an impulsive reaction to their argument at Derby on the Saturday. Had Catterick allowed himself more breathing space and time to reflect, Ball could have remained at the club. There is plenty of evidence to support this theory. First of all the timing of the sale: three days before Christmas was hardly the ideal moment to transfer your best player, given the upcoming programme of games and the holiday period was not exactly conducive to searching for replacements. To make it even more awkward, other clubs were historically reluctant to sell players while they were still in the

FA Cup, and the third round had yet to start.

Secondly, why invite interest from only one club? Ball had a huge number of admirers within the game and Catterick could have circulated his intention to sell amongst potential suitors – both Manchester sides, Arsenal, Spurs and possibly Leeds – with a view to driving up the transfer fee. Bill Shankly would certainly have shown an interest in signing the midfielder, having turned down the opportunity of bringing him to Anfield when Ball was sixteen years of age. His comments support the view that it was a rash decision. 'I would have had Alan Ball if I could,' the Liverpool boss admitted, 'but nobody knew he was available until Arsenal had made their move.' Players like Ball rarely arrived on the market and selling the midfielder after one phone call does not really lend credence to the theory that Catterick had developed an exit strategy for his star man. Instead, it was a snap, impetuous decision.

Finally, and perhaps most pointedly of all, history would bear out that Catterick had no immediate replacement(s) lined up. If selling Ball were a premeditated decision, then the manager would surely have lined up a player of equal stature. As Catterick was well aware, top clubs rarely sold their best players, so there was no chance of getting a like-for-like replacement for the international at short notice. That proved to be the case. Everton subsequently spent six months flailing blindly around the transfer market, eventually landing players who were several classes below Ball and what the Goodison crowd was used to watching. All this is speculation, but his departure came as an incredible blow to supporters – a 'where were you when you found out Alan Ball had been sold' moment – and in the cold light of day it was probably a shock to Catterick.

The transfer left several wounds – there is a case for saying that Ball the player never really recovered from the sale; also, that Everton still carry the scars in many ways. It hastened the end of a glorious era in the club's history, a period that started with the introduction of John Moores and the 'Mersey Millionaires' moniker more than a decade before. During that time Everton's wealth brought status – and success. By moving on the one player known throughout the country, Catterick was in some ways selling the family silver and, by default, also diluting the national standing of the club. True, Everton still paid big money for players – just over two years later breaking the British record again for Bob Latchford – and there was a hugely successful spell in the eighties, but the latter came when both the game's reputation and public interest had plunged to a new low, mainly thanks to the effects of hooliganism and the economic recession. When Everton won the league in 1969/70, 15 million watched top-flight football, by the time of their last title victory in 1986/87 this figure had plunged to nine million, a drop of 40 percent. Although many Everton supporters supported Catterick's action, the concluding paragraphs to one supporter's heartfelt letter to the *Liverpool Echo* summed up the acute sense of loss:

Bally was world class – and we – Everton – were champions of England. Bally meant something wherever football was talked about. A German picked you up just outside Kiel last year when you were hitching round Europe. He couldn't speak English; you couldn't speak German. But you mentioned Liverpool and he said: 'Ja, Alan Ball, Everton.' And you felt that lump in your throat and your eyes began to water as you said: 'Yes, I'm an Evertonian,' and you could see Bally running down the wing in your mind's eye as clearly as if you were standing in the Gwladys Street end. He will still be running down the wing, but he'll be wearing the red and white of Arsenal. You'll still go along next year and give him a cheer – and remember. Because Bally was Everton – he was a part of the family; now he has gone and you've lost a friend.

23.

'I Make the Decisions, I Carry the Can'

EVEN IN THE USUALLY STRESSFUL ENVIRONMENT OF CLUB management, by January 1972 the Everton manager must have been feeling the strain of the job enormously. The decline of the team, the fall-out from the sale of Alan Ball, plus the struggle to bring in players of the required quality must have produced adverse effects on his well-being. His time at Goodison had seen several health scares: as well as the abdominal operation in 1965 and the heavy bout of bronchitis following the Panathinaikos away game there had been several instances of influenza that forced him to miss individual matches.

After two decades of management, the long hours on the road – Catterick reckoned there had been 150 trips to Scotland in ten years alone – must also have taken its toll physically. 'His life, in fact, is nearly given over to football. He takes only a fortnight's holiday a year,' stated Dudley Doust in the *Sunday Times* two years before. Catterick told the American that 'there is seldom an evening when I'm not talking with a parent or watching a football match'. Perhaps more pertinently Catterick also admitted to Doust the rationale of not having a deputy since arriving from Sheffield Wednesday. 'You have to do things yourself,' he explained, 'once you let other people do them, you're slipping.' The obvious comparison here is across the Park, where there was a back-room team good enough to win four European Cups after Shankly's resignation in 1974. The Scot retained Catterick's control, but delegated more.

The by-product of course was that as fortunes slipped the manager felt the full weight of the consequences. 'I wouldn't have a manager's job for a ransom. If the team are doing well then it is because we have good players. If the team are doing badly it is because the manager is at fault. It's a hard life,' John Moores once said. The Littlewoods chief's assessment was correct and by early 1972 Catterick cut an isolated figure, working long hours to turn the club's fortunes round. A natural introvert, Catterick had no safety valve to release the pressure. 'When things are going wrong, he withdraws into his shell even more ... he worries intensely when things aren't going well,' Moores said later. 'It is a bitter blow when the results don't come and it makes him even more withdrawn.' Catterick had previously given Alan Hoby in the *Sunday Express* an insight of the self-inflicted pressures of the job:

People call us hard, tough, and so on, but you know, inside every manager, however hard he may or may not be, is a purist struggling to get out. They all want their teams to play attractive football and show off their skills. They all want to provide entertainment and goals. But any manager worth his salt has to be governed by the playing staff he has available. He would be a fool if he didn't. Don't forget that all sorts of factors are involved ... the players he inherited when he went there ... the money he has to spend ... directors who want results right away ... all kinds of pressures.

It was because of the absence of attractive football, the diminishing quality of the squad and the pressures of the hierarchy that the Everton manager was following a punishing schedule. Concerted efforts to use the funds in strengthening the team, immediately after the sale of Alan Ball, nosedived. In the same week he sold his captain, Catterick failed in an attempt to prise the highly rated striker Mick Channon from Southampton for a new British record fee. Stoke's Tony Waddington also rejected a move for midfield enforcer Mick Bernard, as the Potters were still in both domestic cup competitions, although Catterick would acquire the player in the following summer. During the new year trip to watch Hibernian on the Monday after the visit to Highbury, the Scottish club snubbed a bid of £150,000 for wiry midfielder Alex Cropley and defender John Blackley.

As well as the immediate pressures Catterick faced in rebuilding the team, there was the accumulated stress from two decades of management, during which time he successfully addressed diverse demands from the financial strains of the lower leagues to the burden of instant success at the top. Those pressures would undoubtedly have had a damaging effect on his health. In his ground-breaking book on Spurs, *The Glory Game*, author Hunter Davies reflected on the pressures facing managers in the early 1970s. 'They have complete power over their charges,' he wrote, 'but when it really matters they are helpless. Most players do forget once they get out there playing, but a manager has few releases, few safety valves. Their agony is constant.'

After he retired Matt Busby alluded to a previous conversation with the Everton manager. 'I once remember Harry Catterick saying that people didn't realise the tension and strain for a manager of just one league match. Imagine what it is like for twenty-three [years] of it.' Even rival Bill Shankly acknowledged that fact after learning of the Everton manager's absence from the 1971 semi-final. 'I am sorry Mr Catterick missed the game. When you have so many games to play they are enough to make you ill. The tension we go through is enough to make anybody sick.' Old ally Brian Labone later noted the impact of the rising pressures of being the Everton boss. 'Anyone who thinks a manager's job is a soft number had only to look at Mr Catterick's face to know the real truth. The strain had been showing for some time and he certainly aged in the last few years.' For Labone, the source of the strain was clear, 'I think Mr Catterick's one fault was that he didn't delegate responsibility enough.'

So after the scouting trip to Hibernian, 48 hours later Catterick could be found driving back from Hillsborough, having watched the third epic instalment of the Stoke and West Ham League Cup semi-final. In a remote part of the Pennines the Everton manager suddenly felt severe pain across his chest and left arm. After driving for several miles, Catterick pulled up at an isolated cottage, where a district nurse was fortunately present. A doctor was immediately called for and an ambulance then took the stricken Everton boss to a hospital in Sheffield.

Although there was a degree of mystery in the days that followed, the initial prognosis was that it was nothing particularly serious. Chairman George Watts claimed, 'The reports indicate Mr Catterick's complaint is a minor one. There is no heart trouble, or anything like that. It could well be that he is suffering from the same thing as some of the people in my office – a touch of flu.' Although the club understandably had acted quickly to downplay the incident, Watts' comments slightly contradicted the doctors' opinion at Sheffield, who described Catterick as 'poorly.' Later in the week the Goodison hierarchy was still playing it low key. 'All we do know at the moment is that there is no trace of whatever caused him to feel ill while he was driving his car,' Watts admitted, 'he has been seen by a specialist, given cardiac tests and there is no sign of any heart complaint.'

It later transpired, of course, that the manager had suffered a coronary whilst driving, one that necessitated a six-day spell in intensive care, followed by a further week in Sheffield. After being discharged, Catterick spent another fortnight in a nursing home before completing his recuperation at home. Inevitably in the aftermath there was talk of Catterick's future at Goodison, with stories circulating that he would not be fit enough to return, with Wolves' Bill McGarry taking over the reins. Watts moved quickly to quash the gossip. 'There is no doubt,' he replied when questioned about Catterick's future, 'that he will make an early and complete recovery. All these rumours I have heard are complete nonsense.'

Regarding the club's original insistence that Catterick's health problems were of a minor nature, the length of his recovery bore testimony to their seriousness. It was two months before doctors allowed Catterick to visit Bellefield on a weekly basis, resuming light duties only at the end of March. The home match against Nottingham Forest in May was the first Everton game he had watched since New Year's Day.

There is no doubt that Catterick's health issues were directly linked to the weight of expectation in an increasingly pressurised environment. 'As compared with a business executive, a football club manager presents a balance sheet every Saturday, in terms of the result and the eleven selections he has made,' he told the *Liverpool Echo* in 1976. 'He can get ten out of eleven, and in most standards of business that is good, but in football it is bad.' Also, by the early part of the decade Catterick had enjoyed almost twenty years of prosperity as a manager but the decline of the team had taken him into unchartered territory, one he was ill-prepared for. 'Unfortunately I didn't have a philosophy to help when the going got tough,' he admitted to the *Liverpool Echo* in the same interview, before adding, 'I had other problems apart from the football ones.' Talking about those family issues, Catterick confessed, 'I feel that a very happy domestic life must be a great cushion against the stresses.'

His chairman was cognisant of the burden involved. 'Mr Catterick has had a very trying time, physically and mentally, in the past four weeks,' Watts told the press in early January, 'and it is true that he has been under a lot of pressure and that it hasn't been a good season for him. In my opinion – and I stress that this is his affair and not mine – he does work too hard.' As Catterick once admitted about his profession, 'I don't have anyone sitting at my side holding my hand. The decisions that matter are the ones that only I can make – the team selection and whether I can sign a player – I make the decisions, I carry the can.'

Catterick's health issues were symptomatic of a wider malaise within the playing squad. In the title-winning year and the seasons beforehand the squad had stayed relatively free from injury but that changed in the years that followed, as players aged. Largely through injury, Brian Labone played just twenty league games in the two seasons after the 1970 championship win before retirement. Not only did the absence of his right-hand man affect the dressing room but on the pitch Labone's absence left a massive hole in the back-line. Both John Hurst and the relatively inexperienced Roger Kenyon were more comfortable with a domineering partner and this caused uncertainty in the middle of the defence.

Johnny Morrissey was one of the side's best players in the 1970/71 campaign but in the following season the winger was troubled by an achilles tendon injury and played just 16 league games before moving to Oldham. Catterick felt the absence of the local-born player was crucial to reducing the firepower of the team. 'The loss of Morrissey was obviously something that had a great effect on the strikers,' he told Bob Azurdia on BBC Radio Merseyside at the end of the campaign. With Labone and Morrissey effectively reaching the end of their Everton careers, during the 1971/72 season the treatment room at Bellefield was rarely empty: Tommy Wright was side-lined for 14 games in four spells, Howard Kendall missed nine matches, Jimmy Husband was out for 15 games over four periods while Colin Harvey was side-lined for 26 games in seven. Elsewhere David Johnson missed nine games over three spells while the unlucky Henry Newton had 11 games out in three periods. Consequently, the side was unable to generate any rhythm due to the constant changing of the starting eleven. By 1972 the championship team was literally falling apart.

Transfer troubles

In some respects, some of the pressures had been self-inflicted. Catterick was undoubtedly a great manager in the 1960s, but lost his way after 1970 with the failure to build from a position of strength and not adequately responding when injuries took their toll. The press had reported that Catterick had anything up to £500,000 to spend on players in the summer of 1971 but the Everton manager passed over the opportunity to sign QPR's Rodney Marsh for a club record fee of

£160,000 and, after Everton scouts had watched him closely, rejected Luton Town's Malcolm Macdonald. 'I must reserve judgement as he has been playing for a successful side,' Catterick said, 'The true test of a footballer is how well he plays in a struggling team.'[77] Such a stance was admirable, but Catterick, like other managers, had to gamble at some point. Newcastle did with Macdonald, paying £180,000 in the summer of 1971, the striker scoring a hat-trick on his home debut against Liverpool and becoming the top-flight's leading scorer of the decade. Having failed to bring in new blood during the summer of 1971, the Everton manager still spoke to the press in bullish mood:

There is no reason, barring injuries, why Everton should not enjoy a very successful season. We have available almost all the talent that helped us win the championship two years ago. We are still a comparatively young team and there are players who must be better for the experience they have. To register an improvement you can only talk in terms of top class men. I have a lot of faith in my youth policy. It has proved its worth by the achievements we have had. With our youth and skill, if the ball runs for us, we are liable to win anything and everything.

The manager had conveniently forgotten the collapse in the season before and there was no evidence that the 'youth policy' he was referring to was actually working. Only David Johnson had broken into the team in the previous three seasons and the youngster was still very much a work in progress. There were players like Mike Lyons, Gary Jones and Mick Buckley in the wings, but they were still untried. They were not a 'comparatively young team' either. The average age of the starting line-up in the FA Cup semi-final at Old Trafford in March 1971 was 26 years and four months – discounting substitute Sandy Brown, who was 32 and the oldest player to appear for the club during the decade. The average age was only a couple of months younger than the Liverpool side that had lost to Watford in 1970, a team that was considered ageing and in need of urgent reconstruction.

Even after an injury crisis during the early months of the 1971/72 campaign,

77 Curiously one of Catterick's successors at Goodison, Gordon Lee, held the polar opposite view. At Newcastle, Lee controversially sold 'Supermac' to Arsenal in 1976, justifying the deal to Brian Viner in the latter's book *Looking for the Toffees* by saying that Macdonald needed to be judged in a good side, not a poor one, and had been found wanting. 'I thought he was a good player in a bad team,' Lee said, 'In a bad side, as teams put pressure on them, he'd stand up top in plenty of space. As we became a good side, and started to knock it about, he had nowhere to run.' It was strange that the two men had such diverse views on one player.

Catterick arrogantly rejected calls to bring in new players. 'I won't pay big money for men who, in six weeks' time, when I hope our injury problem eases, will be reserves,' he said. The manager may have had a point, but his follow-up statement, 'I would be interested in George Best or Bobby Moore if they were available, but anything below that standard would not be better than the players we have,' bordered on the delusional, given the club had been in serious decline for the best part of 18 months. As one supporter remarked, 'I am tired of listening to Harry Catterick's continual talk about his injury list. It's time it was realised that the first-team pool isn't good enough. He stated that he has a half a dozen young players in the £100,000 class. I say that is rubbish.'

Catterick's stubbornness led to a number of missed opportunities. Ipswich outbid Everton for centre-half Allan Hunter, who went on to provide more than a decade of sterling service in East Anglia. Looking for a replacement for Johnny Morrissey, Catterick made an offer for Burnley's gifted Dave Thomas, but the deal fell through when the youngster stated a preference for a midfield role, and subsequently went to QPR. Furthermore, Catterick showed no interest in signing Aberdeen captain Martin Buchan, stating he was only intent on strengthening the midfield. This was a ludicrous position. Buchan was a quality player, the inspiring leader at the back that Catterick and the side desperately needed – similar to the role performed by Tommy Smith at Liverpool. The 22-year-old went to Old Trafford instead, where he was a domineering presence for eleven years – six as skipper.

Reading the last Wright

One player Catterick did bring in was John 'Tiger' McLaughlin from Falkirk, a tough-tackling full-back whose receding hairline was the subject of a memorable put-down from the *Sunday Times*. 'McLaughlin is only 23, but because of his bald head he looks like a man who is past it.' Although a reliable performer, it was difficult to see how the signing of the uncapped Scot in October 1971 fitted in with Catterick's mantra that there was only a handful of players who he thought were good enough for the club.

Supporters would say that McLaughlin was a thoroughbred compared to striker Bernie Wright from Walsall – whose move to Goodison is since recognised as symbolising the club's sorry plight in the early years of the decade. Birmingham City had released the weight-lifting youngster in the summer of 1971 and after moving to The Saddlers, Wright impressed the watching Everton scouts – the two teams drawn together in the FA Cup – to such an extent in a third-round replay win against Bournemouth in January 1972 that they recommended his immediate signing. After hardly disgracing himself at Goodison in the next round, Wright moved to Merseyside in a £30,000 deal. 'We had been impressed by his performances in the third division, but we needed to know how he would fare against top-class opposition,' said club executive David Exall, 'the way he played against Everton definitely clinched the deal.'

Nevertheless, the striker effectively left the club at the end of the year following a memorable sequence of events embedded in Goodison folklore. Wright recalled the circumstances of his exit to the *Evertonian* magazine in 2003. 'I was asked by the reserve team trainer at the time, Jack Connor, to go and train with the first team,' the striker said, 'so I went over to Stuart Imlach [the first-team trainer] but he said to me "well, you can come if you want but you won't be playing."' With all his teammates now laughing at him, Wright returned to train with the reserves. The striker then described what happened next. 'The first team were running towards us with Stuart and as they did all the lads were giving me some right stick, saying to me "put one on him, hit him one." So I did.'

Suspended by the club for punching the Everton coach, Wright found further infamy in events shortly afterwards, at the end of December 1972. Legend has it that the drunken forward went looking for Catterick at Bellefield, the manager escaping through the back door. The story then goes that the last sighting of the former Walsall player was on the back of a coal truck heading out of the city. Wright naturally denied the allegations in the same interview:

That's rubbish. I've heard that one and it's the biggest load of junk. I do hear these stories you know, but there is no truth in most of them. I was getting fed up of things, they were just getting on top of me. I thought I'd rather be back at home in Birmingham so I went home one Christmas and I think I came back about five days late. When I did eventually go back they told me to clear off.

Understandably, Wright was trying to airbrush the episode from his Everton career, for in a 1973 interview for the *Sunday People* he confirmed the later recollections of others about the morning he turned up drunk for training. Told he was not fit to join in, Wright explained what happened next, 'I sat moping in the dressing-room alone for a while. Then I exploded, I ran up to the offices, saw Harry

Catterick standing there and really let go at him. I told him exactly what he could do with his club.'

The club suspended Wright and gave the player a fortnight's notice to end his contract. Wright appealed to the Football League but they backed Everton's actions, whose supporting statement read, 'On December 22, when Wright reported for training, he was under the influence of alcohol and created a disturbance. Subsequently he absented himself from training and match duty without permission from December 22 to December 27 inclusive.' Wright's later recollections may have disputed those facts, but there is no doubting that the striker enjoyed a brief, but memorable, stay in the north-west.

Striking problems

Apart from defensive issues, it became apparent in the second half of 1972 that Catterick had an absence of options up front. After the failed bid for Mick Channon following Alan Ball's departure, Catterick still wanted to bring in a quality striker. Trevor Francis, then a Birmingham City *wunderkind*, was one player frequently linked with a move to Goodison, but Catterick felt he 'occasionally gives the impression of lacking determination which explains why interest in him has been nowhere as strong as some reports have indicated'. In the first quarter of 1972 hopes were high that the skilful Nottingham Forest raider and 1967 cup nemesis, Ian Storey-Moore, whose powerful running and ability to cut inside would have been a welcome acquisition, was heading to Goodison. Everton were prepared to pay a British record fee of £260,000 but the move hit the buffers when Forest wanted cash plus players in exchange.

In the following months there were failed bids for Channon (again), Manchester United's Brian Kidd and Wolves' prolific John Richards. Strangely, given the widely held view that Everton were light up front, Catterick failed in his attempt to sell David Johnson to Crystal Palace in August 1972, having already turned down an approach from Liverpool.[78] Johnson subsequently rejected a move after a £100,000 deal with the London side had been agreed, and then did the same

78 This tale is cited as an example of Shankly mischievously taking advantage of Catterick's weakened condition after his health scare. In truth it was probably payback for the Everton manager's attempt to prise Peter Thompson from Anfield twelve months before. This was the second time Everton had tried to sign the winger. Harry Catterick was a massive fan, likening him to a young Tom Finney. John Moores was at Old Trafford in February 1962 when Thompson, then at Preston, was outstanding in a 1-0 FA Cup fifth round second replay victory over Liverpool, scoring the winner. Moores informed the Deepdale chairman after the game he would pay a record £65,000 for the 19-year-old, only to be told 'we need him more than Everton'. Eighteen months later Thompson headed to Anfield for £37,500.

after a further enhanced bid of £120,000 two months later.

After Joe Royle suffered a long-term back-injury in the early months of the 1972/73 campaign, the striker's absence forced Catterick into the market again for another frustrating search for a forward. Having bid once for Manchester City's Francis Lee during the summer, the Everton manager had another record £300,000 offer rejected by his counterparts at Maine Road, who did not intend to sell one of their prize assets. The Everton manager also made an enquiry to Glasgow Rangers about former target Colin Stein. With George Best unsettled at Old Trafford, rumours also abounded that Everton were one of a number of clubs willing to sign the United superstar valued at £300,000. Catterick naturally denied the story, 'I don't discuss other club's players – and that includes Best.' Subsequently the Everton manager told the *Daily Mirror's* Frank McGhee of the difficulties in bringing in a quality spearhead: 'I made up a list of every striker over five foot ten inches in the English and Scottish Leagues, then went through one by one, discarding them for various reasons – too old, not good enough, not brave enough, and so on. I was left with about six. Martin Chivers, Mick Channon class – men their clubs just won't sell.'

The search for a striker eventually took Catterick to Bobby Robson's Ipswich Town. The future England manager was an avowed admirer of David Johnson, phoning Catterick every two weeks to enquire about his availability. 'I think David Johnson will be a great player,' Robson had said twelve months before, 'he has a wonderful future ahead of him. I'd love to have him at Portman Road.' On the final Saturday in October, the two teams drew 2-2 at Goodison and after the game Robson made another plea for a deal involving Johnson, after an unsuccessful £125,000 bid earlier in the year. This time Catterick was more obliging. The performance of the visitors' striker Rod Belfitt had caught his eye – the former Leeds' player had scored and led the line well. Given the paucity of available forwards and his urgent need for reinforcements, it made sense for Catterick to include Belfitt in any discussions. The two clubs came to a deal: a direct swap with Everton collecting a further £50,000.

Like the Bernie Wright transfer, the agreement retains a certain amount of notoriety amongst Everton fans. Belfitt was a 26-year-old who had previously played eight years at Leeds United, appearing in just 73 league games – including the notorious Goodison encounter of November 1964 – and scoring seventeen goals. In 40 league games in East Anglia the Doncaster-born player netted a further thirteen times – not world class but perfectly acceptable for the time. In comparison, Johnson had scored eleven goals in the previous season. For supporters, exchanging a journeyman striker, not considered good enough for one of your biggest rivals, for a hugely promising 21-year-old forward was not progress.

This view ignores the fact that Johnson was expendable – as one of three players, with Whittle and Husband, vying for a place on the wide right of attack – and with Royle injured, Catterick needed Belfitt as a central striker more at the time. For Robson the opposite was true. If anything then, the deal was the Ipswich manager wanting Johnson and offering Belfitt in exchange, rather than the other way round. Nevertheless, quite correctly supporters could later point to Johnson becoming one of the best strikers of his type in the country, hugely effective at running the channels in particular. After an excellent four months at Ipswich – losing just one of his first seventeen league games – Liverpool had another bid rejected in February 1973 and eventually got their man three years later. Meanwhile the limited Belfitt faded into obscurity, another symbol of the post-1970 decline. 'I don't like selling young players,' Catterick later admitted, with no hint of irony, 'you can never be sure how they will develop.'

24.
Fighting the Ghosts

FOLLOWING CATTERICK'S ENFORCED ABSENCE THROUGH ILL-HEALTH, first-team coach Tommy Casey took over managerial duties in January 1972. Although having filled that role for only two months, the Ulsterman had been at the club since 1968 and had brought through some of the younger players now in the first-team, so the appointment made sense. Whilst Catterick remained in a nursing home, there was an upturn in form – the next four matches witnessed two league victories plus a passage into the FA Cup fourth round after a replay triumph against Crystal Palace.

The first game at Selhurst Park was an absolute barnstormer. Even in an era of dirty, malicious encounters, Everton's visit to Crystal Palace for a third-round FA Cup tie took brutality to new heights. 'A shameful match, continual fouling accompanied the hateful sound of malice and rage from 30,000 spectators,' said the *Sunday Times*. Unusually, Joe Royle started the mayhem. A thumping challenge in the early moments on John Jackson left the Palace keeper limping for the rest of the game and with a lump of congealed blood 'the size of a man's fist' at the top of his thigh. After two pitch invasions and fighting on the terraces amongst fans, referee Tommy Dawes lectured the players to cool their belligerence, following vicious challenges by both sides. The atmosphere reached fever pitch when Dawes sent-off the home side's John 'Yogi' Hughes for a second bookable offence just before the hour, after scything down David Johnson by the touchline.

Home fans again ran on the pitch to attack the official five minutes later when Dawes booked Palace's Gerry Queen, the invaders rounded up by players and the police. The exasperated Dawes – who had now lost control of proceedings –

ordered Palace officials to warn fans over the loudspeaker that he would abandon the game should the violence continue. There was actually some football played amidst the carnage. Willie Wallace opened the scoring in first-half injury time before Alan Whittle equalised on fifty minutes, following up after his first shot hit the bar. Wallace scored again twelve minutes from time but Colin Harvey, who was one of the few players to emerge with credit, equalised almost immediately as the match finished 2-2. After the bloodthirsty encounter, Palace boss Bert Head said, 'It was the toughest game I have ever seen in England. That's the nearest I've seen to a riot on a British football ground in all my career.' Meanwhile Head's daughter sneaked Dawes out of the ground in her car. Everton won a well-mannered replay 3-2. 'I am impressed by the new spirit and determination running through the team,' said Catterick from hospital.

By the end of January 1972, the manager was now in direct contact with his coach – Casey had been announcing the team in formation but this had now reverted to the Catterick copyright of alphabetical order.[79] That made no difference at Stamford Bridge on the final Saturday of the month – wearing an odd mix of amber and green, hapless Everton were barely recognisable in both playing style and appearance from their glory days during a humiliating 4-0 defeat to Chelsea. After overcoming Walsall in their next FA Cup tie, and with Catterick still away from Goodison on doctors' orders, Everton faced Tottenham at home in the FA Cup fifth round on the final Saturday in February. Although the players were working hard, there was no midfield control, little penetration up front and mistakes proliferated at the back. There was no surprise when the home side gifted the visitors an opening goal, Kenyon and Lyons failed to clear a long ball, and West spilled Martin Chivers' shot into Alan Gilzean's path. In total control throughout, the London side wrapped up the tie with Martin Peters' goal after the break. 'Everton were again a sad disappointment. They looked lost and confused,' wrote Brian Moore in *The Times*. From his sick-bed Catterick gave a candid assessment of the campaign. 'For the first time in my career,' he admitted, 'I am actually looking forward to the end of the season. These last five months have been a nightmare.'

---

[79] Catterick's predilection for naming his team in alphabetical order before the game, rather than in formation, was treated scornfully by the press, especially as it was obvious what the set-up would be. Sometimes there was no line-up provided before the game. 'For the life of me I cannot see the justification for it or what can possibly be gained,' Horace Yates once wrote in the *Liverpool Daily Post*.

The constant changing and shifting of players had completely disrupted the rhythm and tempo of the team – the key characteristic of Catterick's successful sides. As the team started losing games their confidence fell and, with no senior presence like Brian Labone left to hold the dressing room together, the players entered a downward spiral. Consequently, during Catterick's absence when it seemed Everton had reached the lowest point, the team plumbed new depths. Seven days after the cup loss came the nadir of the whole season, in fact probably of the whole Catterick era. Travelling across the Park to Anfield, Everton produced a display of such staggering ineptitude that only the persevering Kendall was immune from criticism. The game was only 32 seconds old when West, rather than picking up the ball, mis-kicked Kevin Keegan's harmless cross and watched on as it struck a bewildered Tommy Wright and went in. It was 32 minutes before the visitor's first corner and 37 minutes before their first shot. Somehow the score remained 1-0 until twenty minutes from time, when it was John McLaughlin's turn to put into his own net, the defender heading home a Liverpool corner. Goals from Chris Lawler and Emlyn Hughes completed the rout. Horace Yates wrote in the *Liverpool Daily Post*, 'Everton have almost forgotten how to entertain. They are now so defence conscious that it must be an embarrassment for any of them to be labelled a forward.' Asked for his comments after the game, Casey wisely said, 'nothing at all.'

The sight of new signing Bernie Wright entering the fray as a late substitute only reinforced the view that a combination of a caretaker manager, who understandably appeared to be out of his depth, and a squad low on quality and confidence was proving disastrous. The players clearly felt Casey did not have the tools to do the job. As one team member later said, 'Tommy Casey came in and his philosophy of football was "belt it as far as you can up the middle of the park" which was a joke to us. "I only want you to have two touches – one to stop it, and one to kick it."' In response to the Anfield defeat, the caretaker manager symbolically left out championship stalwarts Royle, Hurst, Whittle and Husband for the goalless draw at Manchester United four days later.

On the following Saturday, Wright scored another first-minute own goal in the 2-1 home defeat to Manchester City, when supporters circulated leaflets outside the ground, saying, 'We the people demand success. We are Everton FC. Eighteen months is not just a bad spell.' Confidence in the direction of the club was further eroded when supporters noted the twin strike force for the visit to Huddersfield on April Fools' Day – it was no joke that, two years after clinching the title in the best School of Science tradition, Bernie Wright and a novice Mike Lyons were expected to be the source of goals. Watching from afar, Catterick was a concerned man. 'I was told to rest and relax,' he later said, 'but how could I do that with Everton not only losing matches, but playing football I wanted nothing to do with. Long passes up the middle for Joe Royle to chase, kick and rush stuff just not our style.'

The end of the season could not come quick enough. After defeating Walsall in the FA Cup, Everton won just one of their last sixteen league matches, a victory at Southampton being their first on the road for eighteen months. In mitigation, Everton drew eleven of those, although they scored only nine goals to take their tally in the league campaign to just 37 in 42 games, the lowest since the inaugural season of 1888/89. Amongst the 42 league games there were no less than nine goalless draws, slightly contradicting Catterick's claim to BBC Radio Merseyside's Bob Azurdia. 'I wouldn't like to feel that we are now going away from home and playing with nine defenders. This Everton don't do. We try and play an open type of game.'

Before the end of the season, the Everton board, in response to stories that Catterick may be facing the sack, came out with a public vote of confidence for their manager. Chairman George Watts said, 'I state categorically that no changes whatsoever are necessary, and that we have absolute confidence in the ability of the manager and his staff to put Everton once again at the pinnacle of British football.' For his part the manager said, 'Make no mistake, they [the players] will pick up. There have been lapses of form by key players and we have paid for them. There is only one way to put it right. We must roll up our sleeves and fight back.'

Moores returns – summer of 1972

Refreshed after a holiday in Majorca, Catterick returned to Bellefield in the summer of 1972 with the aim of doing just that. The Everton manager spoke about his health scare to Bob Azurdia before the season started, and was keen to play down the issue. 'I had a blood condition which was a virus initially that I contacted just before the game in Athens against Panathinaikos,' he said, 'En route home I took ill. This blood condition subsequently affected my heart in some measure but doctors assure me I'm in pretty good shape.' Catterick had lost two stone in weight, but as he told Tony Stevens of the *Liverpool Weekly News*, 'the doctor told me earlier I was a stone overweight so it was not as bad as it looks.'

Although given a clean bill of health, it had been an open secret that the club wanted an assistant to support Catterick after his heart scare in the first week of the year. This gave rise to one of the more bizarre stories of his reign at Goodison. Bournemouth's voluble manager John Bond publicly announced that Everton had offered him £8,000 a year to be Catterick's assistant manager and the two had met to discuss terms at Bellefield. The press then reported that Bond had turned down the approach. This was news to the Goodison hierarchy, who claimed they had never met Bond nor offered employment. 'As far as I know, he wasn't offered the job in the first place,' said Catterick. At the time, it seemed a strange tale.[80] Former coach Tommy Eggleston was offered the role though. Having worked with Catterick at both Sheffield Wednesday and Everton before leaving to try his hand at management at Mansfield and in Greece, the appointment was a sensible first step on the road to recovery. This time Eggleston had a more expansive role – it was his job to control training and devise tactics, with Catterick moving to a more general managerial position. Apart from Catterick's good health, equally encouraging was the return of John Moores as chairman.

On coming back to the fold, Moores' sharp business brain told him who was partly culpable for the decline over the previous 24 months. 'I think that over the past two years, the directors may have been too complacent about the way things were going,' he told the annual shareholders' meeting. 'Together with the Everton board, I realise we have a difficult job ahead to put Everton back and on the map again,' Moores informed them, before adding they had to do 'a hell of a lot more to overcome this apparent bad image that we have'. Moores would also have been cognisant of the harsh lessons from business; biographer Barbara Clegg later describing the Littlewoods approach that had led to them avoiding a similar fall from grace:

It was classless; it believed in system and attention to detail; and it never looked back – it was always looking ahead. Stopping to consolidate was not something that John believed in: that was simply stagnation. You consolidated as you went along; if you paused – for whatever reason – you could be overtaken.

---

80 However it later transpired that Bond was offered the job and did turn it down, as a means of obtaining a more lucrative contract at Bournemouth.

Working in tandem in the first half of the 1960s, Moores and Catterick assiduously applied those principles to Everton, bringing the improvements on and off the pitch that brought two league titles. Yet later in the decade, after Moores had resigned, there is an argument that Catterick was indulged somewhat with lengthier contracts and thus lost motivation, incorrectly sticking to his belief that the squad was good enough, with their best years to come, and assumed that Bellefield would produce young stars *ad infinitum*. The manager and directors remained passive in a rapidly changing game and the result was the stagnation that Moores feared, which swiftly turned to regression. Interviewed by James Mossop in the *Sunday Express* in the early weeks of the following season, Moores elaborated on his reasons for returning:

I did not want to become chairman again. But what really made me take over again was the way we played last season. It upset me. It was not so much the bad results, although winning is important. It was the bad football. Besides I am a business man. Our gates had fallen to 29,000 and it simply wasn't good enough. In business, if things go wrong, you have to come up with solutions, or go bust.

Catterick, for his part, reaffirmed his commitment to attacking football, 'Although how successful that may be in terms of results is a little doubtful, but good football always pays. If we can combine good results with attractive football we will be back to 1970, we will be winning championships.' Supporters probably thought that talk of the title was a trifle optimistic after two disastrous campaigns, although bookmakers had Everton as short as 15/1 for the crown. Good results and progressive football needs the right players and the Everton manager had spent the summer trying to add to the squad. Apart from the familiar failure to sign a striker, Catterick's attempt to acquire Sheffield United's flashy midfielder Tony Currie came to nothing. The Everton manager did succeed in bringing in Huddersfield's promising goalkeeper David Lawson for a record fee of £80,000 and long-term target Mick Bernard from Stoke in a £125,000 deal. The purchase of the competitive Potteries ball-winner necessitated a reshuffle in midfield, with Colin Harvey playing the more advanced role.

By failing to address these historic weaknesses at the back and front, Catterick was overseeing an unbalanced squad, with a surfeit of midfielders. That was not a particular worry, as he told Bob Azurdia in August 1972, 'I don't think you can have too many midfield players, as they are adaptable at both front and back.' A fair point, but at the same time this focus on flexibility was at the expense of specialist skills. Keith Newton was a right-back who ended on the left-side, Henry Newton and Bernard midfielders who both ended up at full-back. A decade earlier Catterick bought the best players in their specific role. Now he was saying about Bernard that 'it was not a question of looking specifically for another midfield man, more a feeling that we can't have too many good players'. Time would show that Bernard was probably neither.

The last hurrah

With virtually a full squad of players to select from, Everton started the 1972/73 season strongly. After a solid 1-1 draw at newly-promoted Norwich on the opening day, Everton produced their best performance since the last title-winning season in completely outplaying Manchester City at Maine Road four days later. Winger John Connolly – signed from St Johnstone earlier in the year – scored his first goal for the club in a 1-0 victory that was far more comprehensive than it looked on paper. Geoffrey Green in *The Times* welcomed the return to form. 'A team once again putting the accent on the arts and crafts of football,' he wrote, 'creating space, chasing the ball and using it intelligently, rather than chasing the man as they were last year.'

The fully fit Joe Royle was in the midst of a purple-patch, the big striker scoring in the next five league games as a 2-1 victory at Leicester in the second week of September took unbeaten Everton to the top for the first time since the title-winning campaign. 'They looked the best balanced team I have seen this season,' said Alan Williams in the *Daily Express*.[81] Seven days later the first chinks in the armour appeared during a 1-0 home loss to Southampton, and by the time Everton travelled to Anfield on the back of three defeats in five games, they had dropped to third in the table. In one of the best and most open derby matches of the decade, Catterick's side were much the slicker team and gave as good as they got in the autumn sunshine. Everton missed the two best chances, Larry Lloyd blocking Joe Royle's shot on the line before Kendall shot wastefully over the bar when faced

81 The afternoon in the Midlands was off to a strange start when the front window of the team bus shattered on the way to the game. The coach driver then produced a plastic screen with metal bars to attach around the windscreen. Asked by a supporter what it was for, coach Tommy Eggleston quipped, 'that's to stop the players escaping.'

with an empty net. Not for the last time a visiting team paid for their generosity on the ground, Steve Heighway's cross from the left was out of Lawson's reach and Peter Cormack headed the winner. 'At the end of term, nobody need be surprised if Liverpool and Everton occupy two of the top three places,' predicted Eric Todd in the *Guardian*.

On BBC's *Match of the Day* that night millions of viewers were treated to the surprise sight of Catterick and his Anfield managerial counterpart side by side for the post-match interview, for the first time. 'You can see the Merseyside Morecambe and Wise on TV tonight,' quipped Shankly after the game. For his part, when the camera operator noted that Catterick's chair was a few inches lower than his counterpart's, the Everton manager looked up and said 'well they're that much bigger than us in the league at the moment.' Such a convivial double-act may have been impossible previously, but relations between the two had softened during the summer, as Catterick admitted to the *News of the World* in the week of the game:

While I was in hospital with this heart condition and then a nursing home I heard nothing from Bill and was a bit disappointed. But I hadn't been back long after doctors said I could gradually get the feel of the place again when there a knock at my office door at Bellefield. It was Bill. We talked for more than an hour – all the talk was about football of course and we both enjoyed ourselves tremendously.

Such a visit was not a surprise, of course. Shankly used to boast about watching Everton train at Bellefield, in a public attempt to gain some sort of psychological edge over his close rival. The Liverpool manager was a regular visitor to the venue, usually after Catterick had departed for the day, and the tales have served only to add to the Scot's legend. However, Catterick was well aware of his covert missions. 'He lives over the back of the ground and often calls in, he likes to have a look around, perhaps to see what we are up to,' the Everton manager once said. Their relationship was not full of animosity, as many outsiders were lead to believe. As Catterick admitted to the *Liverpool Echo* after Shankly's surprise resignation, it was one based on mutual respect:

My personal relationship with him was always made out to be one of antagonism which was not true but suited the Merseyside public who thought we should be rivals. But Bill and I always got on reasonably well. He was a straight talker, which suited me. I would like to pay this tribute to him – that I don't think I could have enjoyed managing in a two-club city like this more than I did with Bill Shankly.

In the last chance saloon

The defeat at Anfield left Everton fourth, but a steep decline followed and by the end of November the club was sinking into another crisis in a repeat of the previous campaign – defensively sound, but a lack of goals and an ever-lengthening injury list was sapping confidence. One of the casualties was Joe Royle, who suffered a serious back injury not long after an encouraging goal-scoring display for England against Yugoslavia. By the time of his injury, Royle and winger John Connolly had accounted for eleven of the side's sixteen league goals and the absence of a threat from elsewhere was a big problem, as Catterick admitted. 'In the modern game, scoring goals is done by six men, the front men and the midfield men. Up to now we haven't had one from a midfield player this season.' This lack of penetration continually frustrated the Everton boss. After his skipper missed an excellent late opportunity to equalise in the 1-0 defeat at Arsenal in late November, the manager quipped, 'That Kendall. He's got the best right foot in the game and he puts that one on his left. We've had that sort of a season. Nobody is sticking the ball in the net and we can't win until somebody does.'

Moores may have been content for the time being with Catterick, but the poor run of results had tried the patience of the Everton faithful. In the following game – a 2-1 home loss to West Ham United – there were protests from disgruntled supporters at the end of the match. Catterick was conscious of the impact of the crowd's mood on the fragile morale of the players, as he told the *Liverpool Echo's* Michael Charters, 'No team can be successful without confidence but some of our players have been deeply scarred by the reaction of some Goodison spectators. Many of them seem to come to the ground just to criticise. They seem to take a sort of pleasure in criticising. Players who have come from other clubs are quite genuinely shocked at the treatment they get at Goodison.' The chairman supported his manager, who appealed to fans 'Not to barrack our players. That does no good at all. They have barracked Husband so much that the lad can't play at all at Goodison.' The decline of Husband was particularly sad, the winger failing to build on his immense youthful promise, some saying that he never recovered from Dave Mackay's bad tackle at Derby in a League Cup game in 1968.

Although there was probably some truth to what both men were saying about terrace criticism, they were better admitting it in private. Such public utterances only served to widen the division between the club and supporters, or specifically the manager and fans. One angrily replied to the accusations in the letters page of the *Liverpool Echo*, referencing the poor form of the team. 'It illustrates how out of touch the club is with its supporters,' he wrote, 'recent letters from supporters have all said much the same. Men from all parts of the city who see the game from different angles have been remarkably consistent in their views. Surely they all can't be wrong?'

There was no escaping from the pressures, even away from Goodison. Whilst attending a function in Ormskirk to make presentations to Brian Labone and Roger Hunt, supporters cornered Catterick in the subsequent question and answer session. 'I think Roger had one question to answer,' said Labone, 'I didn't have any, and Harry had about two hundred – all pointed and awkward.' Moores gave Catterick a vote of confidence at this time, tempered by a measured warning. Asked about his manager's future by Gerald Sinstadt on Granada TV's Friday night magazine programme, *Kick Off*, Moores said, 'We are quite happy with Harry Catterick,' before adding a caveat, 'if we had a long run of failure I would do something or get out. I should see the signs and tell the manager that we were not doing well and suggest certain things and if he doesn't respond I must say to him "If we don't improve you had better look for another job."'

Now desperate for a major signing to reinvigorate the season, the Everton boss journeyed north of the border to pursue Aberdeen striker Joe Harper, Scotland's leading domestic marksman with 42 goals in 1971/72 and 27 already in the current campaign. With the Dons prepared to listen to offers for their prolific forward, Everton moved to the front of the queue of six English top-flight clubs to secure the services of the chunky, but mobile, 5 foot 7 inch striker, who was similar in build and style to the great German, Gerd Müller. Travelling to Glasgow airport on the same day as the Saturday home game against Wolves in mid-December, Catterick signed Harper for £180,000 in such secrecy that the club did not know until half an hour after the match, although the press knew in mid-afternoon.

While Catterick was securing the services of the Scot, Everton were falling to a sixth successive defeat, their eleventh of the season, all by the odd goal. To make matters worse, at half-time the tannoy announced the sale of fans' favourite Alan Whittle, to Crystal Palace for a fee of £100,000. The blonde-haired striker, once described by Catterick as 'the best we have had', had lost form since his heroics in the championship run-in. The disastrous piece of public relations drew a lengthy spell of slow handclapping from the 24,000 crowd, who roundly booed the side off at the end of a miserable afternoon. With Catterick away, eight police officers surrounded John Moores' Rolls Royce at the end of the game, in case their protests went too far.

Harper made his debut in the home game against Spurs, a match for which supporters from his former club ordered 200 match programmes. It was an encouraging start. 'His sharpness, readiness to shoot, eagerness to chase every fleeting chance, helped to inspire the team,' wrote Michael Charters about the Scot after a 3-1 victory, the debutant even missing a spot-kick. Man-of-the-match though was his captain. Howard Kendall scored twice for the only time in a league game during his Everton career, confirming his status as the best player at the club at the time by some considerable distance. The signing of Harper formed only part of Catterick's strategy for rebuilding the squad. Another British transfer-record equalling bid for Mike Channon failed, with Everton one of nine clubs attempting to sign the forward from Southampton. Wrexham's precocious teenager David Smallman also rejected a move to Goodison, the talented youngster waiting two further years before joining.

The arrival of Harper brought a short-term improvement in results at the turn of the year – a six-game unbeaten run, with the Scot scoring three goals. There was a 3-2 win over Aston Villa in the third-round of the FA Cup, a victory that gave the Toffees an easy looking fourth-round tie at home to second division Millwall, a team without an away victory in the competition for 22 years. The game proved disastrous and was the darkest day at Goodison in Catterick's time as Everton manager. The home team featured just three players who were first choice in the title-winning season – Tommy Wright, John Hurst and Kendall – plus Roger Kenyon, who had appeared just nine times. The remaining seven had either come through the ranks or were recent Catterick signings. The line-up therefore summed up the decline after 1970. One of the reasons for the rapid deterioration of the championship side was due to a loss of players through injury, retirement and transfer; a youth policy that was not working plus signings that were just not good enough. It was that simple, although why it got to that stage was rather more complex to explain.

Those problems were crystallised in a dreadful ninety minutes. Nevertheless,

Everton were the better team, keeping the visitors penned back in their box for most of the game. The primary problem though was one of physique – Catterick's preference for skilful players, short in stature, was not in keeping with the time. Of the 42 fouls committed in the game, thirty were by Millwall. Although they dominated possession, the shot-shy home team consistently failed to trouble Bryan King in the Londoners' goal and when they did so, they found the visiting keeper in brilliant form, the highlight being an incredible double save from Joe Harper in the first half. [82] The game turned when Kendall went off after 52 minutes, the away side taking the lead on the hour, when veteran Harry Cripps headed home from a free-kick. Following desperate Everton attempts to draw level, the London club scored again near the end in a rare sortie into opposition territory, via Alf Wood with another header from Gordon Bolland's cross. To make matters worse, there were stabbings of a number of Millwall supporters inside the ground.

Cushions and programmes rained onto the pitch at the final whistle, as the majority of the 37,277 crowd vented their frustration at the players, the manager, the directors and the aggressive tactics of the second division outfit. 'It was one of the biggest shocks in the history of the club and their overall performance was so poor that I wonder when and where the reconstruction of the team can develop from here,' wrote Michael Charters in the *Liverpool Echo*. Catterick said little after the game. 'Anything that I might say would be excusing the fact we lost,' the manager admitted, 'for the first twenty minutes we seemed to have things under control, but afterwards things went wrong.' Angry supporters accosted the chairman, his only defence being to say, 'Another bad day,' before promising, 'We're trying to build a better side.' Forty-eight hours later Moores was less accommodating, admitting that the manager and team had three months to sort out the mess. Speaking to the *Liverpool Echo*, Moores said:

I am not happy with anybody at the moment. I am not even happy with myself. Three seasons of disappointment is a long time and we want to end that sequence at the earliest possible moment. We have the money. We have the supporters and this is simply not good enough for them, especially with Liverpool sitting top of the league. I say this and mean it. Now everybody at Goodison is on trial – players, manager, chairman and even the directors. We are all in this together.

---

[82] King ironically became Everton's long-serving Scandinavian scout before leaving the role in January 2017.

Moores' words of warning went unheeded. A goalless draw at Southampton and a 3-0 defeat at Spurs on the last Saturday in February made it two months without a league goal, before the return derby fixture at Goodison in early March. The Toffees stood fourteenth in the table but their local rivals were top, with 44 points from 31 games. The two line-ups made interesting reading, highlighting why Everton had unravelled after 1970 – a watershed year in Liverpool history too. While Catterick's team-building strategy had largely failed to effectively replace and rebuild the squad, Shankly had successfully brought in players from clubs like Bury (Alec Lindsay), Bristol Rovers (Larry Lloyd), Skelmersdale United (Steve Heighway) and, most notably, Scunthorpe United (Kevin Keegan, who followed Ray Clemence's pathway). Everton had been linked with their big money acquisitions – Peter Cormack and John Toshack – before they moved to Anfield.

Shankly's policy, at the time, of bringing in players from down the league was a course of action Catterick failed to employ during his career. This was rooted in his management style and experience. In a results business Catterick expressed no great desire in spending time nurturing talent from lower divisions (even at Sheffield Wednesday) when the finished product was available, albeit at a price. Many years earlier, he spoke about developing players. 'I thought it was possible to change the style of an experienced player,' Catterick said about his time at Crewe and Rochdale, 'But it can't be done, I'm glad I learned that lesson early on.'

As the two teams prepared for the derby, it was apparent that the Liverpool of 1973 vintage were both greater than the sum of their parts and ideally suited to the demands of domestic football of the time. Shankly's outfit were hardworking, hard-running and durable, qualities that Catterick's team, Kendall aside, were now displaying only fleetingly. At Goodison, when for the first time in 45 years the two sides did not come out together, the home team started well – Lyons missing an excellent opportunity after just thirty seconds. As the game developed, the Everton skipper was proving to be the star man, putting in a superb display. 'Kendall's precision play and immaculate passing makes a mockery of the neglect which Sir Alf Ramsey shows towards him,' said the *Guardian*. Elsewhere, goalkeeper Lawson may now have a chequered reputation, but the former Huddersfield stopper enjoyed a decent first season at Goodison, and was outstanding against Shankly's side. Everton encouragingly remained in the game before fading, as Emlyn Hughes painfully struck twice in the last nine minutes to complete Liverpool's first league double over Everton for a quarter of a century.

With no goals in almost ten hours of football, and only eight points to show from fifteen league games, Catterick was in a corner, Moores having effectively already put the manager and players under the microscope. 'It must surely be Mr Catterick himself who faces the biggest trial for managers are traditionally the men who carry the can when things go wrong,' wrote Chris James in the *Liverpool Echo*, 'and they're going very wrong at Goodison Park at the moment.' One supporter's analogy to the same paper summed up the views of many. 'If Catterick had been a manager of one of John Moores' stores and produced goods of the same quality as the Everton team produced on Saturday, he would have been sacked long ago.' Moores, significantly, refused to talk about his manager's future after the game. The attendance at Brian Labone's testimonial against Liverpool, shortly after, reflected the fans' frustrations. The gate of just 25,000 was less than half of Roger Hunt's full house at Anfield twelve months before.

Catterick for his part came out fighting. 'I'm not a quitter,' he said, 'I've never quit at anything in my life. We're having a rough time but I'll fight like hell to get the club out of it.' The manager may have been up for the scrap, but whether the players where was an entirely different matter. The immediate response was encouraging. Seven days later, a brave performance at Leeds produced an unlucky 2-1 defeat, followed by two morale-boosting victories, at home to Sheffield United and at Ipswich Town. A poor performance at West Ham, in a 2-0 loss at Upton Park on the final day of March, left Catterick's side four places and five points off the relegation zone. Despite conceding twice, Everton still had the fourth best defence in the top-flight, having shipped just 36 goals in 34 games, their painful lack of forward power costing them dear.

Inevitably, with the team on the precipice, talk came to the departure of Alan Ball and David Johnson. Although Catterick had brought in new players in the summer of 1972 and deserved praise for not throwing money around, the inadequacy of those replacements forced many to question the decision to sell both men. Johnson had quickly moved to a different level in East Anglia whilst Ball was enjoying a fine season at Highbury. In a piece entitled 'Catterick is fighting the ghosts' Horace Yates speculated about the latter in the *Liverpool Daily Post*. 'Arsenal have revitalised him. Whether Everton could have done as much I don't know,' Yates ventured, before adding wistfully, 'but just now Ball's ghost struts around Goodison.'

25.
Vanishing Point

AFTER A PERIOD OF ECONOMIC BUOYANCY, BY THE START OF THE 1970s Merseyside's long-term slump had begun in earnest. From 1966-1977, more than 350 factories closed in the region as part of the downturn and the wider consequences were shocking: a loss of 75,000 jobs in total, or nearly a fifth of the workforce. Hand-in-hand with that came wider social problems – by the middle of the decade the city had the highest rate of youth crime and unemployment in Europe.

However, the terminal decline of the docks symbolised the area's wider issues, which still exist today. Cunard Line vacated the port in the 1960s and moved to Southampton. Canadian Pacific, the last company operating transatlantic cruises from the city, withdrew in March 1972. In the same year, the first container port opened in Seaforth. The advent of 'containerisation', combined with the break-up of the Commonwealth and Europe replacing the Americas as the country's primary trading route, put the final nails into the docks' coffin. A workforce of 25,000 in 1945 had fallen to just 3,000.

Whilst employment levels dropped alarmingly, also taking place was the disastrous programme of 'slum clearance' within the inner city. Between 1964-1979 almost 80,000 occupancies were demolished – more than a third of Liverpool's stock. Communities were broken up and residents dispersed to perimeter suburbs that later became close to slums themselves as local factories closed. Those who remained in the city centre were housed in unforgiving tower blocks, which quickly became a haven for anti-social behaviour and public health issues. As one commentator said, 'The clearance programmes coincided with the decline of the port and its related industries. In clearing the dock areas the local authority was effectively creating a ghetto of people living off social security.'[83]

The economic and demographic changes also had an adverse effect on the area's population – the 1971 census figure of 600,000 was 70,000 less than ten years before and by 1981 a further 100,000 people had left the city. The population fall and lowering income was bound to impact attendances at Goodison and Anfield, and that proved to be the case, although Liverpool's success masked the problem for several years. In 1969/70 the two teams' aggregate top-flight attendances for the campaign came close to two million spectators but, following steady erosion over the years, by 1983/84 that figure had almost halved, in a season when they shared four major trophies.

During the 1960s the city's musical renaissance directly mapped across to the economic regeneration, so there was no surprise when that too went into freefall as well. The *Merseybeat* era swiftly burned out and thereafter Liverpool was a casual observer as the music scene became increasingly London-centric and the city largely failed to embrace the psychedelic, rock and hippy era.[84]

Whereas Liverpool's rise was more closely associated with the city's rebirth in the 1960s, there was a bitter irony for Evertonians that unfortunately it was their team whose fortunes mirrored the sharp decline of the community in the following years. By April 1973 that curve had become so steep that the Goodison board had a big decision to make.

The Sack

After Manchester City jettisoned Malcolm Allison in October 1980, the *Guardian's* David Lacey wrote that 'Football management is largely about signing players, picking teams and by successful combination of these activities winning more matches than you lose.' In the three years after the 1970 title triumph Catterick had failed to adhere to those basic principles and in that context the Goodison

83 In his epic study of policing inner-city Liverpool, *Spike Island*, author James McClure reported that by the mid-1970s the area had an infant-mortality rate at the national average for 1930 and living standards that equated to those of the rest of the country during the 1940s.

84 John Peel used to talk about the 'dead hand' of the Beatles and how the Fab Four's shadow stifled musical creativity in the city in their aftermath. Even as early as 1971 there was a desperate attempt to recapture the glory days: the poorly-attended 'first annual Mersey Beat Ball' aimed at those largely on the periphery during the early 1960s. Local-born journalist Bernard Falk produced a damning report for the BBC's *24 Hours*. After the city's established stars failed to turn up – Cilla Black was 'in panto' – Falk commented 'So many faces and not a famous name among them – anybody who was anybody didn't come… there are people here who are walking tragedies.'

hierarchy had little choice but to review the manager's position.

Although the first two games in April brought three points against Norwich City and Coventry City to help alleviate the threat of relegation, Moores was not convinced and at a board meeting within 48 hours of the latter game, the chairman asked the directors over the telephone to pass judgement over Catterick's future. They would have had to think deeply over their decision. A decade of being one of the best sides – and biggest clubs – in the country preceded a period of mediocrity that was no longer a blip. The team was playing dull, one-dimensional football in front of falling attendances, two things that concerned Moores on his return. The three home games since the derby defeat had witnessed crowds of little more than 20,000, less than half those of the glory days. Most importantly of all though, after the Millwall cup defeat, the Everton chairman had made clear that everyone was on trial. In the two months since there had been little improvement. Consequently, on the afternoon of Wednesday, 11 April, the Everton hierarchy issued the following statement:

Everton are pleased to announce that they have reached an arrangement with Mr Catterick under which he will continue to serve the club for the term of his present contract, but will act in a senior executive capacity not responsible for team selection.

The directors also showed their terse appreciation of Catterick's tenure 'during a time when Everton achieved success'. It was an inevitable decision, and as one club insider said, 'This just couldn't be allowed to go on. Something had to be done. Everton could not stand another season like the last three.' However, as John Moores recounted in 1978 to Ian Hargraves in the *Liverpool Echo*, the departure came too late:

After Harry was taken ill, we were slow in reacting to the situation. The specialist told us Harry would be fine if we got him a driver and took some of the weight off his shoulders, so we let him soldier on for two more years. In retrospect we made a big mistake because the team fell apart. It may sound cruel, but we should have moved Harry sideways, and appointed a new manager right away. Football is a harsh business, and a man of over fifty with heart trouble just can't cope. Being a manager is a demanding job and only a person who is utterly committed twenty-four hours a day and is willing and able to burn himself out for his club can survive.

Who was going put himself under that pressure at Everton was an interesting question. There was certainly no shortage of contenders. One obvious candidate was Derby County's Brian Clough, but many unsurprisingly considered the charismatic boss as simply too abrasive for the role. There was an approach to Bobby Robson, progressing in impressive fashion at Ipswich, but after offering the future England boss an interview, he stayed at Portman Road on the back of a new long-term contract. Likewise, Jimmy Armfield, manager of newly crowned third division champions Bolton, looked a sound candidate, but one of the great men of English football also turned Everton down. Queens Park Rangers' Gordon Jago also rejected Everton's overtures.

Privately, the hierarchy also admitted they were looking for someone who, in their words, could 'promote' the club's image. This was anathema to an old-style football man like Catterick, who was only interested in winning games. Tony Stevens of the *Liverpool Weekly News* asked Catterick about his reserved manner prior to the start of the season. 'Some managers are always ready to run to the papers and have their names splashed about,' he replied, 'I would describe myself as a quiet type. The real thing is that people love you only when you are a winner.' Catterick was correct, while Everton were successful the public relations role could remain in the shadows, but when results deteriorated then Catterick's continuing apathy and scepticism towards both the written and broadcast media ultimately counted against him.

While the club was finding it difficult to fill the vacancy off the pitch, Catterick puzzlingly retained the managerial reins in the interim. Effectively sacked, that evening Catterick sat in the stands with Moores at the Hawthorns as the relegation-threatened home team ran out 4-1 winners. Three days later, four goals were again conceded in the Midlands, this time in a 4-2 loss at Wolves. After a Goodison victory over Chelsea removed the threat of relegation, Catterick's final home game was against Arsenal and, poignantly, Alan Ball. Four points behind leaders Liverpool, albeit with a game in hand, the visitors were desperate for a victory. There was a resilience about Catterick's final team selection on home turf, which had been sadly missing for some time. Everton forced a goalless draw that ironically increased the chances of the title passing to his great rival across Stanley Park. After the game, both Ball and Catterick had their say, the midfielder criticising his former club. 'It was difficult. I felt there was a defeatist attitude about them,' Ball said, 'They stop teams from playing.' For his manager it was an emotional occasion. 'They couldn't have given me any more,' was all he said in the aftermath. The curtain call for Catterick's twelve years as Everton manager was at the Baseball Ground on the final Saturday of April 1973, in a 3-1 loss.[85] Symbolically, five members of the 1970 championship-winning team were missing through injury and his final team was as follows: *Lawson; McLaughlin, Darracott, Seargeant, Kenyon, Bernard, Jones, Wilson, Lyons, Harper, Connolly.*

That was it. Everton finished seventeenth in the table, relegation avoided thanks primarily to the form of the magnificent Howard Kendall, named the *Daily Express* Star Man of the Season, based on the ratings provided by all the football reporters, a not inconsiderable achievement given the dispiriting nature of the campaign. Tributes to his manager were few after the end of the season, but one from the charismatic and opinionated Ulsterman, Derek Dougan, in the *Liverpool Echo*, was well put:

I shall always remember his comment after winning the 1970 First Division championship: 'We won it by pure football.' Exactly. That's what he personifies – the art of pure football. At a time when standards in the game are not all that they should and could be, he has maintained a style of sportsmanship that makes it a pleasure and honour to play against Everton. He proved by winning the championship that even in this era of hard, often ruthless competitive sport, the basic arts and crafts of the game can triumph.

Courting the Don

Whilst Catterick accepted a vacuous non-executive role, the club continued their search for his replacement. After Jimmy Armfield had turned the job down in the first week in May, Moores approached a new managerial target. Within 72 hours of the Bolton manager rejecting his advances, John Moores was entertaining the Leeds manager Don Revie out of the public eye, at his holiday home in the south of France. On the following Monday, two days before Leeds faced AC Milan in the European Cup Winners' Cup final in Athens, Revie journeyed to Moores' Formby home for more discussions. The visit – indeed perhaps the approach to the Leeds

[85] The most notable feature of the final game was a memorable opening to Roger Kelly's match report in the *Liverpool Daily Post*. 'A police horse bit a woman in Colombo Street, Derby, on Saturday,' he wrote, 'it was a very one-sided contest. Something very similar was happening not 50 yards away inside the Baseball Ground, where Everton completed their third successive depressing season of defeat and disappointment with a humiliating beating.'

manager – could have remained under wraps if it was not for an eagle-eyed member of the public, who contacted the local press to say that a man stopped him and asked for the directions to Freshfield Station, barely five minutes' drive from the Everton chairman's home. Significantly, the driver appeared to have more than a passing resemblance to the Elland Road boss. 'There was no doubt the driver was Revie. He was driving a yellow Mercedes and unless he has a twin it simply had to be him,' the witness said.

The Leeds manager owned a car of that description and credence to the story was given when Revie did not travel with his players from Leeds to Manchester airport, for the flight to Greece 24 hours later. It was no surprise that the press began digging. The details of the offer to restore Everton's fortunes soon emerged, although not via official channels. The deal on the table varied depending on which side of the Pennines you stood. On Merseyside the figure was reported as around £150,000 over five years but in Leeds the *Yorkshire Evening Post* gave a higher amount, £250,000 with a golden 'introductory handshake' of £50,000.

In Athens, before the game against AC Milan, the consensus was that Revie had accepted Everton's formal approach. 'There is no question,' Paul Wilcox confidently predicted in the *Guardian*, 'that now this is only a matter of time before he departs from the club which he has made into one of the strongest in England, Europe, and the world.' In their hotel, 24 hours before the match against the Italian giants, Revie reportedly informed the players and staff that he would be leaving. Indeed not only that, but Revie told Norman Hunter and Trevor Cherry that he wanted them to join him at Goodison. This was a startling development in many ways, but perhaps not a surprise. Revie was on £15,000 a year at Leeds, similar to his peers but perhaps not commensurate with his reputation as the best manager in the country. Keen to secure financial security for his extended family, Revie therefore would have found the offer enormously attractive. Not only that, but there was an opportunity to rebuild an outfit that was, for all his success across the Pennines, still significantly bigger than Leeds.[86] In a one-club football town, one of the best teams in Europe were averaging less than 40,000 a game at Elland Road, a figure comfortably topped by Everton in their glory years.

After Leeds lost the final 1-0, in controversial fashion, the *Yorkshire Evening*

[86] Given the general unpopularity of the Elland Road side, how Everton supporters would have reacted to Revie's appointment is interesting. Perhaps there is a clue in the joke at the time, EVERTON spelt backwards is 'NOT REVE' (sic).

Post said about Revie's position, 'No one expects him to stay with Leeds now. He has told his players he is 95 per cent certain to go.' Then, for some reason, the trail went cold. With Revie now on a two-week holiday in Greece – being courted by Panathinaikos and Olympiakos – and Leeds' chairman Manny Cussins on the French Riviera, there was a power vacuum at Elland Road that did not help Everton. With that in mind, Paul Wilcox provided a further update in the *Guardian*, 'It now seems likely that Don Revie's move to Everton will not be announced publicly until possibly next month. Or maybe never.'

Two weeks after the initial approach there was still no public statement from the Leeds manager on his future, before a bizarre intervention from an unexpected source – the Labour MP Dennis Skinner. At the time, under the government's pay policy a new appointee to a role could not have a higher salary than the previous incumbent. Although the offer to Revie was not officially confirmed, it was certainly substantially greater than Harry Catterick's reputed salary of £12,000 per annum. That fact did not go unnoticed to the legendary 'Beast of Bolsover'. In the midst of the economic crisis of 1973, Skinner, who is still an MP in his eighties, took it upon himself to bring to the House of Commons' attention the subversive developments at Goodison Park. Faithfully recorded in Hansard for 23 May 1973, the following exchange took place with Robin Chichester-Clark, Minister of State for Employment:

Everton Football Club (Manager's Remuneration)

Mr Skinner asked the Secretary of State for Employment whether he will submit the remuneration of the manager of Everton Football Club to the Pay Board; and by what amount it exceeds the Government's formula.

Mr Chichester-Clark: The details of remuneration applicable to this appointment are not known but the Price and Pay Code which is operated by the Pay Board stipulates that new recruits to existing jobs should not be paid more than those they replace.

Two days after this incongruous conversation, Revie telephoned Leeds from Greece to confirm that he would remain as manager of the Yorkshire club. Revie also contacted Everton, giving his reasons for staying at Elland Road as 'personal', although as the *Guardian* reported this 'could be translated to mean anything'. On face value, why Revie appeared to change his mind remains a bit of a mystery. However, given that it came immediately after questions in the House it seems safe to assume that doubts over his salary at Goodison came into play – understandably the future England boss was unwilling to agree a deal that could see the original salary offer close to being halved after government intervention.

However, also in Greece was the former Everton player Billy Bingham, nearing the end of his contract as national team boss and mulling over an offer from AEK Athens. With options limited, club officials made contact with the Ulsterman within 24 hours of Revie turning down the role. The 41-year-old immediately returned to England to agree terms – a £20,000 signing-on fee and a five-year contract, worth £50,000. Having ended a seven-week search for a successor to Catterick, John Moores broke his silence, with a degree of damage limitation vis a vis Revie:

We drew a shortlist of three men four weeks ago. It consisted of Don Revie, Billy Bingham and Jimmy Armfield. The job has only been offered to both Revie and Bingham. We had a discussion with Armfield but it never reached the stage of offering him the position. We ended our discussion with Revie, not the other way round. We gave him a time limitation for him to make up his mind. When he hadn't been in touch with us by then we told him the matter was closed. We never offered the job to Bobby Robson, the Ipswich manager. After we ended our discussions with Revie, we turned to Bingham.

The chairman's comments are interesting, if only because at no point was Bingham ever linked with the manager's post and the appointment appeared to be based more on coincidence than planning. Moores argued that they did not pursue their interest initially as they were unsure of the contractual position of their former player, although for somebody with his means it surely could have been easy to find out. Consequently, the club appeared to have landed a new figurehead more by accident than design. In many ways they had gone a full circle too, as Bingham had been on the playing staff when Catterick arrived twelve years before. The first words of the new boss reflected the challenge of the role. 'No one need tell me that I have taken on a big job. But it is always a big advantage to believe in what you are doing. Everton expect me to bring them success and the pressures will be great.'

The statement was eerily reminiscent of the sentiments of his immediate predecessor on taking up the same post. Catterick was able to rise to the challenge and pressure in brilliant fashion, while unfortunately it was a step too far for the

Irishman and his successor, Gordon Lee. It took the appointment of another of Catterick's former players, Howard Kendall, in 1981 to bring back the glory days of two decades before. Thereafter the club declined in the first decade of the Premier League before the progress and stability of the David Moyes years, when Everton operated on a shoestring compared to their super rich rivals in the upper echelons of the Premier League.

However, the purchasing of a 49 percent stake in the club by the Iranian billionaire Farhad Moshiri in 2016 promised an investment in the club not seen for more than half a century. Indeed, when the new major shareholder said in his statement on joining the club that 'I have committed to providing additional funds for transfers and retaining our key players to ensure that we have a strong core to build on for the future,' he was penning words that could have been spoken by John Moores in 1960. Although there have been early difficulties, if the subsequent years offer anything like the excitement of those heady days produced by the Mersey Millionaires, then Everton supporters are in for quite a ride.

26.
Postscript – the Mersey Millionaires

IN HIS LANDMARK 1968 BOOK *THE FOOTBALL MAN*, ARTHUR Hopcraft famously wrote, 'The way we play the game, organize it and reward it reflects the kind of community we are.' At a time of unprecedented social change, no decade reflected that statement more than the 1960s. In a wider football sense, The Rise of the Mersey Millionaires acts as a bridge between the dour, pallid 1950s and the technicolour, glamour and prosperity of the decade that followed. It is probably no coincidence that Everton's first title triumph, in some ways seen as revolutionary, occurred in 1963 – the tumultuous year of Profumo, of the Beatles, of JFK.

Boardroom affairs

The success needed the collective input of two men: John Moores and Harry Catterick. The Everton chairman provided the money, his manager the footballing wherewithal. In the early years of Catterick's tenure it provided a compelling narrative. 'Among the reasons these two men have developed such a successful partnership is that they are both efficient, knowledgeable and plain speaking,' said Horace Yates in the *Liverpool Daily Post*. 'They have a common aim – to take Everton right to the top and keep them there, and it would be difficult indeed to find a more forceful and enterprising direction of football club affairs anywhere.'

Moores was the most demanding chairman in the game. After sacking his third manager, Billy Bingham, in 1977, the *Sunday Telegraph's* Colin Malam maintained that 'Moores' extremely successful business philosophy – hard work, value for money and an unwillingness to accept second best – has the ingredients of a situation in which only a truly remarkable manager can hope to survive for long.' Malam's point that 'they [Everton] may want success too badly for their own good', undoubtedly led to a degree of insecurity at all levels in the club, from the playing staff through to the directors. Individual players (especially in the early days) must have wondered if their days were numbered when Catterick had such easy access to the chequebook, whilst the aggressive attitude of the press to the club certainly caused both the manager and board to be, if not paranoid, then distrustful of outsiders and changes within the game. No wonder one shareholder accused the board of being 'anti everything' in the early 1970s.

In February 1973 when Catterick's reign was entering its final weeks, one interviewer asked Moores if any club had a divine right to be in the top six year after year. The chairman replied, 'Our fans expect it,' before adding, 'We are not like some clubs content to be in the First Division and get nowhere. We have had three years of failure.' Given the number of teams vying for a top six position at the time, continually satisfying those demands was always going to be difficult. As one journalist remarked, 'It is an unfortunate mathematical fact of life that you cannot squeeze a pint into a half-pint pot ... Everton may believe they ought to be in the elite, but virtually make it a condition of employment is to make life intolerable for the manager, whoever he may be.' The fact Catterick lasted twelve years in that environment is testimony to his skills as both a manager and diplomat on and off the pitch.

That said Catterick held Moores in the highest regard. After signing a new contract in 1964, the manager proclaimed, 'I wanted to be sure that Mr John Moores would again be chairman of the club. He is the best chairman in the world. It was one of the greatest things that has happened in British football when he decided to take an active part in administrative affairs.' Even after departing the club, Catterick still spoke with a certain amount of fondness about his former boss. 'I always had an amicable relationship with Mr Moores,' the former Everton manager told the *Liverpool Echo* in 1976, 'I had high respect for him, and I think he had some for me and what I did for the club. He was straightforward and forthright in his views. He allowed the manager to manage, which is the all-important thing.'

Although Moores retained a close interest after leaving his role in 1965, the departure disturbed the equilibrium and Catterick was indulged to a degree, being rewarded with a seven-year agreement in 1967 and an astonishing nine-year contract two years later. There is a risk that giving any employee a lengthy deal at the age of fifty can lead to a degree of complacency, and that may have happened at Goodison. After twenty tiring years in the management game, knowing he was effectively fireproof may have given Catterick little incentive to rebuild after 1970, especially as his health was failing. The Everton manager's response was strangely passive. As Alan Ball said on the subject after leaving, 'For me, he's felt all along that the same players would all come good again and blind the world for a second time.' By the time Moores had realised that was not going to happen and returned to the fold in 1972 it was too late, but it did not erase the memories of one of football's most fascinating and compelling partnerships, with the manager's contribution acknowledged by Moores after Catterick's death in March 1985:

He was the man who gave us what we wanted at Goodison – a successful team playing the attractive soccer fans demand. Harry was a strict disciplinarian. He found the right players and was able to motivate them in such a way that made us successful. Good directors do not make a successful club and we will always be grateful for the success he brought us.

Live by the chequebook, die by the 'second-raters'

After the former Everton manager passed away in 1985, the *Guardian's* David Lacey said, 'For Catterick the use of the chequebook was the essence of good management rather than the coaching certificate.' Those words sum up his philosophy in the transfer market perfectly: better to go with racing certainties costing a significant premium than run the risk of purchasing developing players who may not reach the required standard.

Catterick had previously described his methods for squad development in a match programme from May 1967. 'A dual plan of developing our own stars and yet never hesitating to meet the strongest of challenges in going for established (but only established) stars.' The key phrase is within the brackets. Any signing would have to bring in a guaranteed level of performance; there was no scope for unlocking potential. Although former players have commented that Catterick was not a tracksuit manager at Everton and did not develop them as footballers, in his view there was no need to coach his stars. Having paid big money for finished articles then that was not required. There was an opposite approach to developing youngsters. 'It's always best to have a player brought through the club and thoroughly indoctrinated,' he told the *Daily Telegraph*'s Robert Oxby in 1969.

In many ways that mirrored Liverpool's ethos in the late 1970s, sign the best players, combine with talented youngsters, and take it from there. Immediately before his Liverpool debut in 1978, Graeme Souness recalled asking coach Joe Fagan (who started under Catterick at Rochdale) what his role would be, having not been told all week. 'We've spent all this money on you and you ask me how to play football?' Fagan replied. That was very much Catterick's attitude to his senior players.[87]

Catterick's philosophy also required a steely confident approach and, unlike many managers, handling star players held no fears. 'Harry was good at signing players who believed in themselves,' Ray Wilson later recalled. 'What's more, he had no problem signing perceived "big heads." Because once you signed for him he'd bring you down and quickly make it clear he was the man in charge.'

Therefore, with Moores' backing, in the first half of the 1960s Catterick identified the areas of the pitch that needed improving, and simply bought like-for-like replacements to do just that: West for Dunlop, Kay for Brian Harris, Scott for Bingham and Stevens for Collins. The beauty of that strategy is that it did not disturb the balance of the team, and it was only following the system changes instigated following the acquisition of the Fred Pickering that problems occurred. By the middle of the decade, with lessons from the 1966 World Cup, Catterick knew midfield power was the key to success on the park, and this was behind the signing of Alan Ball and Howard Kendall, effectively his last meaningful deals as Everton manager.

By the end of the decade, the transfer market had changed considerably from the early 1960s. With more money in the game there was no need for clubs to sell their top players. In that context Catterick's belief that the side should be based around a core of young home-developed talent was laudable, but experience was still required. Don Revie used to say that a skilful manager could perhaps develop

[87] Indeed, although there well documented differences with Bill Shankly, the Everton manager had many similarities with his successor Bob Paisley – aside from both being rarely seen on the training pitch they were essentially quiet men who let their football teams do their talking, with the emphasis on a balanced midfield. Indeed the 'pass and move' tactics associated with Paisley's team, refined over endless games of five-a-side at Melwood, mirrored those of Everton a decade before. Although, for different reasons and to varying degrees, both men lived in the shadow of Shankly, they were inherently more ruthless than the Scot was.

eight of his own young players, but he has to buy the rest. 'And you'd better buy the best,' the Leeds manager said, 'for second-raters can kill you.' Revie had done this, adding Bobby Collins, John Giles and Allan Clarke at various times to the talented youngsters already there when he took up the job. Catterick himself had followed suit – Ball and Kendall joining the squad as the crop of Bellefield youngsters were becoming first-team regulars. But afterwards the system still required the acquisition of top-class players, and that proved problematical.

The 1962/63 team was hugely underrated

The problem with the title victory in 1963 was the press felt it was more about the price of the team, not their quality. The accusations that Everton bought the title dogged the club at the time and in the years that followed the received wisdom was that it was possible to guarantee success via the chequebook. Later experience with other clubs showed this was a fallacy. However, even John Moores fell into the trap on occasions. 'You can't buy success in football,' he one admitted to Mike Langley in the *Daily Express*, 'well, not immediately.'

All this does a major disservice to a fine side that had quality reserve strength. Brian Labone, Alex Parker, Roy Vernon and Alex Young will always get a mention when any all-time Everton best XI is compiled. With Ted Sagar, Gordon West vies for the title of the second best Everton keeper after Neville Southall, whilst the right-hand flank of Jimmy Gabriel and Dennis Stevens was hugely effective and perfectly suited for the time. Then there was Tony Kay, the midfield general Catterick craved. Jimmy Greaves, for one, thought the 1963 team was a better outfit than the 1970 champions.

When there are discussions around the greatest ever Everton team, naturally thoughts turn to the 1969/70 and 1984/85 sides. But the title winners of 1962/63, which had elements of both, also merit consideration.

The post-1970 decline

In some ways, it is the most asked question of the whole Catterick reign. Why did a team, with the world apparently at its feet in April 1970, crash and burn in spectacular fashion in such a narrow timeframe? There is a sense that the side's finely-tuned style of play was always going to produce an outfit that would shine very brightly for a short time but then fade out quickly. Brian Labone referred to this in an interview with the *Liverpool Echo's* Charlie Lambert in 1977:

That team was a bit brittle, in retrospect. There were so many various talents in it. I think we were lucky to see it working at top efficiency for that brief spell. There were so many different temperaments and different sorts of skills and clashes of character, there would always have been some cogs running out of alignment.

The club skipper was undoubtedly correct, but the cogs were misaligned after the title victory primarily because the team was in fact ageing in key areas and in need of urgent reinforcement after three years of transfer inactivity. The problem for Catterick was the market had changed in the interim. The availability of top-class talent had significantly diminished by the early 1970s, and his established strategy of combining expensive stars and highly-talented youngsters was doomed to failure, magnified by the drop in standards of the Bellefield production line – to paraphrase Revie, the 'second-raters' Catterick acquired in that time ultimately lead to his downfall.

Consequently, the clubs moving forward brought in players from down the leagues, or reinvigorated the careers of those whose best days were behind them, whilst developing their own talent. Liverpool (especially in the early 1970s), Ipswich Town, Stoke City and Southampton fall into that category, as did Brian Clough's Derby County and Nottingham Forest. This was not Catterick's forte. In his top-flight managerial career, you would be hard-pressed to find any player from another club, who was not the finished article, that developed and flourished under his tutelage. Catterick's inability to adapt to the changing market forces therefore is the major contributor to the failure to halt the post-1970 decline.

Within that, there were myriad other reasons: the challenge of psychologically lifting the players in the summer of 1970 after a draining twelve months of 52 league games and for some, two trips to Mexico. This probably contributed to the fatigue and lengthy injury list in the two years that followed, affecting the middle of the park in particular. As Catterick told *Goal* Magazine in the summer of 1972, 'It's like taking the engine out of the car, putting down the bonnet and asking what's the matter when the thing doesn't run. Our engine-room went.' Then there was the changing tactics and playing styles. Teams set up in a 4-4-2 formation were now smothering the Everton midfield, whilst the emphasis on work rate, not individual skill, which followed the 1966 World Cup victory was alien to Catterick's beliefs.

Then there was the manager himself, who was now into his sixth decade. After the 1970 title victory, Catterick said, 'The ultimate thing with a manager is to take boys from school...and see them growing into a side that can win the championship.' The question therefore is whether, having achieved his aim, the manager had the same desire to remain at the top, and perhaps reaching that peak diluted his hunger after the second title triumph. Also, there is no doubt that rapidly declining health affected his judgement and took away the fight and ruthlessness required to rebuild the team.

Since 1971, there has been talk of the team 'dying' after the double cup setback. Unfairly, perhaps, that has led to accusations of the side lacking heart and resilience. The very best dust themselves down after a defeat, regardless of circumstance, and move on. Leeds United, for example, suffered many setbacks around this time but remained competitive. But the exits to Panathinaikos and Liverpool were the effects, rather than a cause, of the decline.

But the 1970s were not that bad

The 1960s were a golden age of English football, a period of great managers and players producing success on the continent and at Wembley in 1966. The industrial north – buoyed by the income from big gates and Europe, and able to attract the best players after the abolition of the maximum wage – was the dominant club force. After Ipswich won the title in 1962 the crown went to Merseyside (4 times), Manchester (3) and Leeds in the next eight years. As well as providing the champions, clubs from the big northern cities also vied for the top six places with their rivals from London, although only when Arsenal emerged under Bertie Mee did the south provide a credible title challenger.

The sustained success of those clubs was founded on the long-serving managerial greats: Busby at Manchester United, Catterick and Shankly on Merseyside, Revie at Leeds and Bill Nicholson at Spurs. But the big test was how their clubs adapted as the capability of those individuals waned or after they had left. This succession planning became more difficult due to the scarcity of available talent, the changing transfer market and as the general economic decay of the early 1970s neutralised their previous financial advantages.

All the big 1960s clubs, apart from Liverpool, largely failed to manage this change and it is remarkable how the vast majority went into immediate decline. Manchester United were relegated in 1974, Chelsea went down in the following season and Spurs followed suit in 1977. Although Jimmy Armfield provided some initial continuity at Leeds when he succeeded Brian Clough in 1974, the Elland Road outfit were relegated in 1982 and Manchester City suffered the same fate twelve months later. Even Arsenal faded in the mid-1970s, finding themselves bottom of the table at one stage and in relegation battles, finishing sixteenth in 1974/75 and a place below that in the following campaign. European trophy winners in the 1960s like Newcastle and West Ham United also went down.

The decline in Catterick's last three seasons has to be seen in that context. Although Everton supporters hold the years from 1971-1983 in a certain amount of disrepute, compared to most of their rivals from the previous decade they positively flourished, with three FA Cup semi-finals, a League Cup final appearance and three seasons in the top four. Everton's problem was with their historical rivals now out of the picture, Liverpool had the league almost to themselves with only the smaller provincial clubs as their main competitors.[88] But the decision in 1983 allowing home teams to keep all gate receipts (previously the away club received 20 percent) favoured the traditional giants and gradually they regrouped from the mid-1980s onwards: Everton, then Arsenal and finally Manchester United, although it took the additional riches derived from the Premier League to re-establish the natural order that existed in Catterick's time.[89]

The Catt and Sir Alf

They may not have been on good terms professionally, but Harry Catterick and Sir Alf Ramsey had many things in common. That is even setting aside their clipped speaking tones – with rumours of elocution lessons – and the fact both men had a deep-seated distrust of the press. If anything with Sir Alf the cynicism was even more entrenched, and he was more open about it.

Their careers followed remarkably similar trajectories after starting on the management trail during the 1950s. Both achieved success at the end of the decade: Ramsey won the third division (south) with Ipswich in 1957/58, Catterick won the second division with Sheffield Wednesday in 1958/59, and the future

[88] For proof look at the teams who finished runners-up to Liverpool from 1976-84, they included QPR (1976), Nottingham Forest (1979), Ipswich Town (1982), Watford (1983) and Southampton (1984). The point here is not to denigrate Liverpool's achievements, but to show they occurred in a competitive environment far removed from a decade or so before.

[89] To such an extent that in 2012 when Manchester City won their first title since 1968, it was noted the same nine clubs had finished in the top 10 in both seasons, the exception being Leeds who were replaced by Fulham 44 years later.

England manager followed suit two years later. In 1961/62 Ramsey took Ipswich to the title, as did Catterick twelve months after. With Ramsey now England manager, both men enjoyed their finest hour at Wembley in 1966 before perhaps having their best teams four years later.[90]

It was in the years following 1970 that their similar managerial beliefs converged to damaging effect. Like Catterick, Ramsey abhorred the destructive effects of defensive, physical football. After the loss to a hostile Yugoslavia at the European Championships in 1968, Ramsey said, 'When it comes to rough play, we have a great deal to learn. But I don't wish to play that way.' Those words could have come from the Everton manager. Furthermore, in his book, *The Anatomy of England: A History in Ten Matches*, author Jonathan Wilson outlined Ramsey's fall from grace after the World Cup victory:

Perhaps the hardest thing for any triumphant manager is to continue evolving, to dismantle what has brought trophies and make it new in response to changes in the evolution of the game; Ramsey, by 1972, seems to have been unable to adapt, cautiously protecting himself with the tried and tested and making England increasingly moribund as he did so.

Substitute Ramsey for Catterick and England for Everton and the statement could easily apply to the scenario played out at Goodison. Like the World Cup winner, Catterick did not respond to the changes in the game, whilst failing to reinvigorate the team with quality newcomers. In the first-leg of their European Championships quarter-final at Wembley in the spring of 1972, Ramsey deployed three ball-playing midfielders against West Germany at Wembley and saw Günter Netzer run amok as the visitors won 3-1. In the second leg the England manager over-compensated and uncharacteristically filled his team with hardmen and garnered a sterile goalless draw that signalled the end of an era. That fortnight was a microcosm of the two years after 1970, when Catterick went from the School of Science to the School of Hard Knocks. As David Miller commented in the *Sunday Telegraph* following their ruthless display of tackling at Highbury on New Year's Day 1972, 'Everton, who after several seasons of refinement, and protestations about the

90 Taking comparisons to another level, in 1970 both men suffered damaging defeats from 2-0 up to their closest rivals that indicated a changing of the guard, England against West Germany at Leon in June 1970, Everton at Anfield five months later.

violence of others, now chopped everything above the grass and added some cynical shirt-pulling for good measure.'

Ultimately, the two men came into conflict because they were both managerial winners totally committed to their respective roles. Underneath there would have been enormous respect. Ramsey particularly was a huge admirer of Catterick's work. In 1971 the England manager said, 'When one thinks of football in the sixties there are five clubs which spring to mind – Spurs, Manchester United, Liverpool, Leeds and Everton. Outside of these five there hardly seems to be any that have done anything.' Subsequently asked to comment on the fact that many thought his management style similar to the Everton boss, Sir Alf responded, 'I am flattered that people should say that.'

Blackpool was Catterick's Oxford

Liverpool are the top team in the country whilst Everton are struggling, supporters unhappy that a once-great club is dropping down the table on the back of some miserable football. Under pressure to succeed, you have had the dreaded vote of confidence from your chairman. There is an argument therefore that Harry Catterick in January 1966 and Howard Kendall in January 1984 were in similar positions. Kendall won in the FA Cup at Stoke whilst the Oxford away game in the League Cup was seen as a turning point, after Kevin Brock's back-pass allowed Adrian Heath to equalise.

As for the Blackpool away game in January 1966, whether there was an attack on Catterick is not relevant, it is the fact that the supporters' protests forced the manager to go back to basics. Having trialled some younger players, Catterick returned to those who were tried and trusted and saw an immediate improvement in results, with the 3-0 home win against Sunderland in the FA Cup a key game. Like Kendall in 1984, the end of the season brought an FA Cup final triumph at Wembley, with a promise of future glories ahead.

A crisis of identity

Why, for all their achievements and permanent presence within the elite of English football throughout the 1960s, are Everton often left out of the list of those clubs who lit up such a sparkling and competitive decade? Setting aside the bad publicity surrounding their away supporters, the hostile atmosphere at Goodison Park and 'buying' the title in 1963 – as if that is not enough – there is another reason why Everton are often unfairly ignored. During the decade they lacked a positive reference point for the media and footballing public, one that also crossed over into wider consciousness.

Their rivals across the Park had Shankly, the Kop and their association with the explosion of the city as a centre of popular culture during the middle of the decade. Manchester United had Busby and the triumvirate of Best, Law and Charlton, as well as their 1968 European Cup victory at Wembley. Spurs' legacy was their 1961 double team and the feel-good factor derived from being the first English side to lift a European trophy two years later. Leeds had the white shirts, their reputation for 'professionalism' and a sobriquet of 'Dirty Leeds' that still resonates today. Chelsea were – and still are – linked to the fashionable Kings Road, the epicentre of the 'swinging sixties' in the capital. Manchester City had the charismatic Malcolm Allison and the trio of Bell, Lee and Summerbee. Even West Ham had the World Cup winning trio of Moore, Peters and Hurst, and a song about bubbles.

All these cultural symbols kept alive the contributions of those clubs to a glorious era in the decades that followed. Yet, Everton, who were statistically as successful as any side, did not really provide anything in comparison, other than being the Mersey Millionaires – consequently they are not as remembered to anything like the same degree. The great opportunity was in the European Cup campaign of 1970/71, had they played in the final against the great Ajax team of Johan Cruyff at Wembley then it could have all been so different.

Why Harry Catterick is a great manager

Those who claim that Catterick is regularly left of the list of great managers of the 1960s cite his failure to play the media game as one of the main contributory factors. That was true to a degree, but there were other more nuanced reasons that were apparent at the time. Firstly, in the early part of the decade, the world of football put Catterick's success down to Moores' money, and this view stuck for several years. The manager's reputation also suffered, indirectly, because of the bad publicity that surrounded Everton during this period as well.

In addition, Catterick's reputation was tainted by the painful decline of his last three years in charge. His legacy, if not in tatters, was seriously damaged on departure. In comparison, his peers bowed out as winners: Matt Busby left Manchester United in the warm glow of the 1968 European Cup victory, his work at the club done. Shankly won the league, the UEFA Cup and the FA Cup in his last two seasons, whilst Don Revie also won the league in his final campaign at Leeds in 1973/74. Bill Nicholson's departure is the closest in comparison to the Everton manager, the Spurs' boss resigning after a poor start to the 1974/75 campaign, but in the previous four seasons the Yorkshireman had won three trophies and reached a European final. None had the steady decay of Catterick's last three seasons. The old saying about history is written by the victors applies here.

All four of those peers enjoyed success in European football, which in less partisan times was often a cause for national celebration. In contrast, Catterick's disdain for continental competition was not hidden, reflected in his failure to understand the allure of floodlit contests against Europe's finest.[91] Yet the strange thing was this was not always the case. Asked about European football in 1964, Catterick replied, 'It's a fantastic experience as we learned in Milan. The [FA] Cup Final is a mere training stint by comparison.' However, by the end of the decade he was saying, 'As far as I am concerned, these European competitions are overrated. Blown up out of all proportion. It seems to me the big attraction about European games is the money.' Why the big change? Setting aside that both Catterick and Moores felt disadvantaged in the way the continental giants – unlike English clubs – could scour the globe for the best talent, there is no doubt that the exposure to the rough-house tactics of the opposition and dubious officiating left their scars on a soccer purist. 'There is also the question of interpretation of the laws of the game,' Catterick said in 1970, 'In European football it is quite possible for a referee to lose a match for you.' But all his peers faced the same issues, and this insularity counts against him in the final reckoning.

However, these are mere footnotes in comparison to Catterick's achievements across a managerial career lasting more than two decades. If the club's former centre-forward had never returned to Goodison in 1961, his work at Sheffield Wednesday provided enough evidence that here was a manager of the highest class, capable of providing success on a shoestring budget. Quite correctly though, it is the twelve years at Everton, under immense pressure to succeed, that define him and in comparison to his illustrious opposition he achieved two things they

---

[91] Catterick's stance towards European football was another example of where his and Bill Shankly's views coincided. The Liverpool manager's mistrust of foreigners is well documented and like his managerial rival Shankly thought foreign football was overrated. In 1973 Red Star Belgrade won 2-1 at Anfield in one of the best performances seen by a visiting team on the ground, but their sparkling display failed to impress the Scot, his statement that 'If every English side played as Red Star played, there would be no one to watch matches. Spectators are not interested in possession football,' was right out of the Catterick phrasebook.

arguably did not. Firstly, it was success at two clubs in those two completely different scenarios. Although it is understandable that his achievements at Everton are used as a comparator with those of Busby *et al*, this ignores the work done in getting Sheffield Wednesday from the second division to runners-up in the top-flight in less than three years, with an FA Cup semi-final and a fifth place finish in 1959/60.

Secondly, although not as clear-cut, is the way those managers won their titles. Revie, Shankly, Busby and Nicholson had their own styles of play they employed throughout the period. Leeds and Liverpool were alike in many ways; both teams were hugely effective but largely relied on grim, relentless efficiency to grind down their opponents – taking their lead from the sterile tactics of European football, where a goalless away draw was the desired result. By comparison, in 1970 Geoffrey Green said in *The Times*, 'On their day this Everton side can produce the most entertaining football in the country. Certainly they do not play the sort of percentage game that has made Leeds United the most consistent side in England over the past six years.' That said, Revie's team at their brilliant best after 1969 were eminently more watchable than before. Twelve months prior to Green's observations the *Guardian's* Paul Fitzpatrick commented about Shankly's side: 'Looking at Liverpool on Saturday was about as inspiring as watching a concrete mixer at work.' Such a description would never have applied to Everton at the time. Nicholson and Busby were more attuned to Catterick's way of thinking: success achieved through attractive, skilful football, albeit whilst still needing a strong defence.

However, unlike his rivals, Catterick's titles were achieved through differing methods. His 1963 team were set up in response to the immediate must-win demands of the Moores regime. To the stars inherited from Carey the new manager added steel where needed – Stevens, Kay and Morrissey. The result was a physically powerful squad, tough as teak and perfectly suited to the playing conditions of the time. But with players like Vernon and Young a side that was also capable of playing attractive, inventive football.

The title victory, in football terms, bought Catterick time and he used the subsequent years to refine the team's style in keeping with his wish to play enterprising, graceful football. As he said during this period, 'Everton's hopes continue to be based on skill. This is our tradition: we have no room for the strong-arm type of player and we believe we can succeed with skill.' Catterick's team in the two-and-half years from January 1968 did just that, their 1970 title victory a shining beacon in a period of defensive destroyers, work-rate and midfield ball-winners and where results came before entertainment. 'One of the best things that has happened for the game is Everton winning the League championship with entertaining football,' proclaimed Brian Clough in 1970, which was praise indeed.

By its very nature that style could not last but by winning the title with such panache, seven years after triumphing in a manner regarded as being tough and uncompromising, Catterick showed his versatility as a manager – both as a pragmatist and an idealist. Not only that but, having been unfairly accused of buying the title in 1963, the Everton boss went out and won it with a corps of homegrown players seven years later.

Therefore, from 1951-70, and arguably to a greater degree than his competitors, Catterick displayed the full range of the football management arts: obtaining value for money on a tight budget, tact, diplomacy, strategic thinking, bringing in the right players, team-building, developing young talent, knowing when to sell and buy, getting the balance right, man-management of stars and, most importantly, knowing how to get results.

Those achievements make Catterick a great manager under any criteria, especially given the inherent pressures of the job and the sublime talents of his rivals. Old Everton teammate and managerial rival Joe Mercer best summed up that single-mindedness in a generous epitaph: 'He had to satisfy hungry fans, aristocratic club tradition and directors with money and power. He did it the Harry Catterick way.'

Bibliography

Books

Liverpool 1960-64: Football, Popular Music and Extraordinary Success, Tommy Allen

The Unforgiven: The Story of Don Revie's Leeds United, Rob Bagchi/Paul Rogerson (Aurum Press, 2003)

Playing Extra Time, Alan Ball (Sidgwick & Jackson, 2004)

Kings of the King's Road: The Great Chelsea Team of the 60s&70s, Clive Batty (Vision Sports Publishing, 2004)

Are You Watching the Match Tonight?: The Remarkable Story of Football on Television, Brian Barwick (Andre Deutsch Ltd, 2013)

Everton v Liverpool: A celebration of the Merseyside derby, Brian Barwick/Gerald Sinstadt, (BBC Books, 1988)

The Football Manager: A History, Neil Carter (Routledge, 2006)

The Official Everton Autobiography, compiled by James Cleary (Sport Media 2012)

The Man Who Made Littlewoods: The Story of John Moores, Barbara Clegg (Hodder & Stoughton, 1993)

The Everton Encyclopedia, James Corbett (deCoubertin, 2012)

Everton: The School of Science, James Corbett (Macmillan, 2003)

The Glory Game, Hunter Davies (Weidenfeld & Nicolson, 1972)

Nottingham Forest in the Sixties: The Forgotten Decade, Andrew Dolloway (Primedia, 2015)

Liverpool - Wondrous Place, Paul Du Noyer (Virgin Books, 2002)
Matches of the Day 1958-83, Derek Dougan/Pat Murphy (J.M. Dent, 1984)
Wednesday! Keith Farnsworth (Sheffield City Libraries, 1982)
Gwladys Street's Blue Book, David France (Skript, 2002)
Both Sides of the Border - My Autobiography, Archie Gemmill (Hodder & Stoughton, 2005)
A Football Man – My Autobiography, John Giles (Hodder & Stoughton, 2010)
The Great and the Good, John Giles (Hachette Books, 2013)
Champions of Europe, Brian Glanville (Guinness, 1991)
The Sixties Revisited, Jimmy Greaves/Norman Giller (Queen Anne Press, 1992)
Yours Sincerely, Ron Greenwood (HarperCollins, 1984)
Hardaker of the League, Alan Hardaker/Bryon Butler (Pelham Books, 1977)
The Great Derby Matches: Liverpool versus Everton, Michael Heatley/Ian Welch (Dial House, 1996)
Clough and Revie: The Rivals Who Changed the Face of English Football, Roger Hermiston (Mainstream Publishing, 2011)
The Everton Football Book, Derek Hodgson (Stanley Paul, 1970)
The Football Man, Arthur Hopcraft, (Collins, 1968)
Soccer in the Dock, Simon Inglis (Willow Books, 1985)
Everton, The Official Complete Record, Steve Johnson (deCoubertin, 2010)
Jules Rimet Still Gleaming? England at the World Cup, Ken Jones (Virgin Books, 2003)
2008 Reasons Why Merseyside Is the Capital of Football, John Keith/Gavin Buckland (Robson Books, 2007)
Colin Harvey's Everton Secrets, John Keith/Colin Harvey (Trinity Mirror Sport Media 2005)
It's Much More Important Than That: Bill Shankly, The biography, Stephen F. Kelly (Virgin Books, 1997)
Love Affairs and Marriage, My Life in Football, Howard Kendall (deCoubertin, 2013)
Forever Boys: The Days of Citizens and Heroes, James Lawton (Wisden Publishing, 2015)
Scientific Soccer in the Seventies, Roger MacDonald/Eric Batty (Pelham Books, 1971)
Sir Alf, Leo McKinstry, (HarperCollins, 2006)
When England Ruled the World: 1966-1970: Four Years Which Shaped the Modern Game, Steve Mingle (Pitch Publishing, 2016)

The Team Makers, Peter Morris (Pelham Books, 1971)
Match of the Day: The Complete Record from 1964, John Motson (BBC Books, 1992)
Don Revie: Portrait of a Footballing Enigma, Andrew Mourant (Mainstream Publishing, 2003)
The Soccer Syndrome: English Football's Golden Age, John Moynihan (McGibbon and Kee, 1966)
Everton in Europe 1962 - 2005: Der Ball Ist Rund, Mike Owen (Countyvise Ltd, 2005)
Manchester City: The Mercer-Allison Years, Ian Penney (Breedon Books, 2001)
Everton Player by Player, Ivan Ponting (Hamlyn, 1998)
Everton, The Official Centenary History, John Roberts (Granada Publishing/Mayflower Books, 1978)
Shankly – My Story, John Roberts (Arthur Barker Limited, 1976))
Sod This, I'm Off to Marbella, John Roberts (Trinity Mirror Sport Media, 2010)
Football Managers, John Rogan (Queen Anne Press, 1989)
Goodison Glory, Ken Rogers (Breedon Books, 2000)
Joe Royle – The Autobiography, Joe Royle (BBC Books, 2007)
Bobby Collins – The Wee Barra, David Saffer/Bobby Collins (Tempus Publishing, 2004)
Harry Catterick, The Untold Story of a Football Great, Rob Sawyer (deCoubertin, 2014)
Bill Nicholson – Football's Perfectionist, Brian Scovell (John Blake Publishing, 2011)
The Worst of Friends: The Betrayal of Joe Mercer, Colin Shindler (Mainstream Publishing, 2010)
Three Sides of the Mersey, Rogan Taylor/John Williams/Andrew Ward (Robson Books, 1993)
Alan Ball: The Man in White Boots, David Tossell (Hodder & Stoughton, 2017)
Big Mal: The High Life and Hard Times of Malcolm Allison, David Tossell (Mainstream Publishing, 2009)
Seventy-One Guns: The Year of the First Arsenal Double, David Tossell (Mainstream Publishing, 2003)
The Breedon Book of Football Managers, Dennis Turner/Alex White (Breedon Books, 1993)
Under Auntie's Skirts: The Life and Times of a BBC Sports Producer, Alec Weeks (Book Guild Publishing, 2006)

The Ernie Hunt Story: Joker in the Pack, Chris Westcott (The History Press, 2004)

Red Men: Liverpool Football Club – The Biography, John Williams (Mainstream Publishing, 2010)

Rothmans Football Yearbooks, Tony Williams/Roy Peskett/Jack Rollin/Leslie Vernon (Queen Anne Press, 1970-73)

Brian Clough: Nobody Ever Says Thank You, Jonathan Wilson (Orion, 2011)

Inverting the Pyramid, Jonathan Wilson (Orion, 2009)

The Anatomy of England: A History in Ten Matches, Jonathan Wilson (Orion, 2011)

Everton's FA Cup 100 (Trinity Mirror Sport Media, 2006)

Newspapers

Daily Express
Daily Mail
Daily Mirror
Daily Telegraph
Liverpool Daily Post
Liverpool Echo
News of the World
Sunday Express
Sunday Mirror
Sunday Telegraph
Sunday Times
The Guardian
The Observer
The People
The Times

Periodicals

Charles Buchan's Football Monthly
Evertonian Magazine
Everton Programmes
Goal
Shoot

Acknowledgements

I WOULD LIKE TO THANK ALL THOSE AT THE LIVERPOOL CENTRAL Library, the Manchester Central Library and the library staff at the British Museum in London, also to the wonderful David France for making the Everton Collection such an invaluable resource. Finally to James Corbett and assistant editor, Jack Gordon Brown, for his checking of the original manuscript and invaluable assistance and advice, plus Leslie Priestley for typesetting of the text and plate sections.

Index

deCoubertin BOOKS
www.decoubertin.co.uk